THE B:SIDE WAY

MASTERING LEADERSHIP FOR MODERN TIMES

TRANSFORMING TEAMS WITH PURPOSE AND PRECISION

CHRISTOPHER MYERS

Dedicated to my father, who taught me my first lessons on leadership, and to my wife, for her steadfast love and support.

CONTENTS

PREFACE

In 2020, as the world was grappling with the challenges of the COVID-19 pandemic, I found myself stepping into a new and significant role: CEO of Colorado Lending Source. It was a move that represented both an exciting opportunity and a daunting challenge. I was transitioning from being the CEO of a tech company I co-founded— where I had built everything from the ground up—to leading an established organization in a completely different industry. I was stepping into someone else's creation, inheriting a team that had worked closely together for many years.

This team was exceptional, composed of some of the most talented and dedicated individuals I've ever encountered. Their expertise and commitment were a true testament to the hiring skills of my predecessor. But as I got to know them, I realized something crucial: while they excelled in their respective roles, they didn't see themselves as leaders. In order for us to grow, to expand, and to thrive in a rapidly changing world, we needed to redefine what leadership meant within our organization. It became clear that every person had to recognize the vital role they played in driving our collective success.

Drawing from my experience as an entrepreneurial CEO and as a professor of management and entrepreneurship at Arizona State

University, I knew that the key to unlocking the potential of this team lay in cultivating a new kind of leadership—one that was rooted in personal accountability, adaptability, and a commitment to continuous learning. These are principles I had seen work time and again in the entrepreneurial world, where the ability to innovate, adapt, and lead is not just an advantage, but a necessity.

At Arizona State University, I have the privilege of teaching students who were eager to challenge the status quo, to think differently, and to drive change. This academic experience reinforced my belief that leadership is not confined to titles or positions—it's about mindset, behavior, and the willingness to take ownership. These ideas, tested in both the classroom and the boardroom, formed the basis of the philosophy I brought to Colorado Lending Source.

We rebranded to B:Side, signaling not just a new name, but a new approach. Along with this rebranding, we worked together to define the behaviors and protocols that would become known as "The B:Side Way." These were not just abstract concepts, but actionable principles that we tied directly to our core values.

At B:Side, our core values are the foundation of everything we do. They shape how we approach business, leadership, and personal development. We believe in being our own bosses, embracing change for growth, and embodying a service mentality. These values aren't just words on paper; they are the driving force behind our dynamic and innovative culture.

Through ownership and accountability, we empower each team member to take responsibility and lead, no matter their title. By embracing change, we stay adaptable, always ready to innovate and solve the challenges that come our way. And with a relentless focus on continuous learning, we ensure that we are always growing, both as individuals and as an organization.

"The B:Side Way" is more than just a leadership philosophy—it's a blueprint for how we operate, how we interact, and how we succeed. It's a commitment to creating a culture where every member of the team is encouraged to thrive, innovate, and contribute to our collective success.

Reflecting on this journey, I see the deep connections between my experiences as an entrepreneurial CEO, an educator, and now, the leader of B:Side. These roles have taught me that true leadership is about empowering others, fostering adaptability, and cultivating a continuous drive for improvement. These are the principles that I've tried to instill at B:Side, and they are the principles that have guided our transformation.

As I look back, I am filled with a profound sense of gratitude. Gratitude for the incredible team that welcomed me and embraced this vision. Gratitude for the challenges that have pushed us to redefine ourselves and grow stronger. And most importantly, gratitude for the opportunity to lead such an extraordinary group of people who have made "The B:Side Way" not just a philosophy, but a way of life.

Thank you to everyone who has been a part of this journey. Your dedication, hard work, and belief in what we are building together make everything possible. It's an honor to lead such a remarkable team, and I look forward to all that we will achieve together.

HOW TO READ
THIS BOOK

This book is designed with flexibility in mind, allowing you to jump in wherever you feel drawn, rather than needing to follow a traditional linear path. Whether you're looking to hone your leadership skills, improve your ability to give feedback, or embrace change in your organization, you'll find that each section stands alone, offering valuable insights and actionable advice.

Each chapter is broken down into concise, focused sections that tackle specific aspects of leadership and organizational development. Following each of these short sections, you'll find a recap of the key actions discussed. These summaries are meant to reinforce the main points and provide a quick reference that you can easily return to whenever needed.

In addition to the key actions, each section includes discussion questions designed to provoke thought and spark conversation. These questions can be used for personal reflection, or as a tool to facilitate deeper discussions with your team. They are crafted to challenge your assumptions, encourage critical thinking, and inspire meaningful dialogue about how you can apply these principles in your own leadership journey.

Finally, you'll find exercises at the end of each section. These exercises are practical activities you can undertake to practice and master the skills discussed. They are designed to help you move from theory to action, enabling you to internalize the concepts and apply them in real-world scenarios.

Feel free to skip to the sections that resonate most with you or address the challenges you're currently facing. This book is a toolkit—use it in the way that best suits your needs. Whether you're diving deep into a specific topic or just skimming for a quick refresher, "The B:Side Way" is structured to support your growth as a leader, no matter where you start.

CHAPTER 1
EARN THE RIGHT TO LEAD

Leadership isn't just about holding a title or wielding authority. It's about influence—specifically, the kind of influence that inspires people to follow you willingly. But why would anyone choose to follow you? That's the real question, and the answer boils down to one word: credibility.

Credibility as the Cornerstone of Leadership

Credibility is the bedrock of effective leadership. Without it, you're just a person in a position of power, barking orders that may or may not be heeded. With credibility, you become a leader who people choose to follow, someone who can guide a team to achieve great things. But credibility isn't something you're born with or simply handed when you get a promotion. It's something you earn, every day, through your actions, words, and decisions.

People don't follow leaders because of titles or organizational charts. They follow leaders because they believe in them. They see someone they can trust, someone whose knowledge, expertise, and character they respect. That's what makes a leader credible, and that's why credibility is so essential.

Understanding What Makes You Credible

So, what exactly makes a leader credible? It's not just about knowing your stuff—though competence is a big part of it. Credibility is a blend of expertise and character.

1. *Expertise:* Your team needs to see that you know what you're talking about. Whether you're in finance, tech, marketing, or any other field, your knowledge and competence are crucial. But expertise alone isn't enough.
2. *Character:* People also want to follow someone they respect. They need to believe that you're a person of integrity, fairness, and good values. They need to trust that you're not just looking out for yourself but for the team as a whole.

Credibility, then, is about being both knowledgeable and trustworthy. It's about being the kind of leader who can make tough decisions while still being fair and ethical. And it's about continuously proving, through your actions and decisions, that you are worthy of the trust and respect your team places in you.

Building and Sustaining Credibility

Building credibility isn't a one-time thing. It's a continuous process that requires self-reflection, honesty, and a commitment to personal growth.

1. *Self-Reflection:* Take the time to evaluate yourself honestly. What are your strengths? Where do you need to improve? Understanding your own capabilities and limitations is the first step in building credibility.
2. *Perception Management:* It's not enough to believe in your own credibility; you need to ensure that others see it too. How do your team members perceive you? Do they see you as competent, fair, and trustworthy? If not, what can you do to change that perception?
3. *Consistency:* Credibility is earned through consistent behavior. This means sticking to your principles, making

fair decisions, and continuously demonstrating your expertise. It's about being reliable in both good times and bad.

4. *Earning Discretionary Effort:* People don't work hard just for a paycheck; they work hard for leaders they believe in. If you want your team to go the extra mile, you need to show them that you're worth it. This means being someone who not only helps them achieve their goals but also makes them feel valued and respected.

The Timeless Truth of Credibility

The importance of credibility isn't new. Even 2,500 years ago, Aristotle talked about the two dimensions that make someone credible: virtue (character) and expertise (competence). And despite all the changes in society and business since then, these two elements remain the foundation of credible leadership today.

To be an effective leader, you must continuously earn your credibility. This isn't something you can take for granted. It's something you build through your actions, prove through your decisions, and sustain through your character.

So, ask yourself: Why are you worthy of following? What about you makes you credible in the eyes of your team? If you can answer those questions confidently and honestly, you're on the right path to becoming a leader who truly inspires.

Tips for Building Credibility

The key actions that contribute to a leader's credibility include:

1. *Integrity:* Always do what's right, even when it's difficult. Integrity builds trust, and trust is the foundation of credibility.
2. *Fairness:* Treat everyone with fairness and respect. This doesn't mean treating everyone the same, but rather giving each person what they need to succeed.
3. *Subject-Matter Expertise:* Continuously build your knowledge

and skills. Stay up-to-date in your field and be the go-to person for expertise in your area.

4. *Consistency:* Be consistent in your actions and decisions. Inconsistency breeds doubt, while consistency builds trust and respect.

5. *Transparency:* Be open and honest with your team. Transparency fosters trust and shows that you have nothing to hide.

Remember, credibility isn't something you achieve and then forget about. It's something you have to maintain through your ongoing actions and decisions. By focusing on these key actions, you can ensure that you remain a leader worth following.

LEAD BY EXAMPLE

Leadership isn't about titles or authority. It's about credibility. And that credibility doesn't come from sitting behind a desk or issuing commands. It comes from leading by example—showing that you're never above the tasks you ask of others.

The Heart of Leadership: Credibility

Credibility is the bedrock of effective leadership. People won't follow someone they don't trust or believe in. But what makes a leader credible? It's a blend of knowledge and character.

Knowledge is the expertise and competence you bring to the table. It's knowing your stuff, whether it's the intricacies of a business plan or the details of a strategic initiative. But knowledge alone isn't enough. Character is equally important. It's about being trustworthy, honest, and willing to do what you ask of others.

Trust isn't a one-way street. It's built on reciprocity. When you demonstrate that you're willing to get in the trenches alongside your team, it reinforces your credibility. It shows you're not just talking the talk—you're walking the walk.

Leading by Example: Walking the Walk

Let's face it: Actions speak louder than words. If you expect your team to be punctual, you'd better be the first one in the room. If you value service to others, you need to be ready to roll up your sleeves and help out whenever needed. This isn't just about setting a good example; it's about building unity and teamwork.

Take Meriwether Lewis, for instance. As the leader of the Lewis and Clark expedition, Lewis wasn't just a figurehead. He was right there with his men, doing the hard work, facing the same challenges, and not shirking any responsibility. His willingness to do what he asked of his team built trust and camaraderie, which played a significant role in the success of their mission.

In the modern world, the principles remain the same. Leaders must earn their credibility. It's not just about being the smartest person in the room or having the most experience. It's about showing that you're a person of character, someone who can be trusted to lead by example.

Building Trust and Respect

When you demonstrate credibility through your actions, you inspire your team to follow you—not because they have to, but because they want to. This kind of trust and respect is essential for achieving common goals and driving success.

As you climb the ranks, it can be tempting to delegate tasks you once did yourself. But as your status and authority grow, it becomes even more important to show that you're not above doing the work. This is what keeps your team connected to you and ensures that your leadership is respected and effective.

Never Lose Sight of the Basics

Credibility can be fragile. It's easy to undermine it if you start thinking certain tasks are "beneath" you. Leaders who lose touch with the day-to-day realities of their team risk losing the trust they've worked hard to build.

Never let the perks of leadership—status, seniority, or authority—distract you from the fundamentals. Your team needs to see that you're still willing to do the heavy lifting, that you're still part of the team. This doesn't mean you micromanage or take on tasks that others are better suited to handle. It means you stay connected, remain approachable, and always lead by example.

The Final Word: Leading with Integrity

In the end, leadership is about integrity. It's about being the kind of person your team wants to follow because they respect you, trust you, and believe in you. Remember, you're never above what you ask of others. By leading with credibility—through knowledge, character, and example—you build a team that's ready to follow you anywhere.

Key Actions

- **Lead by Example**: Always be willing to do the same tasks that you ask of your team. This demonstrates that you're not above the work and builds credibility.
- **Be Specific in Expectations**: Clearly articulate what you expect from your team and ensure you meet those expectations yourself.
- **Engage in Reciprocal Trust**: Show trustworthiness by engaging in the same tasks and responsibilities as your team, fostering mutual trust.
- **Demonstrate Consistent Character**: Uphold honesty, reliability, and fairness in all interactions. Own mistakes and work to correct them, reinforcing your credibility.
- **Stay Connected to the Work**: Remain aware of and engaged with the daily realities of your team's work to maintain credibility and approachability.
- **Foster Unity through Shared Effort:** Participate in shared tasks to build a sense of camaraderie and teamwork, creating a strong, cohesive unit.

Discussion Questions

1. How can leaders effectively balance the need to delegate tasks while still demonstrating that they're never above the work they ask of others?
2. What are some practical ways leaders can stay connected to the day-to-day realities of their team's work without micromanaging?
3. In what ways does leading by example impact the trust and credibility a leader has with their team? Can you think of any examples from your own experience?
4. How can a leader's willingness to do the same tasks as their team contribute to fostering unity and a strong team dynamic?

5. What challenges might arise when a leader tries to maintain credibility through actions, and how can these challenges be overcome?

Practice Exercises

1. The Mirror Test

- **Objective**: To ensure that your actions align with what you ask of others.
- **How to Do It**: At the start of each week, write down three tasks or behaviors you expect from your team (e.g., punctuality, attention to detail, collaboration). Throughout the week, consciously practice these behaviors yourself. At the end of the week, reflect on whether you lived up to your own expectations. Ask yourself: "Did I model the behavior I expect from my team?" Adjust your approach based on your findings

2. Shadow Day

- **Objective**: To stay connected to the daily realities of your team's work.
- **How to Do It**: Set aside one day each month to shadow a team member or participate directly in their tasks. During this day, perform the same duties they do, ask questions about their challenges, and gain insights into their work. After the shadow day, reflect on what you learned and how it might inform your leadership decisions and interactions.

3. Trust-Building Feedback Loop

- **Objective**: To foster reciprocal trust and demonstrate consistent character.
- **How to Do It**: Choose one team member each week and ask for their honest feedback on your leadership—specifically,

how well you model the behaviors you expect from the team. In return, provide them with specific, actionable feedback using the "more of" or "less of" framework. This exchange not only builds trust but also helps you stay accountable to the standards you set for the team.

SMALL ACTS, BIG IMPACT

Leadership isn't just about big speeches or grand gestures; it's often about the small, seemingly unimportant actions that, over time, build or break your credibility. Credibility, at its core, is a mix of competence and character. But it's more than just being good at your job or having a strong moral compass. It's about trust—a trust that's built not in a day, but through a thousand tiny actions. And here's the kicker: trust is reciprocal. You give it, you earn it.

Your actions—big and small—are constantly speaking for you. They're a window into your values, showing the world who you are and what you stand for. People are always watching, always noticing. Consistency in what you do and say, both publicly and privately, is crucial. It's the thread that weaves credibility into the fabric of your leadership.

The Front Stage and Backstage of Leadership

Erving Goffman, a sociologist, painted an intriguing picture of human behavior. He argued that we all have a "front stage" and a "backstage" self. The front stage is the polished version we show the world, while the backstage is where our true selves reside. The most effective leaders, though, have little to no difference between these two selves. They're consistent in their actions, whether they're in the spotlight or behind closed doors.

But this kind of authenticity isn't easy. It requires a deep self-awareness and a commitment to staying true to your values, even when no one is watching. It's easy to put on a show, but the real challenge is to be the same person, regardless of the audience.

Using Power Responsibly

Leadership comes with power, and with power comes responsibility. It's easy to get caught up in the dynamics of hierarchy and authority. But true leadership is about using that power ethically and responsibly. It's about treating everyone with respect and fairness, especially when there's no apparent benefit to you.

This might seem trivial, but it's anything but. The way you treat people in those small moments, when the stakes are low and the spotlight is dim, speaks volumes about your character. And people remember. It's in these moments that trust is either strengthened or eroded.

The Humility to Learn and Grow

Leadership isn't a destination; it's a journey. And like any journey, it requires constant self-reflection and a willingness to learn and grow. This means being open to feedback, even when it's uncomfortable. It means recognizing your own biases and actively working to overcome them.

But it's more than just personal growth. It's about fostering an environment where everyone feels included and valued. Inclusivity isn't just a buzzword; it's a cornerstone of credibility. When people see that you're committed to creating a diverse and inclusive environment, they're more likely to trust you and follow your lead.

Building Credibility Brick by Brick

In the end, credibility and trust aren't built overnight. They're the result of consistent actions and behaviors over time. It's about showing up, day after day, and doing the right thing, even when it's hard. It's about being the same person, whether you're on the front stage or backstage.

And most importantly, it's about understanding that the little things—the way you treat people, the way you handle power, the way you respond to feedback—are what truly define you as a leader. So, treat the unimportant importantly, because in leadership, nothing is ever truly unimportant.

Key Actions

- **Consistency in Actions**: Maintain consistency in your behavior and actions, whether in public or private, to build credibility and trust.
- **Authenticity**: Strive to align your front stage (public image)

and backstage (authentic self) behaviors, minimizing the difference between them.

- **Ethical Use of Power**: Use your position of power responsibly, treating everyone with respect and fairness, especially when there's no immediate benefit to you.
- **Attention to the Little Things**: Recognize that small actions and behaviors, even those that seem unimportant, contribute significantly to your overall credibility.
- **Openness to Feedback**: Be open to receiving feedback and use it as a tool for self-reflection and growth.
- **Commitment to Inclusivity**: Actively work towards creating a diverse and inclusive environment, as it reinforces your credibility and trustworthiness.
- **Continuous Self-Improvement:** Engage in constant self-reflection and strive for personal growth to become a better leader.

Discussion Questions

1. How can leaders ensure that their front stage and backstage behaviors are consistent, especially in high-pressure situations?
2. In what ways do small, everyday actions contribute to a leader's overall credibility, and why are they often overlooked?
3. What challenges might a leader face when trying to use their power responsibly, and how can they overcome these challenges?
4. How can leaders foster an inclusive environment that not only enhances team dynamics but also reinforces their credibility and trustworthiness?
5. Why is it important for leaders to be open to feedback, and how can they effectively integrate this feedback into their leadership style?

Practice Exercises

1. Consistency Check

- **Objective**: To ensure consistency between your public and private behaviors.
- **How to Do It**: At the end of each day, reflect on your interactions and decisions. Ask yourself if your actions were consistent with your values and how you present yourself to others. Identify any discrepancies between your front stage and backstage behaviors and make a plan to address them. Over time, work towards reducing these gaps.

2. Power Reflection

- **Objective**: To use power ethically and responsibly in leadership.
- **How to Do It**: For one week, consciously reflect on how you use your authority in various situations. At the end of each day, jot down instances where you made decisions or took actions that impacted others. Consider whether you treated everyone with respect and fairness, especially when the stakes were low. Identify areas where you could improve and make a commitment to adjust your approach in future situations.

3. Inclusive Leadership Practice

- **Objective**: To actively foster inclusivity and build trust within your team.
- **How to Do It**: Once a week, set aside time to engage with team members you don't usually interact with as much. Focus on listening to their perspectives and understanding their unique challenges. Take note of any biases you might have and consider how you can create a more inclusive environment. Implement one small change based on these interactions to make your team feel more valued and included.

PROTECT YOUR PEOPLE

Being a leader is about more than just guiding a team to success. It's about creating an environment where people feel safe, respected, and valued. When you're in charge, no one should ever feel embarrassed or humiliated on your watch. Yet, it's all too common for teams to fall into patterns where harmless actions become fodder for ridicule, turning small missteps into big moments of discomfort. This "fishbowl effect" can quickly erode trust and morale.

As a leader, your actions set the tone for the group dynamic. Public criticism, calling someone out in front of others, or leaving a team member to struggle alone—all these behaviors can undermine your credibility and damage the trust within your team. When someone is humiliated, it's not just that person who suffers; your entire team feels the impact. People may rally around the person who was wronged, but this often comes at the cost of your authority and the group's sense of safety.

The Silent Damage of Public Embarrassment

Good leaders understand that safety is the bedrock of a productive team. When people feel safe, they're more willing to speak up, share ideas, and take risks—all of which are essential for innovation and growth. Your job as a leader is to be a beacon of safety, ensuring that your presence is synonymous with respect and support.

There are several key actions that can help you maintain this environment. First and foremost, ensure that all interactions—whether in meetings, feedback sessions, or casual conversations—are rooted in respect. When you critique, do so constructively and privately. Group debriefs or project analyses should never devolve into a blame game. Start by setting a tone of respect yourself; your team will follow your lead.

Next, be vigilant in protecting your team from situations that could lead to embarrassment. If someone misspeaks or makes a mistake, don't allow it to become a spectacle. Step in with grace, offering explanations or perspectives that diffuse tension. The best leaders make stumbles look like dances, turning potential embarrassment into moments of learning or even humor.

Finally, be proactive in gauging the safety of your team. Ask your team members directly if they feel more or less safe when you're around. This isn't just about managing your image; it's about genuinely understanding the impact of your leadership on the team's dynamics. If people feel they can be themselves and take risks without fear, you're doing something right.

The Lasting Impact of a Safe Environment

Creating a safe and inclusive environment is more than just a nice-to-have; it's a fundamental responsibility of leadership. When people feel safe, they're not just more productive—they're more creative, more collaborative, and more committed to the team's goals. Safety isn't just about preventing embarrassment; it's about fostering a culture where everyone can contribute their best without fear of judgment.

By adopting key actions—like respecting others in every interaction, mitigating potential embarrassment, and actively gauging the safety of your environment—you can build a team that trusts you and each other. This trust will drive collaboration and innovation, helping your team achieve great things together.

In the end, leadership is about more than just guiding a team to success. It's about creating a space where everyone feels valued and respected, where no one ever gets embarrassed on your watch. When you can achieve this, you'll not only lead a successful team—you'll lead a happy, engaged, and loyal one.

Key Actions

- **Root Interactions in Respect**: Ensure all interactions, whether in meetings, feedback sessions, or casual conversations, are conducted with respect. Set the tone by leading with respect yourself.
- **Critique Constructively and Privately**: When offering

feedback or critique, do so in a constructive and private manner to avoid public embarrassment or humiliation.

- **Protect the Team from Embarrassment**: Be vigilant in preventing situations that could lead to embarrassment. If someone makes a mistake, step in with grace to diffuse tension and turn the situation into a learning moment.
- **Make Stumbles Look Like Dances**: Turn potential moments of embarrassment into opportunities for learning or humor, ensuring that mistakes don't become sources of ridicule.
- **Gauge the Safety of the Team**: Proactively ask team members if they feel safe when you're around. This helps you understand the impact of your leadership on the team's dynamics.
- **Foster a Safe and Inclusive Environment:** Strive to create a culture where everyone feels valued, respected, and free to contribute without fear of judgment.

Discussion Questions

1. What are some specific strategies you've seen leaders use to maintain respect during team interactions? How effective were they in fostering a positive environment?
2. How can leaders balance the need for constructive feedback with the risk of embarrassing or humiliating a team member? What are some best practices you've observed or experienced?
3. Have you ever witnessed a situation where a leader successfully turned a potential moment of embarrassment into a positive learning experience? What did they do, and what was the outcome?
4. How can leaders proactively gauge the safety and trust within their team? What methods can be used to ensure that team members feel comfortable expressing themselves openly?
5. In what ways can creating a safe and inclusive environment impact a team's overall performance and creativity? Can you share examples where this approach led to significant positive outcomes?

Practice Exercises

1. Respectful Feedback Simulation

- **Objective**: To practice delivering constructive feedback in a way that is respectful and private.
- **How to Do It**: Role-play with a colleague or friend where you take turns giving each other feedback on a hypothetical project. Focus on being specific, constructive, and ensuring the feedback is delivered privately. After each session, discuss how the feedback made you feel and what could have been done to improve the delivery.

2. Embarrassment Diffusion Role-Play

- **Objective**: To develop the ability to gracefully manage situations that could lead to embarrassment within your team.
- **How to Do It**: Create scenarios where a team member makes a mistake or misspeaks during a meeting. Practice stepping in to diffuse the situation, either by redirecting the conversation, offering a supportive comment, or turning the mistake into a learning moment. Reflect on how well you handled the situation and what you could improve.

3. Team Safety Check-In

- **Objective**: To regularly gauge the level of safety and trust within your team.
- **How to Do It**: Schedule one-on-one meetings with team members to ask open-ended questions about how safe they feel in the team environment. Questions might include, "Do you feel comfortable sharing your ideas in meetings?" or "Is there anything I can do to make our work environment more supportive?" Take notes on their responses and identify patterns or areas for improvement. Implement changes based

on the feedback and follow up in future meetings to assess progress.

Pay Attention

In a recent podcast, a futurist proposed an intriguing idea: money, at its core, is a measure of time. Since time is the only fixed and finite quantity we have, how we spend it reflects what we truly value. This idea struck a chord with me, especially when I thought about the time we spend with those we care about.

Time, after all, is the one resource that we can never get back. Unlike money, which can be earned, lost, and regained, time is irreversible. Every moment we spend, whether on work, relationships, or distractions, is a reflection of our priorities. And in a world that's more connected yet more distracted than ever, how we choose to allocate our time has never been more important.

The Cost of Distraction

Let me share a personal story that brought this concept into sharp focus. One day, I was driving my son to a cross-country meet. Like many of us, I was juggling multiple tasks—checking emails, responding to messages, and half-listening to him as he talked. When we arrived, he looked at me and said, "Dad, you weren't really listening, were you?"

That comment hit me like a ton of bricks. He was right—I hadn't been listening. My attention was split, and even though I was physically present, I was mentally checked out. In that moment, I realized that my distraction wasn't just a minor inconvenience; it was a barrier to connection. My son deserved my full attention, but instead, I had given him only the leftovers of my focus.

This experience was a wake-up call. It made me see how often I allowed distractions—especially technology—to interfere with my most important relationships. It wasn't just about missing out on conversations; it was about sending a message that those around me weren't worth my full attention. And if I was doing this with my son, how often was I doing it with my team, my colleagues, and my friends?

The Power of Undivided Attention

In our distraction-filled world, giving someone your undivided attention is a rare and powerful gift. It's more than just being polite—it's a leadership trait that can set you apart. When you focus entirely on the person in front of you, you're telling them, "You matter. What you're saying is important." And this simple act of focusing can have a profound impact.

I decided to put this into practice. The next time I was with my son, I left my phone in the car. I gave him my full attention, listening to him without any distractions. The change was immediate and noticeable. Our conversation was richer, more meaningful, and our bond felt stronger. It was a small shift in behavior that made a big difference.

This lesson applies to leadership as well. Back in my fintech entrepreneur days, I once worked with a leader at a bank who could barely give me his attention for more than a few seconds at a time. Every meeting was a rushed, superficial exchange, and it left me feeling undervalued and unimportant. Contrast this with the best leaders I've worked with—those who made you feel like the only person in the room when they spoke to you. Their ability to focus, even for a short time, made a lasting impact.

Undivided attention builds trust. It shows respect. It fosters deep, meaningful relationships. And in a business setting, it can significantly boost team performance. When people feel heard and valued, they're more likely to be engaged, motivated, and loyal.

Of course, it's not always possible to give everyone your undivided attention all the time. But when it matters—when you're in a one-on-one meeting, when a team member is sharing a challenge, or when your child is telling you about their day—it's crucial to be fully present. Make a conscious effort to eliminate distractions and focus on the moment.

Intentional Presence as a Leadership Practice

The practice of giving others your undivided attention goes beyond just being a good listener. It's about being intentionally present. This means making a deliberate choice to prioritize the person in front of you over the countless other demands on your time. It's about creating a space where the other person feels seen, heard, and valued.

In leadership, this practice can transform your relationships and, by extension, your organization. When leaders model intentional presence, it sets a standard for others to follow. It creates a culture where people feel respected and appreciated, which can lead to higher morale, better collaboration, and more effective communication.

But being intentionally present requires discipline. It means putting away your phone, closing your laptop, and resisting the urge to multitask. It means giving someone your full focus, even when it's inconvenient or difficult. And it means understanding that the quality of your attention directly impacts the quality of your relationships.

The next time you're in a conversation, try this: Pause before you respond. Make eye contact. Listen not just to the words, but to the meaning behind them. Engage fully with the person in front of you, and notice the difference it makes. You might find that this simple practice of undivided attention becomes one of the most powerful tools in your leadership toolkit.

By being fully present, you're not just managing your time better—you're investing it wisely. And that's a return on investment that pays dividends in every area of your life.

Key Actions

- **Prioritize Quality Time**: Recognize that time is a finite resource and prioritize giving your full attention to those who matter most, especially in personal and professional relationships.
- **Eliminate Distractions**: Make a conscious effort to remove

distractions, such as phones or emails, when engaging with others to ensure that your attention is fully on them.

- **Be Present in the Moment**: Practice intentional presence by fully engaging in conversations, listening actively, and responding thoughtfully to demonstrate that you value the person and the interaction.
- **Model Focused Attention**: As a leader, set an example by giving undivided attention in interactions, which can foster a culture of respect, trust, and deeper connections within your team.
- **Invest in Relationships:** Understand that the quality of your attention directly impacts the quality of your relationships, both in personal and professional contexts, and make a deliberate effort to enhance these through focused engagement.

Discussion Questions

1. How does the concept of time as a finite resource influence the way we prioritize our interactions with others, both personally and professionally?
2. What strategies have you found effective in eliminating distractions during important conversations or meetings? How do these strategies impact the quality of your interactions?
3. Can you share a personal or professional experience where giving someone your undivided attention made a noticeable difference in the outcome? What did you learn from that experience?
4. In what ways can leaders model intentional presence in their daily interactions, and how might this behavior influence the broader organizational culture?
5. How can we balance the demands of multitasking with the need to be fully present in our relationships? What challenges do you face in maintaining this balance, and how do you address them?

Practice Exercises

1. The Focused Listening Exercise

- **Objective**: Improve your ability to give undivided attention during conversations.
- **How to Do It**: Choose one person each day to practice focused listening with. During your interaction, put away all distractions (phone, laptop, etc.) and focus entirely on what the other person is saying. Make a conscious effort to maintain eye contact, avoid interrupting, and listen not just to the words, but to the emotions and intent behind them. After the conversation, reflect on how the interaction felt different from your usual conversations.

2. The Digital Detox Challenge

- **Objective**: Reduce distractions from technology to enhance your presence in interactions.
- **How to Do It**: Set aside specific times each day where you completely disconnect from all digital devices. For example, during meals, meetings, or family time, leave your phone in another room or turn it off. Start with a small time frame, like 30 minutes, and gradually increase it. Notice how this digital detox affects your ability to focus and connect with those around you.

3. The Intentional Presence Practice

- **Objective**: Cultivate the habit of being fully present in your interactions.
- **How to Do It**: Before starting any significant conversation or meeting, take a few moments to center yourself. Take deep breaths and set an intention to be fully present. During the interaction, focus on being mindful of your body language, tone of voice, and the other person's non-verbal cues.

Afterward, assess the quality of the interaction and any improvements in communication or relationship dynamics. Repeat this practice regularly to build the habit of intentional presence.

SHARE CREDIT, SHINE THE SPOTLIGHT

Success isn't a solo act. It's a team effort, built on the shoulders of many, some of whom you may not even see. The best leaders get this. They don't just shine the spotlight on their own achievements or even on their immediate team—they go beyond that. They make it a point to recognize everyone who played a part, especially those who usually go unnoticed. These behind-the-scenes contributors might not be in the limelight, but their work is crucial. And when a leader takes the time to share credit with them, it's not just a nice gesture; it's a smart strategy.

The Power of Shared Credit

When you share credit with others, especially those in less visible roles, you send a powerful message: everyone's contribution matters. This isn't just about being polite or ticking a box. It's about building a culture where people feel seen and valued, regardless of their position. That feeling of recognition can transform a workplace, turning it into a place where people are motivated to give their best because they know it's appreciated.

Think about it this way: a football coach might be praised for a winning season, but behind that success is a whole team of people—trainers, equipment managers, even the person who handles travel logistics. These roles may not be glamorous, but they're essential. By acknowledging these contributions, the coach shows that they understand what it takes to succeed. They're saying, "I see you, and I appreciate what you do."

Going Beyond the Obvious

It's easy to give credit to those in the spotlight—the star players, the team leaders, the ones who deliver the final product. But true leadership goes beyond the obvious. It means looking deeper and recognizing the people who don't usually get a thank you. This might be the administrative assistant who ensures meetings run smoothly, or the IT specialist who keeps everything running behind the scenes.

The key is to be specific and sincere. Don't just throw out a generic "thank you." Take the time to understand what each person did and why it mattered. Verbal recognition is great, but written acknowledgments can be even more powerful. A personal note or a shoutout in a meeting can make a huge difference. And if you want to go the extra mile, consider symbolic gestures like giving a game ball to someone who isn't on the field but played a crucial role in the team's success.

Building a Culture of Inclusion and Appreciation

When leaders consistently share credit with everyone involved, they create a ripple effect. It fosters a culture of inclusion and appreciation, where everyone feels their work is meaningful. This kind of environment isn't just nice to have; it's a game-changer. People who feel valued are more engaged, more committed, and more likely to go above and beyond.

Inclusion goes hand in hand with shared credit. It's about more than just recognizing contributions; it's about making sure everyone's voice is heard. This means actively seeking out and considering the perspectives of all team members, regardless of their role or visibility. By doing this, leaders can tap into a wealth of ideas and insights that might otherwise go unnoticed.

The ability to share credit is a crucial leadership skill, one that goes beyond basic recognition. It's about understanding the collective effort required to achieve success and making sure everyone involved feels valued. When leaders practice this, they don't just boost morale—they build a culture of collaboration and support that drives long-term success.

So, the next time you're celebrating a win, take a moment to think about everyone who helped make it possible. Seek them out, acknowledge their contributions, and make sure they know they're appreciated. Because when you share credit, you're not just lifting others up—you're lifting the whole team, yourself included.

Key Actions

1. Recognize Everyone's Contributions: Acknowledge not just the visible team members but also those who work behind the scenes. Their efforts are crucial to success.
2. Be Specific and Sincere: Go beyond generic statements of appreciation. Take the time to understand what each person did and why it mattered, and express your gratitude in a meaningful way.
3. Use Various Forms of Recognition: Verbal recognition, written acknowledgments, and symbolic gestures like giving a game ball are effective ways to show appreciation.
4. Foster Inclusion: Actively seek out and consider the perspectives and ideas of all team members, regardless of their role or visibility.
5. Build a Culture of Appreciation: Consistently sharing credit creates a workplace where everyone feels valued, leading to greater engagement and commitment.

Discussion Questions

1. Why is it important for leaders to recognize the contributions of team members who are not in the spotlight? How can this impact overall team morale?
2. In what ways can a leader go beyond the obvious when sharing credit? Can you share examples from your own experience where someone acknowledged a less visible contributor?
3. How does the act of sharing credit contribute to building a culture of inclusion within a team or organization? What are some challenges leaders might face in fostering this culture?
4. What are the potential consequences of failing to acknowledge the contributions of those in less visible roles? How might this oversight affect team dynamics and performance?

5. How can leaders ensure that their recognition of others is both specific and sincere? What strategies can be used to make sure that all team members feel valued and appreciated?

Practice Exercises

1. Weekly Recognition Roundup

- **Objective**: To practice identifying and acknowledging contributions from less visible team members.
- **How to Do It**: At the end of each week, take 15 minutes to reflect on your team's work. Identify at least three individuals whose efforts were crucial but not immediately visible. Write a personalized note or send a quick message to each, specifically mentioning what they did and why it mattered. This exercise will help you develop the habit of looking beyond the obvious when giving credit.

2. Inclusion in Team Meetings

- **Objective**: To ensure all team members feel heard and valued, regardless of their role or visibility.
- **How to Do It**: In your next team meeting, make a deliberate effort to include input from everyone, especially those who usually stay quiet or are less visible. Before the meeting, review the agenda and think about how each team member's role relates to the topics at hand. During the meeting, specifically ask for their insights or feedback. This exercise will help you practice fostering a culture of inclusion.

3. Symbolic Gestures of Appreciation

- **Objective**: To develop the habit of using symbolic gestures to recognize and appreciate team members.
- **How to Do It**: Choose a symbolic gesture that resonates with your team culture—this could be something like a "team MVP" award, a "game ball," or even a simple but meaningful

token of appreciation. Each month, present this to someone who has made significant contributions behind the scenes. When presenting it, explain why this person's work was crucial to the team's success. This exercise will help you cultivate a culture of appreciation through meaningful, tangible recognition.

RECOGNIZE CONSTRAINTS

Being a leader isn't just about having the right answers or being the best at the tasks your team performs. It's about building trust, guiding effectively, and knowing when to lean on the expertise of others.

When you first step into a leadership role, you might find yourself in familiar territory. Maybe you've done the job your team is doing, and you can confidently say, "I've been in your shoes, and I know what it takes to get the job done." This experience helps you earn respect and trust. You're seen as a "player-coach," someone who's not just giving orders from a distance but who truly understands the work.

But as you climb the ladder, things start to shift. Suddenly, you're managing people who are doing things you've never done—and may never do. It's tempting to try to learn these tasks quickly, to present yourself as an expert in areas you're not familiar with. You might think this will bolster your credibility, but it's a risky move.

The Thin Veil of Pretend Competence

Let's be honest: pretending to know something you don't is a short-lived strategy. Your team can see through it. They know when you're out of your depth, and if you're not careful, this can erode your credibility faster than you might think. The advice you give could come across as hollow or disconnected from the realities of their work. Instead of earning respect, you risk becoming the leader they joke about when you're out of the room.

So, what's the alternative? How can you lead a team when you don't have firsthand experience with their tasks?

Acknowledging Limitations: The Path to True Credibility

Here's the good news: you don't need to have all the answers. In fact, acknowledging that you don't know everything can be one of your greatest strengths as a leader. It shows humility, a willingness to learn, and respect for the expertise of your team.

Imagine leading a group of human resources professionals. You might not know the ins and outs of employee benefits or workplace policies. Instead of bluffing your way through, you admit what you don't know and seek out the right resources—whether that's consulting with HR experts or diving into the employee handbook. By doing this, you show your team that you value their knowledge and are committed to making informed decisions.

This approach doesn't just protect your credibility; it enhances it. Your team will respect you more for being honest and seeking their input than for pretending to be an expert when you're not.

Leading Through Constraints

The real mark of a great leader isn't their ability to do everyone's job but their ability to understand what's getting in the way of those jobs getting done. That's where your focus should be.

Think about it: the people you lead face obstacles daily—tight deadlines, resource limitations, conflicting priorities, and so on. When you take the time to understand these challenges, you're showing that you're invested in their success. You're not just issuing directives; you're actively working to remove barriers and make their jobs easier.

Ask questions, observe processes, and listen carefully to your team's frustrations. By understanding the constraints they're working under, you can offer advice and solutions that are truly helpful. This makes your leadership relevant and valued, even in areas where you don't have direct experience.

Evolving Credibility: From Doer to Supporter

Early in your career, your credibility might stem from your ability to do the job as well as—or better than—those you lead. But as you grow into more senior roles, your credibility must evolve. It becomes less about being the best at the tasks and more about being the best at supporting your team in doing theirs.

This shift requires a mindset change. Instead of trying to be the expert in every area, focus on being the expert in removing obstacles and enabling success. When your team knows you're in their corner—understanding their pressures and constraints—they'll seek your guidance and value your leadership.

Leadership Beyond the Task

In the end, leadership isn't about knowing how to do everyone's job. It's about knowing what's needed to help everyone do their jobs better. When you understand the constraints your team faces and work to alleviate them, you demonstrate a deeper level of competence and earn lasting credibility.

The next time you're faced with leading a team whose work is unfamiliar to you, resist the urge to fake it. Instead, embrace the opportunity to learn from your team, understand their challenges, and lead by supporting them. This is the path to becoming a leader who is respected not just for what they know, but for how they help others succeed.

Key Actions

- **Acknowledge Your Limitations**: Don't pretend to know everything. Admitting what you don't know and seeking out the necessary resources shows humility and builds trust with your team.
- **Seek Out Expertise**: Leverage the knowledge and experience of your team members by consulting with them and using available resources to make informed decisions.
- **Understand the Constraints**: Focus on understanding the obstacles, challenges, and pressures your team faces. This helps you provide relevant and effective guidance.
- **Ask Questions and Listen**: Engage with your team by asking questions and listening to their concerns. This allows you to gain insight into the challenges they encounter and how you can help address them.
- **Shift from Doer to Supporter**: As you progress in your leadership role, focus less on doing the tasks yourself and

more on supporting your team in achieving their goals by removing obstacles and enabling success.

- **Invest in Your Team's Success:** Show your commitment to your team by actively working to remove barriers and make their jobs easier, demonstrating that you are invested in their success.

Discussion Questions

1. What are some challenges leaders face when managing teams in areas they have little or no experience with, and how can they effectively navigate these situations?
2. How does acknowledging your limitations as a leader impact your credibility and relationship with your team? Can you share an example from your experience?
3. Why is it important for leaders to focus on understanding the constraints and obstacles their teams face rather than trying to master every task themselves?
4. In what ways can leaders effectively shift from being 'doers' to 'supporters' as they advance in their careers, and what are the potential benefits of this approach?
5. How can leaders strike a balance between relying on their team's expertise and providing their own guidance without undermining their credibility?

Practice Exercises

1. Active Listening Sessions

- **Objective**: Improve your ability to understand the constraints and challenges your team faces by practicing active listening.
- **How to Do It**: Schedule one-on-one meetings with team members where your sole focus is to listen to their concerns and challenges. Ask open-ended questions to encourage them to share details about their work processes and obstacles. Resist the urge to offer solutions immediately. Instead, take

notes and follow up later with thoughtful guidance or support based on what you've learned.

2. Humility in Action

- **Objective**: Practice acknowledging your limitations and seeking out the expertise of others.
- **How to Do It**: Identify an area of your team's work that you are not familiar with. During a team meeting, openly acknowledge your lack of expertise in this area and ask for the team's input and guidance. Commit to learning from their expertise by participating in a workshop, training session, or even just a collaborative discussion where they lead the conversation. Reflect on how this approach impacts your team's perception of your leadership.

3. Obstacle Mapping

- **Objective**: Develop a deeper understanding of the constraints your team faces and how you can help alleviate them.
- **How to Do It**: Create a visual map or list of the common obstacles your team encounters in their daily work. Gather this information through team surveys, discussions, or observation. Once you have identified the key obstacles, work with your team to brainstorm potential solutions. Prioritize these solutions and create an action plan to address the most critical barriers. Regularly review and update this map to ensure you are continually supporting your team's success.

REFOCUS AFTER WINS AND LOSSES

As a leader, one of your most critical roles is to help your team make sense of their experiences, especially in the wake of success or failure. These moments—whether they're marked by victory, defeat, or somewhere in between—are ripe with opportunities for growth, learning, and reorientation. How you guide your team through these experiences shapes their understanding of what's important and reinforces the core values that drive your organization forward.

The Power of Perspective: Shaping Meaning in Victory and Defeat

Success and failure are two sides of the same coin. Each has the potential to teach valuable lessons, but only if approached with the right mindset. After a big win, it's easy for teams to get caught up in the euphoria, while a loss can lead to frustration and doubt. As a leader, it's your job to cut through the noise and bring focus back to what truly matters.

Consider a scenario where your team just landed a major client. The temptation might be to celebrate the outcome and bask in the glory. But effective leaders dig deeper. Instead of merely acknowledging the success, you might highlight the specific strategies that led to the win —whether it was the persistence of a team member, the creative approach to problem-solving, or the careful attention to client needs. This reinforces the behaviors that align with your organization's values and ensures the success isn't seen as a fluke, but rather the result of intentional actions.

On the flip side, after a setback, the focus should be on extracting lessons rather than dwelling on the failure. Perhaps a project didn't pan out as expected due to unforeseen challenges. The goal here is to help your team understand what went wrong, not to assign blame, but to learn. Did the team rush through a critical planning phase? Was there a communication breakdown? By pinpointing these factors, you help your team avoid similar pitfalls in the future and encourage a culture of continuous improvement.

Separating Outcome from Lesson: Avoiding the Trap of Misguided Learning

In environments where metrics reign supreme, it's easy to conflate outcome with decision quality. A positive result can sometimes mask poor decision-making, while a negative outcome might obscure the fact that the right approach was taken. This is where your leadership comes into play—ensuring that the right lessons are learned, regardless of the outcome.

Imagine your team made a risky decision that paid off in the short term. The outcome was positive, but the decision-making process was flawed—perhaps it relied too heavily on assumptions or ignored key data. As a leader, it's crucial to help your team recognize that the success was due to luck, not strategy. Without this clarification, your team might mistakenly believe that reckless decisions are acceptable, leading to repeated mistakes.

Conversely, if a well-considered decision doesn't yield the desired result, it's important to reinforce that the process was sound. This helps to build confidence in decision-making frameworks and prevents the team from becoming discouraged by a single negative outcome. The focus should always be on refining the approach, not just on the immediate result.

Creating Meaning Through Stories and Personal Anecdotes

One of the most powerful tools at your disposal as a leader is storytelling. By sharing personal experiences and anecdotes, you can create a lasting impact on how your team perceives and internalizes the values you deem important.

For instance, let's say you've experienced a car accident in the past. You might share this story with your team to illustrate the importance of prioritizing safety over material concerns. The crumpled car can be repaired or replaced, but the value of human life and well-being is irreplaceable. This kind of story not only conveys a lesson but also humanizes you as a leader, making your values more relatable and tangible to your team.

Stories like these resonate because they tap into emotions and lived experiences, making abstract values concrete. They also provide a context that purely logical explanations often lack, helping your team to connect on a deeper level with the principles you want to instill.

Guiding Your Team Toward Purpose and Direction

At the heart of effective leadership is the ability to provide guidance and context, helping your team make sense of their experiences in a way that fosters a sense of purpose and direction. When your team understands not just the 'what' but the 'why' behind their actions, they're more likely to stay engaged and aligned with the organization's goals.

This clarity leads to better decision-making because your team isn't just chasing outcomes—they're making choices that reflect the core values of the organization. Over time, this builds a culture of trust and cohesion, where every success is seen as a step forward in a shared journey, and every failure is viewed as a lesson learned.

Leading Through Success and Failure

In the grand scheme of leadership, your ability to reorient your team around what really matters—especially in moments of success and failure—is what sets you apart. It's easy to let outcomes dictate the narrative, but the true test of leadership lies in how well you can shape meaning, create context, and ensure that the right lessons are learned.

By focusing on the values and principles that underpin your organization, you help your team navigate the ups and downs with a clear sense of purpose. This doesn't just lead to better outcomes; it builds a stronger, more resilient team that's equipped to handle whatever challenges come their way. And that's what really matters in the end.

Key Actions

- **Shape Meaning After Success and Failure**: As a leader, guide your team in making sense of their experiences, particularly after victories or setbacks. Emphasize the lessons and values that matter most, ensuring that the focus is on growth and learning rather than just the outcome.

- **Reinforce the Right Behaviors**: After a success, highlight the specific actions and strategies that led to the positive outcome. This ensures that the team understands the intentional behaviors behind the success, rather than attributing it to luck.
- **Extract Lessons from Setbacks**: When things don't go as planned, help your team identify what went wrong and what can be improved. Focus on learning from the experience rather than assigning blame.
- **Separate Outcome from Decision Quality**: Make sure your team understands the difference between a successful outcome and good decision-making. Acknowledge when luck played a role in success and when a sound decision-making process didn't yield the desired result.
- **Use Storytelling to Convey Values**: Share personal anecdotes and stories to illustrate important values and lessons. This helps to humanize leadership and makes abstract principles more relatable and tangible for your team.
- **Provide Context and Purpose**: Guide your team by providing clear context and explaining the 'why' behind their actions. This fosters a sense of purpose and alignment with the organization's goals, leading to better decision-making and stronger team cohesion.

Discussion Questions

1. How can leaders effectively separate the outcome of a situation from the quality of the decision-making process, and why is this important for long-term success?
2. In what ways can storytelling and personal anecdotes be used by leaders to reinforce core values within a team? Can you share an example from your own experience?
3. How should a leader handle a situation where a poor decision

leads to a positive outcome? What steps can be taken to ensure the team learns the right lesson from this experience?

4. What strategies can leaders use to help their team reorient and focus on what truly matters after a significant success or failure? How can this influence the team's future performance?

5. How does providing context and purpose behind actions impact team cohesion and decision-making? Can you think of a time when understanding the 'why' behind a decision changed your approach or attitude?

Practice Exercises

1. Outcome Reflection Exercise

- **Objective**: Improve your ability to separate outcomes from decision quality and reinforce the right lessons.
- **How to Do It**: After every major project or decision, take time to reflect on both the outcome and the decision-making process. Write down the specific actions that led to the result, whether positive or negative. Identify if the outcome was a result of sound strategy, execution, or luck. Discuss these reflections with your team, emphasizing the lessons learned and reinforcing the behaviors that align with your organization's values.

2. Storytelling Practice

- **Objective**: Enhance your ability to use storytelling to convey values and lessons effectively.
- **How to Do It**: Choose a value or lesson you want to instill in your team. Think of a personal story or anecdote that illustrates this value. Practice telling this story in a way that is engaging and relatable, focusing on how it connects to the lesson you want your team to learn. Share this story in a team meeting or one-on-one conversation, and observe how it

resonates with your audience. Ask for feedback to improve your storytelling skills.

3. Purpose and Context Alignment Exercise

- **Objective**: Strengthen your ability to provide context and align your team with the organization's purpose.
- **How to Do It**: Before your next team meeting, take a recent decision or project and break down the 'why' behind it. Outline how this decision or project aligns with the organization's goals and values. During the meeting, present this context clearly, explaining the purpose behind the actions taken. Encourage your team to ask questions and discuss how understanding the 'why' influences their motivation and approach. Make this a regular practice to reinforce the importance of context and purpose in everyday actions.

RESPECT EXPERTS

Leadership is not about knowing everything. It's about knowing who to turn to when you don't. Recognizing the limits of your expertise isn't a weakness; it's a strength. In an increasingly complex world, no single person can master every domain. The most effective leaders understand this and leverage it to their advantage.

They don't just rely on their own knowledge—they surround themselves with experts from various fields. These leaders become curators of talent, building strong, trusted relationships with individuals who have specialized skills and knowledge. By doing so, they position themselves to navigate challenges and make informed decisions with the help of those who truly know their stuff.

Collecting Experts: The Key to Informed Leadership

One of the most critical behaviors of successful leaders is their ability to tap into a network of experts when needed. Rather than trying to muddle through complex issues alone, they reach out for guidance. This approach not only leads to better decision-making but also strengthens their ability to support and lead others effectively.

The best leaders don't just surround themselves with experts; they actively cultivate these relationships. They understand that having a wide-ranging network is like having a toolkit—each expert represents a different tool that can be used when the situation demands it. This approach turns the leader into a kind of generalist-specialist, someone who knows how to access and apply specialized knowledge as needed.

Communicating with Experts: The Art of Collaboration

Having access to expertise is one thing; effectively communicating with experts is another. Leaders must be able to clearly articulate their needs and questions, but more importantly, they need to listen. Truly listening to those with specialized knowledge requires humility and a willingness to learn.

Effective leaders foster a culture of collaboration, where ideas and knowledge flow freely. They encourage open dialogue, ask the right questions, and create an environment where experts feel valued and heard. This not only improves decision-making but also strengthens the entire organization by promoting a continuous learning mindset.

Knowing Who Knows: The Real Expertise

True expertise in leadership isn't just about what you know—it's about knowing who knows. This means that leaders don't need to have all the answers at their fingertips, but they do need to know where to find those answers quickly.

Effective leaders build a diverse network of experts across a wide range of fields. This includes traditional areas like law, finance, and medicine, but also extends to more niche topics like technology, nutrition, or even parenting. The broader and more diverse the network, the better equipped the leader is to handle any situation that arises.

But collecting experts is just the first step. Leaders must keep these relationships active and alive. This means regularly engaging with their network, maintaining trust, and ensuring that lines of communication are always open. In doing so, they not only become more informed but also more effective in their roles.

Growing Through Expertise

At the core of great leadership is the recognition that growth is a never-ending process. By continuously seeking out new knowledge and building strong relationships with experts, leaders can evolve and adapt in an ever-changing world.

This growth isn't just personal; it's organizational. As leaders grow, so too does their ability to guide and develop their teams. By respecting true expertise—both in themselves and others—leaders create an environment where learning, collaboration, and informed decision-making become the norm.

In the end, leadership is about making the right choices for the right reasons. And often, the best choice a leader can make is to reach out to someone who knows more than they do. By doing so, they not only improve their own understanding but also elevate the entire team or organization. That's the power of respecting true expertise.

Key Actions

- **Recognize the Limits of Your Expertise**: Understand that you can't know everything and that it's a strength, not a weakness, to acknowledge this.
- **Surround Yourself with Experts**: Build a network of individuals with specialized knowledge and skills across various fields.
- **Cultivate Relationships with Experts**: Actively maintain and strengthen your connections with these experts, treating them as valuable resources.
- **Tap into Your Network When Needed**: Reach out to your network of experts for guidance and advice rather than trying to navigate complex issues on your own.
- **Communicate Effectively with Experts**: Clearly articulate your needs and questions while being open to listening and learning from those with specialized knowledge.
- **Foster a Culture of Collaboration**: Create an environment where ideas and knowledge flow freely, and experts feel valued and heard.
- **Know Who Knows**: Understand that true leadership expertise includes knowing who has the answers, not just having all the answers yourself.
- **Keep Relationships Active and Alive**: Regularly engage with your network to maintain trust and ensure open lines of communication.
- **Promote Continuous Learning**: Embrace and encourage a mindset of ongoing growth and development, both for yourself and your organization.

Discussion Questions

1. How can leaders effectively balance their own expertise with the need to rely on the expertise of others?

2. What strategies can be used to build and maintain a diverse network of experts across various fields?

3. In what ways can leaders foster a culture of collaboration where experts feel valued and ideas flow freely?

4. How does knowing who to reach out to, rather than having all the answers, impact a leader's decision-making process?

5. What are some practical steps leaders can take to ensure they are continuously learning and growing alongside their network of experts?

Practice Exercises

1. Expert Network Mapping

- **Objective**: Identify and expand your network of experts across various fields.
- **How to Do It**: Start by listing the current experts you know and categorize them by their area of expertise (e.g., law, technology, finance). Identify gaps in your network where you may need additional expertise. Set a goal to reach out to at least two new experts each month, whether through networking events, professional associations, or referrals. Regularly review and update your network map to ensure it remains diverse and robust.

2. Active Listening Practice

- **Objective**: Improve your ability to effectively communicate and collaborate with experts.
- **How to Do It**: Choose a conversation or meeting with an expert as an opportunity to practice active listening. During the discussion, focus entirely on what the expert is saying without interrupting. Take notes if necessary. After the expert has finished speaking, summarize what you heard and ask clarifying questions to ensure you fully understand their perspective. Reflect on the conversation afterward to identify

what you learned and how it can be applied in your leadership role.

3. Decision-Making with Expert Input

- **Objective**: Develop the habit of integrating expert advice into your decision-making process.
- **How to Do It**: Identify a decision you need to make that falls outside your primary area of expertise. Reach out to relevant experts in your network for their input on the decision. Synthesize the advice you receive and weigh it against your own knowledge and the context of the decision. Make your decision and afterward, reflect on how the expert input influenced the outcome. Consider whether this approach can be applied to future decisions.

CELEBRATE REAL EXCELLENCE

Excellence is one of those things everyone chases but few can truly define. It's elusive, often hidden, and even harder to recognize. But here's the kicker: being able to spot excellence—whether it's in yourself, your team, or even in the most unexpected places—sets a leader apart. It's not about who benefits. It's about seeing greatness, no matter where it comes from, and giving it the recognition it deserves.

The Sharp Eye: Seeing Excellence in Unlikely Places

Great leaders possess a rare skill: the ability to recognize excellence even in areas where they might not be experts. This isn't just about acknowledging brilliance within their own industry or team; it's about seeing it anywhere, in anyone. Imagine a CEO who can spot outstanding customer service in a front-line employee at a completely different company. That's more than just good leadership; it's a sign of real competence. It shows the leader can assess talent objectively, without letting ego or self-interest cloud their judgment.

When a leader recognizes excellence in places others might overlook, they're not just acknowledging a job well done. They're sending a message: excellence matters, no matter where it comes from. This kind of recognition is rare and, when done right, can set a leader apart as someone who truly understands what it means to be great.

Humility in Leadership: Knowing When You Don't Know

Another hallmark of a competent leader is the ability to admit their own limitations. No one knows everything, and the smartest leaders are the ones who know what they don't know. These leaders aren't afraid to seek out advice, guidance, and support from experts in other fields. They understand that learning doesn't stop at the boundaries of their own knowledge.

By surrounding themselves with people who are smarter or more experienced in certain areas, these leaders make better decisions. They're not just making informed choices; they're setting an example for their teams. It's a clear signal that learning, growth, and openness to new ideas are valued.

This approach also has a practical benefit: it increases the leader's credibility. People are more likely to follow someone who admits they don't have all the answers and shows a willingness to learn from others. It's a sign of strength, not weakness.

Unbiased Recognition: Even When It's Tough

Here's where the rubber meets the road: recognizing excellence when it's inconvenient, or even when it hurts. It's easy to praise someone you like or someone who's on your team. But what about a competitor? Or someone who's fallen out of favor? A true leader acknowledges excellence wherever it's found, even if it's in someone they don't particularly respect.

This kind of recognition requires objectivity and a deep commitment to valuing excellence above personal feelings. When a leader can do this, it sends a powerful message: that they're committed to fairness, and that excellence will always be recognized, no matter who it comes from.

This approach doesn't just build trust; it attracts top talent. People want to work with leaders who are fair, objective, and committed to recognizing and rewarding true excellence. By valuing achievement in all its forms, leaders create an environment where high-performing individuals want to be.

The Payoff: A Culture of Excellence

At the end of the day, excellence is a rare quality that not everyone can see. But when a leader has the competence to recognize it, the humility to seek it out in others, and the integrity to acknowledge it—even when it's tough—they set themselves apart.

These leaders build credibility, foster a culture of learning, and attract top talent. They're not just making their own success more likely; they're paving the way for the success of everyone around them. By embracing and celebrating excellence in all its forms, these leaders create an environment where excellence can thrive—and that's a win for everyone involved.

Key Actions

- **Recognize Excellence Everywhere**: Effective leaders can spot excellence in any individual or situation, even in areas outside their expertise or where they wouldn't normally expect to see it.
- **Objective Assessment**: Leaders should be able to assess talent and excellence without letting ego or self-interest influence their judgment. This includes recognizing excellence in competitors or in people they may not personally respect.
- **Acknowledge Limitations**: Competent leaders admit their own limitations and seek out advice, guidance, and support from experts in other fields, demonstrating an openness to learning and growth.
- **Unbiased Recognition**: Leaders must be willing to acknowledge excellence even when it's inconvenient or challenging, showing a commitment to fairness and objectivity.
- **Promote a Culture of Excellence**: By consistently recognizing and celebrating excellence, leaders foster an environment where high-performing individuals want to work, thereby attracting top talent and encouraging overall success.

Discussion Questions

1. How can leaders develop the ability to recognize excellence in areas outside of their expertise? What strategies or habits can they adopt to sharpen this skill?
2. In what ways can acknowledging one's own limitations and seeking advice from experts in other fields enhance a leader's credibility and decision-making process?
3. Why is it important for leaders to recognize excellence in competitors or individuals they may not personally respect?

How can this practice influence the overall culture of an organization?

4. Discuss the challenges leaders might face when recognizing excellence in situations where it might be inconvenient or uncomfortable. How can they overcome these challenges?

5. How can leaders create and sustain a culture of excellence within their organization? What role does consistent recognition and celebration of excellence play in attracting and retaining top talent?

Practice Exercises

1. Daily Excellence Spotting

- **Objective**: Improve your ability to recognize excellence in unexpected places.
- **How to Do It**: Each day, make it a point to identify at least one instance of excellence outside of your immediate field or team. This could be in a different department, a competitor, or even in your personal life. Reflect on why you consider this instance as excellence and how it can be applied or acknowledged in your own context. Document these observations in a journal to track your progress.

2. Seek Out Expert Opinions

- **Objective**: Enhance your openness to learning and improve decision-making by acknowledging your limitations.
- **How to Do It**: Identify an area where you feel less confident in your knowledge or expertise. Reach out to an expert in that field—this could be through reading their work, attending a seminar, or having a direct conversation. After gathering insights, reflect on how this new knowledge can inform your leadership decisions. Implement this habit regularly to build a network of experts you can rely on.

3. Unbiased Acknowledgment Drill

- **Objective**: Strengthen your ability to objectively recognize excellence, even in challenging situations.
- **How to Do It**: Think of a person or organization you don't particularly admire or have had conflicts with in the past. Identify something they've done that can be considered excellent, no matter how small. Write a note or email acknowledging their achievement. This exercise helps train your mind to be objective and fair in recognizing excellence, regardless of personal feelings.

HOLD YOUR OPINIONS

When you've been in the game long enough, certain patterns start to emerge. One that I've seen time and again, both in others and in my own leadership journey, is the tendency to overlook the impact our actions have on our teams. It's easy to fall into this trap—especially when you're used to moving fast, making decisions, and getting things done. But here's the catch: this can lead to a dangerous habit, one that stifles the very thing that makes a team thrive—open dialogue.

The Trap of Dominating Conversations

High-performing leaders are often the sharpest minds in the room. They know what they want, and they know how to get it. But this strength can quickly become a weakness when it leads to dominating conversations and decision-making processes. You've probably seen it happen: a leader walks into a meeting, mind already made up, and subtly or not-so-subtly steers the discussion toward their preferred outcome.

The result? The conversation becomes one-sided. Instead of a free exchange of ideas, the team ends up focusing on how to execute the leader's plan. And while efficiency is great, it's not the same as effectiveness. In fact, it can kill creativity and block the flow of fresh, potentially game-changing ideas.

The Silent Cost of Preemptive Opinions

It's important to remember that leaders hold a lot of sway in any discussion. When you, as a leader, express your opinion right out of the gate, you unintentionally set the tone for the entire conversation. Your team members, consciously or not, will likely align their views with yours. They may hold back opposing viewpoints or critical data that could challenge your perspective. After all, who wants to be the one to contradict the boss?

This isn't just about people-pleasing. It's about the psychological pressure that comes from knowing that your leader has a strong preference.

And the higher the stakes, the stronger that pressure becomes. Suddenly, the meeting isn't about finding the best solution; it's about aligning with the leader's view and moving on. The risk? You miss out on insights that could make all the difference.

The Power of Withholding Judgment

The best leaders know that great ideas don't always come from the top. They also understand that their role isn't just to make decisions, but to cultivate an environment where every voice can be heard—where the magic of collaboration can happen.

One of the simplest, yet most powerful, strategies to achieve this is to hold back your opinion. That's right—keep your thoughts to yourself, at least at first. Let your team explore the problem from every angle. Encourage them to share their ideas, no matter how unconventional. Ask questions, listen actively, and show genuine interest in what they have to say.

By withholding your judgment, you're giving your team the space they need to think creatively and speak freely. This doesn't just lead to better solutions; it builds trust. Your team members will feel more valued and more willing to share their ideas in the future, knowing that their contributions truly matter.

Creating an Environment for Innovation

Innovation thrives in environments where ideas can flow freely without fear of judgment or reprisal. As a leader, it's your job to create that environment. That means recognizing the weight your words carry and being intentional about when and how you express your opinions.

Instead of jumping in with your ideas right away, try this approach:

- *Start by asking questions*: What do you think? How would you approach this? What are we missing?
- *Listen with an open mind:* Really hear what your team is saying. Don't just listen for the sake of responding.

- *Encourage debate:* Let your team challenge each other's ideas, and even yours. Debate is healthy and often leads to the best outcomes.
- *Reserve your opinion:* Once all ideas have been fully explored, then—and only then—share your thoughts. And when you do, be open to revising them based on what you've heard.

By taking these steps, you're not just leading—you're facilitating a process where the best ideas can surface, no matter where they come from. This isn't just good for your team; it's good for your business.

The Long-Term Benefits

Leaders who consistently hold back their opinions and allow their teams to explore ideas fully will see long-term benefits. Your team will become more engaged, more innovative, and more confident in their abilities. They'll feel ownership over their work, knowing that their input is valued and can make a real impact.

Moreover, by fostering a culture of open communication and collaboration, you'll find that your team is more adaptable and resilient in the face of challenges. They'll be better equipped to handle uncertainty and will approach problems with a solution-oriented mindset.

At the end of the day, leadership isn't about being the smartest person in the room or having all the answers. It's about guiding your team toward the best possible outcome by creating a space where ideas can be freely exchanged and explored. It's about recognizing that your role is to facilitate, not dominate.

So, next time you're in a meeting, remember: keep your opinions to yourself—at least for a little while. You might just be surprised by what your team comes up with when given the space to think and speak freely.

Key Actions

1. **Avoid Dominating Conversations**: Refrain from steering discussions towards your pre-determined solutions. Allow the

conversation to flow freely to encourage the exchange of diverse ideas.

2. **Hold Back Your Opinion Initially**: Delay sharing your thoughts or opinions until all ideas and perspectives have been fully explored by the team.

3. **Ask Open-Ended Questions**: Start the conversation by asking questions like, "What do you think?" or "How would you approach this?" to encourage input from your team.

4. **Listen Actively**: Pay close attention to what your team is saying without immediately formulating a response. Show genuine interest in their ideas.

5. **Encourage Healthy Debate**: Allow your team to challenge each other's ideas, and even yours. Promote debate as a way to explore all possible solutions.

6. **Recognize the Weight of Your Words**: Understand that your opinions carry significant influence and should be shared thoughtfully to avoid stifling creativity and open dialogue.

7. **Facilitate, Don't Dominate**: Focus on guiding your team toward the best outcome by creating an environment where everyone feels comfortable sharing and exploring ideas.

Discussion Questions

1. How can leaders strike a balance between being decisive and allowing for open dialogue within their teams?

2. What are some potential consequences of a leader sharing their opinion too early in a discussion? How might this impact team dynamics and decision-making?

3. In what ways can leaders encourage team members to share their ideas and challenge the status quo without fear of retribution?

4. How can holding back your opinion as a leader lead to more innovative solutions within a team? Can you think of any real-life examples where this approach has been successful?

5. What strategies can leaders use to actively listen and engage

with their teams during discussions, ensuring that all voices are heard?

Practice Exercises

1. The Silent Leader Exercise

- **Objective**: To practice withholding your opinion to foster open dialogue and creativity within your team.
- **How to Do It**: In your next team meeting, consciously decide to refrain from sharing your opinion until the very end of the discussion. Focus on asking open-ended questions and encouraging others to share their thoughts first. After the meeting, reflect on how this approach impacted the quality of the conversation and the variety of ideas presented.

2. Active Listening Drill

- **Objective**: To improve your ability to listen actively and engage with your team members' ideas.
- **How to Do It**: During a one-on-one or team discussion, commit to not interrupting or interjecting your own thoughts while someone else is speaking. Instead, focus on truly understanding their perspective. After they finish, summarize what they said to confirm your understanding before offering any feedback or opinion. This practice will help you develop stronger listening skills and build trust within your team.

3. Debate Facilitation Practice

- **Objective**: To encourage healthy debate and ensure all perspectives are considered before making a decision.
- **How to Do It**: During a team meeting, introduce a topic or problem that needs to be addressed. Assign different team members to argue for and against various solutions, even if it's

not their personal viewpoint. Your role is to facilitate the debate by asking probing questions and ensuring everyone participates. After the exercise, discuss as a group how the debate influenced their thinking and whether new ideas emerged that might not have otherwise been considered.

CHAPTER 2
BREAKING THE NICENESS TRAP

Have you ever worked somewhere where leaders and teams bend over backward to avoid candid conversations about performance? Yeah, me too.

When I first joined Colorado Lending Source, we had a culture like that. We've made strides since then, but those old habits die hard. Sure, we want a positive culture. But here's the thing: it has to be a positive, high-performing, and growth-oriented culture to be real. When politeness and cheerleading become the default in every conversation, the message is clear: being nice matters more than being honest. And that's where things start to fall apart. We end up in a culture where giving honest feedback or discussing performance issues is practically taboo.

Cultures of niceness can feel good, even supportive, but they're a trap. They keep people and teams from growing and hitting their full potential. Poor performance gets ignored, or worse, swept under the rug. Honest conversations about performance become rare, and because results aren't the focus, these "nice" cultures don't excel at much beyond being polite.

I call this the "niceness trap." It breeds mediocrity. Those who want to achieve real results either fall in line or leave, because asking for accountability in a culture of niceness is seen as rude. And when market conditions shift, and the organization's edge dulls, that polite culture sticks around, making it almost impossible to rekindle the honest conversations needed for real results.

But it doesn't have to be this way. Even in a niceness culture, leaders can learn to give candid feedback and hold others accountable while still being positive and supportive. Overcoming a tradition of politeness is less about mindset and more about leadership skill. Leaders can remind their teams that you can be polite and candid at the same time, and that politeness shouldn't be an excuse to dodge honest conversations.

So, how do we start? First, we need to understand why we avoid frank conversations in the first place. It's pretty simple: we want to be liked.

The need to be liked can be a fatal flaw for leaders in these cultures. All humans want to be liked, but when this desire becomes too strong, it can stop leaders from delivering tough messages, being honest in confrontations, and making hard decisions. Being liked isn't the problem; it's when the need to be liked interferes with a leader's ability to manage and hold others accountable that things go wrong. This need can warp decision-making and make it tough for leaders to make unpopular choices about team members they see as "friends."

The truth is, successful leaders strive to be likable, not liked. They act on strong values and principles, doing the right thing all the time. Speaking candidly and making sound choices is always the right thing to do. The urge to be liked is something leaders have to resist if they want to be effective. Having a likable style is good, but when the need for acceptance takes over, leadership suffers. As one leader puts it, "Don't set yourself on fire to keep others warm." Be a likable leader who doesn't need to be liked.

This desire to be liked often comes from a poor understanding of conflict. Handling conflict effectively is hard—it takes time, energy, and courage. It's always easier to avoid it. Conflicts are messy, complex, and often leave everyone feeling worse. And let's face it, addressing conflict increases the risk of not being liked, which can sting.

When teams aren't taught how to handle conflict in a healthy way, delivering tough messages becomes almost impossible. We'll tap-dance around the issue and, if we're lucky, manage to send an ambiguous message that leaves everyone thinking, "Well, that was weird, but I guess everything's fine."

The worst part of avoiding conflict is the mental gymnastics we do to keep from ruffling feathers. We'll go along with people even though we disagree with them. We support and maintain the status quo even when we know it's not working.

Let's not mince words: this is cowardice, plain and simple. Once you're branded gutless, it's nearly impossible to shake that label. You lose credibility, and it undermines everything you do in the eyes of your team and peers.

Remember, the purpose of feedback is to make people better. That brings us to a key principle in giving frank, high-quality feedback:

Criticism is a compliment.

That might sound counterintuitive, but dig a little deeper, and you'll see why it's true.

It's simple. It takes effort to identify and evaluate what actions are needed for real improvement. Developing a feedback-positive skill set is hard work. It's always easier to ignore problems and smooth things over. That's what you do when you don't care or think someone's a lost cause.

The highest compliment you can pay someone is the effort you're willing to put in to help them succeed. Sometimes that means giving tough feedback. Caring enough about someone to offer feedback is no small gesture. It's the essence of leadership.

Leadership is a two-way street. You have to want to lead, and people have to want to follow. True leadership asks you to do both. You need to care enough to want your team to succeed, and you need to be self-aware enough to know that the feedback you receive comes from a good place. This is hard, but that's why you need to do it.

Elite, player-led teams fight back against the poisonous tyranny of niceness, the desire to be liked, and the fear of both giving and receiving feedback. They know that failing to do so keeps everyone from reaching their full potential.

Only by mastering these behaviors can we create a culture where honest conversations and accountability lead to better performance, stronger results, and personal fulfillment.

In the following sections, I'm going to dive into how you can make your team better through feedback, what holds the team back, and what you can do to sharpen your feedback skills with the people you lead, your peers, and those who lead you.

TURN TOUGH TALKS INTO GROWTH

Let's face it: Giving and receiving feedback is no walk in the park. When we offer criticism, it often feels like we're stepping onto a minefield—essentially telling someone, "You're wrong, and I'm right." That's not just uncomfortable; it can be downright intimidating, especially if we're not completely confident in our own stance. It's easy to get lost in the gray areas, tempted to stay silent and avoid the conflict altogether. But here's the catch: If you take the easy way out, nobody grows.

Feedback, when used well, is one of the most powerful tools in a leader's arsenal. It's not just about pointing out mistakes; it's about sparking growth, improvement, and mutual understanding. Whether you're a parent, partner, coach, teacher, or manager, you're constantly giving feedback—even if you don't realize it. Sometimes it's in the form of a raised eyebrow, a sigh, or an offhand comment. Other times, it's more formal, like a performance review or a post-project debrief. Regardless of the format, feedback has the potential to drive change. At its best, it helps everyone involved become better. At its worst, it can ignite conflict, breed resentment, and drive a wedge between people who need to work together.

So how do we ensure that feedback leads to growth rather than discord? The good news is that the art of giving constructive, meaningful feedback can be mastered.

Involve the Recipient in the Process

The first step in mastering feedback is to shift the dynamic from a one-sided critique to a two-way conversation. Instead of simply telling someone what they did wrong, involve them in the discussion. Make them an active participant rather than a passive recipient. This means focusing on specific behaviors or actions instead of vague generalities or personal attacks. It requires a deep understanding of the people you're working with and a genuine commitment to their growth and success.

Ask for Permission

Here's a strategy that might surprise you: ask for permission before giving feedback. At first glance, this might seem overly cautious or even unnecessary, but there's a method to the madness. People learn best when they're ready to learn. By asking, "Is now a good time for some feedback?" you give the other person a sense of control over the conversation. This simple step can make them more open and receptive, turning what could be a tense interaction into a productive dialogue.

Focus on Behavior, Not the Person

It's crucial to separate the person from the behavior. Critique the action, not the individual. This takes practice, but it's essential for effective feedback. For example, instead of saying, "You're always so negative," it's more constructive to say, "I noticed you frowned during the meeting when we discussed the new project. Can we talk about that?" This approach makes the feedback more actionable and less likely to be perceived as a personal attack.

Own the Feedback

Another powerful tactic is to frame the feedback from your own perspective. Starting with "I" instead of "you" can soften the message and make it less confrontational. For example, saying "I felt concerned when the deadline was missed" is much more constructive than "You missed the deadline." This approach shows empathy and opens the door for a more open and honest conversation.

Ditch the "Sandwich" Approach

You've probably heard of the "sandwich" approach: cushioning negative feedback between two positive comments. While the intent is to soften the blow, this method often backfires. It can come across as insincere or even manipulative. Think about it—how do you feel when someone gives you "sandwiched" feedback? Probably patronized. Instead, be straightforward and genuine. Focus on specific behaviors that can be improved without sugarcoating the message.

Timing Is Everything

Timing plays a crucial role in how feedback is received. Ideally, feedback should be given as soon as possible after the behavior or event in question. This ensures that the details are fresh in everyone's mind, allowing for more immediate adjustments. However, timing isn't just about promptness; it's also about context. As I often tell my son, "Read the room." If someone is stressed out, exhausted, or overwhelmed, it's not the best time to pile on additional feedback. It takes emotional intelligence to gauge the situation and choose the right moment.

Create a Context of Openness and Safety

While the "what" and "when" of feedback are often situational, the "how" is universal. The best leaders foster an environment where feedback is seen as a tool for growth, not as a weapon. This requires creating a context of safety, balance, and openness. Specific leadership routines—such as regular check-ins, open-door policies, and transparent communication—can help establish this environment. When people feel safe, they're more likely to take feedback to heart and make meaningful changes.

Respect Through Actionable Feedback

Giving thoughtful, actionable feedback is one of the highest forms of respect you can show someone. It signals that you care enough to help them improve. On the flip side, avoiding necessary conversations or diluting your message out of discomfort does a disservice to everyone involved. Effective feedback is a catalyst for growth and development —if delivered with sincerity and clarity.

The Essence of Leadership

At the end of the day, leadership is about making the people and situations around you better. Don't shy away from giving feedback, but do so in a way that's supportive and constructive, not judgmental or punitive. This requires a deep understanding of the individuals you're working with and a genuine commitment to helping them succeed. When done right, feedback doesn't just improve performance—it builds trust, strengthens relationships, and fosters a culture of continuous improvement.

In essence, turning tough conversations into growth opportunities is what separates good leaders from great ones. Embrace the discomfort, master the art of feedback, and watch how it transforms not just your team, but your entire organization.

Key Actions

- **Involve the Recipient in the Process**: Engage the person in the feedback conversation by focusing on specific behaviors and making them an active participant.
- **Ask for Permission**: Before giving feedback, ask the recipient if they are open to it, allowing them to feel more in control and receptive.
- **Focus on Behavior, Not the Person**: Critique the specific action or behavior rather than making it personal, to ensure the feedback is constructive.
- **Own the Feedback**: Use "I" statements to frame feedback from your own perspective, which helps to soften the message and show empathy.
- **Ditch the "Sandwich" Approach**: Avoid cushioning negative feedback between positive comments, as this can come across as insincere. Instead, be direct and genuine.
- **Timing Is Everything**: Provide feedback as soon as possible after the event, while also being mindful of the recipient's current state and the context.
- **Create a Context of Openness and Safety**: Foster an environment where feedback is viewed as a tool for growth by establishing leadership routines that encourage openness and balance.
- **Respect Through Actionable Feedback**: Deliver feedback that is specific, actionable, and aimed at helping the recipient grow, rather than avoiding discomfort.

Discussion Questions

1. How can involving the recipient in the feedback process change the outcome of a tough conversation? Can you share an example from your experience?
2. What are the potential benefits and challenges of asking for permission before giving feedback? How might this approach impact the receptiveness of the recipient?
3. Why is it important to focus on behavior rather than the person when giving feedback? How might this distinction affect the relationship between the feedback giver and receiver?
4. What are the risks associated with using the "sandwich" approach to feedback? Can you think of a situation where this method might have backfired or been misunderstood?
5. How can leaders create a culture of openness and safety that encourages constructive feedback? What specific routines or practices have you found effective in fostering this environment?

Practice Exercises

1. Role-Playing Feedback Scenarios

- **Objective:** To practice giving and receiving feedback in a controlled environment, allowing you to refine your approach and build confidence
- **How to Do It:** Pair up with a colleague or friend and take turns role-playing different feedback scenarios. One person acts as the feedback giver, and the other as the recipient. Focus on involving the recipient in the conversation, using "I" statements, and avoiding the "sandwich" approach. After each role-play, discuss what worked well and what could be improved. Repeat this exercise with various scenarios to build versatility in your feedback delivery.

2. Ask for Permission Before Giving Feedback

- **Objective:** To build the habit of asking for permission before delivering feedback, making the recipient more open to the conversation.
- **How to Do It:** In your daily interactions, consciously practice asking for permission before offering feedback. For example, say, "I have some thoughts on how we could improve this. Would now be a good time to discuss them?" Observe how this affects the recipient's receptiveness and the overall tone of the conversation. Reflect on the outcomes and adjust your approach as needed.

3. Document and Reflect on Feedback Conversations

- **Objective:** To improve your feedback delivery by analyzing past interactions and identifying areas for growth.
- **How to Do It:** After giving feedback, take a few minutes to jot down what you said, how the recipient responded, and what the outcome was. Reflect on whether you focused on behavior rather than the person, if you used "I" statements effectively, and how timing influenced the conversation. Review these notes regularly to spot patterns and make adjustments to your feedback approach over time.

FEED FORWARD, NOT BACKWARD

Feedback is an essential tool for leadership. It helps people recognize their strengths and see where they can do better. But let's be honest: giving feedback can be tough. Most of us avoid it because we fear conflict or don't want to hurt someone's feelings. The problem is, when we shy away from giving honest feedback, we miss the opportunity to help others grow.

To overcome this, I recommend a strategy I call "feed forward." It's all about focusing on solutions and future steps rather than dwelling on past mistakes or performances. This approach shifts the conversation from blame to action, from defensiveness to progress.

Why "Feed Forward" Works

One of the biggest challenges with traditional feedback is that it often triggers defensiveness. When someone feels attacked or criticized for something they did in the past, their natural response is to defend themselves. They'll explain why they made certain choices or argue about the accuracy of the feedback. This back-and-forth can easily spiral into resistance and, ultimately, a stalemate.

"Feed forward" sidesteps this issue. By focusing on the future—what can be done differently or better—leaders can help individuals engage in the conversation without feeling the need to protect their egos. The past can't be changed, but the future is full of potential. This shift in focus makes it easier for people to listen, absorb, and act on the feedback.

Empowerment Through Optimism

There's little value in litigating the past. Rehashing old mistakes rarely leads to progress. Instead, by adopting a "feed forward" approach, leaders can make individuals feel more in control and empowered to take action. When people feel like they have a say in what comes next, they're more likely to take ownership of their actions and commit to improvement.

At its core, "feed forward" is about optimism. It's grounded in a belief in the individual's potential. By focusing on what can be achieved moving forward, leaders send a powerful message: "I believe in you and your ability to grow." This belief can be a strong motivator, boosting confidence and encouraging a proactive attitude.

Navigating the "Why"

Naturally, people will ask "Why?" when receiving feedback. They want to understand the reasoning behind it, and this curiosity can sometimes lead them to dig into past events. While it's important to be prepared to answer these questions, leaders should steer the conversation back to the future as quickly as possible. Providing clear and concise explanations can satisfy the need for context without getting bogged down in the past.

Striking the Right Balance

When it comes to delivering feedback, remember the mantra from Cobra Kai: "Strike hard, strike first, no mercy." Well, maybe not the "no mercy" part. Mercy is critical, but don't dance around the truth. Be direct, be honest, and don't sugarcoat the message. People appreciate honesty, even when it's tough to hear.

Too often, we soften our feedback to avoid conflict, thinking it will make the situation easier. But in doing so, we dilute the message. The best leaders deliver feedback with clarity and courage, fostering trust and respect in the process. It's like ripping off a band-aid—it might sting at first, but it's better than dragging it out.

Leading by Example

Finally, it's essential for leaders to be open to feedback themselves. If you expect others to take your feedback seriously, you must be willing to listen and learn from theirs. This not only helps you grow as a leader but also sets a positive example for your team. A culture of continuous improvement starts at the top.

"Feed forward" is a powerful tool for leaders. It's about helping people see their strengths, understand where they can improve, and motivate them to reach their full potential. By focusing on solutions, reducing defensiveness, and conveying optimism in their future, leaders can create a positive, supportive environment that encourages growth and success.

So, next time you're faced with giving feedback, remember to look forward. Guide the conversation toward what can be done, not what went wrong. Your team will thank you, and you'll find that progress comes more naturally when everyone is focused on the future.

Key Actions

- **Focus on the Future:** Shift the conversation from past mistakes to future actions and solutions.
- **Reduce Defensiveness:** Avoid triggering defensive reactions by emphasizing what can be done differently moving forward.
- **Empower Individuals:** Give people a sense of control and ownership over their next steps, which increases their engagement and commitment.
- **Convey Optimism:** Show belief in the individual's potential to improve and succeed, using feedback as a tool for motivation.
- **Answer the "Why" Quickly:** Provide clear and concise explanations for feedback without getting bogged down in past events.
- **Be Direct and Honest:** Deliver feedback with clarity and courage, avoiding sugarcoating or softening the message.
- **Be Open to Feedback Yourself:** Lead by example by being receptive to feedback and demonstrating a willingness to learn and grow.

Discussion Questions

1. How can leaders effectively balance the need to address past performance while keeping the focus on future solutions?
2. In what ways can focusing on the future rather than the past reduce defensiveness during feedback conversations?
3. How does conveying optimism in an individual's potential influence their response to feedback? Can you share a personal experience where this approach made a difference?
4. What strategies can leaders use to answer the inevitable "Why?" questions without derailing the focus on future actions?
5. How can leaders cultivate a culture of openness to feedback within their teams, and what role does modeling this behavior play in that process?

Practice Exercises

1. Future-Focused Feedback Role-Playing

- **Objective:** To practice shifting the conversation from past performance to future solutions.
- **How to Do It:** Pair up with a colleague or friend. One person plays the role of the leader giving feedback, and the other plays the role of the employee. The leader should practice giving feedback by focusing entirely on what can be done moving forward rather than dwelling on past mistakes. After the exercise, switch roles and discuss what worked well and what could be improved.

2. Optimism Reinforcement Journaling

- **Objective:** To develop the habit of conveying optimism and belief in others' potential during feedback.
- **How to Do It:** Keep a daily journal where you reflect on a feedback conversation you had or plan to have. Write down the key points you want to address, followed by a positive,

future-focused statement that reinforces your belief in the individual's ability to improve. Review these entries regularly to reinforce this mindset.

3. The "Why" Anticipation Exercise

- **Objective:** To improve your ability to quickly and effectively answer the "Why?" questions during feedback without losing focus on the future.
- **How to Do It:** Think of a recent scenario where you needed to give feedback. Write down the feedback you would give and list potential "Why?" questions the person might ask. Then, draft concise, clear responses that provide enough context without getting stuck in the past. Practice delivering these responses aloud to reinforce your ability to handle these questions smoothly in real situations.

MASTERING SPECIFIC FEEDBACK

Man, I hate performance reviews. They're a tough spot for both the person on the receiving end and the one giving it. The pressure to strike the right balance between constructive criticism and praise is real. And it's so easy to slip into vague, general statements that feel safe but are ultimately useless. After all, most of us want to be liked more than we want to lead.

But here's the thing: how we deliver feedback can make or break how it's received. And there are some tried-and-true strategies that can make feedback not just bearable but actually effective.

The Golden Rule: Get Specific

The most crucial piece of advice is simple: be specific. Avoid general statements like the plague. And yeah, I get that the metaphor might hit differently these days, but the point stands. Saying "Great job" or "That didn't go well" isn't going to help anyone improve. Think about the times you've received vague feedback. Your reaction was probably either "Phew, dodged that one" or "No kidding, Sherlock."

Generic feedback is a copout. It doesn't push anyone to do better, and it's a disservice to the person you're trying to help.

Instead, I recommend using a "more of" or "less of" framework. This approach zeroes in on specific behaviors or actions the person can increase or decrease in the future. For example, rather than saying, "You need to be more organized," you could say, "I'd like to see more organization in the layout of your project presentations going forward." This kind of feedback gives the person a clear action to take, something tangible they can work on.

The Valence Factor: Positive and Negative Feedback

Another crucial aspect of giving feedback is understanding its valence —whether it's positive or negative.

Positive Valence Feedback: Praise can be incredibly motivating, but only if it's specific. General praise like "Great job" doesn't do much. Instead, try something like, "I really appreciated the clear structure and visuals you used in the presentation." This feedback is more meaningful and helps the person understand exactly what they did well.

Negative Valence Feedback: Criticism is tougher to swallow but can be invaluable if delivered with the right intent. Again, avoid being vague. Instead of saying, "You need to be more professional," opt for something like, "I'd like to see more timely responses to emails and a more professional tone in your written communications." This approach provides a clear, actionable path to improvement.

The Litmus Test: Is It Useful?

Here's a doozy of a question that's often overlooked: Is the feedback useful? It may seem obvious, but in my experience, it's worth asking.

Useful feedback is actionable—it leads to positive change. Vague feedback, on the other hand, can actually be counterproductive. Take "You need to be more of a team player," for example. It's too broad and puts the person on the defensive. Instead, say something like, "I'd like to see more collaboration and contribution to group discussions in meetings." This specific feedback is far more likely to prompt the desired change.

That said, there are times when the best feedback is none at all. Feedback needs to be targeted and delivered in the right doses. I'm not suggesting you hold back, but I do want you to think about the value, context, and timing of your feedback.

The Silent Impact of Formal Feedback

Let's recap the essentials: The key to delivering effective feedback is to be specific and focus on actionable improvements rather than making general statements. The "more of" or "less of" framework is a simple yet powerful way to make feedback both useful and actionable, leading to better performance and growth. By considering the valence and usefulness of your feedback, you can communicate your observations in a way that helps the person understand how they can improve.

Now, one last point that's often overlooked: In formal feedback situations, like year-end performance reviews or postmortem debriefs after a project, what isn't said often carries the most weight. Research shows that people interpret formal feedback differently from day-to-day comments. In these scenarios, people tend to see any feedback as either positive or negative—there's no middle ground. Neutral statements don't exist when it comes to formal feedback. So, be mindful of this when delivering your assessments.

In the end, whether you're giving praise or criticism, the goal is to be clear, specific, and constructive. It's not just about pointing out what went wrong or right; it's about helping the person grow and improve. And when done right, even the most dreaded performance review can become a powerful tool for development.

Key Actions

- **Be Specific:** Avoid vague and general statements in feedback. Use a "more of" or "less of" framework to provide clear, actionable advice.
- **Understand the Valence:** Recognize whether the feedback is positive or negative and deliver it in a way that is specific and actionable.
- **Ensure Feedback is Useful:** Make sure the feedback is actionable and leads to positive change. Avoid broad or defensive feedback and instead, offer specific suggestions for improvement.
- **Consider the Impact of Formal Feedback:** In formal settings, understand that feedback is often seen as either positive or negative with no middle ground. Be mindful of this when delivering assessments to ensure they are clear and constructive.
- **Focus on Growth and Improvement**: The ultimate goal of feedback is to help the person grow and improve, making the feedback process a powerful tool for development when done correctly.

Discussion Questions

1. How can the "more of" or "less of" framework improve the effectiveness of feedback in your team? Can you share an example where this approach might have been useful in past feedback sessions?
2. In what ways can vague feedback be counterproductive? How can we train ourselves to avoid giving vague feedback, especially under pressure?
3. Why is it important to consider the valence (positive or negative) of feedback when delivering it? How does the valence affect the receiver's response and subsequent actions?
4. What are the potential risks of giving neutral or vague feedback in formal settings like performance reviews? How can we ensure our formal feedback is interpreted as intended?
5. How can leaders balance the need to be liked with the responsibility to provide honest, specific feedback? What strategies can be used to make feedback both constructive and well-received?

Practice Exercises

1. Specific Feedback Exercise

- **Objective**: Improve your ability to provide specific, actionable feedback.
- **How to Do It**: Choose three examples from recent work interactions where you've given or received feedback. Rewrite the feedback using the "more of" or "less of" framework. For instance, if the original feedback was, "You need to be more organized," revise it to something like, "I'd like to see more organization in your project timelines by setting clear milestones." Practice delivering this revised feedback out loud.

2. Valence Awareness Exercise

- **Objective**: Increase your awareness of the emotional impact of positive and negative feedback.
- **How to Do It**: Over the next week, consciously track the feedback you give to colleagues, noting whether it is positive or negative. For each piece of feedback, ask yourself: Was it specific? Did it provide a clear path to improvement or reinforcement of good behavior? At the end of the week, review your notes and identify patterns in how you deliver feedback. Reflect on how you can make your feedback more balanced and effective.

3. Litmus Test Exercise

- **Objective**: Develop your ability to ensure feedback is useful and actionable.
- **How to Do It**: Before giving any feedback, ask yourself: "Is this feedback useful?" Apply the litmus test by evaluating if the feedback is specific, actionable, and likely to lead to improvement. If the answer is no, revise the feedback until it meets these criteria. Practice this process with a peer or mentor by sharing your feedback and discussing how it could be improved to be more useful.

BALANCE CRITICISM

Feedback is, at its core, a form of low-intensity conflict. It can be a minefield for both the giver and the receiver, as it touches on a person's work, decisions, and sometimes even their character. This delicate nature makes it essential to approach feedback with care and balance, always keeping in mind the goal: to foster growth and improvement without damaging the relationship or morale.

Understanding the Sensitivity of Feedback

We all know people tend to overreact to criticism. A piece of constructive feedback can be taken as a personal attack if it's not presented thoughtfully. The problem intensifies when the feedback is unbalanced, skewed heavily toward the negative without acknowledging what's going well. But here's the thing: there's no magical ratio of praise to criticism that guarantees success. It's more about the quality and context of the feedback than the quantity.

Balancing the Conversation and the Relationship

Instead of adhering to a strict ratio of criticism to praise, the real goal should be finding balance—both in the feedback session itself and in the overall relationship. This means ensuring that your positive comments are just as vivid, specific, and thoughtful as your critiques. It's about treating the entire conversation as a nuanced dialogue, rather than a checklist where you need to tick off a certain number of praises to offset a criticism.

Earlier, we touched on the pitfalls of the "sandwich" approach, where criticism is sandwiched between two layers of praise. This method often comes across as insincere, diluting the impact of both the praise and the critique.

Instead of resorting to this formulaic approach, aim to balance the scales by providing specific, detailed, and genuine positive feedback alongside your critiques. This strategy not only builds trust but also encourages the recipient to remain open to coaching and improvement. By giving equal weight to compliments and criticisms, you create an environment where feedback is seen as a tool for growth, not as an attack.

The Power of Language, Setting, and Tone

It's not just what you say, but how you say it. The language, setting, and tone used when delivering feedback can drastically alter its impact. A monotone delivery or a negative tone can cast a shadow over even the most constructive feedback, making it hard for the recipient to absorb the message.

Emotionally intelligent leaders understand the importance of context. They've seen how a poorly timed or delivered piece of feedback can provoke strong emotional reactions—anger, tears, or defensiveness— often rooted in the recipient's unseen stresses or challenges. This is where the ability to "read the room" comes into play.

By taking a quick temperature check of the situation, leaders can gauge whether the moment is right for feedback. This doesn't mean walking on eggshells; it means using discretion and good judgment to find the best time and approach to delivering your message.

Striking the Right Balance in Leadership Relationships

Striking a balance in your feedback isn't just about the conversation— it's about the overall relationship. If the ratio of criticism to praise leans too heavily on the negative, people may withdraw, feeling like nothing they do is good enough. Over time, they might stop trying altogether. On the flip side, if the ratio is too positive, even the slightest critique can feel like a crushing blow, causing the recipient to overreact or place undue weight on the criticism.

As a leader, assessing and striving for the right balance in your relationships is essential. It's a dynamic process, requiring ongoing attention and adjustment. The goal is to create a feedback culture where people feel supported and challenged in equal measure, fostering both personal growth and organizational success.

Approaching feedback with care, consideration, and balance is key to creating a culture of growth. By balancing criticism with specific, detailed positive feedback and carefully considering the language, tone, and context, leaders can foster an environment where feedback is welcomed rather than feared. Striking the right balance in both the conversation and the relationship is crucial to nurturing the development of those around you, ultimately leading to a more positive and effective team dynamic.

Key Actions

1. **Approach Feedback with Care and Balance**: Treat feedback as a nuanced dialogue, ensuring that both positive comments and criticisms are specific, vivid, and thoughtful.
2. **Avoid the "Sandwich" Approach**: Rather than using a formulaic method of sandwiching criticism between praise, balance your feedback with genuine, detailed positive comments alongside your critiques
3. **Use Appropriate Language, Setting, and Tone**: Pay attention to how you deliver feedback. The tone, language, and setting can significantly impact how the message is received
4. **Read the Room and Adjust Accordingly**: Take quick temperature checks to gauge the recipient's emotional state and the context. Use discretion and good judgment to choose the best time and approach for delivering feedback.
5. **Strive for Balance in Leadership Relationships**: Maintain a balanced ratio of praise to criticism over time to ensure that your feedback is both supportive and challenging, fostering a positive and effective team dynamic.

Discussion Questions

1. How do you determine the right balance between positive feedback and criticism in your leadership role? Can you share an example where this balance led to a successful outcome?
2. What strategies do you use to "read the room" before delivering feedback, and how has this influenced the effectiveness of your feedback?

3. Have you ever encountered a situation where the tone or setting of your feedback overshadowed the content? How did you address or learn from that experience?
4. In what ways can leaders ensure that their positive feedback is as detailed and impactful as their criticisms? Why is this important for fostering a culture of growth?
5. What are your thoughts on the "sandwich" approach to feedback? How can leaders move beyond this method to create more meaningful and effective feedback conversations?

Practice Exercises

1.Feedback Reflection Journal

- **Objective**: Improve your ability to balance criticism with positive feedback.
- **How to Do It**: After each feedback session you conduct, write a brief reflection in a journal. Note the balance between criticism and positive comments, the language and tone used, and the recipient's reaction. Over time, review your entries to identify patterns and areas for improvement.

2. Role-Playing Scenarios

- **Objective**: Practice reading the room and adjusting your feedback approach accordingly.
- **How to Do It**: Partner with a colleague or mentor to role-play various feedback scenarios. Take turns giving and receiving feedback in different contexts (e.g., a stressed-out employee, a high performer, etc.). After each scenario, discuss what worked well and what could be improved in terms of timing, tone, and balance.

3. Specificity Drill

- **Objective**: Enhance your ability to provide specific and detailed feedback.

- **How to Do It**: Choose a recent project or task completed by someone on your team. Write two versions of feedback: one that is vague and general, and another that is specific and detailed. Compare the two, and consider how the recipient might react to each version. Practice consistently using the specific and detailed version in real feedback sessions.

MASTER THE "HOW" QUESTION

Feedback. It's the lifeblood of growth, but make no mistake, can it be a minefield. You want to be honest and direct, sure, but there's a fine line between being helpful and being hurtful. The goal isn't to pat yourself on the back for being right; it's to help your team get better, without piling on unnecessary stress or discomfort.

So, how do you strike that balance? Enter the "how" question—a simple yet powerful tool for delivering feedback that gets results without raising defenses.

The Magic of "How"

Here's the deal: people naturally resist criticism. Tell someone they need to improve, and you might as well be waving a red flag in front of a bull. But ask them how they can improve, and suddenly the conversation shifts. "How" questions embed the critique in a way that feels less like a slap and more like a nudge. The criticism is still there, but it's wrapped in a question that invites the recipient to take control.

Let's say you think your team needs more talent. You could bluntly say, "Your team lacks talent," and watch the walls go up. Or, you could ask, "How will you upgrade the talent on your team?" Now, the ball is in their court. By answering the question, they're accepting the need for improvement and taking ownership of the solution. It's subtle, but incredibly effective.

Why "How" Questions Work

There's a tug-of-war happening inside all of us. We know we need to grow, but we bristle at having our flaws pointed out. "How" questions bridge this gap. They guide people to self-identify areas for improvement, making the feedback feel less like a critique and more like a collaborative problem-solving session.

Self-driven realizations always stick better than imposed advice. When someone comes to their own conclusion about what needs to change, they're more likely to commit to making that change happen. Smart leaders know this and use "how" questions to lead people to those lightbulb moments.

It's About Empowerment, Not Manipulation

Let's be clear: this isn't about clever tricks or manipulating your team into compliance. The goal is to build a culture where accountability and openness to feedback are part of the fabric of your organization. When feedback is framed as a question, it shifts the dynamic from "I'm telling you what to do" to "Let's figure this out together." That's powerful.

Inquiry-based approaches, like using "how" questions, empower your team to take charge of their own growth. And when people feel empowered, they're more engaged, more motivated, and ultimately, more successful.

The Long Game

The beauty of this approach is that it benefits everyone in the long run. When your team members feel responsible for their own development, they're not just doing it for you—they're doing it for themselves. This kind of intrinsic motivation leads to better performance, stronger skills, and a team that's aligned and driven toward a common goal.

So, the next time you're faced with giving feedback, ditch the direct critique and embrace the "how" question. It's a small shift that can make a big difference in how your feedback is received and acted upon. And in the end, that's what it's all about—helping your team be the best they can be.

Key Actions

- **Use "How" Questions to Deliver Feedback:** Frame feedback as a question, asking "how" the person will address the issue, to make the feedback feel collaborative and less confrontational.
- **Encourage Self-Identification of Improvement Areas:** Guide team members to recognize areas where they can

improve on their own, leading to greater ownership and commitment to change.

- **Empower, Don't Manipulate:** Focus on creating a culture where feedback is seen as a tool for growth, not a tactic for control. Use questions to empower team members to take charge of their development.
- **Shift the Dynamic from Directive to Collaborative:** Use inquiry-based feedback to transform the conversation from one of instruction to one of mutual problem-solving.
- **Promote Intrinsic Motivation:** Foster an environment where team members are motivated by their own desire to grow and improve, rather than just external directives.

Discussion Questions

1. How can the use of "how" questions change the dynamic of feedback in a team setting? Can you think of a situation where this approach might have been more effective?
2. In what ways does framing feedback as a question encourage personal ownership of the problem? How might this influence a team member's willingness to act on the feedback?
3. What are the potential risks or downsides of using "how" questions in feedback? How can a leader avoid these pitfalls while still maintaining an open and constructive dialogue?
4. How can leaders ensure that their use of "how" questions is seen as empowering rather than manipulative? What steps can be taken to build a culture of trust around feedback?
5. Reflecting on your own experiences, how does intrinsic motivation differ when feedback is delivered through a collaborative approach versus a directive approach? How can leaders foster this intrinsic motivation within their teams?

Practice Exercises

1. Reframe Criticism as a Question

- **Objective:** To practice embedding criticism within a constructive question.
- **How to Do It:** Think of a piece of feedback you need to give to someone on your team. Instead of stating the criticism directly, reframe it as a "how" question. For example, instead of saying, "You need to be more organized," ask, "How could you improve the organization of your projects?" Write down a few different examples and practice delivering them in a conversational tone.

2. Role-Playing Feedback Sessions

- **Objective:** To improve comfort and effectiveness in using "how" questions during feedback.
- **How to Do It:** Partner with a colleague or friend to role-play a feedback session. Start by giving traditional, direct feedback, then switch to using "how" questions. After each round, discuss how the feedback was received and how it felt to deliver it. Reflect on the differences and work on refining your approach.

3. Self-Reflection on Past Feedback

- **Objective:** To build awareness of how past feedback could have been more effective using "how" questions.
- **How to Do It:** Reflect on a time when you gave or received feedback that didn't go as well as you hoped. Rewrite the feedback as a "how" question, focusing on making it more collaborative and less confrontational. Consider how this rephrasing might have changed the outcome. Repeat this exercise with several past examples to build your skill in naturally framing feedback as questions.

ASK FOR HELP, GIVE FEEDBACK

Giving feedback is one of the most important yet delicate tasks in leadership. How you approach it can make or break a team member's growth. One of the biggest traps leaders fall into is focusing too much on what they say, without considering what goes unsaid. Just like in a courtroom, it's often the gaps in the conversation—the things that aren't said—that can have the most significant impact on the outcome.

The Hidden Meaning of Feedback

Feedback is rarely taken at face value. It's open to interpretation, and team members will often read between the lines, trying to decipher what you really mean. This is where things can go sideways. While your intention might be to offer constructive criticism, if you're not careful, your words can be twisted into something else entirely—something impractical, pointless, or even insulting.

The Danger of Vagueness

When feedback lacks specificity, it's easy for the person on the receiving end to feel attacked rather than supported. Vague criticisms can come across as inflammatory and aggressive, making the person defensive and resistant to change. This is why the best leaders are hyper-aware of the potential pitfalls in giving feedback and work hard to eliminate any comments that could be seen as unhelpful or hurtful.

Words to Avoid

Certain phrases are guaranteed to derail a feedback session. Statements like "This seems like a pattern with you," "This is lousy work," or "I can't imagine what has gotten into you" do more harm than good. These kinds of remarks aren't just unproductive; they're destructive. They offer no clear path forward and instead leave the team member feeling lost, demoralized, and uncertain about what to do next.

How to Reframe Your Feedback

To ensure your feedback is effective, you need to attach specificity and practicality to any criticism. Instead of saying, "This is lousy work," try something like, "I noticed that the report was missing some key data points. Let's go over it together and see where we can make improvements." This approach not only identifies the issue but also opens up a dialogue for collaboration and improvement.

Another strategy is to reframe feedback as a request for help. For example, instead of saying, "You need to dramatically improve," you could say, "I could use your help in improving this project. What ideas do you have to make it stronger?" By asking for their input, you empower the team member to take ownership of the situation, turning what could have been a negative experience into a positive, collaborative one.

The Power of What Goes Unsaid

Finally, remember that sometimes it's what doesn't get said that matters most. If you're constantly pointing out what's wrong without acknowledging what's right, your team members may start to feel undervalued. Balance your criticism with genuine praise where it's due. Highlighting strengths alongside areas for improvement shows that you're paying attention to the whole picture, not just the flaws.

In conclusion, giving feedback isn't just about correcting mistakes; it's about guiding your team toward growth and improvement. By being mindful of your words—and the gaps in them—you can offer feedback that is not only constructive but also empowering. And when in doubt, ask for help. It turns a critique into a conversation, fostering a sense of partnership and shared responsibility.

Key Actions

- **Be Mindful of What Goes Unsaid**: Recognize that feedback isn't just about what you say; the gaps in your message can have a significant impact. Pay attention to what's left unsaid and how it might be interpreted.
- **Avoid Vagueness**: Eliminate vague criticisms that can be seen as inflammatory or aggressive. Focus on being clear and specific to avoid misinterpretation.

- **Eliminate Destructive Phrases**: Steer clear of phrases that are unproductive and potentially destructive, such as "This seems like a pattern with you" or "This is lousy work." These comments offer no clear path forward and can demoralize the recipient.
- **Attach Specificity and Practicality to Criticism**: Ensure that any criticism you offer is specific and practical, providing a clear path for improvement. Replace broad statements with detailed, actionable feedback.
- **Reframe Feedback as a Request for Help**: Instead of making demands or issuing harsh criticisms, ask for the team member's help in improving the situation. This approach fosters collaboration and empowers the individual to take ownership of the outcome.
- **Balance Criticism with Praise**: Don't just focus on what's wrong. Acknowledge and highlight strengths alongside areas for improvement to show that you value the team member's overall contributions.

Discussion Questions

1. How can the unsaid aspects of feedback impact a team member's perception and response? Can you think of a time when what wasn't said affected how you interpreted feedback?
2. What are some specific phrases or types of feedback you've received that felt vague or unhelpful? How did that impact your motivation or performance?
3. Why is it important to avoid destructive phrases in feedback, and how can leaders reframe their language to be more constructive and actionable?
4. How does asking for help from team members during feedback sessions change the dynamic of the conversation? Can you share an example where this approach led to a positive outcome?
5. In your experience, how does balancing criticism with genuine praise affect the overall effectiveness of feedback?

What strategies can leaders use to ensure they are highlighting both strengths and areas for improvement?

Practice Exercises

1. Feedback Reframing Exercise

- **Objective:** Improve your ability to turn vague or negative feedback into specific, actionable suggestions.
- **How to Do It:** Take a piece of feedback you've given or received that was vague or potentially harmful (e.g., "This work isn't good enough"). Write it down, then reframe it using a more constructive and specific approach (e.g., "The report needs more detailed data on customer demographics to strengthen our analysis"). Practice this reframing with different types of feedback until it becomes second nature.

2. Ask for Help Feedback Simulation

- **Objective:** Develop the habit of turning feedback into a collaborative process by asking for help.
- **How to Do It:** Role-play a feedback session with a colleague or friend. Instead of delivering traditional feedback, frame your comments as requests for assistance (e.g., "Can you help me understand what could be improved in this presentation?"). Practice this in different scenarios, focusing on fostering collaboration and mutual problem-solving.

3. Positive-Negative Balance Check

- **Objective:** Cultivate a balanced approach to delivering feedback by pairing criticism with praise.
- **How to Do It:** Reflect on recent feedback sessions you've conducted or participated in. Write down the criticisms and see if you paired them with genuine praise. If not, go back and identify positive aspects you could have highlighted.

Practice balancing feedback in future sessions by consciously preparing both constructive criticisms and specific praise points ahead of time.

THROW PROBLEMS BACK

As a leader, the quality of your leadership is often reflected in the kinds of questions that come your way. When people seek your input, it's a sign of respect for your knowledge, wisdom, and experience. But how you respond to these questions can have a lasting impact on your team's development and the overall culture of your organization.

Encouraging Open Communication

A key aspect of leadership is fostering an environment where open communication thrives. You want your team to feel comfortable asking questions and sharing their views. This isn't just about being approachable; it's about creating a space where curiosity and learning are valued. However, the way you respond to questions is critical. Your tone, language, and even body language play a significant role in how your message is received. If you're not careful, a well-intentioned response can be perceived as dismissive or condescending, which can shut down communication and lead to defensiveness.

The Power of Throwing Problems Back

One effective way to encourage deeper thinking and problem-solving within your team is to throw problems back at them rather than providing immediate answers. When someone comes to you with a question, resist the urge to solve the problem on the spot. Instead, ask them what they think. What are their instincts telling them? What have they done in similar situations in the past? What do they believe is the best course of action?

This approach does a few important things:

1. *Promotes Ownership*: By encouraging your team to come up with solutions, you're helping them take ownership of their challenges. This builds confidence and self-reliance, which are critical for personal and professional growth.
2. *Encourages Critical Thinking*: When you throw the problem back, you're pushing your team to think critically. They have

to analyze the situation, weigh different options, and make decisions. This kind of deep thinking leads to better problem-solving skills over time.

3. *Fosters a Culture of Learning:* When you consistently ask your team to think through their challenges, you're creating a culture where learning and development are part of the everyday process. Your team will start to approach problems with a mindset of curiosity and growth rather than fear or hesitation.

Navigating Power Dynamics

Of course, this approach only works if you're mindful of the power dynamics at play. In any organization, there's a natural hierarchy, and sometimes people might hesitate to ask questions or challenge your views because they don't want to rock the boat. As a leader, it's your job to level the playing field.

To encourage open dialogue, create a safe environment where people feel comfortable expressing their thoughts and ideas. This means actively listening, providing non-judgmental feedback, and being willing to engage in honest discussions. When your team knows they can speak up without fear of repercussions, they're more likely to take the initiative and ask those important questions.

Responding Constructively

While throwing problems back is a powerful tool, it's equally important to consider how you respond when your team does ask questions. A positive and constructive response can build trust and reinforce the idea that their input is valued. On the flip side, a negative or dismissive response can have the opposite effect, discouraging further questions and stifling growth.

When responding, focus on being clear, specific, and constructive. If someone suggests a solution that isn't quite right, don't just shoot it down. Instead, ask probing questions that help them refine their thinking. Guide them toward a better solution without taking over the process. This way, they learn from the experience and feel empowered to tackle future challenges.

The Long-Term Impact

By encouraging your team to ask questions and thoughtfully throwing problems back at them, you're not just solving the issue at hand—you're investing in their long-term development. You're helping them build the skills and confidence they need to navigate complex situations on their own. This approach fosters a culture of continuous improvement, where learning and growth are part of the fabric of your organization.

As a leader, your ultimate goal is to develop the talent around you. Sometimes, that means stepping back and letting your team wrestle with the problem. By staying in the question for a few moments longer, you're not only building credibility and trust but also cultivating a team that's equipped to handle whatever comes their way.

In the end, leadership isn't about having all the answers—it's about empowering others to find their own.

Key Actions

- **Foster Open Communication:** Encourage your team to ask questions and share their views by creating an environment where curiosity and learning are valued.
- **Be Mindful of Your Responses:** Pay attention to your tone, language, and body language when responding to questions to avoid unintended defensiveness or resistance.
- **Throw Problems Back:** Instead of providing immediate answers, ask your team what they think, encouraging them to develop their problem-solving skills and take ownership of challenges.
- **Promote Ownership:** Help your team take ownership of their challenges by encouraging them to come up with solutions, which builds confidence and self-reliance.
- **Encourage Critical Thinking:** Push your team to think critically by asking them to analyze situations, weigh options,

and make decisions, leading to better problem-solving skills over time.

- **Foster a Culture of Learning:** Create a culture where learning and development are part of the everyday process by consistently encouraging your team to think through their challenges.
- **Level the Playing Field:** Navigate power dynamics by creating a safe environment where everyone feels comfortable expressing their thoughts and ideas.
- **Respond Constructively:** Focus on clear, specific, and constructive feedback when responding to questions, guiding your team to refine their thinking without taking over the process.
- **Invest in Long-Term Development:** Use the approach of throwing problems back as a way to develop your team's skills and confidence for navigating complex situations on their own.

Discussion Questions

1. How can leaders strike the right balance between providing guidance and encouraging independent problem-solving within their teams?
2. What are some practical ways to create a safe and open environment where team members feel comfortable asking questions and challenging ideas, despite existing power dynamics?
3. In what situations might it be more effective for a leader to provide direct answers rather than throwing problems back to the team? How can a leader recognize these moments?
4. How can leaders ensure their tone, language, and body language convey support and openness when responding to questions or feedback?
5. What are the potential long-term benefits of fostering a culture of learning and critical thinking within an

organization, and how can leaders actively contribute to this culture?

Practice Exercises

1. Role Reversal Problem-Solving

- **Objective**: Improve your ability to throw problems back to your team and encourage their independent thinking.
- **How to Do It**: The next time a team member comes to you with a problem or question, instead of giving them the answer, ask them what they think should be done. Follow up with questions like, "What are the possible options?" or "What have you tried so far?" This exercise will help you practice guiding your team to think critically and take ownership of solutions.

2. Active Listening and Feedback Reflection

- **Objective**: Enhance your awareness of your tone, language, and body language when responding to questions or feedback.
- **How to Do It**: During your next meeting or one-on-one session, focus on listening actively. After the conversation, take a few minutes to reflect on how you responded. Consider whether your tone, language, and body language were supportive and constructive. Write down any areas where you could improve and make a conscious effort to adjust in future interactions.

3. Open Dialogue Simulation

- **Objective:** Create a more open and inclusive environment for your team to express their thoughts and ideas.
- **How to Do It:** Set up a simulated scenario where you invite your team to discuss a challenging topic or decision. Before the

discussion, emphasize that the goal is to explore different perspectives with respect and openness. During the session, practice active listening, provide non-judgmental feedback, and encourage everyone to share their thoughts. Afterward, ask your team for feedback on how comfortable they felt and what could be done to improve the environment. This exercise will help you build a culture of open communication and mutual respect.

BIG PICTURE, SMALL FIX

Feedback and coaching are crucial tools for improving performance and guiding people toward success. But while they share the common goal of helping others grow, they are fundamentally different processes. Understanding these differences and how to use them effectively can make all the difference in how they're received and acted upon.

Feedback: Direct and Actionable

Feedback is essentially a direction or evaluation from someone with expertise or authority—think of a teacher guiding a student, or a leader advising a team member. The purpose of feedback is to help someone improve by pointing out specific areas for change. It's often a one-way street, where the person giving the feedback tells the recipient what needs to be done differently. The underlying message is, "Here's what you need to change; now go and do it."

The nature of feedback means it usually comes from someone in a position of power or with more experience. This dynamic can create resistance or defensiveness in the recipient, particularly if the feedback isn't delivered carefully. To make feedback effective, the person giving it needs to do more than just point out what's wrong—they need to establish context, explain why the change is necessary, and how it ties into the bigger picture.

Imagine telling someone to change a single piece in a jigsaw puzzle without showing them the whole image. They might change it, but they won't understand why it matters. Effective feedback paints the broader picture first, making it clear how the small correction contributes to the overall goal. Then, it zooms in on the specific behavior or action that needs to change, followed by another pullback to show how this adjustment will help achieve the larger objective. It's a process of anchoring the feedback in the bigger picture, focusing on the correction, and then returning to the bigger picture to reinforce its importance.

Coaching: Collaborative and Developmental

Coaching, on the other hand, is a more collaborative process. Instead of directing someone to make changes, a coach guides individuals toward discovering their own solutions. The coach acts more like a partner in the journey, asking questions that encourage self-reflection and problem-solving. This approach fosters a sense of ownership over one's development, making the individual more invested in their growth.

Coaching thrives on an equal power dynamic. Unlike feedback, which can feel hierarchical, coaching is more about facilitating a conversation. The coach isn't telling the individual what to do; instead, they're helping them figure out what they need to do themselves. This not only helps in skill development but also builds confidence, as the individual learns to trust their judgment and abilities.

A good coach knows that the best solutions are the ones the individual comes up with on their own. By guiding them to these conclusions through thoughtful questions and active listening, the coach empowers the individual to take control of their growth.

The Balance: When to Use Feedback vs. Coaching

Effective leaders understand the importance of both feedback and coaching, and they know when to use each. Feedback is essential when specific, immediate changes are needed—especially when there's no room for error. For example, if a team member is making a mistake that could jeopardize a project, clear, direct feedback is necessary to correct the course quickly.

Coaching is more appropriate when the goal is long-term development. It's about helping someone build the skills and confidence to solve problems independently in the future. Instead of simply correcting mistakes, coaching focuses on developing the individual's ability to think critically and creatively.

In practice, the best leaders blend feedback and coaching. They use feedback to address immediate issues and provide clear direction. Then, they switch to a coaching approach to help the individual understand why those changes are important and how they can apply the lessons learned to other areas of their work.

Creating a Supportive Environment

Both feedback and coaching are about growth, and for either to be effective, they need to happen in a supportive environment. This means fostering a culture where team members feel safe to receive feedback and encouraged to engage in the coaching process. Leaders can do this by being clear, specific, and consistent in their feedback, and by making coaching an ongoing conversation rather than a one-time event.

In the end, whether you're giving feedback or engaging in coaching, the goal is to help people succeed. By understanding the nuances of each approach and using them effectively, you can create an environment where your team not only performs better but also grows in confidence and capability.

Key Actions

- **Establish Context Before Giving Feedback**: When providing feedback, start by explaining the bigger picture and why the change is necessary. This helps the recipient understand the importance of the feedback and how it ties into the overall goal.
- **Be Specific in Feedback**: Focus on the exact behavior or action that needs to be changed. Avoid vague statements and provide clear, actionable guidance on what needs to be done differently.
- **Use the Big Picture, Small Correction, Big Picture Model**: Anchor the feedback in the broader context, zoom in on the specific issue, and then return to the big picture to reinforce the importance of the change.
- **Foster a Collaborative Coaching Environment**: Engage in a back-and-forth process during coaching, asking questions that encourage the individual to think critically and develop their own solutions.

- **Balance Power Dynamics in Coaching**: Ensure that coaching maintains an equal power dynamic, where the coach acts as a partner rather than an authority figure, helping the individual take ownership of their development.
- **Blend Feedback and Coaching**: Use feedback for immediate, specific changes and coaching for long-term development. Recognize when each approach is appropriate and combine them to support both immediate performance improvement and ongoing growth.
- **Create a Supportive Environment**: Cultivate a culture where team members feel safe to receive feedback and are encouraged to engage in the coaching process. Make feedback clear, specific, and consistent, and treat coaching as an ongoing conversation.

Discussion Questions

1. How can leaders effectively balance the use of feedback and coaching when working with their team members? Can you share examples of when one approach might be more effective than the other?
2. In what ways can establishing the bigger picture before giving feedback improve how the feedback is received and acted upon? Have you seen this approach used effectively in your own experience?
3. What are some strategies for ensuring that feedback is specific and actionable? How do you think vague feedback impacts the recipient's ability to make meaningful improvements?
4. How does the power dynamic differ between feedback and coaching, and how can leaders navigate these dynamics to ensure both approaches are effective?
5. What are some ways leaders can create a supportive environment that encourages both the giving and receiving of feedback and coaching? What role does consistency play in this process?

Practice Exercises

1. The Feedback Loop

- **Objective:** Improve your ability to give clear, specific, and actionable feedback.
- **How to Do It:** Identify a recent situation where you had to provide feedback, either in a professional or personal context. Reflect on how you delivered the feedback and whether it was specific and tied to the bigger picture. Rewrite the feedback using the "Big Picture, Small Correction, Big Picture" model. Practice delivering this revised feedback to a colleague, friend, or mentor, and ask for their thoughts on its clarity and impact.

2. Coaching Conversations

- **Objective:** Develop your ability to engage in effective coaching by fostering a collaborative and supportive environment.
- **How to Do It:** Set aside time to practice a coaching session with a peer or team member. Instead of offering direct solutions, focus on asking open-ended questions that encourage the other person to think critically and explore their own solutions. Pay attention to the power dynamic—ensure the conversation feels like a partnership rather than a directive. Reflect afterward on how well you facilitated the other person's self-discovery and what you could improve.

3. Feedback and Coaching Role-Play

- **Objective:** Strengthen your ability to discern when to use feedback versus coaching and practice both skills in a controlled setting.
- **How to Do It:** Pair up with a colleague or friend and take turns role-playing different scenarios that require either feedback or coaching. One person plays the role of the leader,

while the other plays the team member. Start with a scenario that clearly requires feedback, then switch to one that lends itself to coaching. After each role-play, discuss which approach was used, why it was chosen, and how effectively it was delivered. Repeat this exercise with different scenarios to build versatility in using both feedback and coaching effectively.

TIME YOUR FEEDBACK

Feedback is one of the most powerful tools in a leader's toolkit. When used correctly, it can guide team members toward better performance, sharpen their skills, and drive the entire organization forward. But as powerful as feedback is, its effectiveness is all about timing. Giving feedback during a performance—while someone is actively engaged in a task—can actually do more harm than good.

This might seem counterintuitive. If someone is struggling, isn't it better to step in and help them correct their course? The answer, surprisingly, is no. Experienced leaders and coaches know that the timing of feedback is just as important as the content of the feedback itself.

Don't Critique in the Heat of the Moment

The urge to provide feedback in the middle of a performance is understandable, especially when things are going off track. You want to help, to prevent mistakes, and to guide the individual toward success. But offering critiques while someone is performing can damage their confidence, disrupt their focus, and ultimately undermine the performance you're trying to improve.

Think about sports. Coaches rarely give detailed feedback during a game. Instead, they save their observations for pre-game pep talks, halftime huddles, or post-game reviews. Why? Because mid-performance feedback can distract athletes, causing them to overthink actions that should be automatic. This kind of distraction often leads to more mistakes rather than improvements.

I've seen this play out in youth sports with my own kids. My son's fourth-grade baseball team had a player whose father couldn't resist shouting instructions from the stands: "Keep your elbow up!" "Watch the ball!" The result? Every time the kid stepped up to bat, his concentration was shattered by his father's well-meaning advice. Instead of helping, the constant stream of feedback caused him to falter, striking out more often than not.

The same dynamic occurs in professional settings. I've witnessed leaders receiving feedback in the middle of a presentation or a meeting, and the effect is almost always negative. They become self-conscious, their flow is interrupted, and their performance suffers. It's clear that critiquing someone during their performance rarely leads to the desired outcome.

The Power of Timing

Timing is everything when it comes to feedback. Delivered immediately before or after a performance, feedback can make a strong impact and be highly effective in improving future efforts. But when given during the performance, it often has the opposite effect.

Why does this happen? Feedback during a performance forces individuals to think about actions that should be automatic. Instead of focusing on the task at hand, they start overanalyzing their movements, decisions, or words. This overthinking slows them down, makes them second-guess themselves, and ultimately hinders their ability to perform at their best.

Think about the performances we all engage in daily: writing, speaking, cooking, driving, even simple tasks like cleaning or reading. Imagine someone interrupting you with critiques during any of these activities. It would likely disrupt your flow, causing frustration and making the task harder than it needs to be.

Leaders must recognize that the same principle applies to their teams. By reserving feedback for moments before or after a performance, leaders allow their team members to focus fully on the task at hand, leading to better results.

How to Time Your Feedback for Maximum Impact

So, how can you ensure your feedback has the intended impact? Here's a simple framework to follow:

1. *Before the Performance:* Set clear expectations and provide guidance before the task begins. This prepares the individual

with a roadmap of what's expected and allows them to perform with confidence.

2. *During the Performance:* Observe quietly. If you see something that needs addressing, make a mental note or jot it down. Resist the urge to interrupt the flow of performance with critiques.

3. *After the Performance:* Offer reflections and suggestions for improvement once the task is complete. This is the time to discuss what went well, what didn't, and how they can improve next time.

This approach supports better performance and creates an environment where individuals feel confident and capable, knowing they won't be critiqued in the middle of their work.

The Long-Term Benefits of Timing Feedback Well

The ultimate goal of feedback is to help people grow and succeed. When leaders understand the importance of timing, they ensure that their feedback is not only heard but also acted upon. This leads to continuous improvement and long-term success.

By mastering the art of timing, you'll become a more effective leader, helping your team members reach their full potential without the setbacks caused by poorly timed feedback. In the end, it's not just about what you say, but when you say it that makes all the difference.

Key Actions

- **Avoid Giving Feedback During the Performance**: Refrain from offering critiques while someone is actively engaged in a task, as it can disrupt their focus and negatively impact their performance.
- **Set Expectations Before the Performance:** Provide clear guidance and set expectations before the task begins to prepare the individual for success.
- **Observe Quietly During the Performance:** During the

performance, observe without interrupting. Make mental notes or jot down observations for later discussion.

- **Provide Feedback After the Performance**: Offer reflections and suggestions for improvement once the task is complete, ensuring the individual can process and act on the feedback without distraction.
- **Focus on Timing to Enhance Effectiveness**: Understand that the timing of feedback is crucial. Delivering it before or after a performance maximizes its effectiveness and helps the individual grow and succeed.

Discussion Questions

1. How does the timing of feedback affect an individual's performance?
2. Why might offering feedback during a performance be counterproductive?
3. How does setting expectations before a task influence the effectiveness of feedback?
4. What challenges might leaders face when withholding feedback during a performance?
5. When is the best time to provide feedback to maximize its impact?

Practice Exercises

1. Feedback Timing Awareness

- **Objective:** Develop a heightened awareness of the timing of your feedback and improve your ability to withhold critiques during performances.
- **How to Do It:** Over the next week, observe your natural tendencies when it comes to giving feedback. Each time you feel the urge to provide feedback during someone's performance (whether it's a colleague in a meeting, a family member during an activity, or even yourself), pause and ask yourself: "Is this the best time to offer feedback?" Make a

conscious decision to wait until after the performance. Reflect at the end of each day on how withholding feedback affected the outcome and the individual's performance.

2. Pre-and Post-Performance Feedback Practice

- **Objective:** Practice delivering feedback effectively before and after a performance to reinforce positive behavior and address areas of improvement.
- **How to Do It:** Identify a few situations where you typically provide feedback (e.g., team meetings, project presentations, or coaching sessions). Before the performance begins, offer clear guidance and set expectations. After the performance, provide specific, constructive feedback focusing on what went well and areas for improvement. Note how the timing of your feedback influences the recipient's response and overall performance.

3. Role-Playing Mid-Performance Interventions

- **Objective:** Understand the impact of mid-performance feedback by simulating scenarios and reflecting on the outcomes.
- **How to Do It:** Partner with a colleague or friend and create role-playing scenarios where one person performs a task (such as giving a presentation or completing a project). The other person interrupts with feedback during the performance. After the exercise, discuss how the interruption affected the performer's focus, confidence, and overall effectiveness. Repeat the scenario with feedback provided only before or after the performance, and compare the results. Use these insights to improve your timing in real-life situations.

ASK DEEP QUESTIONS

Leadership isn't just about giving orders or feedback on the fly. It's about fostering growth, encouraging self-reflection, and enabling those around you to find their own paths forward. One of the most under-appreciated yet effective tools in a leader's arsenal for achieving this is the echo question.

Echo questions are designed to prompt deep thinking. They don't hand the answers over on a silver platter. Instead, they create a mental space where individuals can ponder, reflect, and eventually arrive at their own conclusions. This type of questioning goes beyond the superficial and digs into the heart of self-reflection. It's not about the leader telling someone what they should do; it's about guiding them to discover it for themselves.

Crafting and Timing Echo Questions

But here's the thing—echo questions need to be used wisely. They're not one-size-fits-all, and they shouldn't be fired off like a machine gun. The goal isn't to overwhelm someone with deep, existential queries. Instead, these questions should be thoughtfully crafted and strategically timed to prompt meaningful reflection.

For instance, when asking, "What do you think is holding you back from being promoted?" you're not just fishing for a quick answer. You're planting a seed. The real growth happens in the time between when the question is asked and when it's answered. This process allows the individual to take ownership of their development. They're not just parroting back what they think you want to hear; they're engaging in an internal dialogue that leads to genuine insight.

But timing matters. Drop a heavy question and immediately demand an answer, and you're likely to get something half-baked. People need time to let the question resonate, to mull it over, and to explore the layers of their own thinking. That's where the "echo" comes in—it's that lingering effect that stays with them, challenging their assumptions and encouraging deeper reflection.

Implementing Echo Questions for Sustainable Growth

Echo questions can be a game-changer, but like any tool, they must be used with skill. Here's how to effectively integrate echo questions into your leadership style:

1. *Know When to Echo:* Echo questions are best used when you want someone to engage in self-reflection. Whether it's about career growth, team dynamics, or personal development, the key is to ask questions that lead to introspection rather than immediate answers. For example, "What do you think are the obstacles in your way to achieving your goals?" is a powerful question that prompts the individual to explore their own barriers rather than waiting for you to point them out.

2. *Be Patient:* Patience is critical. After posing an echo question, give the person time—days, weeks, or even months—to think about it. You're not just looking for a quick response; you're after a well-considered answer that reflects genuine introspection. This waiting period allows the question to "echo" in their mind, leading to deeper insights.

3. *Follow Up Thoughtfully:* When you do follow up, don't just jump straight to the answer. Start by revisiting the question, asking what thoughts or realizations have come up since it was first posed. This reinforces the value of the process and keeps the conversation focused on growth rather than judgment.

4. *Create a Safe Reflection Space:* While the term "safe space" might not be your go-to (it certainly causes my skin to crawl), the concept is vital. Make sure the person feels comfortable exploring these questions without fear of immediate judgment or repercussions. The idea is to encourage open, honest reflection. You might frame it as "a place for candid exploration" or "an opportunity for self-assessment."

5. *Use Echo Questions Sparingly: Not* every situation calls for an echo question. Overuse can dilute their impact. Reserve them for moments when you want to inspire deep thinking and personal growth, rather than day-to-day decision-making.

Examples of Effective Echo Questions

To wrap this up, here are a few examples of echo questions you can use to encourage meaningful self-reflection:

- *Career Development:* "What's stopping you from reaching the next level in your career?"
- *Personal Growth:* "Why do you think people respond to you the way they do?"
- *Team Dynamics:* "What are the values that guide us as a team, and how do we embody them?"
- *Leadership Potential:* "How can you act like a leader even before you're given the title?"

When you ask these questions, you're not just looking for an answer. You're sparking a process—a journey of self-discovery that can lead to profound growth. And the beauty of it is that when the individual finally arrives at their answer, it's truly theirs. They own it, and that ownership is the foundation of sustainable, long-term development.

The Lasting Impact of Echo Questions

So, why are echo questions so effective? Because they shift the responsibility for growth from the leader to the individual. Instead of spoon-feeding answers, you're helping people discover their own paths, fostering a sense of ownership and self-reliance that's crucial for long-term success.

In the end, leadership isn't just about directing—it's about guiding, nurturing, and sometimes stepping back to let the echoes do the work. When used thoughtfully, echo questions can be one of the most powerful tools in your leadership toolkit, leading to deeper reflection, better insights, and ultimately, more meaningful growth.

Key Actions

- **Know When to Echo**: Use echo questions in situations where you want to inspire self-reflection and personal insight, rather than seeking immediate answers.

- **Be Patient**: Allow time for the person to process the echo question, giving them the space to arrive at a thoughtful and introspective answer.
- **Follow Up Thoughtfully**: Revisit the question during follow-up discussions, focusing on the insights and realizations that have emerged rather than seeking immediate conclusions.
- **Create a Safe Reflection Space**: Encourage open and honest exploration by ensuring the individual feels comfortable reflecting on the echo question without fear of immediate judgment or consequences.
- **Use Echo Questions Sparingly:** Reserve echo questions for significant moments when deep thinking and personal growth are desired, avoiding overuse to maintain their impact.

Discussion Questions

1. How can leaders balance the use of echo questions with more direct feedback to ensure effective communication and growth?
2. In what situations have you found echo questions to be particularly effective or ineffective in your leadership experience?
3. What strategies can leaders use to create a comfortable environment for self-reflection without causing anxiety or stress when posing echo questions?
4. How might the timing of follow-up conversations impact the effectiveness of echo questions in fostering personal growth?
5. What are some potential challenges of using echo questions, and how can leaders overcome these to ensure meaningful self-reflection and development?

Practice Exercises

1. Echo Question Brainstorm

- **Objective**: To develop the ability to craft effective echo questions tailored to different scenarios.
- **How to Do It**: Identify three different leadership scenarios, such as career development, team dynamics, or personal growth. For each scenario, create three potential echo questions that encourage deep reflection. Evaluate each question by considering whether it prompts introspection without leading to immediate answers. Share these questions with a trusted colleague or mentor for feedback on their effectiveness.

2. Patient Reflection Practice

- **Objective**: To improve patience and timing when using echo questions.
- **How to Do It**: During your next one-on-one meeting, ask an echo question relevant to the individual's current challenges or goals. Instead of seeking an immediate response, encourage the person to take time to think about it and schedule a follow-up discussion. Reflect on your own response to waiting—note any impatience or anxiety—and practice mindfulness to remain calm and focused. During the follow-up, assess how the additional reflection time impacted the quality of the answer and the person's growth.

3. Creating a Reflection Space

- **Objective**: To cultivate an environment conducive to deep reflection and honest dialogue.
- **How to Do It**: Choose a regular meeting or coaching session and set the intention to create a space for reflection. Begin the session by clearly stating that the purpose is to explore ideas without judgment, emphasizing that there are no right or

wrong answers. Pose an echo question and observe how the person responds in this reflective environment. After the session, assess how the reflective space influenced the conversation and how it might be improved for future sessions.

CHAPTER 3
DRIVE ACCOUNTABILITY, ELEVATE PERFORMANCE

As leaders, our responsibilities extend far beyond managing our own tasks. We are entrusted with the growth and development of our teams and organizations. This requires not only setting clear goals but also establishing a culture of accountability. To elevate performance, we must first create clarity around our objectives. Without clarity, our efforts become scattered, and our teams can lose focus. Clarity in goals ensures that everyone understands the objectives we aim to accomplish, and these goals should challenge us without being overwhelming.

One of the most critical roles we play as leaders is that of a teacher. Our actions, decisions, and behaviors serve as a model for our teams. By teaching and guiding others, we help them develop their skills and abilities, creating an environment ripe for success. This process isn't just about instruction; it's about fostering a mindset of continuous learning and improvement.

Setting Clear Expectations: The Foundation of Success

Setting clear expectations is the cornerstone of performance elevation. When team members know what is expected of them, they can align their efforts with the organization's goals. This alignment is crucial for driving the company forward. Clear expectations also eliminate ambiguity, reducing the chances of miscommunication and mistakes.

But setting expectations isn't enough. We must ensure that these expectations are realistic and attainable. Goals should stretch our capabilities, pushing us to grow, but they should also be achievable. When goals are too lofty or unclear, they can lead to frustration and burnout. The balance lies in setting goals that are challenging yet within reach, encouraging progress and motivating the team.

The Role of Accountability in Performance Improvement

Accountability is the engine that drives performance improvement. It's not just about holding people responsible for their actions but about creating a culture where accountability is valued and embraced. When team members are held accountable, they understand that their contributions matter. This understanding fosters a sense of ownership and responsibility, leading to higher levels of commitment and performance.

However, holding others accountable can be challenging, especially when it comes to addressing poor performance. It's easy to shy away from difficult conversations, but avoiding them only exacerbates the problem. Effective leaders tackle these issues head-on, using accountability as a tool for growth rather than punishment.

Learning and Teaching: The Core of Leadership

All great leaders are teachers at heart. Leadership is not just about directing others; it's about imparting knowledge, sharing experiences, and helping others grow. The process of improvement is inherently tied to learning. As leaders, we must create an environment where learning is encouraged and mistakes are seen as opportunities for growth.

Teaching isn't limited to formal training sessions. It's embedded in our daily interactions with our teams. Every feedback session, every decision explained, and every mistake corrected is a teaching moment. By consistently modeling the behaviors and skills we want to see in our teams, we set the stage for continuous improvement.

Managing by Objectives: A Proven Approach

One effective strategy for driving performance is managing by objectives, a method popularized by Peter Drucker in the 1950s. This approach involves supervisors and subordinates collaborating to set clear goals and expectations. Together, they create action plans to achieve these goals, ensuring that everyone is on the same page.

Managing by objectives is still widely used today because it works. It provides a structured framework for performance management, making it easier to track progress and make adjustments as needed. By involving team members in the goal-setting process, we empower them to take ownership of their work and contribute to the organization's success.

Creating a Supportive Climate for Success

For performance to truly elevate, the environment must be one of support and encouragement. A supportive climate doesn't mean coddling or lowering standards; it means providing the resources, feedback, and encouragement needed for team members to succeed. It's about creating a space where people feel safe to take risks, make mistakes, and learn from them.

Supportive leadership is proactive. It anticipates challenges and provides the tools and guidance needed to overcome them. It's about being present, approachable, and invested in the success of each team member. When leaders create a supportive environment, they pave the way for higher levels of performance and accountability.

Addressing Poor Performance Effectively

Addressing poor performance is one of the most challenging aspects of leadership, but it's also one of the most important. Ignoring poor performance sends a message that mediocrity is acceptable, which can quickly erode team morale and productivity.

When dealing with poor performance, it's essential to approach the situation with a mindset of improvement rather than punishment. The goal should be to help the individual understand where they went wrong and how they can improve. This involves clear communication, setting specific expectations, and providing the necessary support for improvement.

The Continuous Cycle of Improvement

Leadership is a continuous cycle of setting expectations, holding people accountable, and fostering a culture of learning and growth. It's about creating clarity, not just in goals but in the behaviors and standards we expect from our teams. It's about being a teacher, not just in formal settings but in every interaction. And it's about creating a supportive environment where accountability is seen as a positive force for improvement.

As leaders, our ultimate goal is to elevate performance, both in ourselves and in others. By following these principles, we can create a culture where excellence is the norm, and continuous improvement is a shared value. After all, as Jack Clark, a Hall of Fame rugby coach, wisely said, "Getting better is the best feeling in the world." And it's a feeling that, as leaders, we have the privilege and responsibility to inspire in others.

POWER OF A SIMPLE QUESTION

Holding people accountable is one of the most important—and often challenging—responsibilities of leadership. It's not just about making sure things get done; it's about fostering a culture of responsibility, transparency, and progress within your team. The most effective leaders understand that accountability isn't achieved through complex systems or heavy-handed management techniques. Instead, it often boils down to one simple tool: asking the right questions.

The Power of a Well-Timed Question

Accountability starts with a conversation. Simple, direct questions like "What's the status of that?" or "How is that going?" are powerful tools in a leader's arsenal. These questions do more than just check the box; they signal to your team that you're paying attention and that their work matters.

By asking these questions frequently, you create a rhythm of communication that keeps everyone on their toes. It's not about micromanaging; it's about staying connected and showing that you care about the outcomes. The key is to ask these questions consistently, so they become a natural part of your interactions with your team.

The Accountability List: A Leader's Secret Weapon

To make these check-ins more effective, it's essential to keep a simple, yet comprehensive, tracking list. This list should include all direct reports, family members, or colleagues who have responsibilities within your purview. By jotting down what each person is responsible for, you ensure that nothing slips through the cracks.

Every day, make it a point to review this list. Whether through email, text, phone calls, or face-to-face conversations, these regular check-ins reinforce the idea that accountability is an ongoing process, not a one-time event. This simple habit keeps you informed, your team engaged, and your projects on track.

Nudging Toward Progress

People generally want to do good work, but they sometimes need a little nudge in the right direction. Asking these simple questions isn't just about gathering information; it's about creating momentum. When you ask, "How is that going?" you're not just looking for a status update—you're encouraging action. You're reminding your team that they're responsible for their tasks and that you're here to support them in achieving their goals.

However, accountability also means being prepared to step in when things aren't going as planned. If the answers you get indicate that someone is falling behind or struggling, it's crucial to address it promptly. Have an open and honest conversation about what's happening, and work together to develop a plan to get back on track. Avoiding these conversations only compounds the problem.

Tracking Progress: The Key to Accountability

For accountability to work, leaders need to know where things stand at all times. This is where your tracking list becomes invaluable. Regularly reviewing and updating this list ensures that you're always aware of the status of your team's responsibilities. It's hard to hold someone accountable if you're not sure what they're supposed to be doing or how far along they are.

This practice doesn't just keep you informed; it also helps your team stay focused. When people know their progress is being monitored, they're more likely to stay on top of their tasks. It's a gentle reminder that their work is important and that you're invested in their success.

The Bottom Line: Simplicity Drives Accountability

In the end, holding people accountable is about more than just keeping tabs on your team. It's about creating a culture where responsibility is shared, progress is monitored, and success is celebrated. By asking simple questions, maintaining a tracking list, and being ready to take action when needed, you can lead your team to consistently meet and exceed their goals.

The most effective leaders don't rely on complex systems to drive accountability. They use straightforward tools and consistent communication to keep everyone on track. And sometimes, all it takes is a simple question to make a big difference.

Key Actions

- **Ask Direct Questions**: Use simple, direct questions like "What's the status of that?" or "How is that going?" to check in on progress and signal that their work matters.
- **Create a Tracking List**: Maintain a simple, comprehensive list of responsibilities for your direct reports, colleagues, or team members, and review it regularly to stay informed.
- **Engage in Regular Check-ins**: Make daily or frequent check-ins through various communication channels to reinforce accountability and keep projects on track.
- **Encourage Action**: Use questions not just to gather information but to nudge your team toward progress and remind them of their responsibilities.
- **Address Issues Promptly**: If a team member is falling behind, have an open conversation to identify the problem and work together on a plan to move forward.
- **Monitor Progress Consistently**: Regularly review and update your tracking list to ensure you're aware of the status of your team's tasks, helping both you and your team stay focused and on track.
- **Foster a Culture of Responsibility:** Use straightforward tools and consistent communication to build a culture where accountability is shared, progress is monitored, and success is celebrated.

Discussion Questions

1. How do you currently hold your team members accountable, and how might the approach of asking simple, direct questions improve your effectiveness?

2. What challenges have you faced in maintaining a consistent tracking system for your team's responsibilities, and how could a daily review process help overcome these challenges?

3. In what ways can regular check-ins with your team foster a culture of responsibility and progress, rather than being perceived as micromanagement?

4. How can you ensure that your accountability conversations are both supportive and action-oriented, especially when addressing issues where team members are falling behind?

5. What strategies can you implement to monitor progress consistently without creating unnecessary pressure on your team, ensuring that they stay focused and motivated?

Practice Exercises

1. Daily Accountability Check-in

- **Objective**: Improve your ability to hold team members accountable through consistent communication.
- **How to Do It**: Start your day by reviewing a simple tracking list that includes each team member's responsibilities. Choose one or two items to follow up on, and ask direct questions like "What's the status of that?" or "How is that going?" Make sure these check-ins are brief and focused, aimed at both gathering information and encouraging progress. Repeat this exercise daily to build a habit of consistent accountability.

2. The "Nudge" Practice

- **Objective**: Enhance your ability to encourage action and progress within your team.
- **How to Do It**: Select a task or project that is currently in progress. Instead of waiting for a formal update, proactively reach out to the responsible team member with a question designed to nudge them forward, such as "What's your next step on this?" or "How can I support you in moving this

forward?" Reflect on the impact of this nudge, and observe how it helps create momentum. Practice this exercise regularly with different team members.

3. Progress Tracking Routine

- **Objective**: Strengthen your skills in monitoring progress and maintaining a comprehensive view of your team's responsibilities.
- **How to Do It**: Dedicate 15 minutes at the end of each day to update your tracking list with the latest information on each team member's tasks. Take note of any areas where progress seems stalled or unclear. The following morning, use this updated list to guide your check-ins and ensure that you're consistently informed about the status of each responsibility. By making this a daily routine, you'll sharpen your ability to monitor progress effectively.

MENTAL MODELS FOR MASTERY

Mental models are the unsung heroes in the world of learning and leadership. They are mental shortcuts that simplify the complex, helping us to grasp new concepts, solve problems, and make better decisions. If you want to fast-track your growth—or that of your team —learning how to cultivate and apply mental models is a game changer.

The Power of Storytelling in Learning

Humans have relied on storytelling for thousands of years to pass down wisdom, teach lessons, and make sense of the world. There's a reason for that. Our brains are hardwired to respond to stories because they present information in a way that's both engaging and easy to remember. Good leaders are often good storytellers. They use narratives to illustrate concepts, making abstract ideas concrete and relatable.

But stories do more than just entertain or inform. They shape our understanding, influence our beliefs, and guide our actions. When a leader uses storytelling effectively, they can help their team internalize new ideas, remember key concepts, and see the world from a fresh perspective. It's a method that works because it taps into the way our brains naturally process and retain information.

Understanding Mental Models

So, what exactly are mental models? At their core, mental models are representations of how we think things work. They are simplified versions of reality that help us navigate the complexities of the world. Think of them as internal blueprints that guide our thoughts, decisions, and actions.

These models can take many forms—images, diagrams, or structured stories—and can be highly specific to a particular field, like the scientific method in research, or more general, like the concept of supply and demand in economics. No matter the form they take, mental models serve as frameworks for understanding and approaching problems. They help us break down complicated issues into manageable parts, making it easier to learn and apply new concepts.

Why Models and Stories Work So Well

Models and stories resonate with us because they offer a clear example of how to succeed. They show us the steps someone else took to overcome a challenge or achieve a goal, setting a standard for us to follow. When we see a model of success, whether in a story or a diagram, it gives us something to emulate. It lights the path forward, making it easier for us to learn and adopt new behaviors.

In essence, both models and stories provide a roadmap. They tell us, "Here's how it's done," and allow us to follow along, learning as we go. By giving us this framework, they can dramatically speed up the learning process.

The Role of Practice in Solidifying Learning

But learning doesn't stop at understanding. To truly internalize new models and behaviors, practice is essential. This is where leaders come into play. A leader's role is not just to share models or tell stories but also to create an environment where practice is encouraged and supported.

This might involve giving specific, constructive feedback, setting clear and attainable goals, or providing the resources needed to succeed. Practice helps solidify what has been learned. It turns abstract concepts into real-world skills.

Leaders who recognize this and actively encourage practice see better results. They help their team members move from understanding to mastery.

The Need for a Diverse Set of Mental Models

No single mental model can solve every problem. That's why it's crucial for leaders to have a diverse set of models to draw from. Different situations call for different approaches, and what works for one person might not work for another. By having a variety of models at their disposal, leaders can tailor their guidance to the unique needs and learning styles of their team members.

This adaptability not only accelerates learning but also ensures that it is more effective. It's like having a toolbox full of different tools. The more options you have, the better equipped you are to handle any challenge that comes your way.

Accelerating Learning Through Mental Models

Mental models and storytelling are among the most powerful tools in a leader's arsenal. They help simplify the complex, making it easier for team members to grasp new concepts and apply them in their work. But these tools are most effective when combined with practice and a diverse set of models tailored to the situation at hand.

By using mental models strategically, leaders can accelerate the learning process, helping their team members not only understand new ideas but also adopt and master new behaviors. This approach not only fosters growth but also builds a strong foundation for continuous improvement.

In the end, the goal is simple: to create an environment where learning is accelerated, understanding is deepened, and growth is constant. With the right mental models and a commitment to practice, that goal is well within reach.

Key Actions

- **Use Storytelling to Illustrate Concepts**: Leverage the power of storytelling to make abstract ideas concrete and relatable, helping team members internalize and remember new information.
- **Apply Mental Models for Simplification**: Utilize mental models to break down complex issues into manageable parts, providing a clear framework for understanding and solving problems.
- **Emulate Success Through Models and Stories**: Provide examples of excellence through models and stories, offering a

roadmap that team members can follow to learn and adopt new behaviors.

- **Encourage Practice to Solidify Learning**: Foster an environment where practice is encouraged, supported by specific feedback, clear goals, and the necessary resources to turn understanding into mastery.
- **Adapt Guidance Using a Diverse Set of Models:** Have a variety of mental models at your disposal to tailor guidance to the unique needs and learning styles of team members, ensuring more effective learning and problem-solving.

Discussion Questions

1. How can storytelling be used effectively in a leadership role to enhance team learning and communication.
2. What mental models do you currently use in your work, and how have they helped you simplify complex problems or tasks.
3. In what ways can leaders encourage their team members to practice new behaviors or skills to solidify their learning?
4. Why is it important for leaders to have a diverse set of mental models, and how can this diversity impact the way they guide their teams?
5. How do models and stories serve as roadmaps for success, and what are the potential risks of relying too heavily on them?

Practice Exercises

1. Storytelling for Impact

- **Objective**: Improve your ability to use storytelling as a tool for teaching and leadership.
- **How to Do It**: Identify a complex concept or lesson you want to communicate to your team. Craft a story that illustrates this concept in a relatable and engaging way. Practice telling this story to a colleague or friend, focusing on

clarity, emotional engagement, and relevance. Reflect on their feedback and refine your story for future use.

2. Mental Model Mapping

- **Objective**: Develop the habit of applying mental models to simplify and solve complex problems.
- **How to Do It**: Choose a problem or challenge you're currently facing at work. Identify at least two mental models that could be applied to understand and address the issue. Create a visual map or diagram showing how these models interact with the problem and lead to potential solutions. Review this map regularly as you work through the challenge, adjusting your approach as needed.

3. Practice and Feedback Routine

- **Objective**: Enhance your ability to encourage and support practice among your team members.
- **How to Do It**: Set up a regular routine where you provide your team with specific, actionable feedback on their work. Start by identifying one skill or behavior they need to develop. Encourage them to practice this skill daily or weekly, and provide clear, supportive feedback on their progress. Track their development over time and adjust your feedback to help them continue improving.

ROOT OUT POOR PERFORMANCE

Poor performance is like a pebble in a shoe—it may seem small, but it can cause big problems if left unchecked. In a team setting, one person's lackluster performance can throw off the whole group, slowing progress and dampening morale. But before you rush to label someone as a "poor performer," it's crucial to step back, assess the situation, and approach the issue constructively.

Rather than pointing fingers, a more effective strategy involves focusing on specific behaviors and setting clear, actionable goals. By doing this, you can guide individuals toward improvement and, ultimately, contribute to the team's success.

The Power of Asking for Information

When performance dips, the first instinct might be to issue a reprimand. But a more effective approach often starts with a simple request for information. This isn't about micromanaging or piling on paperwork. Instead, it's about using information gathering as a tool to diagnose the problem and guide improvement.

For example, imagine you have a salesperson whose numbers are consistently below average. Instead of jumping to conclusions, you might ask them to provide a daily call summary. This request serves multiple purposes: it increases accountability, encourages reflection on daily activities, and provides you with data to analyze the situation.

If the numbers don't improve after a few weeks, you can delve deeper. Ask for additional details, like the content of those calls or the objections they're facing. The goal here isn't to catch them in the act of underperforming but to identify where the breakdown is occurring. Are they not making enough calls? Are they struggling with closing deals? Is there a pattern in the types of leads they're handling? The information you gather can pinpoint the root cause of the issue, allowing for targeted coaching and support.

Setting Clear Goals and Expectations

Once you've identified the specific behaviors that need improvement, it's time to set clear, achievable goals. Vague instructions like "do better" or "increase sales" won't cut it. You need to be specific. For instance, instead of telling the salesperson to "increase their numbers," you might set a goal of making 20 additional calls per week or securing at least five new client meetings.

Clear expectations don't just give the individual something to aim for —they also provide a benchmark for evaluating progress. And when these goals are met, they serve as a confidence booster, showing that improvement is not only possible but within reach.

Addressing Systemic Issues

Sometimes, the root cause of poor performance isn't just the individual's behavior—it's the environment they're working in. Inadequate resources, unclear processes, or a lack of proper training can all contribute to underperformance. As a leader, it's your job to recognize these systemic issues and address them.

For example, if the salesperson is struggling because they aren't getting enough quality leads, that's a problem you need to solve at an organizational level. Maybe the marketing team needs to adjust their strategy, or perhaps the sales process itself needs tweaking. By addressing these broader issues, you create an environment where high performance isn't just possible—it's inevitable.

Creating a Supportive Environment

At the end of the day, the goal is to build a positive, supportive environment where everyone can thrive. This means open, honest communication, ongoing feedback, and a commitment to helping each team member succeed.

When you focus on specific behaviors and gather the right information, you can provide targeted feedback that drives improvement. Combine this with a willingness to address systemic issues, and you'll create a culture that not only tolerates but actively fosters high performance.

In short, addressing poor performance isn't about pointing out flaws—it's about identifying opportunities for growth and helping your team reach their full potential. By taking a thoughtful, informed approach, you can turn even the most challenging situations into stepping stones toward success.

Key Actions

- **Focus on Specific Behaviors**: Avoid labeling individuals as "poor performers" and instead focus on the specific behaviors contributing to low performance. This approach allows for targeted improvement and constructive feedback.
- **Request Information Thoughtfully**: Use information gathering as a tool to diagnose performance issues, rather than as a means of micromanaging. Asking for specific details can help identify the root cause of the problem.
- **Set Clear, Achievable Goals**: Establish specific and actionable goals that provide clear direction and measurable benchmarks for improvement, rather than vague instructions like "do better."
- **Identify and Address Systemic Issues**: Recognize that poor performance may stem from broader organizational problems such as inadequate resources, unclear processes, or insufficient training. Address these issues to create an environment conducive to high performance.
- **Foster a Supportive Environment:** Promote a positive and supportive environment through open communication, ongoing feedback, and a commitment to helping team members succeed, ensuring that everyone has the opportunity to thrive.

Discussion Questions

1. How can focusing on specific behaviors, rather than labeling someone as a "poor performer," change the way we address performance issues within our teams?
2. What are some effective ways to request information from team members without making them feel micromanaged? Can you share an example from your own experience?
3. How do clear, achievable goals impact individual performance, and what are some strategies for setting these goals in a way that motivates team members?
4. In what ways can systemic issues within an organization contribute to poor performance, and how can leaders identify and address these issues to improve overall team success?
5. What steps can leaders take to create a supportive environment that encourages open communication and continuous improvement, especially when dealing with performance challenges?

Practice Exercises

1. Behavioral Observation and Documentation

- **Objective**: Improve your ability to identify and focus on specific behaviors that contribute to performance issues.
- **How to Do It**: Spend a week observing the performance of a team member or colleague. Take detailed notes on specific behaviors, actions, and outcomes related to their performance. Avoid making generalizations or assumptions. At the end of the week, review your notes and identify the key actions that may be contributing to their performance levels. Practice articulating these behaviors in a constructive and non-judgmental way.

2. Goal-Setting Practice

- **Objective**: Enhance your ability to set clear, achievable goals that provide direction and motivation.
- **How to Do It**: Choose a current project or task you're working on. Break it down into smaller, specific goals with clear benchmarks and deadlines. For each goal, write down the exact steps needed to achieve it. Practice this exercise with different projects or tasks over a month, and reflect on how setting clear goals impacts your progress and motivation.

3. Systemic Issue Identification

- **Objective**: Develop the skill of identifying and addressing systemic issues that may contribute to poor performance.
- **How to Do It**: Take a recent example of a performance issue within your team or organization. Analyze the situation by asking yourself what broader organizational factors might have contributed to the problem (e.g., lack of resources, unclear processes). Create a list of potential systemic issues, and brainstorm possible solutions or improvements. Discuss these with a colleague or your team to see how addressing these issues might improve overall performance.

BREAKING SKILLS DOWN

Excellence isn't about mastering one big thing—it's about perfecting a lot of little things. Great performance is often built on a foundation of specific skills and their smaller components, or sub-skills. These sub-skills are the individual actions or routines within a broader skill that can be isolated and refined to improve overall performance. The best coaches and leaders understand this well. They know that breaking skills down into 20 or 30 sub-skills and drilling on them is the path to true excellence.

The Power of Sub-Skills

Imagine you're watching a world-class golfer. Their swing looks effortless, but what you don't see are the countless hours spent perfecting the grip, stance, and weight distribution—each a sub-skill crucial to their success. When performance drops, it's often because one of these sub-skills is slipping. Identifying and focusing on these specific components can lead to significant improvements in overall performance.

Whether in sports, communication, or leadership, breaking down skills into their sub-components and working on them individually can yield powerful results. This approach allows for targeted practice, which is far more effective than trying to improve the whole skill at once.

The Swing Thought: Narrowing Focus for Improvement

One effective method to enhance a sub-skill is through what golfers call a "swing thought." This means focusing on a single aspect of a skill during practice to improve it. For instance, in public speaking, instead of trying to perfect the entire speech at once, you might focus solely on improving eye contact with the audience. By narrowing your focus, you can make more substantial progress in that specific area, which will then elevate your overall performance.

This principle applies broadly. Think of relationship-building. It's a complex skill with many sub-skills like conversational flow and active listening. Focusing on one of these at a time, like improving how you take turns in a conversation, can make you more effective in connecting with others. The same goes for tasks like hitting a golf ball —breaking down the skill into grip, stance, and swing mechanics, and focusing on improving each individually leads to better overall performance.

Drilling Down: The Art of Repetition

Repetition is the mother of skill. The famous Moscow tennis school understands this, having students simulate the perfect swing for two years before they ever play a competitive game. This kind of focused, repetitive practice is what leads to mastery. The same principle applies to any field, whether it's sports, academics, or business.

For instance, consider the skill of studying. It's not just about hitting the books; it's about mastering the sub-skills that make studying effective, such as note-taking and reading comprehension. Drilling these sub-skills through repetition can significantly boost a student's academic performance. The same is true in business—sub-skills like time management and effective communication are critical to success. Drilling these through deliberate practice can lead to a noticeable improvement in overall performance.

The Devil Is in the Details: Why Leaders Must Focus on Sub-Skills

Great leaders pay attention to the details—the small things that often make a big difference. Take a division manager struggling with higher turnover rates than other departments. A sharp leader might dig into the specifics—like the sub-skills related to team management or employee engagement—to find the root cause and address it. It's often these small, overlooked details that, when improved, can lead to significant gains in overall performance.

For example, if a team's project presentations lack impact, the leader might not just ask for better presentations. Instead, they'll focus on specific sub-skills like the organization of ideas or the clarity of visual aids. By improving these details, the overall quality of the presentations will naturally rise.

Building a Foundation: The Role of Sub-Skills in Competence

Skills are the building blocks of competence—the more finely tuned these blocks are, the stronger the overall structure. By breaking down complex skills into teachable and learnable sub-skills, leaders can help their teams develop more quickly and effectively. The process of learning, drilling, and refining these sub-skills through simulation and real-time experience is what drives improvement.

In the end, it's not about making sweeping changes overnight but about understanding that greatness comes from getting the small things right. By teaching and focusing on sub-skills, leaders empower their teams to become more skillful, leading to greater overall performance and success.

The Path to Excellence

Excellence isn't a one-time achievement; it's a continuous journey of refining and perfecting sub-skills. By breaking down skills into their components and focusing on improving each one, leaders can drive significant improvements in performance. Whether through drills, focusing on specific swing thoughts, or paying attention to the details, the approach is the same: master the small things to achieve great results. In doing so, leaders can help their teams reach new heights of performance and competence.

Key Actions

- **Break Down Skills into Sub-Skills**: Identify and isolate the specific components or routines within a broader skill to improve overall performance.
- **Focus on a Single Aspect (Swing Thought)**: Narrow your focus to a single sub-skill or specific aspect of a skill during practice to make substantial progress in that area.
- **Use Repetition to Master Sub-Skills**: Emphasize repetitive practice of sub-skills to build mastery, understanding that repetition is crucial for improvement.
- **Pay Attention to Small Details**: Leaders should focus on the

small details within sub-skills, as these often have a big impact on overall performance.

- **Practice Sub-Skills Through Simulation and Real-Time Experience:** Engage in deliberate practice, including drills and simulations, to refine sub-skills and build competence.

Discussion Questions

1. How can breaking down complex skills into sub-skills improve overall performance in a team or organization? Can you provide an example from your own experience?
2. What are some challenges you've encountered when trying to focus on a single sub-skill (or "swing thought") during practice? How did you overcome them?
3. In your opinion, how important is repetition in mastering sub-skills? Can you think of a situation where repetitive practice led to significant improvement?
4. Why do you think leaders sometimes overlook the small details within sub-skills, and how can paying closer attention to these details impact overall performance?
5. How can leaders effectively implement drills and simulations to help team members practice and refine sub-skills? What strategies have worked well in your experience?

Practice Exercises

1. Sub-Skill Identification Exercise

- **Objective**: Improve your ability to break down complex skills into their sub-components.
- **How to Do It**: Choose a skill relevant to your work or personal life (e.g., public speaking, project management, or a sport). List all the sub-skills that make up this larger skill. For example, if you choose public speaking, identify sub-skills like tone of voice, pacing, eye contact, and audience engagement. Practice identifying sub-skills regularly with different tasks to build this skill.

2. Focused Practice with a Swing Thought

- **Objective**: Enhance your ability to focus on a specific aspect of a skill to improve overall performance.
- **How to Do It**: Select one sub-skill from a larger skill you want to improve. For example, if you're working on your golf swing, focus solely on your grip during a practice session. Set aside dedicated time to practice this sub-skill, keeping it as your main focus for the entire session. Repeat this exercise with different sub-skills to gradually improve the overall skill.

3. Detail-Oriented Leadership Drill

- **Objective**: Develop your ability to pay attention to and improve small details within sub-skills as a leader.
- **How to Do It**: Choose a task or project that your team is working on and identify one or two small details within the sub-skills that could be improved. For instance, if you're leading a team presentation, focus on the clarity of the visual aids or the structure of the narrative. Provide specific feedback on these details and work with your team to refine them. Practice this regularly by focusing on different details in various tasks.

PRIORITIZE FOR SUCCESS

In leadership, the ability to set and manage priorities is a cornerstone of success. Priorities serve as the guiding light for teams, helping them focus on the tasks that matter most. By clearly defining these priorities, leaders can channel their team's energy toward achieving significant results. But setting and recalibrating priorities isn't always straightforward—especially for those new to a role or environment. It's a challenge that requires a keen understanding of both the immediate needs and long-term goals of the organization.

The Leader's Role in Prioritization

Leaders play a crucial role in helping their teams navigate the often complex landscape of priorities. This isn't just about issuing directives; it's about engaging in open and explicit communication. Effective leaders regularly check in with their team members, asking them directly about their current priorities. This dialogue helps ensure that everyone is aligned and focused on tasks that drive the most progress toward the organization's goals.

Priorities are not static. What is critical today might shift tomorrow, depending on changing circumstances or new information. The best leaders understand this fluidity and are skilled at recalibrating priorities as needed. This flexibility ensures that the team remains on course, even as the organizational landscape evolves.

Measuring and Aligning Performance

While there are many tools leaders can use to measure performance—such as goals, objectives, key performance indicators (KPIs), and critical success factors—the emphasis on individual priorities is particularly powerful. Priorities represent the highest and best use of time. Unlike daily responsibilities, which are often routine, priorities are the tasks that will have the most significant impact in the short term. They are the key to unlocking long-term success.

A results-focused leader knows that getting priorities right leads to immediate action, which is essential for achieving long-term goals.

However, it's important to recognize that not everyone is naturally skilled at determining what their priorities should be. This is where leadership truly shines. By frequently asking team members about their top priorities and offering guidance on how to elevate or adjust them, leaders can significantly enhance performance.

The Ripple Effect of Prioritization

The ability to set and recalibrate priorities doesn't just apply to professional settings—it can be equally valuable in personal relationships. Leaders can apply the same principles with family and friends by thoughtfully exploring what matters most and suggesting a focus on tasks that deserve higher attention. This approach can strengthen relationships and ensure that important matters are addressed with the care they deserve.

The Essential Skill of Prioritization

Setting and managing priorities is not just a skill—it's an essential leadership quality that drives progress and ensures success. By helping team members understand and align their priorities with the organization's goals, leaders create a culture of performance and accountability. This focus on what truly matters enables teams to make meaningful strides toward their objectives, both in the short term and for the long haul. Whether in a professional context or in personal life, the ability to prioritize effectively is a powerful tool that can lead to significant, lasting results.

Key Actions

- **Engage in Open Communication**: Regularly check in with team members about their current priorities and ensure they align with organizational goals through explicit and open dialogue.
- **Be Adaptable and Recalibrate Priorities**: Recognize that priorities are fluid and need constant reassessment to stay aligned with evolving circumstances and long-term goals.
- **Focus on High-Impact Tasks**: Identify and emphasize tasks

that represent the highest and best use of time, driving short-term actions essential for long-term success.

- **Guide and Support Team Members**: Help team members identify and adjust their priorities by frequently asking about their focus areas and offering guidance on how to elevate or recalibrate them.
- **Apply Prioritization in Personal Relationships**: Use the same prioritization skills in personal relationships by exploring what matters most and suggesting a focus on tasks that deserve higher attention.
- **Create a Culture of Performance**: Establish a culture where priorities are clear, aligned with larger goals, and drive a performance-focused environment.

Discussion Questions

1. What strategies do you use to help your team members align their priorities with the broader goals of the organization?
2. How do you approach recalibrating priorities when unexpected changes or challenges arise in your work environment?
3. Can you share an example of a time when focusing on short-term priorities directly contributed to achieving a long-term goal?
4. How do you ensure that the priorities you set are the highest and best use of your team's time?
5. In what ways can the skills of setting and managing priorities be applied to strengthen personal relationships outside of work?

Practice Exercises

1. Priority Mapping

- **Objective**: To improve your ability to identify and align priorities with long-term goals.

- **How to Do It**: Start by listing your current tasks and responsibilities. Next, categorize them into urgent, important, and non-essential. For each item, ask yourself, "How does this task contribute to my long-term goals?" Adjust your list by prioritizing tasks that have the most significant impact on your long-term objectives. Practice this exercise weekly to refine your prioritization skills.

2. Recalibration Check-In

- **Objective**: To develop the habit of regularly reassessing and adjusting priorities as circumstances change.
- **How to Do It**: Set aside 15 minutes at the end of each week to review your priorities. Ask yourself what has changed in your work environment and whether your current priorities still align with your long-term goals. If necessary, adjust your priorities to reflect these changes. This exercise helps you stay adaptable and focused on what truly matters.

3. Priority Dialogue

- **Objective**: To strengthen your communication skills around discussing and aligning priorities with others.
- **How to Do It**: Schedule a one-on-one meeting with a team member or peer. Begin the conversation by asking them about their top three priorities. Listen actively, then provide feedback or suggestions on how their priorities could be better aligned with broader goals. Practice this exercise regularly to enhance your ability to guide and support others in their prioritization process.

HARNESS IMPATIENCE

Impatience is a trait that most leaders wrestle with daily. On the surface, it can seem like a superpower, propelling teams to meet tight deadlines, achieve high standards, and produce quick results. But this double-edged sword can also slice through team morale, leaving a trail of defensiveness and underperformance in its wake. The challenge for leaders is learning how to wield impatience wisely—using it to drive progress without alienating those around them.

The Misuse of Impatience

We all know someone whose impatience comes off as a constant storm, creating an atmosphere of tension and anxiety. Take the example of a former colleague I worked with—let's call him John. John was known for his rapid response times and relentless push for results. On paper, this sounds like a dream client, right? But in reality, John's impatience earned him a reputation as a "jerk." People dreaded his emails and avoided his calls, and the quality of work he received suffers because no one wants to engage with him. His impatience, instead of motivating his team, made them defensive and resistant.

Impatience, when mishandled, can damage relationships and stifle creativity. It turns what could be constructive urgency into destructive pressure. People become more concerned with avoiding blame than solving problems, and the leader's credibility erodes over time. The key issue here isn't the impatience itself, but how it's communicated and directed.

Channeling Impatience Productively

Impatience doesn't have to be a liability. When used correctly, it can be a powerful motivator, creating a sense of urgency that drives performance and excellence. The trick is in how you express it.

First and foremost, impatience should be focused on the outcome, not on the people involved. Your impatience should be about achieving results, not about blaming individuals for delays or mistakes. This distinction is crucial. It allows you to maintain high standards without making your team feel like they're constantly under attack.

One way to do this is through clear, open, and honest communication. Instead of expressing frustration at what hasn't been done, shift the focus to what can be done. Ask questions like, "What do you need to hit this deadline?" or "How can I help you move this forward?" This not only shows that you're invested in the outcome but also that you're willing to support your team in achieving it.

Balancing Impatience with Empathy

Impatience, when balanced with empathy, can create a high-performing environment where people feel motivated rather than demoralized. It's about pushing for results while also understanding the challenges your team faces. Empathy doesn't mean lowering your standards; it means recognizing the human side of work—the pressures, the setbacks, and the unexpected hurdles that can slow progress.

Leaders who balance impatience with empathy are able to set high expectations without making their team feel like they're walking on eggshells. They create a culture where people are driven to succeed because they know their leader has their back, not because they're afraid of disappointing them.

The Power of Self-Reflection

One of the most effective ways to use impatience as a tool rather than a weapon is to turn it inward. Instead of asking, "Why aren't they doing this faster?" ask yourself, "What can I do to help them get this done?" This shift in mindset makes your impatience about your own actions, not someone else's shortcomings. It keeps the focus on the goal while also demonstrating your commitment to the team's success.

When you frame your impatience as a challenge to yourself, it becomes a catalyst for improvement rather than a source of stress for your team. It also sets an example for your team members to reflect on their own actions and take responsibility for their contributions to the overall effort.

Turning Impatience Into a Leadership Asset

Impatience isn't inherently a bad trait—it's all in how you use it. By focusing on outcomes, communicating supportively, and balancing impatience with empathy, you can turn what might seem like a leadership flaw into a powerful asset. In the end, it's not about stifling your impatience but about channeling it in a way that pushes your team to perform at their best, without cutting them down in the process.

Key Actions

- **Focus on Outcomes**: Direct impatience toward achieving specific results rather than blaming individuals for delays or mistakes.
- **Supportive Communication**: Use open and honest communication that shifts the focus to what can be done, offering help and resources rather than expressing frustration.
- **Balance Impatience with Empathy**: Push for results while understanding the human side of work, recognizing challenges, and setting high expectations without creating unnecessary stress.
- **Self-Reflection**: Channel impatience inward by asking how you can better support your team's progress, turning impatience into a personal challenge rather than a source of stress for others.

Discussion Questions

1. How can a leader balance the urgency of impatience with the need for empathy in their communication?
2. What are some practical ways to shift impatience from being people-focused to outcome-focused in a team environment?
3. Can you think of a time when impatience from a leader led to either positive or negative outcomes? What was the impact on the team?
4. How does self-reflection help a leader channel their impatience in a more constructive way?

5. In what ways can leaders ensure that their impatience drives creativity and problem-solving, rather than stifling it?

Practice Exercises

1. Outcome-Focused Communication Exercise

- **Objective**: To practice directing impatience toward outcomes rather than individuals.
- **How to Do It**: The next time you feel impatient with a situation at work, pause before speaking. Write down the outcome you want to achieve and craft your communication around that goal. For example, instead of saying, "Why isn't this done yet?" you might say, "What do we need to get this completed by the end of the day?" Practice this approach in different scenarios and observe the impact on your team's response.

2. Empathy Balance Challenge

- **Objective**: To develop the ability to balance impatience with empathy.
- **How to Do It**: In your next team meeting or one-on-one conversation, consciously acknowledge the challenges your team members are facing before expressing your expectations. For example, start with, "I understand that the deadline is tight, and you've been juggling multiple tasks," then follow up with, "What can I do to help you meet this deadline?" Reflect on how this approach affects the team's motivation and engagement.

3. Self-Reflection Journal

- **Objective**: To enhance your ability to channel impatience inward and focus on personal improvement.
- **How to Do It**: Keep a daily journal where you note instances when you felt impatient during the day. Reflect on how you

handled each situation and ask yourself what you could have done differently to support your team better. Write down actionable steps you can take in similar situations in the future. Over time, review your entries to track your progress and identify patterns in your behavior.

PEER EVALUATION MATTERS

Peer evaluation is the practice of having individuals at the same level or status in an organization assess and provide feedback on each other's work. It's more than just a tool for critique; it's a powerful mechanism for growth. While peer pressure often gets a bad rap, when channeled correctly, it can be a potent force for pushing people to excel. I learned this firsthand while teaching leadership and conflict processes at Arizona State University.

In classes, I introduced a simple yet revealing exercise. Students were required to take their papers to a copy center, make copies for their peers, and then have those peers grade each other's work—with no commentary. The results were eye-opening. The students, acting as evaluators, were far tougher on each other than I, or any leader, could have been. They held each other to incredibly high standards, scrutinizing every detail. The outcome? Better quality papers and a clear demonstration of how peer evaluation can drive excellence.

The Impact of Peer Judgment

People are highly sensitive to how they're perceived by their peers. Research and experience show that peers often grade performance more harshly than leaders do. The possibility of being judged negatively by someone of equal status can be a powerful motivator. It pushes individuals to put in more effort, to be more diligent, and to aim higher. That's why smart leaders incorporate peer evaluation as a strategy to elevate overall team performance. It's rare to find a high-performing team that doesn't leverage this dynamic to its advantage.

Crafting Effective Peer Evaluation

The best leaders don't just encourage peer evaluation; they create structured opportunities for it. They design processes where peers can assess each other's work and offer constructive feedback. However, it's crucial to set clear ground rules. Without them, peer evaluation can slip into judgmental or even cruel behavior, which is counterproductive.

One effective approach is to separate the grading aspect from the feedback. Grading can sometimes feel punitive, whereas feedback is intended to be constructive. When individuals know that feedback is meant to help them improve, rather than to rank them, they're more open to accepting it without becoming defensive.

Peer Opinion in the Professional World

In professional settings, the opinion of peers carries significant weight, especially in organizations where there aren't many opportunities for formal feedback. Here, peer evaluations can fill the gap, providing valuable insights and helping individuals improve. The best leaders involve their peers in evaluations and reviews, whether it's through debriefing sessions, post-mortems, or backcasting exercises. These peer-driven assessments bring diverse perspectives to the table, fostering creativity and guarding against groupthink.

The Positive Use of Peer Pressure

But let's not forget: while peer pressure is a powerful motivator, it must be used carefully. It should never be wielded in a way that is harmful or demeaning. When used positively, peer pressure can create a culture of excellence within an organization. It pushes everyone to do their best while fostering a supportive environment.

Interestingly, team members are generally less sensitive to more passive forms of peer evaluation, such as 360-degree feedback or cross-evaluations. These methods, while valuable, don't carry the same immediate impact as direct peer assessment. The key is to balance these different forms of evaluation, using each where it's most effective.

Harnessing Peer Power for Growth

The power of peer evaluation lies in its ability to drive improvement and achieve better results. When leaders involve peers in the evaluation process and establish clear guidelines, they can harness this power in a constructive and supportive way. The result is a team that not only performs better but also grows together, pushing each other to new heights.

Remember, peer evaluation isn't just about assessment—it's about fostering a culture where excellence is the norm, and continuous improvement is a shared goal. When done right, it becomes one of the most valuable tools in a leader's arsenal.

Key Actions

- **Encouraging High Standards**: Peer evaluators often hold each other to high standards, which drives better quality work.
- **Setting Clear Ground Rules**: Establishing clear guidelines for peer evaluation to prevent judgmental or cruel behavior.
- **Separating Grading from Feedback**: Distinguishing between the grading process and constructive feedback to reduce defensiveness and encourage improvement.
- **Involving Peers in Evaluations**: Actively including peers in evaluation processes like debriefing sessions, post-mortems, or backcasting exercises to gain diverse perspectives and avoid groupthink.
- **Using Peer Pressure Positively**: Leveraging peer pressure in a way that motivates without being harmful or demeaning, fostering a supportive culture of excellence.
- **Balancing Evaluation Methods**: Understanding the different impacts of direct peer assessment versus more passive methods like 360-degree feedback, and using each appropriately.

Discussion Questions

1. How can peer evaluation be structured to ensure it remains constructive rather than becoming overly critical or judgmental?
2. In what ways does peer pressure differ from traditional top-down evaluation, and why might it be more effective in certain situations?
3. What are the potential risks of peer evaluation, and how can

leaders mitigate these risks while still encouraging high standards?

4. How does the separation of grading and feedback influence the effectiveness of peer evaluations in promoting growth and improvement?

5. In your experience, how does the involvement of peers in evaluation processes like debriefings or post-mortems impact team dynamics and creativity?

Practice Exercises

1. Peer Evaluation Role-Play

- **Objective**: To practice giving constructive and specific feedback in a peer evaluation setting.
- **How to Do It**: Pair up with a colleague or friend and exchange a piece of work, such as a presentation or a written document. Take turns acting as the evaluator, providing feedback that is specific and focused on improvement. Use the "more of" or "less of" framework to guide your feedback. After the exercise, discuss how the feedback was received and what could be improved in the delivery.

2. Create Ground Rules for Peer Feedback

- **Objective**: To develop clear and effective guidelines for peer evaluations in your team or organization.
- **How to Do It**: Gather your team and brainstorm a set of ground rules that will govern peer evaluations. Consider aspects such as tone, specificity, and the separation of grading from feedback. Once you've agreed on the rules, implement them in a small, controlled peer evaluation session and observe how they impact the feedback process.

3. Conduct a Peer Debriefing Session

- **Objective**: To practice leading a peer-driven evaluation session that fosters creativity and avoids groupthink.
- **How to Do It**: After completing a team project or significant task, organize a debriefing session where peers provide feedback on each other's contributions. As the leader, encourage open and honest discussions while ensuring the feedback remains constructive. Pay attention to how diverse perspectives are shared and how they influence the group's insights and future strategies. Reflect on the session's outcomes and identify areas for improvement in facilitating such discussions.

PRACTICE WITH PURPOSE

We've all heard the phrase "practice makes perfect," but that's not quite right. Practice doesn't necessarily lead to perfection, but it does lead to permanence. Whether in sports, business, or life, the more you repeat a task, the more ingrained it becomes in your mind and muscles. The catch is that practice needs to be done strategically—close to the real deal—to ensure those repeated actions are worth something in the real world.

Your brain doesn't care if the experience is real or simulated as long as it feels real enough. That's why simulators are a game-changer. They allow you to practice high-stakes tasks without the real-world consequences. Pilots have been using flight simulators for decades, perfecting their craft without putting lives or aircraft at risk. Today, anyone with a decent computer can use these tools to sharpen their flying skills. But it's not just about aviation; this principle applies to any skill that demands precision.

Simulators Are Only as Good as the Feedback They Provide

The real magic of simulators lies in their ability to provide immediate feedback. When you make a mistake in a simulation, you can see the consequences right away and adjust your behavior accordingly. This creates a powerful feedback loop—practice, mistake, correction, repeat —that's essential for learning.

Take John Gagliardi, the legendary football coach who became the winningest coach in NCAA history. Gagliardi's teams didn't waste time on brute-force drills. Instead, they focused on precise execution—footwork, hand placement, and other critical skills—over and over again. They used film to catch mistakes immediately, making corrections on the spot. It was like a mental and physical flight simulator for football, embedding the right actions deep into the players' muscle memory.

Build Your Own Simulator for Success

In the workplace, leaders can take a page from Gagliardi's playbook. Identify the key tasks or outcomes that are critical for your team's success and create a "simulator" for them. This could be role-playing scenarios, mock presentations, or even sophisticated software that mimics real-world challenges. The key is to ensure these simulations are as realistic as possible and that they allow for mistakes—because mistakes are where the learning happens.

Feedback is crucial here. Just like in a flight simulator, immediate feedback allows individuals to correct their course and improve rapidly. This approach helps to build proficiency in those foundational skills that are at the core of your team's work. By practicing these key actions in a controlled, feedback-rich environment, your team will be better prepared for the real thing.

Bruce Lee, the martial artist, understood this better than most. He wasn't afraid of the person who practiced 10,000 different kicks once; he respected the one who practiced one kick 10,000 times. That's the kind of precision and repetition we're talking about. It's not about quantity; it's about quality—repeating the right things in the right way until they become second nature.

Mastery Through Simulated Experience

Whether in personal growth or professional development, the path to mastery lies in repetition, practice, and immediate feedback. Simulators and other practice tools allow you to refine your skills in a risk-free environment. By identifying the key actions your team needs to succeed and focusing on precise repetition, you can create your own version of a flight simulator. This approach doesn't just prepare you for success—it makes it inevitable.

Key Actions

- **Strategic Practice**: Engaging in practice that closely mimics real-world tasks to ensure that skills learned through repetition are applicable in real situations.
- **Feedback-Driven Learning**: Using immediate feedback from simulations or practice sessions to identify and correct mistakes in real-time, creating a powerful learning loop.
- **Precise Execution**: Focusing on the exact execution of critical skills, such as footwork, hand placement, or other foundational tasks, and repeating them until they become second nature.
- **Realistic Simulation**: Creating or utilizing simulators that are as close to real-life scenarios as possible, ensuring that practice is relevant and effective.
- **Repetition of Foundational Skills**: Concentrating on the repeated practice of essential behaviors or skills, reinforcing them through consistent and focused repetition.
- **Continuous Improvement:** Emphasizing the importance of ongoing practice and refinement, with an understanding that mastery comes from repeatedly honing specific skills.

Discussion Questions

1. How can leaders in non-technical fields apply the concept of simulators to improve their team's performance and decision-making?
2. What are some examples of tasks in your own work or personal life where strategic repetition could lead to better outcomes?
3. How does immediate feedback during practice sessions influence the effectiveness of skill development? Can you

think of a situation where delayed feedback might be less effective?

4. John Gagliardi focused on precise execution rather than brute-force drills. How can this approach be translated into a business setting, particularly in team training and development?

5. Bruce Lee valued the repetition of a single skill over practicing many different ones. Do you agree with this approach? How might it apply to mastering a complex task in your professional life?

Practice Exercises

1. Simulated Decision-Making Scenarios

- **Objective**: Improve your ability to make quick, effective decisions in high-pressure situations.
- **How to Do It**: Identify a challenging scenario you might face in your work, such as a critical client negotiation or a sudden project crisis. Create a detailed, realistic simulation of this scenario, either alone or with colleagues. Go through the scenario step by step, making decisions as you would in real life. After completing the simulation, review your decisions, identify any mistakes, and discuss alternative approaches. Repeat the exercise with different scenarios to build confidence and proficiency.

2. Focused Skill Repetition

- **Objective**: Develop deep expertise in a key skill by practicing it repeatedly.
- **How to Do It**: Choose one foundational skill that is critical to your success (e.g., public speaking, analytical thinking, or a technical skill like coding). Set aside dedicated time each day to practice this skill with intentional focus. For example, if public speaking is your focus, practice delivering a short presentation or speech repeatedly, refining your delivery each

time. Record yourself to identify areas for improvement. Continue this daily practice for several weeks, aiming for small, incremental improvements each time.

3. Immediate Feedback Loop

- **Objective**: Enhance your learning process by incorporating immediate feedback into your practice.
- **How to Do It**: When practicing a particular skill, seek out or create opportunities for immediate feedback. For instance, if you're working on improving your leadership communication, record a conversation or meeting you lead. Review the recording immediately afterward, noting areas where you can improve. Alternatively, work with a mentor or colleague who can provide real-time feedback as you practice. Use this feedback to adjust and refine your approach, then practice again with the new insights in mind. Repeat this process until the adjustments become second nature.

LEARN IT, DO IT, TEACH IT

Learning is more than just absorbing new information; it's about fully understanding and internalizing that knowledge. One of the most effective ways to cement new learning is to teach it to someone else. This approach, often summarized as "learn it, do it, teach it," transforms passive learning into active mastery.

The concept isn't new. The Roman philosopher Seneca famously said, "When we teach, we learn." The act of teaching forces us to clarify our understanding, articulate our thoughts, and, ultimately, prove to ourselves how well we grasp the material. But there's more to it than just reinforcing knowledge—teaching also deepens our connection to the content and turns learning into a shared experience.

Learning, Doing, and Teaching: The Full Circle of Mastery

When you learn something new, you're in the early stages of building a skill or understanding a concept. Doing is the next step—it's where you apply what you've learned in a practical setting. But the process isn't complete until you teach what you've learned to others. This final step transforms you from a mere student into a mentor, and it's in this role that you truly master the material.

Think about it like this: When you teach, you have to organize your thoughts, anticipate questions, and find ways to make the material relatable to your audience. This forces you to engage with the content on a deeper level than if you were just learning or doing it yourself.

Applying the Concept: Real-World Examples

The "learn it, do it, teach it" approach isn't just an abstract idea—it's a practical tool you can use every day, both personally and professionally.

Take my experience with my youngest son, Will. When he was learning about the solar system in school, I would ask him to teach me what he had learned each day. He would explain the orbits, the planets, and other key concepts. By teaching me, he wasn't just repeating information; he was reinforcing his understanding, identifying gaps in his knowledge, and building confidence in his communication skills.

This method worked wonders for him, and it's a strategy that can be applied far beyond the classroom. In a professional setting, encouraging team members to teach what they've learned can lead to a stronger, more cohesive team. It helps ensure that critical knowledge isn't siloed, and it allows for the free exchange of ideas that can lead to innovation.

Creating a Learning Environment: Fostering Trust and Collaboration

For this approach to work, it's crucial to create an environment where people feel safe and supported in sharing their knowledge. Teaching and learning should be seen as collaborative processes, where feedback is constructive, and ideas are exchanged freely.

Encouraging a culture where teaching is valued can help prevent groupthink and foster creativity. When team members are asked to explain and teach new concepts, they are more likely to offer fresh perspectives and challenge the status quo. This kind of environment not only promotes learning but also drives innovation.

The Shift from Student to Advocate

There's a significant shift that happens when we move from being a student to becoming a teacher. Teaching requires us to take ownership of the material and become advocates for the ideas we're sharing. This level of engagement turns learning into a mission, where the goal isn't just to understand but to inspire others.

When we teach, we are no longer passive recipients of information—we become active participants in the learning process. This shift in mindset empowers us to take charge of our education and motivates us to continue learning, doing, and teaching.

Embrace the Role of a Teacher

Whether you're learning a new skill, developing a deeper understanding of a concept, or leading a team, embracing the role of a teacher can enhance your learning and strengthen your mastery. The "learn it, do it, teach it" approach transforms knowledge into wisdom and makes the learning process more dynamic and impactful.

So, the next time you learn something new, don't just keep it to yourself. Share it, teach it, and watch how your understanding deepens and your influence grows

Key Actions

- **Engage in Active Learning**: Move beyond passive absorption of information by actively engaging with new concepts and skills.
- **Apply What You've Learned**: Practice and implement new knowledge to reinforce understanding.
- **Teach What You've Learned**: Share your newly acquired knowledge with others to deepen your comprehension and solidify your mastery.
- **Organize and Articulate Thoughts**: When teaching, focus on clearly explaining the material, which helps to clarify your understanding and anticipate questions.
- **Create a Collaborative Learning Environment**: Foster a culture where teaching and learning are collaborative processes, encouraging the free exchange of ideas and constructive feedback.
- **Take Ownership of the Material**: Embrace the role of a teacher and become an advocate for the ideas you're sharing, which leads to a deeper connection with the content.
- **Encourage Team Learning**: In a professional setting, promote teaching among team members to ensure knowledge is shared and innovation is encouraged.
- **Shift from Student to Mentor:** Transition from simply learning to actively teaching, which enhances personal growth and leadership skills.

Discussion Questions

1. How has the act of teaching something you've recently learned impacted your understanding of the material? Can you share a specific example?
2. What are the challenges you've encountered when trying to teach a new concept to others, and how did you overcome them?
3. In what ways can we foster a culture of teaching and knowledge sharing within our team or organization? What specific steps can we take to create a supportive environment for this?
4. How do you think the "learn it, do it, teach it" approach can be applied to your personal growth outside of work? Can you think of an area where you could implement this strategy?
5. What are some potential benefits and drawbacks of encouraging team members to teach what they've learned to others? How can we maximize the benefits while minimizing any negative impacts?

Practice Exercises

1. Daily Reflection and Teaching

- **Objective**: To reinforce daily learning by teaching it to others.
- **How to Do It**: At the end of each day, reflect on something new you learned or a skill you practiced. Then, find a colleague, friend, or family member, and take 5-10 minutes to explain the concept to them as if they were unfamiliar with it. Focus on clarity and simplicity in your explanation. If no one is available, consider recording a short video of yourself explaining the concept.

2. Peer Teaching Sessions

- **Objective**: To build confidence and mastery by teaching peers in a structured environment.
- **How to Do It**: Organize a weekly or bi-weekly session with a group of peers where each person takes turns teaching a concept or skill they've recently learned. Prepare your session by breaking down the material into digestible parts and anticipating potential questions. Encourage feedback and discussion to further deepen your understanding.

3. Teach-Back Method in Meetings

- **Objective**: To enhance understanding and retention of information shared in meetings or training sessions.
- **How to Do It**: After a meeting or training session, volunteer or assign a participant to summarize and teach back the key points to the group. This can be done immediately after the session or as a follow-up at the next meeting. The focus should be on how well the material is understood and communicated, rather than just repeating information. Use this method regularly to build a habit of reinforcing learning through teaching.

CHAPTER 4
INSPIRE, DON'T JUST MANAGE

Inspiring others isn't just a nice-to-have; it's the heart of effective leadership. There are many ways to get the best out of people, but understanding what truly drives them is the key. Different things motivate different people. Some thrive on rewards and recognition, while others are fueled by the opportunity to have influence and autonomy. But what makes people give their best, not just today, but over the long haul?

While universal principles of inspiration exist, it's crucial to remember that everyone is unique. What's effective for one person might not work for another. Yet, one thing seems to resonate with everyone: the idea of a leader who genuinely cares. When we believe our efforts are valued and feel part of something bigger than ourselves, it can be incredibly motivating.

Understanding What Drives People

Being a great leader starts with understanding your team's needs and motivations. It's not about making grand speeches or using incentives to push people into action. It's about connecting on a personal level, creating a sense of belonging, and helping others see their own potential. When you do this, you move beyond mere management; you inspire greatness.

Leadership is about more than just getting things done. It's about creating an environment where people want to do their best because they believe in what they're doing. When people feel valued and supported, they're naturally more motivated. This sense of purpose and belonging is what drives long-term success.

Leading by Example

The best leaders don't just talk the talk; they walk the walk. They work hard for their team, leading by example and showing that they're invested in everyone's success. This isn't just about being a boss; it's about being a fan of your people. Even on their bad days, you're there, cheering them on. This kind of support builds a strong relationship based on mutual respect and trust, allowing for tough conversations without damaging the overall bond.

One key to consistently inspiring others is to be their biggest advocate. When your team knows you're in their corner, they're more likely to push themselves and strive for excellence. It's this unwavering support that creates a culture where people feel safe to take risks and grow.

The Power of Internal Motivation

It's important to recognize that true motivation comes from within. While external factors like incentives can be effective in the short term, they're not sustainable over the long haul. The best leaders understand this and focus on creating a culture where people are motivated because they believe in the mission and values of the organization. When people feel that their work matters, they're inspired to give their best every day.

Creating a Culture of Belonging and Purpose

The secret to inspiring others lies in creating a culture where everyone feels like they belong and have a purpose. This doesn't happen overnight, and it certainly doesn't happen by accident. It requires a leader who is intentional about building connections and fostering an environment where people feel valued.

Let's take a cue from some of the most admired leaders in history. These leaders were always in the corner of those they led. They weren't just there to give orders; they were there to support, cheer, and believe in their people. This kind of leadership is powerful because it taps into something deeper than mere compliance—it taps into the human desire to be part of something meaningful.

Real-World Example: Spielberg's Steady Ascent

Consider film director Steven Spielberg. When he was starting out, he didn't rush into making feature films. Instead, he chose to start in television, gaining valuable experience and preparing for the challenges ahead. This decision laid the foundation for his success as one of the most influential film directors of all time.

Spielberg's story highlights the importance of understanding what drives you and your team. He didn't take the flashy, fast route; he took the path that allowed him to grow and develop, and that's what made all the difference. As a leader, recognizing the unique motivations of each person on your team and being flexible in your approach can lead to greatness.

The Role of the Leader

Ultimately, inspiring and motivating others is about being a leader who truly cares. It's your job to create an environment where people feel valued, supported, and inspired to do their best work. When you consistently exhibit behaviors that motivate others and foster a culture of belonging, you can achieve remarkable results.

One story that sticks with me is about a leader I once had the pleasure of learning from. He was an investor in the company I co-founded, and happened to be a former Secretary of Defense. This man had seen it all and had a successful career as an executive at a Fortune 500 company. Before a large town hall event with people from across the organization, told those around him, "I always remember one thing in a moment like this. They can fire me a lot more quickly than I can fire them. All they have to do is not do their best."

That simple statement encapsulates what it means to be a leader. It's not about holding power over others; it's about understanding that your team's success is your success. By inspiring and motivating others, you help them reach their full potential, which in turn leads to remarkable outcomes for the entire organization.

The Path to Remarkable Results

In the end, the secret to inspiring others isn't really a secret at all. It's about being a leader who truly cares, who helps people believe in themselves, and who creates a culture where everyone feels they belong and have a purpose. When you do that, you don't just lead—you inspire greatness. And that's when remarkable results happen.

STRENGTHS OVER WEAKNESSES

Leading a team is as much about boosting confidence as it is about setting direction. Think back to moments when you faced a high-pressure situation—a big presentation, an important meeting, or even an athletic competition. What made the difference between feeling overwhelmed and rising to the occasion? Often, it's that extra boost of confidence, that small reminder of what you do best, that tips the scales in your favor.

As a leader, your job is to help your team find that edge. This means guiding them to focus on their strengths just before they step into the spotlight. It's a simple yet powerful technique that can shift their mindset from fear of failure to excitement about the opportunity.

The Power of Specific Encouragement

General praise like "You've got this" is nice, but it's not enough. For encouragement to be truly effective, it has to be specific and credible. Your team needs to believe in the strengths you're highlighting, and that belief only comes when your words resonate with their own understanding of their abilities.

Let's say you're preparing your team for a big client presentation. Instead of saying, "Do your best," try something like, "Your attention to detail is second to none. The client is going to love how thorough you've been in preparing this." By pointing out a specific strength, you're not just boosting their confidence; you're giving them something tangible to focus on, something they know they can rely on.

This approach isn't limited to the workplace. Imagine telling your child before their soccer game, "You're the fastest kid on the field. You're going to outrun everyone today." Or before your spouse heads into a social gathering, "Your warmth and ability to connect with people will make tonight a great success." These aren't just empty compliments—they're targeted affirmations that help shift the focus from anxiety to anticipation.

Support Beyond Words

However, recognizing strengths is only part of the equation. To help your team truly excel, you need to provide the tools, resources, and support necessary for success. Confidence without competence is a recipe for disaster. Make sure your team is well-prepared, trained, and equipped to handle the tasks ahead. This might mean offering additional training, setting up practice sessions, or simply being available to answer questions and offer guidance.

Creating a positive and supportive environment is also crucial. People perform better when they know they're in a safe and encouraging space. Foster a culture where strengths are celebrated, and challenges are met with constructive support rather than criticism.

Lead by Example

As a leader, managing your own confidence is just as important as boosting your team's. The pressure of leadership can easily lead to self-doubt, especially when the stakes are high. But just like your team, you need to focus on your strengths and remind yourself of past successes.

Break down large tasks into manageable steps, and visualize yourself succeeding in each one. Remember, the confidence you exude will set the tone for your team. If they see you handling pressure with poise and focusing on what you do best, they'll be more likely to do the same.

A Real-World Example

Consider the story of a senior employee responsible for strategic partnerships at a large company. She had worked tirelessly to secure a major corporate partnership that would benefit students nationwide. The night before her big presentation, her boss pulled her aside and said, "You've done an incredible job on this. No one knows this material like you do. Tomorrow, you're going to nail it."

This wasn't just a pep talk—it was a targeted boost of confidence that reminded her of the hard work she'd put in and the expertise she had developed. The next day, she delivered a flawless presentation, securing the partnership and furthering her career.

The Takeaway

The key to helping others perform at their best lies in your ability to emphasize their strengths and provide the necessary support. Be specific in your encouragement, and make sure it's relevant and believable. Create an environment where strengths are highlighted and resources are readily available. And don't forget to manage your own confidence—because your team will follow your lead.

By focusing on these strategies, you can foster a culture of confidence and success within your team, helping each member reach their full potential while also ensuring you perform at your best.

Key Actions

- **Provide Specific Encouragement**: Avoid general praise and instead focus on highlighting specific strengths that are credible and relevant to the individual. This helps shift their focus from anxiety to anticipation and boosts their confidence.
- **Recognize Strengths Before Performance**: Emphasize the strengths of your team members just before they are about to perform, whether it's a presentation, a game, or a social event. This targeted affirmation helps them focus on what they do best.
- **Support with Resources and Training**: Confidence must be backed by competence. Ensure that your team has the necessary tools, resources, and training to succeed. Offer guidance and create practice opportunities to help them prepare.
- **Foster a Positive and Supportive Environment**: Create a culture where strengths are celebrated, and challenges are met with constructive support. This environment encourages your team to perform at their best.

- **Manage Your Own Confidence**: As a leader, focus on your strengths and past successes to manage your own confidence. Break down tasks into manageable steps and visualize success. Your confidence will set the tone for your team.
- **Lead by Example**: Demonstrate poise and focus under pressure. Your behavior as a leader will influence how your team handles their own challenges, so lead by example to inspire confidence in others.

Discussion Questions

1. How can specific and credible encouragement from a leader impact an individual's performance compared to general praise? Can you share a personal experience where this made a difference?
2. In what ways can leaders balance the emphasis on strengths with providing the necessary resources and training to ensure their team members are fully prepared?
3. How does the environment a leader creates affect the confidence and performance of their team? What are some practical steps leaders can take to foster a positive and supportive atmosphere?
4. Why is it important for leaders to manage their own confidence, and how can their behavior influence the confidence levels of their team?
5. What are some challenges leaders might face when trying to highlight strengths before a performance, and how can they overcome these challenges to effectively boost their team's confidence?

Practice Exercises

1. Strengths-Focused Feedback

- **Objective**: Improve your ability to provide specific and credible encouragement that highlights individual strengths.

- **How to Do It**: Identify three people in your team and take note of their key strengths. Before their next major task or presentation, provide each of them with specific feedback that highlights one of these strengths. For example, instead of saying "Good luck," say something like, "Your ability to analyze data thoroughly will make your report stand out." After the task, reflect on how your feedback impacted their performance and confidence.

2. Environment Audit

- **Objective**: Assess and improve the supportiveness of your work environment.
- **How to Do It**: Take a step back and observe the environment you've created for your team. Are strengths regularly acknowledged? Are resources and support easily accessible? Conduct a quick survey or hold a discussion with your team to gather feedback. Based on this input, identify one or two areas where you can make changes to foster a more positive and supportive environment. Implement these changes and monitor the impact over time.

3. Self-Confidence Visualization

- **Objective**: Enhance your ability to manage your own confidence under pressure.
- **How to Do It**: Before a high-pressure situation (like a presentation or meeting), take 10 minutes to visualize yourself succeeding. Break the task down into manageable steps in your mind, and recall past successes where you handled similar situations well. Focus on the strengths that have helped you succeed before. Practice this regularly before key events, and notice how it influences your confidence and performance.

EXTEND CELEBRATIONS

Recognizing and celebrating achievements is a vital part of leadership. It boosts morale, motivates your team, and sets a positive tone for the entire organization. But there's a difference between simply acknowledging a win and making that success last. Great leaders know how to extend the lifespan of outstanding accomplishments, keeping the momentum alive long after the initial celebration fades.

The Art of Keeping Good News Alive

It's easy to celebrate a win in the moment—maybe you throw a team dinner, hand out a bonus, or send a congratulatory email. These are all good practices, but they're short-lived. The best leaders go further. They find ways to keep those achievements in the spotlight, ensuring that the positive energy doesn't dissipate after the applause dies down.

One simple yet impactful way to prolong the celebration is through a heartfelt letter. A well-written letter can be revisited time and time again, serving as a lasting reminder of the accomplishment. Imagine the impact of a college football coach who writes a letter to each senior player, detailing their contributions, growth, and what they've meant to the team. These letters become cherished keepsakes, read and reread until the paper is worn thin. It's a tangible way to keep the good news alive and remind the players of their value and achievements long after the season ends.

Creative Commemorations

But letters are just the beginning. There are countless ways to creatively commemorate success. Maybe it's naming something—a conference room, an award, or even a project—after the person or the achievement. This not only honors the individual but also sets a lasting legacy that others can aspire to. You could create a custom screensaver that rotates images or quotes related to the success, or even design a special t-shirt that people can wear with pride.

These tangible reminders keep the memory of the accomplishment fresh. They turn a single moment of recognition into an ongoing source of motivation and inspiration.

Meaningful Connections

Another powerful method to prolong the life of an accomplishment is to reflect on the journey that led to it. Take, for example, a leader who, after a significant professional milestone, writes personal letters to everyone who supported them along the way. These letters do more than just thank the recipients; they reinforce the leader's gratitude, strengthen relationships, and allow the leader to relive and celebrate their success repeatedly.

Small Gestures, Big Impact

It doesn't always have to be grand gestures. Small, meaningful traditions can have a huge impact. Celebrate anniversaries of big wins, create a special drink in honor of the team's success, or start a tradition that brings the team together to reminisce about past victories. Even something as simple as a photo on the wall can serve as a daily reminder of what the team has achieved.

These gestures may seem small, but they're powerful. They show that you're not just a leader who recognizes success—you're a leader who values it deeply, who understands the importance of keeping that success alive and front of mind.

Balancing Celebration with Challenges

Leadership isn't just about pointing out what's going wrong; it's equally important to highlight what's going right. The best leaders know how to balance constructive criticism with genuine celebration. They understand that while challenges are inevitable, so too are opportunities to recognize and prolong success.

By consistently acknowledging and celebrating the wins within your team, you create an environment that's not just positive, but also resilient. People work harder, not just to avoid failure, but to achieve the kind of success that's celebrated, remembered, and valued.

The Lasting Impact of Prolonged Recognition

In the end, prolonging the lifespan of outstanding accomplishments isn't just about making people feel good—it's about creating a culture where success breeds more success. It's about keeping motivation high and reminding everyone of what they're capable of.

So, as you look for ways to celebrate your team's achievements, think beyond the immediate. How can you keep that good news alive? How can you ensure that the positive impact lasts, inspiring not just the individual, but the entire organization?

The answer lies in the details—the letters, the traditions, the little things that, when done consistently, make a big difference. By prolonging the celebration of accomplishments, you're not just recognizing success; you're building a legacy of excellence that will last far beyond the moment.

Key Actions

1. **Extend Recognition Beyond the Moment**: Go beyond immediate celebrations by finding ways to prolong the recognition of achievements, such as writing heartfelt letters or creating lasting commemorations.
2. **Use Creative Commemorations**: Implement creative methods to keep the memory of accomplishments alive, like naming a project or creating tangible reminders (e.g., screensavers, t-shirts) to inspire ongoing motivation.
3. **Strengthen Connections Through Reflection**: Reinforce relationships and gratitude by reflecting on the journey to success and expressing appreciation to those who contributed, often through personalized gestures like writing letters.
4. **Incorporate Meaningful Traditions**: Establish small yet significant traditions, such as celebrating anniversaries of achievements or creating special rituals, to maintain motivation and keep past successes in the team's consciousness.

5. **Balance Criticism with Celebration**: Maintain a healthy balance between addressing challenges and celebrating successes to create a positive and resilient work environment.

6. **Foster a Culture of Continuous Motivation**: Focus on creating a culture where success is regularly acknowledged and celebrated, which in turn inspires further accomplishments and builds a lasting legacy of excellence.

Discussion Questions

1. How can leaders ensure that the recognition of accomplishments has a lasting impact on team motivation and morale?
2. What are some creative ways to commemorate achievements in the workplace, and how can these methods enhance team culture?
3. In what ways can small traditions or rituals help keep the memory of past successes alive within an organization.
4. How can leaders balance the need for constructive criticism with the importance of celebrating successes, and why is this balance crucial for team dynamics?
5. What are the potential long-term benefits of consistently prolonging the celebration of outstanding accomplishments, and how can this practice influence the overall success of an organization?

Practice Exercises

1. Personalized Recognition Letters

- **Objective**: Improve your ability to create meaningful, lasting recognition for team members.
- **How to Do It**: Choose one team member who has recently accomplished something significant. Write a personalized letter highlighting their specific contributions, growth, and the positive impact they've had on the team. Focus on being sincere and specific. Give the letter to the individual and

observe their reaction. Reflect on how this gesture might influence their motivation in the long term.

2. Create a Commemorative Tradition

- **Objective**: Develop your skill in creating traditions that keep accomplishments alive within your team or organization.
- **How to Do It**: Identify a recent team success and think of a simple yet memorable way to commemorate it—such as naming a meeting room after the project or creating a recurring event that celebrates the achievement. Implement this tradition and encourage your team to participate. Monitor how the tradition influences team spirit and morale over time.

3. Balanced Feedback Practice

- **Objective**: Enhance your ability to balance constructive criticism with celebration.
- **How to Do It**: Over the course of a week, make a conscious effort to balance every piece of constructive feedback you give with a celebration of something that has gone well. After giving feedback, follow up with a specific acknowledgment of something positive. Reflect on how this balanced approach affects your interactions with your team and their overall engagement.

MAKE OTHERS SHINE

As leaders, one of our most essential duties is recognizing and celebrating the achievements of our team. It's easy to hand out praise or throw a celebration after a big win. These moments are crucial—they boost morale and make people feel valued. But the best leaders don't stop at recognition. They understand that true motivation comes from keeping those positive moments alive long after the initial applause fades.

Going Beyond Simple Recognition

Sure, a congratulatory email or a bonus is nice, but what if we could extend the impact of those moments? What if we could make those feelings of accomplishment and pride linger, not just for the individual but for the entire team?

One powerful way to do this is by finding creative, lasting ways to celebrate achievements. Maybe it's something as simple as writing a heartfelt letter that the recipient can keep and revisit whenever they need a boost. Or perhaps it's naming something significant—a conference room, a project, even a new initiative—after the person or team responsible for the success. By creating tangible reminders of accomplishments, we keep the motivation alive. It's not just about the moment of victory; it's about keeping that feeling of success front and center, so it continues to inspire.

A Mentor's Lifelong Guidance

Imagine a seasoned business mentor who, after years of guiding young entrepreneurs, started a tradition of giving each mentee a unique journal. In the first few pages, he would write a personal message reflecting on their journey together, offering advice tailored to their strengths and challenges. These journals became valued companions—many mentees would continue to fill them with their own thoughts and experiences as they ventured into their careers. This practice wasn't just about marking the end of their mentorship; it was about equipping them with a lasting source of wisdom and encouragement as they faced new challenges ahead.

Celebrating with a Personal Touch

Another example comes from a professional who, after achieving significant success, took the time to write letters to everyone who had helped him along the way. This wasn't just about saying thank you; it was about reflecting on his journey and keeping the celebration alive. These letters reinforced his relationships and allowed him to savor his success over time, not just in a fleeting moment.

The lesson here is that there's no one-size-fits-all approach. Whether it's through celebrating anniversaries, creating a special tradition, or even something as simple as taking a team photo to commemorate a big win, what matters is that the celebration continues. Great leaders find ways to keep these positive moments alive, showing their team members that they're not just a passing thought—they're a priority.

Making Others Look Good

But let's take it a step further. The most impactful leaders don't just celebrate their team members' achievements—they make them look good to the people who matter most in their lives. Whether it's in front of a spouse, a close friend, or a valued client, showing off the talents and qualities of our team members in front of those who are important to them can have a profound impact.

Imagine the pride a team member feels when their expertise is acknowledged not just in the workplace but in front of their loved ones. It's one thing to be recognized by your boss, but when that recognition is shared with the people who matter most to you, it takes on a whole new level of significance. It deepens the loyalty, trust, and motivation of the individual, making them feel truly valued and appreciated.

The Key to Lasting Motivation

In the end, the secret to effective leadership is not just in recognizing and celebrating success but in finding ways to extend that celebration in meaningful, lasting ways. When we go beyond the simple "well done" and find ways to make our team members look good in front of those they care about, we tap into a deeper well of motivation and loyalty.

It's about creating a culture where success isn't fleeting but is remembered and cherished. By doing so, we not only inspire our team to continue striving for greatness but also build stronger, more meaningful relationships that form the foundation of a truly positive and productive work environment.

Key Actions

- **Extend Recognition Beyond the Moment**: Don't just acknowledge achievements in the moment. Find creative and lasting ways to celebrate success to keep the motivation alive.
- **Create Tangible Reminders**: Use physical or symbolic gestures like letters, named spaces, or traditions to commemorate achievements and ensure they are remembered.
- **Personalize the Celebration**: Tailor recognition to the individual and the situation, making it meaningful and memorable for the person involved.
- **Showcase Team Members to Those They Value**: Highlight the expertise and qualities of team members in front of people who are important to them, deepening their sense of pride and motivation.
- **Build Lasting Motivation**: Focus on creating a culture where successes are not fleeting but are remembered, celebrated, and used as ongoing sources of inspiration.

Discussion Questions

1. How can leaders balance the need for immediate recognition with the goal of creating lasting motivation within their teams?
2. What are some creative ways you've seen or implemented to extend the celebration of achievements in the workplace?

3. In what ways can making team members look good in front of those they value most impact their long-term motivation and loyalty?

4. How can leaders personalize recognition to make it more meaningful for individual team members?

5. What are the potential challenges or pitfalls of extending recognition and keeping achievements alive, and how can they be addressed?

Practice Exercises

1. Personalized Recognition Writing

- **Objective**: Improve your ability to create meaningful and lasting recognition for your team members.
- **How to Do It**: Choose one team member each week and write a personalized letter acknowledging their recent achievements and unique qualities. Focus on making the recognition specific and personal. Afterward, reflect on how this personalized approach impacted your relationship with the team member and their motivation.

2. Creative Celebration Planning

- **Objective**: Develop your skill in extending celebrations in ways that keep motivation alive.
- **How to Do It**: Identify a recent team success or individual achievement and plan a creative, ongoing celebration around it. This could involve creating a small ritual, naming something after the achievement, or establishing an anniversary tradition. Implement the plan and observe how it affects team morale over time.

3. Public Recognition Practice

- **Objective**: Enhance your ability to showcase your team members' strengths to those who matter most to them.

- **How to Do It**: Select a team member and find an opportunity to publicly recognize their contributions in front of someone important to them, such as a spouse, client, or senior leader. Pay attention to how the team member responds and how it influences their engagement and performance. Reflect on the experience to identify what worked well and what could be improved.

MEMORABLE REWARDS

In the hustle of daily business, it's easy to focus solely on the tangible rewards—salaries, bonuses, benefits. But let's face it: while money pays the bills, it's not what fuels the soul. People remember how you made them feel, not just how much you paid them. This is where rewarding your team with memorable experiences comes into play.

Rewarding employees with special experiences is more than just a gesture; it's a powerful way to show that you care about their growth, happiness, and well-being. These experiences can build a deep sense of loyalty and appreciation within your team, something that money alone can't buy. The best leaders understand this and go out of their way to create opportunities that resonate on a personal level.

It's Not Just About the Money

Traditional compensation—salaries, bonuses, benefits—will always be important. But if that's all you're offering, you're missing a critical piece of the puzzle. The truth is, people crave experiences that enrich their lives and expand their horizons. It's not just about handing out cash; it's about creating moments that matter.

Take a moment to consider this: What if you could give your team something that money can't buy? Something that they'll remember long after the paycheck is spent? The best leaders recognize that people value unique experiences—meeting a personal hero, attending a once-in-a-lifetime event, or even receiving insider knowledge that elevates an ordinary moment into something special. These experiences don't just happen by accident; they require effort, planning, and most importantly, a deep understanding of what makes your team tick.

Facilitating Memorable Experiences

Understand What They Value

The first step in rewarding your team with experiences is under-standing what they truly value. Not everyone is going to be thrilled by the same things. Some might crave professional development opportu-nities, while others might cherish the chance to pursue personal passions or hobbies. The key is to listen—really listen—to what your team members are excited about.

Take the time to ask them directly: "What experiences would be most meaningful to you?" You might be surprised by what you hear. For one person, it might be a meeting with an industry leader they admire; for another, it could be the chance to volunteer at a charity they care about. Whatever it is, make a note of it. These are the experiences that will make your rewards personal and impactful.

Make Existing Experiences Special

Sometimes, the experiences your team craves are already on their radar. They might have plans to attend an event, participate in a conference, or meet someone influential. As a leader, you have the power to enhance these experiences. Share insider knowledge, offer tips on how to make the most of the event, or even provide background information that adds depth and meaning to their experience.

For instance, if an employee is attending a conference, don't just send them on their way. Give them a rundown of the key players they should meet, the sessions they shouldn't miss, and the historical context behind the event. This extra layer of preparation can turn a routine trip into a memorable and enriching experience.

Create New Opportunities

Leaders who excel at rewarding with experiences don't just wait for opportunities to present themselves—they create them. This could mean arranging a meeting between a team member and someone they've always admired, or setting up a lunch with an expert in a field they're passionate about. Sometimes, it's as simple as facilitating a conversation that sparks new ideas and perspectives.

The best part? Many of these experiences don't require a huge financial investment. They require your time, attention, and a willingness to go the extra mile. For example, if you know a team member is passionate about community service, you might help them join a local board or volunteer group. If someone is eager to learn more about a specific industry, introduce them to your contacts in that field. These gestures may seem small, but they can have a huge impact on your team's morale and loyalty.

Recognize and Celebrate

It's important to remember that recognition plays a huge role in the effectiveness of these experiences. Make sure to acknowledge the effort and growth that comes from these opportunities. Publicly celebrate their achievements and make it clear that you value their personal and professional development. This not only reinforces the impact of the experience but also sets a positive example for the rest of the team.

Balance with Traditional Compensation

While experiences can be incredibly rewarding, they're not a substitute for fair pay and benefits. The key is to balance these two elements. Competitive salaries and benefits will attract top talent, but memorable experiences will keep them engaged, loyal, and motivated. By offering both, you create a holistic approach to employee satisfaction that addresses both their financial needs and their deeper desires for personal growth and fulfillment.

Why It Matters

Rewarding your team with memorable experiences isn't just a feel-good strategy—it's a business strategy. A team that feels valued and appreciated is more likely to be engaged, productive, and innovative. These experiences can differentiate your company from competitors, making it a more attractive place to work. In a world where top talent is always in demand, this could be the edge you need.

At the end of the day, the best leaders know that people are more than just their job titles or paychecks. They're individuals with dreams, passions, and unique desires. By recognizing this and rewarding them with experiences that matter, you're not just building a team—you're building a community that's committed to shared success.

Key Actions

- **Understand What They Value**: Take the time to listen to your team members and understand what experiences are most meaningful to them, whether they relate to professional development, personal passions, or hobbies.
- **Make Existing Experiences Special**: Enhance the experiences your team is already planning to have by providing insider knowledge, historical context, or specific tips that can make the experience more memorable and enriching.
- **Create New Opportunities**: Be proactive in creating new and meaningful experiences for your team members, such as arranging meetings with admired figures, facilitating conversations with experts, or helping them participate in community activities.
- **Recognize and Celebrate**: Acknowledge and celebrate the growth and achievements that come from these experiences, making it clear that you value their personal and professional development.
- **Balance with Traditional Compensation**: Ensure that rewarding with experiences complements, rather than replaces, fair pay and benefits, creating a holistic approach to employee satisfaction that addresses both financial needs and personal growth.

Discussion Questions

1. What are some unique experiences that have had a lasting impact on your personal or professional life? How did they shape your growth?
2. How can leaders effectively identify the experiences that will be most meaningful to their team members? What strategies can be used to ensure they are listening and understanding their team's desires?

3. In what ways can leaders enhance existing experiences for their team members to make them more special and memorable? Can you share an example of how this has been done effectively?

4. What are the potential challenges in creating new opportunities for team members, and how can leaders overcome these challenges to provide meaningful experiences?

5. How can a company balance traditional compensation with rewarding experiences to create a motivated and loyal workforce? What are the risks of relying too heavily on one over the other?

Practice Exercises

1. Empathy Mapping

- **Objective**: To better understand what your team members value and what experiences would be meaningful to them.
- **How to Do It**: Choose one team member and create an empathy map with four quadrants: *Says*, *Thinks*, *Does*, and *Feels*. Gather information by observing their behavior, listening to their conversations, and asking direct questions about their interests and aspirations. Identify potential experiences that align with what they value based on the insights you've gathered. Repeat this process for different team members to gain a well-rounded understanding of what drives each individual.

2. Experience Enhancement Workshop

- **Objective**: To practice making existing experiences more special and meaningful for your team members.
- **How to Do It**: Select an upcoming event or experience that a team member is planning to attend. Research the event thoroughly, gathering relevant information, tips, and historical context. Share your insights with the team member, offering suggestions on how to maximize their experience

(e.g., key people to meet, sessions to attend, or background information that adds value). Follow up with the team member afterward to discuss how the additional information impacted their experience.

3. Proactive Opportunity Creation

- **Objective**: To develop the habit of creating new and meaningful opportunities for your team members.
- **How to Do It**: Identify a team member who could benefit from a new experience, such as meeting a mentor, learning a new skill, or participating in a community project. Plan and facilitate the opportunity—this could be setting up a lunch meeting, arranging a training session, or connecting them with an organization they're passionate about. Monitor the impact of the experience by gathering feedback from the team member and assessing any changes in their motivation or performance. Make this a regular practice by continuously seeking out and creating new opportunities for different team members.

GIVE A STAGE TO SUCCESS

Recognizing and rewarding employees with unique experiences is a powerful way to show your support and commitment to their growth. Too often, leaders rely on traditional forms of compensation like raises or bonuses to express appreciation. But the best leaders understand that people crave more than just monetary rewards—they crave meaningful experiences. These experiences don't have to be extravagant; they just need to be thoughtful and tailored to what truly matters to the individual.

The Power of Shared Success

I remember a time from my own life that really drove this point home. When I was in eighth grade, I hit a two-run home run in a baseball game. It was one of the greatest moments of my young life. But when I looked around, my parents weren't there to see it. The elation of the moment quickly deflated. I wanted someone to witness my success, to share in that triumph. We've all had those moments—times when we wish someone was there to see us at our best, to celebrate our achievements with us.

As leaders, it's our job to be there for those moments for our team members. The best leaders go out of their way to create opportunities for their team to shine. They recognize that everyone has their own unique strengths and passions, and they work to provide opportunities for these to be showcased.

Tailoring Experiences to Individual Desires

Think about what truly motivates your team. It might be something as simple as setting up a meeting with a mentor or as elaborate as sending them on a trip to learn from industry leaders. It could be the chance to take the lead on a major project, or even something personal like the opportunity to drive a particular car on a racetrack. The key is to understand what your team members value and find ways to make those experiences happen.

For example, one of your employees might be passionate about community service. Facilitating their involvement in a local board or charity could be incredibly fulfilling for them. Another team member might be fascinated by health and wellness. Arranging a session with a top nutritionist or fitness coach could be the experience they've been longing for.

Enhancing Existing Experiences

Sometimes, the experiences don't need to be new; they just need to be enriched. Adding context or knowledge can elevate an otherwise ordinary event into something memorable. If a team member is attending a conference, share some background on the speakers or the history of the event to make it more engaging. Offer them tips on how to network effectively or what sessions might be particularly valuable.

The best leaders act like the biggest fans of their team members. They understand what their people are passionate about and go the extra mile to make those passions come alive. This kind of attention to detail can be a powerful motivator and foster deep loyalty and appreciation within the team.

Balancing Traditional and Experiential Rewards

Of course, it's important to acknowledge that experiential rewards are just one piece of the puzzle. Salaries, benefits, and other traditional forms of compensation still play a crucial role in attracting and retaining top talent. But when leaders combine these traditional rewards with tailored, meaningful experiences, they create a more holistic and supportive environment that drives success.

Leading Through Shared Experiences

I've had the privilege of sharing in some truly special experiences with my team. I remember a time when one of my colleagues was nervous about a big meeting with a client. I offered to attend the meeting with her, not just as moral support but as a way to show that I was invested in her success. The meeting went well, and the shared experience brought us closer. It's moments like these that help build trust and loyalty within a team.

As a leader, I encourage you to think beyond the conventional. Find ways to reward your team with experiences that allow them to grow, showcase their skills, and pursue their passions. By doing so, you'll not only create a more motivated and engaged team, but you'll also foster a deeper sense of connection and loyalty that can propel your organization forward.

Key Actions

- **Recognize and Reward Through Experiences**: Understand that meaningful experiences can be more impactful than traditional rewards. Tailor these experiences to what matters most to the individual.
- **Be Present for Successes**: Actively participate in your team members' successes. Celebrate their achievements and share in their triumphs to build deeper connections.
- **Tailor Opportunities to Individual Passions**: Identify what your team members value and create opportunities that align with their unique strengths and passions
- **Enhance Existing Experiences**: Enrich standard experiences with additional knowledge or context to make them more engaging and memorable.
- **Act as a Supportive Leader**: Show your team that you are invested in their success by offering support, whether through attending important meetings or facilitating growth opportunities.
- **Balance Traditional and Experiential Rewards**: Combine traditional compensation with meaningful experiences to create a more supportive and motivating environment.
- **Foster Connection and Loyalty:** Use shared experiences to build trust, loyalty, and a stronger sense of connection within the team.

Discussion Questions

1. How can leaders identify the unique passions and strengths of their team members to create meaningful experiences?

2. What are some examples of experiences that have been more motivating or rewarding for you than traditional forms of compensation? Why were they impactful?

3. How can a leader effectively balance the need for traditional rewards (like salaries and bonuses) with the creation of personalized experiences for their team?

4. In what ways can enhancing an existing experience (e.g., providing additional context or knowledge) make it more memorable and valuable for an employee?

5. How can leaders ensure they are present and actively supporting their team members during key moments of success? What impact does this have on team dynamics and loyalty?

Practice Exercises

1. Personalized Experience Mapping

- **Objective**: To understand what motivates your team members and how to tailor experiences that resonate with them.
- **How to Do It**: Spend time with each team member in a one-on-one setting. Ask open-ended questions about their interests, passions, and what experiences they find most rewarding. Create a personal map for each person, detailing potential opportunities you can facilitate that align with their desires. Regularly update this map based on new insights and observations.

2. Experience Enrichment Workshop

- **Objective**: To practice enhancing existing experiences with additional context and knowledge.
- **How to Do It**: Identify an upcoming event or opportunity for one of your team members, such as a conference, meeting, or project. Research relevant background information, historical context, or strategic insights that could enhance

their experience. Schedule a brief session where you share these insights with the team member before the event. Afterward, discuss how the added context influenced their experience.

3. Shared Success Reflection

- **Objective**: To build a habit of being present and supportive during your team members' successes.
- **How to Do It**: At the end of each week, reflect on your team's achievements and identify moments where you could have been more present or involved. Plan for the upcoming week by pinpointing potential successes (e.g., presentations, meetings, milestones) and making a conscious effort to be there to support and celebrate with your team. Track your involvement over time to see how it strengthens relationships and morale.

The Ripple Effect

As a leader, one of the most meaningful gifts you can give your team is feedback. But not just any feedback—genuine, thoughtful feedback that acknowledges their contributions and helps them grow. We often talk about constructive criticism, the kind that points out areas for improvement, but equally important is positive reinforcement that lets people know they're on the right track. Unfortunately, this kind of feedback is sometimes too rare. The best leaders, however, recognize the value in letting their team members know when they've made an impact. It's more than just a pat on the back; it's about showing that you see them, that their efforts matter.

The Power of Being Seen

Think back to a time when you achieved something significant. Did you crave recognition from those around you? Most of us do. I remember a moment from my own life that drives this point home. It was eighth grade, and I was on the baseball team. I wasn't the star player, but I gave it my all and improved as the season went on. In the second-to-last game, I hit a two-run home run—the game-winning hit. It should have been a moment of triumph, but my parents weren't there to see it. I felt a twinge of disappointment. But what I really wanted was for my teammates and coaches to recognize what I had done. That recognition was what made the success feel real.

This need for acknowledgment isn't unique to kids playing baseball. It's universal. We all have talents and skills that we want others to notice. As a leader, your role is to be the biggest fan of your team members. This means going out of your way to understand what they're good at and giving them opportunities to shine.

When Leaders Learn from Their Teams

Great leaders don't just recognize the achievements of their team—they also acknowledge the influence their team has on them. This can be something as simple as borrowing a metaphor or phrase that someone else on the team uses. Or it might mean seeking advice from a team member who has expertise in a particular area. When you admit that you've learned something from someone on your team, even if they're junior to you, it's a powerful display of humility. It shows that you're open, receptive, and willing to grow. This kind of vulnerability builds trust and rapport, making your leadership more effective.

Show, Don't Just Tell

Another way to show your appreciation for your team is by taking an active interest in their skills. If you've heard that someone on your team is great at client presentations, don't just take it on faith—ask to sit in on one of their presentations. If someone is a fantastic cook, ask if you can watch them in action. These small acts of interest do more than just boost morale; they build a strong sense of loyalty and support. It tells your team that you're not just passively observing their work—you're invested in it.

The Full Picture of Motivation

Of course, feedback and appreciation are just one part of the puzzle when it comes to motivating and supporting your team. Traditional forms of compensation, like salaries and benefits, still play a crucial role in attracting and retaining top talent. But by recognizing the value of unique, personal experiences and facilitating these for your team, you create a deeper sense of connection and appreciation. This, in turn, drives success in ways that a paycheck alone never could.

In the end, the impact you have as a leader isn't just about the decisions you make or the results you deliver. It's about the connections you forge, the recognition you give, and the way you make people feel valued. These are the things that leave a lasting mark, rippling through your team and beyond.

Key Actions

- **Give Genuine Feedback**: Provide thoughtful feedback that includes both constructive criticism and positive reinforcement, helping team members know their efforts are seen and valued.
- **Be the Biggest Fan of Your Team**: Go out of your way to understand what your team members are good at and provide opportunities for them to showcase their abilities.
- **Acknowledge the Influence of Your Team**: Recognize and admit when you've learned something from someone on your team, even if they're junior to you. This shows humility and openness.
- **Take an Active Interest in Team Members' Skills**: Actively engage with your team's talents by observing their skills in action, which reinforces their sense of value and loyalty.
- **Balance Traditional and Personal Motivation:** Understand that while traditional compensation is important, personal experiences and recognition create a deeper sense of connection and motivation within the team.

Discussion Questions

1. How can leaders balance giving constructive criticism with

providing positive reinforcement in a way that feels genuine and impactful to their team members?

2. In what ways can a leader actively demonstrate that they are the "biggest fan" of their team members? Can you share an example from your own experience?

3. Why is it important for leaders to acknowledge when they've been influenced or learned something from their team? How does this impact team dynamics and trust?

4. How can leaders effectively show interest in their team members' skills and talents without coming across as micromanaging or intrusive?

5. What are some non-traditional ways leaders can motivate and support their team beyond standard compensation, and how can these methods contribute to long-term success?

Practice Exercises

1. Daily Feedback Practice

- **Objective**: To improve your ability to give genuine, balanced feedback to your team members.
- **How to Do It**: Each day, choose one team member to observe during their work. Identify one thing they did well and one area where they could improve. At the end of the day, provide them with specific feedback, using the "more of" or "less of" framework. This exercise helps you develop a habit of giving specific, actionable feedback regularly.

2. Influence Reflection

- **Objective**: To become more aware of how your team members influence your thinking and decisions.
- **How to Do It**: At the end of each week, reflect on the interactions you had with your team. Write down at least three instances where you borrowed an idea, phrase, or approach from someone on your team. Note how these influences impacted your work or leadership style. Share one

of these examples with the team member involved, acknowledging their contribution.

3. Skill Showcase Request

- **Objective**: To deepen your connection with your team members by showing interest in their unique skills.
- **How to Do It**: Identify one skill or talent a team member possesses that you haven't yet seen in action. Approach them with genuine curiosity, asking if you can observe them using this skill. Whether it's a professional ability like presenting or a personal talent like cooking, this exercise helps you build rapport and show your appreciation for their abilities.

PRAISE THAT MATTERS

When it comes to recognizing and encouraging your team, third-party compliments are like secret weapons. Unlike the direct praise you might give in person, these compliments come through someone else, making them feel more sincere and carrying a surprising amount of weight.

So, why do these indirect compliments hit harder?

No Strings Attached

First, third-party compliments don't come with the usual strings attached. Imagine telling a team member, "Great job on that project, but…" That "but" tends to undercut the praise, leaving the person feeling less appreciated. On the other hand, when someone hears that their boss praised them to someone else, the compliment feels unfiltered and genuine—no qualifiers, no backhanded remarks. It's just pure recognition.

The Element of Surprise

Another reason third-party compliments are so powerful is the element of surprise. When you give direct praise, people might expect it. They did something well, and they know you noticed. But when the praise comes from someone else—someone they didn't even know was paying attention—it's a whole different story. This surprise element makes the compliment feel more meaningful and sincere, boosting its impact.

How to Make It Work

So, how do you harness the power of third-party compliments? The key is to be intentional. Look for opportunities to mention your team members' successes in conversations with other colleagues, clients, or stakeholders. You could praise a team member to a client, mention someone's hard work to a higher-up, or even compliment a team member to another team member. The trick is to do it naturally, without it coming off as forced.

Be Genuine

Authenticity is crucial. If your compliment isn't sincere, it won't land the way you want it to. Don't just flatter for the sake of it—focus on genuine praise for real achievements. People can tell when you mean it, and that's what makes these compliments so impactful.

Build a Culture of Recognition

Incorporating third-party compliments into your leadership style can do wonders for your team's morale. When you make it a habit to recognize your team's efforts in this way, it creates a culture of appreciation and acknowledgment. This doesn't just boost individual spirits—it lifts the whole team, leading to better performance and a more positive work environment.

The Power of Sincerity

People tend to see third-party compliments as more sincere because they aren't just for show. When someone hears that you've been praising them behind their back (in the best way possible), it means a lot. It's like discovering that someone has been rooting for you without expecting anything in return, and that kind of support is both memorable and motivating.

Creating a Positive Ripple Effect

Using third-party compliments strategically helps to foster a culture where recognition is the norm, not the exception. When people feel valued and appreciated, they're more likely to be engaged and satisfied with their work. This ripple effect can lead to a more motivated team, ready to go the extra mile.

Final Thoughts

Third-party compliments are a simple yet powerful tool in a leader's arsenal. By being strategic, sincere, and consistent in how you use them, you can create a workplace culture that thrives on recognition and appreciation. This, in turn, leads to a more motivated and engaged team, where everyone feels valued and inspired to contribute their

best. So next time you see excellence, don't just keep it to yourself—
tell someone else, and let the compliment work its magic.

Key Actions

- **Avoid Qualifiers in Praise**: When offering direct
  compliments, avoid using qualifiers like "but" that can
  diminish the impact of the praise. Focus on unfiltered,
  genuine recognition.
- **Leverage the Element of Surprise**: Use third-party
  compliments strategically, as they often catch the recipient off
  guard and make the recognition feel more meaningful and
  sincere.
- **Be Intentional with Recognition**: Actively seek out
  opportunities to mention your team members' successes to
  others, whether it's colleagues, clients, or stakeholders. This
  helps amplify the impact of the praise.
- **Ensure Authenticity**: Only offer third-party compliments
  when they are sincere and based on genuine achievements.
  Authenticity is key to making these compliments meaningful.
- **Cultivate a Culture of Recognition**: Incorporate third-party
  compliments into your regular leadership practices to create
  an environment where recognition and appreciation are the
  norm.
- **Foster a Positive Ripple Effect:** Understand that consistent
  use of third-party compliments can lead to increased
  motivation, engagement, and satisfaction within the team,
  creating a positive work environment.

Discussion Questions

1. Why do you think third-party compliments are often
   perceived as more sincere than direct praise? How does this
   perception impact team dynamics?
2. Can you share an example of a time when receiving a third-
   party compliment had a significant impact on you or

someone you know? What made it more meaningful than direct praise?

3. In what ways can leaders be more intentional about incorporating third-party compliments into their regular feedback routines? What are some potential challenges in doing so?

4. How can a leader ensure that their third-party compliments remain authentic and don't come across as forced or insincere? What are the risks of inauthentic recognition?

5. How might cultivating a culture of recognition through third-party compliments affect overall team performance and morale? What steps can leaders take to foster such a culture?

Practice Exercises

1. The Compliment Relay

- **Objective**: To become more intentional about recognizing team members through third-party compliments.
- **How to Do It**: Each day for a week, identify one team member who has done something noteworthy. Instead of praising them directly, share their accomplishment with another colleague, client, or stakeholder. Be specific about what they did well. At the end of the week, reflect on how this practice has influenced your awareness of team members' contributions and how it was received by others.

2. Sincerity Check

- **Objective**: To ensure that your third-party compliments are genuine and impactful.
- **How to Do It**: Before giving a third-party compliment, ask yourself two questions: "Do I truly believe in the praise I'm about to give?" and "Is this compliment specific and focused on a real achievement?" If the answer to either is no, refine your compliment until it feels authentic. Practice this exercise

daily to build the habit of giving sincere, meaningful recognition.

3. Surprise Praise Journal

- **Objective**: To enhance the element of surprise in your third-party compliments.
- **How to Do It**: Keep a journal where you track moments when you notice something praiseworthy about a team member that they might not be aware of. Once a week, find a way to mention these observations to someone else in a position to relay it back to the team member. Review your journal monthly to see how often you've been able to surprise and positively impact your team through this approach.

EXPECT GREATNESS

As a leader, one of your most important responsibilities is to recognize and address the crises of confidence that even the most talented individuals may experience. Whether it's dealing with failure, tackling a challenging opportunity, or simply navigating a moment of uncertainty, everyone occasionally needs an extra boost of encouragement.

This is where the power of anticipation comes into play—through sincere and specific affirmations and predictions of future success, you can significantly influence how others perceive themselves and their potential.

The Power of Specific Affirmations

While general praise can make someone feel good in the moment, it's the specific, forward-looking affirmations that truly empower people to excel. Instead of saying, "Good luck with your presentation," try something more predictive like, "I predict this will be the best pitch you've given in weeks." This kind of specific language does more than just lift spirits; it shapes beliefs. When people hear confident predictions about their success, they start to internalize that belief and act accordingly.

The impact of this approach is well-documented. Many successful individuals credit their mentors, teachers, or parents for consistently affirming their abilities and predicting their future success. These affirmations, delivered at crucial moments, often serve as a catalyst for achieving greatness.

How Leaders Can Anticipate Excellence

To maximize the effectiveness of this approach, consider the following:

1. *Focus on Daily Wins:* While long-term success is important, don't underestimate the power of acknowledging and predicting success in everyday activities. For instance, telling a team member, "I'm confident you'll find a great solution to this problem," or saying to a friend, "I admire how you

handled that challenge today," can have a profound impact. These small, consistent affirmations build a foundation of confidence that accumulates over time.

2. *Be Sincere and Specific:* Generic praise lacks the power to inspire real change. To make your affirmations count, ensure they are both sincere and specific. Instead of vague compliments, offer clear and direct statements that highlight particular strengths or achievements. This not only boosts confidence but also fosters trust and strengthens relationships.

3. *Emphasize Near-Term Success:* It's not just about predicting grand future achievements; near-term success is equally important. Acknowledge the immediate challenges and express optimism about overcoming them. Statements like, "I know you'll master this new skill in no time," can provide the immediate encouragement someone needs to push through a tough spot.

4. *Create a Culture of Confidence:* Leaders who regularly anticipate excellence create an environment where confidence thrives. When people feel that their leaders genuinely believe in their potential, they're more likely to take risks, innovate, and ultimately achieve more than they thought possible. This culture of confidence becomes self-reinforcing, as success breeds more success.

5. *Use Affirmations to Build Stronger Relationships:* Beyond boosting confidence, this approach also deepens the bonds between you and those you lead. When people feel valued and respected, especially by someone they admire, it creates a strong connection. This bond not only enhances individual performance but also strengthens the overall team dynamic.

The Power of Your Words

The words you choose as a leader have the power to shape the future. By consistently expressing sincere and specific affirmations and predictions of success, you can help others overcome self-doubt, build their confidence, and achieve greatness.

It's a simple yet profound way to lead, one that can transform not just individual lives but entire organizations. So, the next time you have the chance, anticipate excellence—because sometimes, all it takes is a few well-chosen words to make a world of difference.

Key Actions

- **Focus on Daily Wins**: Acknowledge and predict success in everyday activities to build a foundation of confidence over time.
- **Be Sincere and Specific**: Ensure affirmations are genuine and detailed, highlighting particular strengths or achievements.
- **Emphasize Near-Term Success**: Recognize immediate challenges and express optimism about overcoming them to provide encouragement.
- **Create a Culture of Confidence**: Foster an environment where people feel their potential is genuinely believed in, encouraging risk-taking and innovation.
- **Use Affirmations to Build Stronger Relationships:** Strengthen bonds by making others feel valued and respected through specific and sincere affirmations.

Discussion Questions

1. How can specific affirmations impact someone's confidence differently than general praise? Can you share an example from your own experience?
2. What strategies can leaders use to consistently recognize and acknowledge daily wins within their teams? How might this practice influence overall team morale?
3. Why is it important to emphasize near-term success in addition to long-term goals? How can this approach help individuals overcome immediate challenges?
4. In what ways can creating a culture of confidence within an organization encourage innovation and risk-taking? How have you seen this play out in your own work environment?

5. How do specific and sincere affirmations help in building stronger relationships? Can you think of a time when receiving such an affirmation made a significant difference in your performance or motivation?

Practice Exercises

1. Daily Affirmation Journal

- **Objective**: Improve your ability to give sincere and specific affirmations.
- **How to Do It**: Each day, take five minutes to reflect on interactions with your team or colleagues. Write down at least three specific affirmations you can share with them based on their actions or achievements. Focus on highlighting particular strengths or behaviors. Then, the next day, make a point to deliver these affirmations in person or through a written note.

2. Near-Term Success Prediction

- **Objective**: Develop the habit of predicting and expressing near-term success to boost confidence in others.
- **How to Do It**: Choose a task or project someone on your team is currently working on. Before they start or during the process, make a specific prediction about their success (e.g., "I believe you'll excel at organizing this event because of your attention to detail"). Follow up with them afterward to see how they felt about your prediction and its impact on their performance.

3. Confidence-Building Conversations

- **Objective**: Practice creating a culture of confidence by engaging in meaningful conversations.
- **How to Do It**: Set aside time each week to have a one-on-one conversation with a team member or colleague. During the

conversation, focus on asking questions that help them reflect on their recent achievements and challenges. Offer sincere and specific feedback that emphasizes their strengths and potential. Encourage them to share their thoughts on how your feedback influences their confidence and motivation.

TRUST AND EMPOWER

As a leader, you're often the one people turn to for approval. They want your stamp on their work, your thumbs-up on their decisions. It's part of the job. But how you respond can make all the difference in the world. The typical options include, "This is great," "Let's tweak this," or the dreaded "We need to start from scratch." But there's a fourth response that can be even more powerful: "I trust you, and I have full confidence in your abilities. You don't need my approval; your opinion is my opinion."

This simple yet profound statement can be a game-changer, especially when dealing with someone junior to you. It signals that you see them not just as a subordinate but as a peer, someone whose judgment you value and respect. It's a subtle way of saying, "I believe in you," and it can transform the relationship dynamic, motivating them to take ownership and drive results with confidence.

The Power of Trust

I once knew an executive who shared a story from his early career that illustrates this point perfectly. Fresh out of college and eager to prove himself, he was asked to provide a deposition in a legal matter. Before doing so, he had to brief the CEO and chairman of the company. The CEO asked him just two questions: "Do you think we did the right thing?" and "Do you think we followed a fair process?"

After the executive answered, the CEO simply said, "Great. That's all I needed to know. I trust you and your supervisor. Now I can brief our legal team."

That brief exchange left a lasting impression on the young executive. The CEO's trust wasn't just in the decision-making process but in the people involved. It shaped the executive's leadership style going forward, teaching him the immense value of empowering others by trusting their judgment.

Real-World Application: Empowering Your Team

Let's consider a more everyday scenario. Imagine a company planning to move into new office space. The team leader, known for being particular about office setup, recognizes that one of the team members has a great eye for design and is exceptional at selecting furniture. When the time comes to choose chairs and tables, the team member seeks the leader's opinion. Instead of diving into details, the leader simply says, "If you like it, I like it."

That's it. No micromanagement, no second-guessing—just trust.

This kind of trust and confidence isn't just a motivational tool; it's a leadership strategy that fosters growth, autonomy, and engagement. By stepping back and showing faith in their abilities, the leader not only empowers the team member but also signals to the entire team that their contributions are valued and trusted.

The Ripple Effect of Empowerment

When leaders adopt this approach, the effects ripple through the organization. Team members who feel trusted are more likely to take initiative, bring new ideas to the table, and make decisions that they stand by. They feel a sense of ownership and pride in their work, knowing that their leader has their back.

Moreover, this trust can transform the leader's role. Instead of being a bottleneck for every decision, the leader becomes a guide, providing direction and support only when needed. This frees up time and mental space for more strategic thinking and allows the team to function more autonomously.

The Big Picture: Building a Culture of Trust

Building a culture of trust starts with small steps, like the ones we've discussed. It's about choosing to empower rather than control, to believe in rather than doubt. Over time, these small choices add up, creating an environment where people feel confident in their abilities and are motivated to contribute their best work.

In the end, leadership isn't just about making decisions or giving orders. It's about building a team of people who trust themselves because they know their leader trusts them. So, the next time someone asks for your opinion, consider responding with, "I trust you. Your opinion is my opinion." You might be surprised at the positive impact it has—not just on the individual but on your entire team.

The key takeaway? Trust empowers. And empowered people drive results.

Key Actions

- **Empower Through Trust**: Show your team members that you trust their judgment by expressing confidence in their decisions, rather than always providing your own opinion or approval.
- **Recognize and Treat Others as Peers**: When appropriate, treat those junior to you as peers, acknowledging their expertise and abilities. This can significantly boost their confidence and motivation.
- **Foster Autonomy**: By stepping back and allowing your team members to make decisions, you encourage them to take ownership of their work and contribute more meaningfully.
- **Communicate Confidence in Abilities**: Let team members know that you trust their skills and knowledge, reinforcing that they don't always need your validation to make the right choices.
- **Build a Culture of Trust:** Consistently choosing to trust and empower your team members helps build a broader culture of trust within the organization, leading to increased initiative and engagement from the team.

Discussion Questions

1. How can leaders effectively communicate trust in their team members' decisions without appearing disengaged or uninterested?

2. What impact do you think treating junior team members as peers can have on their development and performance?

3. In what situations might it be challenging for a leader to fully trust a team member's judgment, and how can these challenges be addressed?

4. How can a leader balance the need for oversight with the desire to foster autonomy and ownership within their team?

5. What are some practical steps leaders can take to build a culture of trust within their organization, and what potential obstacles might they face?

Practice Exercises

1. Delegate with Confidence

- **Objective**: Build trust by delegating tasks without micromanaging.
- **How to Do It**: Identify a task or project that you typically oversee closely. Instead of providing detailed instructions, delegate it to a team member and express your confidence in their ability to handle it. Tell them, "I trust your judgment; make the decisions you think are best." Follow up only to offer support if needed, and avoid checking in excessively.

2. Peer-to-Peer Feedback

- **Objective**: Treat team members as peers and empower their decision-making.
- **How to Do It**: Select a junior team member whose work you respect. In your next interaction, ask for their opinion on a decision or project that you are working on. Show genuine interest in their feedback and consider incorporating their suggestions. This exercise helps shift the dynamic from top-down management to collaborative leadership.

3. Trust-Building Conversations

- **Objective**: Cultivate a culture of trust by reinforcing your confidence in team members.
- **How to Do It**: Set aside time for one-on-one meetings with key team members. During these conversations, make a point to acknowledge their expertise and express your trust in their abilities. Use phrases like "I trust your judgment" or "Your opinion is valuable to me." Reflect on how this approach impacts their confidence and motivation over time.

MASTER SPONTANEOUS REWARDS

Rewards are a big part of what drives us. They push us to reach our goals and achieve our ambitions. But not all rewards are created equal. Most people are familiar with what you might call "calculated rewards," the kind you expect for doing something specific, like a performance bonus at work or a thank-you gift for helping out a friend. These are the rewards we anticipate, but they don't always pack the punch we think they do. In fact, their impact often fades quickly, and the absence of a reward we expected sticks with us longer than the presence of one we received.

The Problem with Expected Rewards

The biggest issue with calculated rewards is that they quickly lose their power. When we start to expect something, it no longer motivates us the same way. The thrill is gone. This is especially true when those expected rewards don't materialize. The sting of not getting something we thought was coming leaves a mark, often more vivid than the memory of getting the reward itself.

For example, I once knew a leader who made a hefty salary. Over time, though, the amount became just a number to him. He couldn't even remember how much he was paid a few years back. But when there was a year where he didn't get the raise he expected, he remembered every detail. The disappointment overshadowed all the years he did receive what he thought he deserved. It's a perfect example of how calculated rewards can turn into a double-edged sword—they can motivate, sure, but they can also demotivate when they don't come through.

Another downside of calculated rewards is the negative feelings they can create when they fall through. If someone's used to a certain reward and suddenly it doesn't happen, it's easy for them to feel unappreciated. This can lead to resentment, a drop in motivation, and even disengagement from their work. It's a slippery slope that can erode trust and damage relationships.

The Power of Spontaneous Rewards

Given the pitfalls of calculated rewards, it's worth considering a different approach: spontaneous rewards. These are the rewards that come out of nowhere, with no strings attached. They're given as a gesture of appreciation, not because someone completed a specific task or hit a milestone, but simply because you value them. And because they're unexpected, they often have a much stronger and longer-lasting impact.

Spontaneous rewards catch people off guard in the best possible way. They create a powerful emotional response because they're surprising and heartfelt. Since these rewards aren't tied to an expectation, they don't lose their effectiveness over time. Instead, they often create a lasting positive memory, strengthening relationships and boosting morale in a way that calculated rewards just can't match.

Real-Life Examples of Spontaneous Rewards

Let me share a couple of stories to illustrate this.

First, there was a leader at a financial institution known for being all business—results-driven and not particularly warm. He worked with a coach to try and develop more empathy, but it didn't seem to make much of a difference. Then, one evening, he noticed a team working late. On a whim, he walked across the street, bought them a bunch of pizzas, and had them delivered to the office.

It was a simple gesture, but it made a huge impact. The team was thrilled, and word spread quickly throughout the organization. This one spontaneous act not only lifted the team's spirits but also started to change how people saw him as a leader. His reputation shifted, and he began to be seen as someone who genuinely cared about his team.

Another favorite story involves a media figure I've known for years, a golf fan like me. She called me out of the blue one Tuesday morning and invited me to join her and her team at the World Golf Hall of Fame induction ceremony in Augustine, Florida. I was blown away by the offer. Unfortunately, I couldn't make it, and had to settle for watching highlights of it online.

A couple of weeks later, I asked her how the trip went. She told me it was amazing—they had been able to attend a private session with some of the greats like Gary Player and Vjay Singh. But what stuck with her most was that she had to ask dozens of people before she found three who could join her. She joked that her only regret was not buying the tickets on Wednesday morning so she could have made even more people feel special.

This story is a perfect example of how spontaneous rewards work. The invitation wasn't tied to any specific accomplishment. It was just a thoughtful, generous offer that made me feel valued, even though I couldn't go. And that's the beauty of spontaneous rewards—they leave a lasting impression and make people feel truly appreciated.

Why Spontaneous Rewards Work

Spontaneous rewards are powerful because they come without expectation. They show that you value people not just for what they do, but for who they are. This helps to foster a sense of belonging and reinforces the idea that team members are appreciated as individuals, not just for their performance.

Calculated rewards, while effective in the short term, can sometimes create a sense of entitlement. People start focusing more on the reward than on the task at hand. In contrast, spontaneous rewards shift the focus back to the individual and the relationship. They encourage a culture of gratitude and strengthen bonds within the team.

In the end, becoming a master of spontaneous rewards isn't about throwing money around or giving out grand gestures. It's about being thoughtful, paying attention to the people around you, and seizing the opportunity to show appreciation when it's least expected. Whether it's buying pizza for a team working late or inviting a colleague to a once-in-a-lifetime event, these small, spontaneous acts can make a huge difference. They remind people that they're seen, valued, and appreciated, which is the most powerful reward of all.

Key Actions

- **Avoid Over-Reliance on Expected Rewards**: Recognize that calculated rewards can lose their effectiveness over time and may even lead to negative feelings if they are not received as expected.
- **Embrace Spontaneity**: Look for opportunities to provide rewards or recognition in unexpected ways. These spontaneous acts can create a more powerful emotional response and leave a lasting impact.
- **Value Individuals, Not Just Performance**: Show appreciation for people as individuals, not just for what they accomplish. Spontaneous rewards help reinforce this idea by focusing on the person rather than the task.
- **Pay Attention to Your Team**: Be observant and aware of the efforts and needs of those around you. This awareness allows you to recognize when a spontaneous reward might be most effective.
- **Seize the Moment**: When you see an opportunity to provide a spontaneous reward, act on it. Even small gestures, when unexpected, can significantly enhance morale and strengthen relationships.
- **Foster a Culture of Gratitude**: Encourage an environment where spontaneous rewards and acts of appreciation are the norm, helping to build a stronger, more connected team.

Discussion Questions

1. How do calculated rewards impact long-term motivation within a team?
2. What are the benefits of using spontaneous rewards over expected rewards in the workplace?
3. Can you share an example of when a spontaneous reward made a significant difference in your work environment?
4. How can leaders effectively balance the use of calculated and spontaneous rewards?

5. In what ways do spontaneous rewards contribute to a positive workplace culture?

Practice Exercises

1. Spontaneous Recognition Journal

- **Objective**: Develop the habit of recognizing opportunities for spontaneous rewards.
- **How to Do It**: Keep a small journal or use a note-taking app to jot down instances where you notice someone going above and beyond or showing exceptional effort. Once a week, review your notes and select one or two people to acknowledge with a spontaneous reward or gesture of appreciation. Reflect on how these actions impact your relationships and the team's morale.

2. Surprise Team Appreciation

- **Objective**: Strengthen team bonds through unexpected acts of kindness.
- **How to Do It**: Identify a time when your team or a specific team member has put in extra effort, such as working late or handling a challenging task. Without announcing it beforehand, surprise them with a small reward, like bringing in coffee, arranging a team lunch, or sending a personalized thank-you note. Observe the reactions and consider how these spontaneous acts improve team dynamics.

3. Personalized Recognition Challenge

- **Objective**: Enhance your ability to recognize and reward individual contributions meaningfully.
- **How to Do It**: For one month, commit to recognizing one team member each week in a personalized way that reflects their unique interests or contributions. This could be through

a handwritten note, a small gift related to their hobbies, or a public acknowledgment during a meeting. After each recognition, assess the impact on that individual's engagement and the overall team atmosphere.

CHAPTER 5
MAKE DECISIONS, OWN OUTCOMES

Making decisions is at the heart of leadership. It's a skill that can make or break a leader. Yet, despite its significance, decision-making often gets sidelined in leadership discussions. Some leaders might think they've got it covered, that they're already making sound decisions, and that there's little to gain from revisiting the topic. But here's the truth: no matter how seasoned you are, you can always sharpen your decision-making abilities by studying what works for others and reflecting on your own methods.

The Art of Decision-Making

Decision-making isn't just about picking the right option from a list of choices; it's about the process that leads you to that choice. Some leaders rely on classic approaches, like listing the pros and cons or gathering input from a range of perspectives. These methods have their place, but they're not without pitfalls.

One of the biggest dangers is paralysis by analysis. This happens when you get so caught up in gathering information and weighing every possible outcome that you freeze. For leaders, who often face decisions that need to be made quickly, this can be disastrous. The key is to find a balance between gathering enough information to make an informed decision and not getting bogged down by it.

Understanding Heuristics and Biases

Another challenge in decision-making is the role of heuristics—the mental shortcuts we use to make decisions more quickly. These short-cuts can be helpful, but they can also introduce biases that skew our judgment.

Take the anchoring bias as an example. This occurs when the first piece of information you receive heavily influences all subsequent decisions. If a leader is too anchored to initial information, they may overlook better options that emerge later.

To combat these biases, leaders must first become aware of them. Once you understand how your mind might be tricking you, you can take steps to counteract these effects. This might mean deliberately seeking out information that challenges your initial assumptions or consulting with others who have different perspectives.

Establishing Decision-Making Routines

One way to improve decision-making is to establish clear routines and practices. For instance, setting aside specific times dedicated to making decisions can help you focus and minimize distractions. This intentional approach ensures that you give each decision the attention it deserves, rather than making hasty choices in the midst of a busy day.

Another powerful practice is to regularly seek out diverse viewpoints. Engaging with people who see things differently can uncover new insights and help you avoid the trap of groupthink. When you surround yourself with people who challenge your assumptions, you're more likely to arrive at a well-rounded decision.

Weighing Risks and Consequences

Every decision carries risk. The key is to not just focus on the potential upside but also to consider the downside risk—the possible negative consequences. It's natural to get excited about the positive outcomes, but responsible leaders take the time to think through the worst-case scenarios as well. By doing this, you can put strategies in place to mitigate potential downsides and make more balanced decisions.

The Continuous Improvement of Decision-Making

Decision-making is not a one-time event but an ongoing process that you can continuously improve. Reflect on past decisions—what went well, what didn't, and why? This reflection can provide valuable lessons that make you a better decision-maker over time.

In summary, decision-making is a crucial aspect of leadership that directly impacts success. While various methods exist, it's important to stay aware of the potential pitfalls like paralysis by analysis and cognitive biases. By establishing thoughtful routines, seeking out diverse perspectives, and weighing risks carefully, leaders can refine their decision-making process and enhance their effectiveness. Remember, even the best leaders can get better at making decisions—it's a skill that's always worth honing.

EVERY DECISION BRINGS PROBLEMS

Every decision you make as a leader is a double-edged sword. Each choice you make carries with it the potential for both positive and negative outcomes. The challenge lies in understanding that these outcomes aren't always immediate or obvious. In fact, they often unfold in ways that are both unexpected and complex.

First, Second, and Third Order Consequences

When you make a decision, the immediate result is just the tip of the iceberg. This is what we call the first-order consequence—the direct, observable effect of your choice. It's the easy part, the outcome you can see coming a mile away.

But here's the catch: decisions rarely operate in isolation. The first-order consequence triggers second-order consequences—those are the effects that come about as a reaction to the initial outcome. These could be unintended benefits, like increased efficiency, or unforeseen problems, like employee burnout.

Then there are the third-order consequences, which can be the trickiest to predict. These are the long-term effects that might not surface until weeks, months, or even years down the road. They're the true test of whether a decision was sound or short-sighted.

Consider this: You decide to cut costs by reducing staff. The first-order consequence is immediate savings. The second-order consequence might be an increase in workload for the remaining employees, leading to stress and decreased morale. The third-order consequence? Over time, this could result in higher turnover rates, costing you more in recruitment and training than you initially saved.

The Art of Anticipation: Thinking Beyond the Immediate

Effective leadership isn't just about making decisions—it's about making decisions that stand the test of time. This requires foresight, a skill that separates good leaders from great ones. When faced with a choice, don't just ask yourself, "What will happen if I do this?" Instead, think in layers: "What will happen next? And after that?"

By considering the first, second, and third-order consequences, you're not only planning for the immediate future but also for the long-term implications of your actions. This kind of strategic thinking helps you navigate the complexities of leadership with a clearer vision.

Embracing the Inevitability of Problems

Here's a hard truth: problems will arise, no matter how carefully you plan. Every decision brings with it a set of challenges, some of which you won't see coming. But this doesn't mean you should shy away from making tough calls. Instead, you should be prepared to deal with the fallout, adjusting your strategy as new issues come to light.

Think of decision-making as a game of chess. Every move you make opens up new possibilities, both good and bad. The key is to stay nimble, ready to pivot when needed, and always thinking several steps ahead.

Reputation Matters: The Long-Lasting Impact of Decisions

Your decisions do more than just solve problems; they shape your reputation. Are you the leader who consistently makes wise, calculated choices? Or are you the one whose decisions create more problems than they solve?

Managing up—working effectively with higher-level leadership—requires you to be mindful of how your decisions reflect on you. Leaders who consistently make thoughtful, well-considered decisions build trust and credibility. They're seen as problem-solvers, not problem-creators.

This is especially important when you're in a position where your decisions affect not just your immediate team but the broader organization. The reputation you build through your decisions can either open doors or close them.

Decision-Making Is a Balancing Act

Leadership is about making decisions, and decision-making is inherently risky. But by thinking through the potential consequences—first, second, and third—you can make choices that lead to positive outcomes and avoid unnecessary pitfalls.

Remember, every decision will have consequences, some of which you can't foresee. The goal isn't to make perfect decisions every time—that's impossible. The goal is to make informed decisions, anticipate potential problems, and be ready to adapt when the unexpected happens. In doing so, you not only navigate the complexities of leadership more effectively, but you also build a reputation as a leader who can be trusted to make the right call, even when the stakes are high.

Key Actions

- **Anticipate Consequences:** Consider not just the immediate (first-order) outcomes of a decision, but also the secondary and tertiary (second and third-order) effects that may unfold over time.
- **Think Strategically:** Look beyond the immediate impact of a decision and consider the long-term implications, planning several steps ahead to navigate potential challenges.
- **Embrace the Inevitability of Problems:** Accept that every decision will bring about new challenges and be prepared to address them as they arise, adjusting your approach as needed.
- **Stay Nimble and Ready to Pivot:** Maintain flexibility in your leadership approach, being ready to change course if unexpected consequences or problems surface.
- **Manage Your Reputation:** Be mindful of how your decisions impact your reputation as a leader, particularly in how they reflect your ability to solve problems rather than create them.
- **Engage in Thoughtful Decision-Making:** Prioritize making informed, well-considered decisions that take into account both immediate and long-term outcomes.
- **Build Trust and Credibility:** Through consistent and wise decision-making, establish yourself as a leader who can be trusted to make sound choices, especially in high-stakes situations.

Discussion Questions

1. How can leaders effectively anticipate the second and third-order consequences of their decisions, and what tools or frameworks can assist in this process?
2. In what ways can a leader's reputation be impacted by the decisions they make, and how can they ensure their choices build trust and credibility within their organization?
3. Can you share an example from your experience where a decision you made had unexpected second or third-order consequences? How did you address these challenges?
4. How does the ability to stay nimble and pivot in response to unforeseen problems influence the overall success of a leader's decision-making process?
5. What strategies can leaders employ to balance the need for quick decision-making with the need for thorough consideration of potential long-term consequences?

Practice Exercises

1. Scenario Mapping

- **Objective**: Improve your ability to anticipate first, second, and third-order consequences of decisions.
- **How to Do It**: Start by identifying a decision you need to make, whether it's in your professional or personal life. Once you have the decision in mind, map out the immediate outcomes, or first-order consequences. Next, consider the potential ripple effects—these are your second-order consequences. Think through how these might evolve over time into third-order consequences. As you explore these layers, reflect on how this understanding might influence or alter your approach to the decision.

2. Decision Retrospective

- **Objective**: Build awareness of the long-term impacts of past decisions to inform future choices.
- **How to Do It**: Choose a significant decision from your past, preferably one that had both positive and negative outcomes. Reflect on the immediate (first-order) effects and then think about the subsequent consequences that followed. As you identify these second and third-order outcomes, consider any unexpected challenges or benefits that emerged. Use this reflection to understand what you might have missed at the time and how you can apply these lessons to improve your future decision-making.

3. Reputation Management Audit

- **Objective**: Strengthen your awareness of how your decisions impact your reputation and relationships with others.
- **How to Do It**: Take a moment to think about recent decisions you've made that had visible impacts on your team or organization. Reflect on how each of these decisions affected your reputation among peers, subordinates, and superiors. Look for patterns in your decision-making that either enhanced or detracted from your credibility. With this understanding, create a plan to reinforce positive behaviors and address any tendencies that could harm your reputation in future decisions.

SEPARATE PROBLEMS FROM SOLUTIONS

Making decisions is at the core of effective leadership. But it's not just about making any decision; it's about making the right decision at the right time. This requires a careful analysis of the situation, where defining the problem accurately is the first and most critical step. It might sound obvious, but for many leaders—especially those who are naturally inclined to act quickly—this step can be easily overlooked. The impulse to jump straight to solutions is strong, but it's a trap that can lead to wasted time, resources, and subpar outcomes.

The Importance of Clarity

Before diving into solutions, it's essential to draw a clear line between problems and solutions. When these two become blurred, the path to resolution becomes muddy. You risk narrowing your focus prematurely, potentially missing out on more effective or innovative approaches. To avoid this, start by defining the problem as clearly and specifically as possible. Ask yourself, "What exactly am I trying to solve?" By doing so, you set the stage for a more thorough exploration of potential solutions.

Recognizing Interconnected Issues

Effective leaders understand that problems rarely exist in isolation. More often than not, they are interconnected with other issues, creating a web of challenges that can be difficult to untangle. The key is to recognize these connections without becoming overwhelmed by them. Identify each problem individually, then address them one by one, starting with the root causes. This methodical approach prevents you from falling into the trap of attempting to solve everything at once, which can lead to superficial fixes that don't address the underlying issues.

Question Everything

Never accept someone else's definition of the problem without digging deeper. This is where your analytical skills come into play. Ask probing questions, challenge assumptions, and don't be afraid to reframe the issue. Sometimes, the problem as presented isn't the real issue at all—it's just a symptom of something deeper. By breaking down complex problems into smaller, more manageable pieces, you gain a better understanding of what you're truly dealing with, making it easier to find a solution that works.

Framing the Problem Shapes the Solution

How you define a problem directly influences the solutions you'll consider. For instance, if you believe the issue with your team stems from a poor working environment, your solutions will likely focus on improving that environment. But if you think the root cause is related to leadership dynamics, you'll approach the problem differently, perhaps by addressing how decisions are made or how power is distributed. This is why it's so important to take your time in defining the problem correctly—because once you've set that framework, it guides the entire decision-making process.

The Power of Multiple Perspectives

No leader makes decisions in a vacuum—or at least, no effective leader does. Seeking input from others is not a sign of weakness; it's a strategic move that broadens your perspective and helps you see the problem from different angles. This can reveal blind spots you hadn't considered and lead to more robust solutions. Additionally, involving your team in the decision-making process fosters buy-in and ensures that the solutions you implement are supported by those who will carry them out.

Evaluating Solutions with an Open Mind

Once you've clearly defined the problem and gathered input, it's time to consider potential solutions. This step requires an open mind and a willingness to entertain ideas that may not align with your initial thoughts. Evaluate the pros and cons of each option, and don't be afraid to go back to the drawing board if none of the solutions seem right. Gathering and analyzing relevant data can provide valuable insights here, but remember that data alone doesn't make decisions—

people do. Your judgment, informed by data, experience, and the input of others, is what will ultimately lead to the best outcome.

The Big Picture of Decision-Making

Effective decision-making is a process that starts with clearly defining the problem and ends with a well-considered solution. Along the way, it involves questioning assumptions, seeking multiple perspectives, and remaining open to alternative viewpoints. By following this approach, you not only make better decisions but also address the root causes of problems, leading to long-term, sustainable results.

Fight the urge to rush to solutions. Instead, take the time to understand the problem in depth, involve others in the process, and evaluate your options carefully. This disciplined approach to decision-making is what sets great leaders apart and ensures that the solutions you choose are not just quick fixes, but enduring ones.

Key Actions

- **Draw a Clear Line Between Problems and Solutions**: Focus on defining the problem accurately before jumping to solutions.
- **Recognize Interconnected Issues**: Identify and address problems individually, starting with root causes.
- **Question Everything**: Challenge assumptions and don't accept someone else's definition of the problem without further analysis.
- **Frame the Problem Carefully**: Understand that how you define the problem will shape the solutions you consider.
- **Seek Multiple Perspectives**: Involve others in the decision-making process to broaden your perspective and ensure buy-in.
- **Evaluate Solutions with an Open Mind**: Consider a range of potential solutions and assess their pros and cons thoroughly.
- **Take a Disciplined Approach to Decision-Making**: Follow

a methodical process from problem definition to solution selection to achieve long-term, sustainable results.

Discussion Questions

1. How can leaders ensure they are accurately defining the problem before moving on to solutions?
2. What are some ways to identify interconnected issues, and how can leaders prioritize which problem to address first?
3. In what situations is it most important to question assumptions and challenge someone else's definition of a problem?
4. How does the way a problem is framed influence the potential solutions?
5. What are the benefits and potential challenges of involving others in the decision-making process?

Practice Exercises

1. Problem Reframing Drill

- **Objective**: Improve your ability to define problems accurately and see them from different angles.
- **How to Do It**: Take a current problem you're facing and write down your initial definition of it. Then, try to reframe the problem in at least three different ways. For example, if the problem is low team morale, consider reframing it as an issue of unclear goals, inadequate communication, or lack of recognition. Reflect on how each reframing changes the potential solutions.

2. Root Cause Analysis Practice

- **Objective**: Strengthen your ability to identify and address the root causes of problems.
- **How to Do It**: Choose a problem you've recently solved or are currently addressing. Use the "5 Whys" technique to dig

deeper into the root cause. For each answer you come up with, ask "Why did this happen?" five times, each time getting closer to the underlying issue. Once you reach the root cause, brainstorm potential solutions and compare them to your original approach.

3. Perspective Gathering Exercise

- **Objective**: Enhance your ability to seek and integrate multiple perspectives in decision-making.
- **How to Do It**: The next time you're faced with a decision, deliberately seek out the opinions of at least three different people who are affected by or knowledgeable about the issue. Make sure to choose individuals with varying viewpoints or roles. After gathering their input, analyze how their perspectives change or reinforce your understanding of the problem and potential solutions. Apply these insights to refine your decision-making process.

CHECKLISTS MAKE DECISIONS

When you're at the helm, every decision you make can have wide-reaching consequences. The stakes are high, and it's all too easy to get caught up in the whirlwind of pressures and opinions. That's why a simple, yet powerful tool can be a game-changer: the checklist.

But before you can whip out a checklist and start ticking boxes, there's an essential first step that can't be overlooked—defining the problem. And not just on the surface. You need to dig deep, get to the root, and really understand what you're dealing with. This involves asking tough, probing questions about what's really going on. Is the issue a symptom or the actual cause? What are the different ways to look at this problem? By taking the time to thoroughly examine the situation, you set yourself up to find the best solution, rather than just putting a band-aid on a bigger issue.

Crafting a Decision-Making Checklist

Once you've defined the problem, it's time to create a checklist of questions that will guide you through the decision-making process. This checklist isn't just a random list of things to consider—it should be tailored to fit the specific situation, your values as a leader, and your organization's principles. Here's what to include:

- **Does this align with our strategy?** Every decision should move your team closer to its goals. If it doesn't, why are you considering it?
- **Is this consistent with my values and the company's principles?** Leaders need to lead by example. Your decisions should reflect the values you preach.
- **How will this impact our customers?** Ultimately, your business exists to serve your customers. Consider their experience with every decision you make.

The Importance of Diverse Input

No leader operates in a vacuum. The best decisions often come from a combination of perspectives. That means involving the right people in the decision-making process. This could include subject matter experts who bring specialized knowledge, team members who will be directly affected by the decision, and even those who might have a completely different point of view. By bringing these voices into the conversation, you can uncover blind spots and think through the implications of your choices more thoroughly.

Data: The Backbone of Good Decisions

In today's world, decisions backed by solid data stand a better chance of succeeding. Whether it's market research, financial analysis, or insights from your team, gathering and analyzing data should be a non-negotiable step in your process. But it's not just about collecting data—it's about interpreting it wisely. Consider potential risks, unintended consequences, and the long-term impact of your decision. A well-informed decision is far less likely to come back to bite you.

Flexibility: The Mark of a Good Leader

Even with the best preparation, not every decision will play out as expected. That's why it's crucial to stay flexible and be willing to revisit and revise decisions as new information comes to light. Being too rigid can cause you to double down on a failing strategy, while flexibility allows you to adapt and pivot, keeping your team on track toward your goals.

The Power of Good Questions

At the heart of good decision-making are good questions. The questions you ask reveal your assumptions, biases, and understanding of the situation. They help you explore the risks and opportunities and lead you toward the best possible decision. On the flip side, poor decision-makers often fail because they don't ask the right questions or any questions at all.

While complex decisions require tailored questions, even everyday decisions can benefit from a set of checklist questions. Whether you're deciding how to allocate your time, respond to a customer complaint, or tackle a tricky problem, having a set of go-to questions can streamline your thought process and ensure you're making choices that align with your goals and values.

Creating Your Own Checklist

Leaders can create their own checklist questions or suggest them to others. For example, before implementing a new process, you might ask:

1. *Is this decision consistent with our team's strategy?*
2. *Does this decision align with my values and the company's principles?*
3. *What will be the impact of this decision on our customers?*

These questions help ground your decisions in what's most important —your strategy, values, and customer impact.

The Role of Checklists in Everyday Leadership

The decision-making process is a vital part of leadership. By using a checklist of quality decision-making questions, you ensure that your choices are thoughtful, informed, and aligned with your long-term goals. This approach not only helps you navigate the challenges and opportunities of leadership but also sets the stage for lasting success for you and your team.

In the end, it's not just about making decisions—it's about making the right decisions. A well-crafted checklist can be your guide, helping you to ask the right questions, involve the right people, and gather the right data. And when you combine that with a willingness to adapt, you'll find yourself making decisions that lead to outcomes you and your team can be proud of.

Key Actions

- **Thoroughly Define the Problem:** Take the time to deeply understand the issue at hand by asking probing questions and identifying the root cause.
- **Create a Decision-Making Checklist:** Develop a tailored checklist of questions that align with the team's strategy, the leader's values, the company's principles, and the potential impact on customers.
- **Involve the Right People:** Engage subject matter experts, team members affected by the decision, and those with differing perspectives to gain a well-rounded understanding.
- **Gather and Analyze Data:** Collect relevant data and interpret it carefully to assess risks, unintended consequences, and long-term impacts.
- **Stay Flexible:** Be open to revisiting and revising decisions as new information becomes available, allowing for adaptability in the decision-making process.
- **Ask Good Questions:** Use thoughtful, specific questions to guide decision-making and ensure alignment with goals, values, and customer impact.
- **Use Checklist Questions Regularly:** Apply checklist questions to both complex and everyday decisions to streamline the thought process and ensure consistent alignment with priorities.

Discussion Questions

1. How can leaders ensure they are identifying the true root cause of a problem rather than just addressing symptoms?
2. What are some examples of checklist questions that could be universally applied across different types of decisions, and why are they effective?
3. In what ways can involving diverse perspectives in the decision-making process improve the quality of the final decision?

4. How can leaders balance the need for thorough data analysis with the risk of over-analyzing and delaying decisions?
5. Why is flexibility important in the decision-making process, and how can leaders cultivate a mindset that allows for adaptation when new information arises?

Practice Exercises

1. Root Cause Analysis Practice

- **Objective**: Improve your ability to identify the true root cause of problems.
- **How to Do It**: The next time you encounter a problem, practice the "5 Whys" technique. Start by stating the problem, then ask "Why?" to uncover the cause. Each answer should lead to another "Why?" until you reach the root cause. Document the process and reflect on whether the root cause you identified is different from your initial assumption.

2. Decision-Making Checklist Creation

- **Objective**: Develop and refine your own decision-making checklist tailored to your leadership context.
- **How to Do It**: Identify a recent decision you made and analyze it using the principles discussed. Based on this analysis, create a checklist of questions that could have guided that decision more effectively. Use this checklist for your next significant decision, and afterward, evaluate its effectiveness and make adjustments as needed.

3. Diverse Perspective Simulation

- **Objective**: Enhance your ability to involve and value diverse perspectives in decision-making.
- **How to Do It**: For your next team decision, deliberately seek input from individuals who typically hold different

viewpoints from your own. Role-play scenarios where you argue from their perspective to better understand their concerns and ideas. After the decision is made, review how these perspectives influenced the outcome and reflect on what you learned from incorporating them.

TIMELINESS VS. PRECISION

When you're in a leadership role, making decisions is inevitable. The stakes are high, and the impact of your choices can ripple throughout your organization. The trick isn't just making decisions but knowing when to make them. It's a delicate dance between waiting for the right information and seizing the moment before it slips away.

The Allure of Optionality

The longer you can keep your options open, the more control you maintain over potential outcomes. This approach, known as preserving optionality, is about holding off on a decision until you have as much information as possible. In theory, this seems like the best way to make informed choices. After all, new data might emerge, or circumstances might shift in your favor. But here's the catch: waiting too long can turn a golden opportunity into a missed one.

Effective leaders understand the importance of this balancing act. They gather data, weigh options, and involve the right stakeholders. But they also know when it's time to stop analyzing and start deciding. Hesitation, while often tempting, can lead to stagnation. The moment you have the necessary information, it's time to act.

The Pitfalls of Perpetual Gray Areas

Making decisions "in the gray" is where many leaders falter. This is the space where options aren't fully preserved, and there's no clear focus on the data at hand. It's a place of indecision, where nothing is fully committed to, and nothing is fully discarded. When you find yourself here, you risk losing momentum and, worse, missing out on the best possible outcomes.

To avoid this trap, set clear timelines for your decision-making process. For instance, if a decision needs to be made by a committee, establish a firm deadline—say 24 hours—for final confirmation. This creates a sense of urgency and forces clarity. It pushes you out of the gray and into action.

The Power of Decisiveness

Decisiveness doesn't mean rushing to judgment. It means knowing when you have enough information to make a sound decision and then committing to that choice with confidence. Whether it's moving quickly to capitalize on an opportunity or taking the time to gather every piece of the puzzle, effective leaders strike the right balance.

Once a decision is made, the work isn't over. The best leaders remain vigilant, ready to reassess and adjust as new information arises. This ongoing process of evaluation ensures that decisions remain relevant and effective as situations evolve.

The Decision-Making Framework

To help you navigate the complexities of decision-making, consider implementing a framework that guides the process:

1. **Preserve Optionality:** Keep your options open until you have the information you need. Don't rush into a decision without sufficient data.
2. **Set Deadlines:** Avoid the gray by setting clear, reasonable deadlines for when decisions need to be made.
3. **Involve Stakeholders:** Ensure all relevant voices are heard. This doesn't mean making decisions by committee, but it does mean considering diverse perspectives.
4. **Commit to Action:** Once you've gathered the necessary information and considered your options, make your decision and move forward. Decisiveness is key to maintaining momentum.
5. **Stay Flexible:** Be willing to revisit and revise decisions as new information comes to light. Flexibility doesn't mean indecision; it means being responsive to change.

The art of decision-making lies in knowing when to wait and when to act. It's about preserving your options as long as possible but recognizing the moment when it's time to commit. Effective leaders don't dwell in indecision. They balance optionality with decisiveness, ensuring that when they do make a decision, it's informed, timely, and poised for success.

Key Actions

- **Preserving Optionality**: Keep options open until you have gathered enough information to make an informed decision.
- **Avoiding the Gray Area**: Prevent indecision by setting clear deadlines for when decisions need to be made.
- **Involving Stakeholders**: Consider diverse perspectives by involving relevant stakeholders in the decision-making process.
- **Being Decisive**: Commit to action once enough information has been gathered, making decisions with confidence to maintain momentum.
- **Staying Flexible:** Remain open to revisiting and revising decisions as new information becomes available, ensuring ongoing relevance and effectiveness.

Discussion Questions

1. How do you balance the need to preserve optionality with the risk of missing out on opportunities by waiting too long to make a decision?
2. Can you share an example from your experience where setting a clear deadline for a decision helped avoid indecision and led to a successful outcome?
3. What are the potential risks of involving too many stakeholders in the decision-making process, and how can these risks be managed effectively?
4. How do you determine when you have gathered enough information to move from analysis to action in your decision-making process?
5. In what ways can staying flexible and revisiting decisions after they are made lead to better long-term outcomes for an organization?

Practice Exercises

1. Decision Timing Drill

- **Objective**: Improve your ability to balance optionality with timely decision-making.
- **How to Do It**: Identify a decision you need to make in your personal or professional life. Set a firm deadline for making that decision, whether it's 24 hours or a week, depending on the complexity. During that time, gather as much relevant information as possible, but once the deadline hits, make your decision. Reflect on the process: Did you gather enough information? Did the deadline push you to be more decisive?

2. Stakeholder Involvement Exercise

- **Objective**: Enhance your ability to involve the right stakeholders without falling into decision paralysis.
- **How to Do It**: Choose a decision that involves multiple people. Before making the decision, list all potential stakeholders and categorize them by importance and impact on the decision. Involve only the most critical stakeholders in the discussion. Afterward, evaluate the effectiveness of their involvement and the quality of the decision made.

3. Flexibility Challenge

- **Objective**: Develop your ability to stay flexible and revisit decisions when necessary.
- **How to Do It**: Take a recent decision you've made and revisit it with any new information that has come to light. Analyze whether the decision still holds up or if adjustments are needed. Practice this regularly with both small and large decisions to build the habit of ongoing evaluation and flexibility.

CONSENSUS FOR SMARTER DECISIONS

When it comes to making decisions, leaders often default to group discussions, thinking that more voices lead to better outcomes. But here's the truth: group decision-making can be a mixed bag. Too often, the wrong voices dominate, the right ones stay silent, and vested interests muddy the waters. That's where the Weigh-In Consensus process comes in—a method that balances inclusivity with decisive leadership.

The Role of the Decision Owner

At the heart of this process is the Decision Owner—the person responsible for driving the decision to its conclusion. This individual might be the leader or an expert in a relevant field, but their role is clear: they own the decision from start to finish. The Decision Owner's job is to guide the team through the process, ensuring that all voices are heard without relinquishing control of the final call.

Creating a Target Position

The process kicks off with the Decision Owner crafting a Target Position—a preliminary solution or strategy that reflects their current thinking. This isn't the final decision but a starting point for discussion. Think of it as a straw man, something tangible that others can respond to, refine, or challenge. The Target Position serves as the focal point for dialogue, allowing the Decision Owner to steer the conversation while remaining open to new ideas.

Engaging the Team: Dialogue and Debate

Once the Target Position is on the table, the real work begins. The Decision Owner engages the team in a structured dialogue, encouraging dissent and alternative viewpoints. This isn't about reaching a quick consensus; it's about exploring different perspectives to refine the initial idea. The best leaders create an environment where team members feel comfortable voicing their opinions, knowing that their input will genuinely influence the outcome.

Building Consensus Through Weigh-In

The next step is the Weigh-In—a process where each team member shares their thoughts on the Target Position. This isn't just a simple thumbs-up or thumbs-down; it's an opportunity for everyone to weigh in on the pros and cons, offer modifications, and highlight potential pitfalls. The Decision Owner listens carefully, taking note of recurring themes, insightful critiques, and innovative suggestions. The goal here is not just to gather input but to build a more robust solution through collective wisdom.

Refining the Decision

Armed with this feedback, the Decision Owner then refines the Target Position, incorporating the best ideas while still steering towards the ultimate decision. This might involve several rounds of discussion, especially if the decision is complex or if there are strong opposing views. The key is that the Decision Owner remains in control, guiding the process towards a conclusion that benefits from diverse input while avoiding the pitfalls of decision-by-committee.

Implementing the Final Decision

Once the Target Position has been refined and consensus is reached, it's time to implement the decision. But here's where the Weigh-In Consensus process shines: because the decision has been shaped by the team, there's a built-in sense of ownership and commitment. The decision isn't just handed down from above; it's the product of a collaborative effort, making buy-in and execution more likely to succeed.

The Pitfalls of Traditional Group Decision-Making

It's worth noting why traditional group decision-making often falls short. In a typical group discussion, the loudest voices can dominate, while quieter, often more thoughtful, perspectives get lost. There's also the issue of groupthink—the tendency for groups to coalesce around a single idea without fully exploring alternatives, just to avoid conflict. And let's not forget the impact of past decisions on the group's willingness to take risks; if a previous decision went poorly, the group might be overly cautious, stifling innovation.

Why Weigh-In Consensus Works

The Weigh-In Consensus process mitigates these issues by assigning clear ownership of the decision while still leveraging the team's collective insights. It ensures that the final decision is well-rounded, considering multiple perspectives, yet remains decisive. The process is inclusive but not diluted by the need to please everyone. It's about making high-quality decisions that stand up to scrutiny and lead to successful outcomes.

Weigh-In Consensus is more than just a method; it's a mindset. It recognizes the value of diverse perspectives while maintaining the decisive leadership necessary for effective decision-making. By utilizing this approach, leaders can make informed, high-quality decisions that not only consider the needs of all stakeholders but also stand the test of time.

Key Actions

- **Decision Ownership**: A single person owns the decision from start to finish, ensuring clarity and accountability.
- **Target Position**: Start with a preliminary idea that others can critique and refine.
- **Structured Dialogue**: Encourage open debate and diverse viewpoints to improve the initial idea.
- **Weigh-In Process**: Gather input from all stakeholders, but keep the Decision Owner in control.
- **Refinement and Consensus**: Use feedback to refine the decision, ensuring it's both inclusive and decisive.
- **Effective Implementation:** A decision shaped by the team is more likely to be executed successfully.

Discussion Questions

1. What are the potential risks of allowing the loudest voices to dominate group decision-making, and how does the Weigh-In Consensus process address these risks?

2. How does the role of the Decision Owner in the Weigh-In Consensus process differ from a traditional team leader in a group decision-making setting?

3. In what ways can the Target Position serve as both a starting point for discussion and a tool for steering the decision-making process?

4. How can leaders create an environment where team members feel comfortable voicing dissenting opinions during the Weigh-In Consensus process?

5. What are some potential challenges a Decision Owner might face when trying to balance inclusivity with decisiveness, and how can they overcome these challenges?

Practice Exercises

1. Target Position Drafting

- **Objective**: Improve your ability to create clear, actionable starting points for decision-making.
- **How to Do It**: Identify a decision you need to make in your work or personal life. Draft a Target Position that outlines your initial thoughts and proposed solution. Share this with a trusted colleague or friend, asking them to critique it as if they were part of a team discussion. Refine your Target Position based on their feedback, focusing on how well it serves as a foundation for further dialogue.

2. Facilitating Structured Dialogue

- **Objective**: Enhance your skills in leading discussions that encourage diverse viewpoints and constructive debate.
- **How to Do It**: In your next team meeting, introduce a topic that requires input from multiple perspectives. Use the Weigh-In Consensus approach: start with a Target Position, then ask each team member to weigh in with their thoughts. Actively manage the conversation, ensuring that quieter voices are heard and dominant voices are balanced. After the

meeting, reflect on what went well and what could be improved in your facilitation technique.

3. Consensus Building Simulation

- **Objective**: Practice the process of refining a decision through multiple rounds of feedback and discussion.
- **How to Do It**: Choose a hypothetical scenario or case study relevant to your field. Assign yourself the role of the Decision Owner and gather input from a small group of peers or mentors, simulating the Weigh-In process. Focus on how you incorporate their feedback into the final decision while maintaining clear ownership. Repeat the exercise with different scenarios to build confidence in your ability to balance inclusivity with decisiveness.

SIMULATE BEFORE COMMITTING

Making decisions is a core responsibility of any leader. But let's be honest—not all decisions are created equal. Some are simple, while others carry significant weight, affecting the future of the entire organization. For those more complex, high-stakes decisions, a different approach is required. One effective strategy is to "live" with a decision before you make it official.

The Traditional Decision-Making Process

The conventional approach to decision-making typically involves arriving at a conclusion, announcing it, and then putting it into action. There's often a gap between the announcement and the implementation—an interval where the decision starts to take shape in the real world. This gap is crucial, but most leaders overlook its potential. They jump straight from making a decision to executing it without fully considering the nuances.

The Power of "Living" With a Decision

So, what does it mean to "live" with a decision? It's about mentally and emotionally committing to a decision as if it's already been made, but without locking it in. You engage with your team, customers, or other stakeholders as though the decision is final. This isn't about waffling or second-guessing; it's about testing the waters before diving in.

Think about it like this: You've decided to promote someone within your organization. Before you make the announcement, start assigning them tasks and responsibilities that align with their new role. Observe how they handle these challenges. Do they rise to the occasion, or do they struggle? How do other team members react to their new authority? This kind of "dry run" allows you to assess the real-world impact of your decision without fully committing.

Avoiding Regret in High-Stakes Decisions

The best leaders understand that the most important decisions often revolve around people—hiring, promotions, and team dynamics.

These decisions can be particularly tricky because they involve emotions, relationships, and the future direction of your team.

For example, when promoting a team member to a leadership role, there's always a risk that they might say or do something in their new position that leads to regret. By "living" with the decision beforehand, you give yourself a chance to catch potential issues early on. If something feels off during this trial period, you can address it before it becomes a larger problem.

How to "Live" With a Decision

1. *Delay the Announcement:* Give yourself a 24-48 hour window before making any public announcements. This buffer time allows you to mentally commit to the decision and explore its implications without pressure.
2. *Engage as If It's Final:* Start interacting with key stakeholders as though the decision has already been made. Assign tasks, discuss plans, and observe how people respond. This step is crucial for gathering real-time feedback on your decision's potential impact.
3. *Assess and Adjust:* Use the insights you gather during this period to refine your decision. If you notice any red flags, take a step back and reassess. This doesn't mean you're indecisive; it means you're thorough.

The Benefits of "Living" With Your Decisions

By "living" with a decision before making it official, you give yourself the chance to fully consider all the implications. This approach helps you avoid the common pitfall of making hasty decisions that lead to regret. It's about being proactive rather than reactive—testing the decision in the real world before committing to it.

This method doesn't just apply to promotions or hiring. It can be used in any situation where the stakes are high and the consequences significant. Whether you're considering a new business strategy, a major investment, or a restructuring of your team, "living" with the decision can provide valuable insights that lead to better outcomes.

Making Better Decisions Without Regret

At the end of the day, the goal is to make decisions that are well-informed and thoughtful. By simulating outcomes and living with a decision before you make it official, you're better equipped to ensure that your choice is the right one. It's not about hesitation or doubt—it's about being strategic and deliberate. And in leadership, that's what separates the good from the great.

Key Actions

- **Mentally Commit to the Decision:** Treat the decision as if it's already made, allowing yourself to engage with it fully before announcing it officially.
- **Delay the Announcement:** Take a 24-48 hour pause before making any public announcements, giving yourself time to assess the decision's implications.
- **Engage as If It's Final:** Interact with stakeholders and team members as though the decision is set in stone to gauge reactions and gather feedback.
- **Assign Relevant Tasks:** Test the decision by assigning tasks or responsibilities aligned with it, particularly when making promotions or role changes.
- **Observe Reactions and Outcomes:** Monitor how the decision plays out in real-time, noting any red flags or positive responses.
- **Assess and Adjust:** Use the insights gained during the trial period to refine or reconsider the decision before making it official.
- **Be Proactive, Not Reactive:** Approach decision-making strategically by simulating outcomes, aiming to avoid regrets and ensure better-informed choices.

Discussion Questions

1. How can "living" with a decision before announcing it help leaders avoid common pitfalls in decision-making?
2. What are some potential challenges leaders might face when delaying the announcement of a decision, and how can they overcome them?
3. In what ways can engaging with stakeholders as if a decision is final provide valuable feedback for refining the decision?
4. How does the practice of "assigning relevant tasks" before making a final decision help in assessing the suitability of a promotion or role change?
5. Can you think of a time when "living" with a decision before making it official could have changed the outcome? What would you have done differently?

Practice Exercises

1. Decision Simulation Exercise

- **Objective**: Practice mentally committing to a decision before making it official.
- **How to Do It**: Choose a low-stakes decision you need to make, such as selecting a new vendor or adjusting a project deadline. Mentally commit to this decision for 24-48 hours as if it's already made. During this period, engage with team members and stakeholders as though the decision is final. Observe your own reactions and the responses of others. After the period ends, assess whether your initial decision still feels right or if you need to make adjustments.

2. Stakeholder Engagement Practice

- **Objective**: Improve your ability to gather feedback by engaging with others as if a decision is final.
- **How to Do It**: Identify a decision you are considering that involves your team or stakeholders, such as implementing a

new process. Without making the decision official, start conversations with key individuals as if the decision has already been made. Ask for their input, reactions, and concerns. Take note of any feedback that could help refine the decision. Practice this regularly with different scenarios to become more comfortable with this approach.

3. Task Assignment Simulation

- **Objective**: Strengthen your ability to assess the suitability of decisions related to role changes or promotions.
- **How to Do It**: Select a team member you are considering for a new role or responsibility. Before making any formal decisions, assign them tasks that align with the new role's demands. Observe how they handle these tasks over a set period (e.g., one week). Reflect on their performance and the reactions of others involved. Use this exercise to gain insights into whether the person is truly ready for the promotion or role change.

CHOOSE STABILITY SOMETIMES

Most decisions in life, whether big or small, fall into a category we often overlook: status quo decisions. These are the moments when, after careful consideration, we choose to keep things as they are. But here's the catch—we tend to underestimate the significance of these choices. We might think that sticking with the current state doesn't require much explanation or fanfare. However, that's a mistake.

Recognizing Status Quo as a Decision

Deciding to change course often gets all the attention, but choosing not to change is just as much of a decision—and it deserves to be treated with the same level of importance. Think about it: when we decide to maintain the status quo, we've likely gone through a rigorous process. We've analyzed the situation, gathered data, consulted with stakeholders, and weighed the alternatives. Yet, despite all this effort, we often fail to communicate the decision effectively.

Admired leaders understand that deciding not to act is still a decision. And like any decision, it needs to be communicated clearly. If we don't, we risk being seen as indecisive or passive. This is especially true in larger organizations where people might be wondering why no action is being taken on a particular issue. If they're left in the dark, they may assume the worst.

The Importance of Communicating the Decision

When it comes to maintaining the status quo, clarity and transparency are your best friends. People need to know not just *what* you decided, but *how* and *why* you arrived at that decision. By explaining the steps you took—how you analyzed the problem, considered alternatives, and ultimately chose to stick with the current approach—you can alleviate concerns and build confidence in your leadership.

One effective way to communicate a status quo decision is by holding a meeting or sending out a memo that lays out your thought process. This isn't just about ticking a box; it's about ensuring that everyone involved understands the reasoning behind your choice. Follow up with your team or stakeholders to address any questions or concerns they might have. This follow-up is crucial because it shows that you're engaged and open to dialogue, even when the decision is to stay the course.

The External Perception

Internal communication is one thing, but don't forget about the external world. How will your decision to maintain the status quo be perceived by customers, clients, or partners? These external parties might not be privy to the same level of detail as your team, but they still need reassurance. In these cases, a more detailed explanation might be necessary to maintain trust and credibility.

For example, if a client is expecting changes or improvements and you've decided to hold off, they need to understand why. Maybe the timing isn't right, or perhaps the current strategy is working well, and a change could disrupt that success. Whatever the reason, communicating it clearly can prevent misunderstandings and reinforce the relationship.

Making a Big Deal Out of It

At the end of the day, a status quo decision isn't a non-decision. It's a conscious choice, often made after careful consideration. And like any other decision, it needs to be communicated effectively to ensure that everyone is on the same page.

By being open, transparent, and thorough in your explanation, you can turn what might seem like an uneventful decision into an opportunity to reinforce trust and credibility. So, the next time you choose to keep things as they are, don't downplay it. Make a big deal out of it —because it is.

Key Actions

- **Recognize Status Quo as a Decision**: Understand that choosing to maintain the status quo is a deliberate decision and should be treated with the same importance as decisions to change course.

- **Communicate Clearly and Transparently**: Ensure that the reasoning behind a status quo decision is clearly communicated, including the analysis and steps that led to the decision.
- **Explain the Decision-Making Process**: Share the thought process, data analysis, stakeholder consultations, and alternative considerations that contributed to the decision to maintain the status quo.
- **Engage in Follow-Up**: Follow up with team members or stakeholders to address any questions or concerns, demonstrating openness and engagement.
- **Consider External Perception**: Communicate the decision effectively to external parties, such as customers or clients, to maintain trust and credibility.
- **Make a Big Deal Out of It:** Treat the decision to maintain the status quo as significant, ensuring it is communicated with the same importance as other decisions.

Discussion Questions

1. Why do you think leaders often overlook the importance of communicating status quo decisions?
2. In what ways can failing to communicate a status quo decision impact team morale or external perceptions?
3. How can a leader effectively balance the need for transparency with the potential risk of over-explaining a decision to maintain the status quo?
4. What strategies can be used to ensure that external parties, such as clients or customers, understand and accept a decision to keep things the way they are?
5. How can making a big deal out of status quo decisions reinforce trust and credibility within a team or organization?

Practice Exercises

1. Status Quo Decision Analysis

- **Objective**: To improve your ability to recognize and articulate the importance of maintaining the status quo.
- **How to Do It**: Identify a recent decision where you chose to keep things the way they are, either in your personal or professional life. Write a brief analysis of the decision-making process, including the problem you faced, the alternatives you considered, and the reasons you chose not to change anything. Share this analysis with a colleague or mentor for feedback on how well you communicated the decision.

2. Communicating the Status Quo

- **Objective**: To practice clear and transparent communication of status quo decisions.
- **How to Do It**: Select a scenario where you've decided to maintain the status quo and prepare a short presentation or memo explaining the decision to your team or a group of peers. Include the rationale, the alternatives considered, and the reasoning behind your final choice. After presenting, ask for feedback on the clarity and effectiveness of your communication.

3. External Perception Scenario

- **Objective**: To enhance your ability to consider and manage external perceptions of status quo decisions.
- **How to Do It**: Think of a status quo decision that might impact external stakeholders, such as clients or customers. Draft a communication plan that includes a detailed explanation of the decision, tailored to these external parties. Consider how you would address potential concerns or questions they might have. Review this plan with a trusted colleague or mentor and refine it based on their feedback.

POWER OF A GUIDING PRINCIPLE

Great leaders often rely on a core set of values to guide their decisions and actions. But the truly exceptional ones take it a step further—they elevate a single, "superseding value" that serves as a beacon for the entire organization. This isn't just another value on a list; it's the value that transcends all others, providing clarity and direction in every situation.

The Superseding Value: Your Organizational Compass

Imagine your organization as a ship navigating through the tumultuous waters of the business world. The superseding value is the North Star that guides your course. By anchoring all decisions to this one principle, you ensure that everyone—from top executives to frontline employees—is aligned and moving in the same direction. This shared focus simplifies decision-making and fosters a strong sense of purpose across the organization.

When a leader identifies and communicates a clear superseding value, it becomes the lens through which all actions and decisions are viewed. For example, if your superseding value is customer service, then every action taken by your team should be measured against how well it serves the customer. This clarity not only empowers team members to make decisions independently but also ensures that those decisions are consistent with the organization's overall mission.

Communicating the Value: Creating Alignment and Accountability

For a superseding value to be effective, it must be communicated clearly and consistently. It can't be just another buzzword or part of a list of generic values that everyone nods along to but quickly forgets. The superseding value needs to be real, actionable, and genuinely embraced by leadership.

A powerful example of this in action is Steve Kerr, the head coach of the Golden State Warriors. Kerr's superseding value is joy. He believes that when his players find joy in their work, both on and off the court, they perform better and create a more cohesive team. Kerr doesn't just talk about joy; he lives it, models it, and expects it from his team. This emphasis on joy has not only cultivated a positive culture within the Warriors organization but has also contributed to their remarkable success.

When a leader consistently communicates and models their superseding value, it resonates with the team. People are naturally drawn to clarity and authenticity, and when they see their leader living out the value they espouse, it creates trust and fosters a deep sense of alignment.

Enhancing Communication and Unity Through a Shared Value

A superseding value does more than guide individual decisions—it enhances communication and fosters unity. When everyone in the organization understands what the most important value is, discussions and decisions become more straightforward. There's no need to guess what the right course of action might be; the superseding value provides a clear standard against which all options can be measured.

This shared understanding also strengthens the bonds within the team. When people are united by a common principle, it creates a sense of belonging and purpose that goes beyond the day-to-day tasks. The organization becomes more than just a place of work; it becomes a community of like-minded individuals working towards a shared goal.

Driving Better Decisions Across the Board

The true power of a superseding value lies in its ability to drive better decisions at every level of the organization. It serves as a touchstone for evaluating options, resolving conflicts, and setting priorities. When faced with tough choices, leaders and team members alike can ask themselves, "Does this align with our superseding value?" The answer to that question provides the clarity needed to move forward with confidence.

Moreover, by holding everyone accountable to the superseding value, leaders can cultivate a positive culture that values consistency, integrity, and excellence. This not only improves decision-making but also enhances overall organizational performance.

Identifying and embracing a superseding value is one of the most powerful tools a leader has at their disposal. It provides a clear, consistent standard that guides decision-making, enhances communication, and fosters unity within the organization. By living out this value and holding others accountable to it, leaders can create a culture that not only drives success but also brings out the best in everyone involved.

Consider what your superseding value might be and how it can elevate your leadership and decision-making. Once you've identified it, make it a central part of your leadership strategy. Communicate it, model it, and watch how it transforms your organization.

Key Actions

- **Elevate a Single Value:** Identify and prioritize one core value that will serve as the guiding principle for the entire organization.
- **Communicate with Clarity:** Consistently articulate the superseding value to ensure everyone in the organization understands and aligns with it.
- **Model the Value in Action:** Demonstrate the superseding value in your own decisions and behaviors to set an example for others.
- **Use the Value as a Decision Filter:** Evaluate all decisions through the lens of the superseding value to maintain consistency and alignment with organizational goals.
- **Anchor Conversations in the Value:** Reference the superseding value during discussions to enhance communication and drive meaningful dialogue.
- **Hold the Team Accountable:** Ensure that all team members adhere to the superseding value, reinforcing its importance within the organizational culture.

Discussion Questions

1. What is a superseding value that you believe could guide your team or organization, and why do you think it would be effective?
2. How can a leader effectively communicate a superseding value without it becoming just another buzzword?
3. Can you share an example from your experience where a clear guiding principle (superseding value) influenced a decision or outcome in your organization?
4. How might holding team members accountable to a superseding value impact the overall culture of an organization?
5. What challenges might arise when trying to establish and maintain a superseding value within a diverse team, and how can they be addressed?

Practice Exercises

1. Identify and Articulate Your Superseding Value

- **Objective**: To clarify and communicate a guiding principle that resonates with your leadership style and organizational goals.
- **How to Do It**: Reflect on your core values and the needs of your organization. Choose one value that you believe should guide all decisions and actions. Write a brief statement explaining why this value is essential and how it will influence the organization. Practice communicating this value in different scenarios, such as team meetings, one-on-one conversations, and written communications.

2. Model the Superseding Value in Daily Decisions

- **Objective**: To practice consistently applying the superseding value in your leadership decisions and actions.

- **How to Do It**: Throughout your day, consciously evaluate decisions you need to make through the lens of your chosen superseding value. For each decision, ask yourself how it aligns with this value and what adjustments might be necessary to stay true to it. Keep a journal to document these decisions, noting how the value influenced your choices and the outcomes.

3. Facilitate a Value-Based Discussion with Your Team

- **Objective**: To engage your team in understanding and aligning with the superseding value, fostering a unified approach.
- **How to Do It**: Organize a team meeting focused on the superseding value. Start by explaining its importance and how it should guide decision-making. Then, lead a discussion where team members share their thoughts on how the value applies to their roles and responsibilities. Encourage them to provide examples of how they've seen the value in action or where they believe it could be better integrated. Use this exercise to reinforce the value and identify areas for improvement.

PREPARE FOR DECISION FATIGUE

Decision fatigue is a sneaky, often overlooked phenomenon that can wreak havoc on the quality of our choices. As leaders, we're constantly bombarded with decisions, big and small. The more choices we face, the more drained we become, and that's when our decision-making starts to slide. The result? Poor choices, reduced focus, and emotional burnout. It's a vicious cycle that can have a serious impact on your effectiveness as a leader.

Let's start by unpacking what decision fatigue is all about.

Understanding Decision Fatigue

Imagine you're on a parole board, deciding whether prisoners should be granted parole. A study found that those who appeared before the board early in the morning were significantly more likely to be granted parole than those who came later in the day. Why? Because the board members were fresher in the morning and could make more considered, objective decisions. As the day wore on and the number of decisions piled up, their mental reserves dwindled, leading to poorer judgment.

This study highlights a crucial point: timing matters when it comes to decision-making, and the more decisions we're forced to make, the worse our choices become.

Why Leaders Are Especially Vulnerable

As a leader, you're responsible for making decisions that can impact your team, your organization, and sometimes, even your industry. The stakes are high, and the pressure is relentless. But here's the kicker: the sheer volume of decisions you're making every day is probably wearing you down more than you realize.

The mental load accumulates, and before you know it, you're making decisions with a brain that's running on empty. This is when mistakes happen—when you give in to short-term fixes instead of considering long-term consequences, or when you default to a "good enough" decision because you just don't have the energy for anything else.

So, how can you protect yourself from decision fatigue and keep your decision-making sharp?

Strategies to Combat Decision Fatigue

1. *Prioritize Morning Decisions:* Start your day by tackling the most critical decisions first. Your brain is at its freshest in the morning, so use that time to focus on tasks that require the most cognitive energy. Leave routine, low-stakes decisions for later in the day when your mental energy is lower.
2. *Pre-decide on the Small Stuff:* Don't waste your mental bandwidth on trivial decisions. Pre-decide on routine choices like what to wear, what to eat for breakfast, or your daily schedule. By reducing the number of decisions you need to make, you free up mental energy for more important tasks.
3. *Manage Your Energy:* Decision fatigue isn't just about the number of choices you make; it's also about your overall energy levels. Take regular breaks, get some exercise, and fuel your body with healthy meals. These simple habits can keep your mind sharp and your decision-making on point.

Staying Effective Amid Constant Choices

Decision fatigue isn't just a "nice-to-know" concept—it's a real challenge that can undermine your leadership if left unchecked. By understanding the science behind it and implementing practical strategies, you can maintain your decision-making edge.

Remember, it's not about avoiding decisions altogether; it's about being strategic in how you approach them. Prioritize the big stuff when your mind is fresh, pre-decide on the small stuff to save energy, and take care of your body so your brain stays sharp.

These steps might seem small, but they add up to a significant improvement in your ability to lead effectively. Decision fatigue is real, but with the right approach, you can minimize its impact and keep your leadership strong.

Key Actions

- **Prioritize Morning Decisions**: Focus on making critical decisions early in the day when your mental energy is at its peak.
- **Pre-decide on Routine Choices**: Reduce mental load by pre-deciding on trivial, everyday decisions like what to wear or what to eat.
- **Manage Energy Levels:** Regularly take breaks, get exercise, and eat healthy meals to maintain your energy and keep your decision-making sharp.
- **Avoid Overloading Yourself with Decisions**: Be mindful of the number of decisions you need to make in a day. Where possible, delegate or automate decisions to conserve mental energy for the most important tasks.
- **Be Strategic with Timing**: Recognize that the timing of your decisions matters. Tackle complex or high-stakes decisions when your energy and focus are highest, typically in the morning.
- **Incorporate Breaks and Downtime**: Regularly step away from work to reset your mental state, which helps to recharge and prevent decision fatigue from setting in.
- **Stay Aware of Decision Fatigue**: Acknowledge when you might be experiencing decision fatigue and adjust your decision-making process accordingly, either by postponing less critical decisions or seeking input from others.

Discussion Questions

1. How have you personally experienced decision fatigue in your role, and what strategies have you found effective in managing it?
2. Why do you think prioritizing decisions in the morning can make such a significant difference in the quality of your decision-making? Can you share an example from your own experience?

3. What routine decisions in your daily life could be pre-decided or automated to reduce mental load? How might this change impact your overall productivity?

4. How do you currently manage your energy levels throughout the day, and what adjustments could you make to better combat decision fatigue?

5. In what ways could recognizing and addressing decision fatigue improve leadership effectiveness within your team or organization?

Practice Exercises

1. Morning Decision Prioritization

- **Objective**: To optimize decision-making by focusing on high-priority tasks when your mind is freshest.
- **How to Do It**: Each evening, list the three most important decisions or tasks you need to tackle the next day. In the morning, commit to addressing these items first, before diving into less critical work. Reflect on how this practice affects the quality of your decisions and overall productivity.

2. Routine Decision Pre-Planning

- **Objective**: To reduce decision fatigue by automating or pre-deciding routine choices.
- **How to Do It**: Identify three routine decisions you make daily, such as what to eat for breakfast, what to wear, or your workout schedule. Create a fixed plan for these decisions (e.g., a weekly meal plan, a go-to outfit, or a workout routine) that you follow without thinking. Over time, evaluate how this change frees up mental energy for more important decisions.

3. Energy Management Check-In

- **Objective**: To maintain high energy levels throughout the day, preventing decision fatigue.
- **How to Do It**: Set three alarms on your phone for different times during the day (e.g., mid-morning, early afternoon, and late afternoon). When each alarm goes off, take a 5-10 minute break to assess your energy level. During this break, engage in a quick recharging activity, such as deep breathing, a short walk, or a healthy snack. At the end of the week, reflect on how these breaks affected your decision-making and overall well-being.

OWN THE PROCESS, NOT JUST OUTCOMES

We live in a world obsessed with results. The scoreboard, the bottom line, the final grade—they all tell us who won and who lost. But when it comes to leadership, there's a critical piece missing in this picture: the decision-making process. Celebrating decisions, not just the outcomes, is a practice that separates great leaders from the rest. It's not just about what you achieve; it's about how you get there. Focusing on the process enriches your team's growth, fosters trust, and keeps you from burning out.

The Real Value Lies in the Process

Let's start with the obvious: Not every decision will lead to a win. Even the best-laid plans can go awry. But if you only celebrate the victories, you're missing out on a treasure trove of learning opportunities. Focusing on the decision-making process, rather than the outcome, encourages a culture of continuous learning. It shifts the spotlight from just results to reflection and growth. When leaders emphasize the process, they give their team permission to dissect what happened— what data was used, what strategies were tried, and how collaboration unfolded. This reflective practice is where real development occurs. People learn not just from what went right but from what went wrong. And in the long run, this mindset sharpens the team's decision-making skills, making them more resilient and adaptable.

Building Trust and Accountability Through Transparency

Trust doesn't come from results alone; it's built through transparency and inclusion in the process. When leaders are open about how decisions are made, the reasoning behind them, and the steps taken, it demystifies the process for the entire team. Even if a decision leads to an undesired outcome, team members are more likely to stand by it because they understand the 'why' behind it. This transparency builds a sense of ownership and accountability. People are more willing to take responsibility when they feel they've been a part of the journey. They're not just cogs in the machine; they're contributors to the collective success.

Judging Decisions and Outcomes Separately: A Critical Distinction

Here's the truth: good decisions don't always yield good results, and bad decisions can sometimes lead to unexpected wins. It's tempting to judge the quality of a decision by its outcome, but that's a trap. Leaders must separate the two to truly understand what's working and what isn't. By evaluating the decision-making process independently of the result, you can identify where the process was strong and where it might need improvement. This objective assessment allows for more consistent and fair evaluations, leading to better decision-making across the board.

Showcasing What Makes a Decision Great

One of the most powerful things a leader can do is to highlight what makes a good decision great. It's not about whether the outcome was favorable but whether the process was sound. Ask yourself: If someone else had the same information and followed the same steps, would they have reached the same conclusion? Was the process thorough and capable of producing a quality decision? By celebrating the decision-making process, even when the results aren't ideal, you reinforce the importance of sound reasoning and thoughtful analysis. This approach not only builds confidence but also encourages a culture of calculated risk-taking and continuous improvement.

The Ripple Effect of Celebrating Decisions

When you celebrate decisions, not just outcomes, you're doing more than just encouraging a specific behavior—you're reshaping your organization's culture. You're telling your team that the journey matters as much as the destination. This mindset fosters an environment where learning is valued, trust is built, and resilience is cultivated. Over time, this approach leads to better decision-making across the organization, driving more consistent success and sustainable growth.

In the end, the process is the true measure of success. By embracing and celebrating the decision-making process, you create a culture that values learning, accountability, and thoughtful decision-making. And that, more than any single outcome, is what drives long-term success.

Key Actions

- **Celebrate the Decision-Making Process, Not Just Outcomes**: Focus on the process of making decisions to encourage continuous learning, growth, and improvement within the team.
- **Encourage Reflection and Growth**: Create opportunities for team members to reflect on the decision-making process, including the data used, strategies employed, and collaboration efforts, to learn from both successes and failures.
- **Build Trust and Accountability Through Transparency**: Be transparent about how decisions are made and the reasoning behind them, which helps build trust and a sense of ownership among team members.
- **Judge Decisions and Outcomes Separately**: Distinguish between the quality of the decision-making process and the results it produces, understanding that good decisions may not always yield favorable outcomes.
- **Showcase What Makes a Decision Great**: Highlight and celebrate the aspects of the decision-making process that demonstrate sound reasoning and thoughtful analysis, regardless of the outcome, to reinforce the value of a strong process.
- **Promote a Culture of Learning and Risk-Taking**: Encourage a culture where calculated risks are taken, and continuous improvement is valued by celebrating well-made decisions even if the outcomes are not ideal.

Discussion Questions

1. How can leaders effectively shift the focus from outcomes to the decision-making process in their teams? What challenges might arise in making this shift?

2. In what ways does transparency in decision-making build trust and accountability within a team? Can you share an example where transparency either strengthened or weakened trust in your experience?

3. Why is it important to judge decisions and outcomes separately? How can this distinction improve the overall decision-making process in an organization?

4. How can leaders encourage their teams to reflect on and learn from the decision-making process, especially when the outcomes are not favorable? What tools or practices can support this reflection?

5. What are some practical ways to celebrate a well-made decision, even if the outcome isn't what was desired? How can this practice influence a team's willingness to take calculated risks?

Practice Exercises

1. Decision Reflection Journal

- **Objective**: To improve your ability to reflect on and learn from the decision-making process.
- **How to Do It**: After making a significant decision, take 15-20 minutes to write a journal entry detailing the steps you took, the information you relied on, and the reasoning behind your choice. Focus on the process rather than the outcome. Then, review these entries weekly or monthly to identify patterns, strengths, and areas for improvement in your decision-making process.

2. Transparency Practice Sessions

- **Objective**: To build trust and accountability through transparent communication.
- **How to Do It**: In your next team meeting, choose a recent decision (successful or not) and walk your team through the entire decision-making process. Explain the factors

considered, the options weighed, and the reasoning behind the final choice. Encourage team members to ask questions and share their perspectives. Make this a regular practice to reinforce transparency.

3. Outcome-Independent Evaluation

- **Objective**: To separate the evaluation of decisions from their outcomes.
- **How to Do It**: Select a past decision where the outcome wasn't as expected. Gather your team and review the decision-making process in detail. Assess the quality of the process without focusing on the results. Ask questions like: "Was the information available used effectively?" and "Were all reasonable options considered?" The goal is to evaluate and learn from the process itself, not just the result.

CHAPTER 6
BUILD RELATIONSHIPS, FUEL GROWTH

Relationships are the lifeblood of leadership. They are the connections that bring meaning to our professional and personal lives, making us more than just our titles or achievements. While some people seem naturally gifted in forming bonds with others, the truth is that building and maintaining strong relationships requires discipline, strategy, and practice. Great leaders know that the value of a relationship isn't just about what you can get from it; it's about recognizing the inherent worth of the connection itself.

The Power of Connection

Research has repeatedly shown that strong relationships are the cornerstone of a fulfilling life. Beyond the obvious benefits of companionship and support, good relationships increase what's known as social capital. This is the intangible value derived from being well-connected within a network. When you're at the center of strong relationships, people are more likely to help you, advocate for you, and be patient with you during tough times. This isn't just a personal advantage—it's a professional one, too.

Honest Communication: The Foundation of Trust

Effective leaders don't just talk—they communicate. They engage in honest, open dialogue with others, making an effort to truly understand the interests and values of those they lead. This isn't something that happens by chance; it's a conscious effort to build trust and rapport.

To maintain these relationships, leaders must go beyond transactional interactions. It's not enough to reach out only when you need something. Relationships require ongoing attention and care, especially when working with people from diverse backgrounds. By showing genuine interest, demonstrating vulnerability, and sharing your own story, you can create bonds that transcend differences and foster a deep sense of trust.

The Legacy of Leadership

At the end of your career, your legacy will be defined not by the results you achieved but by the relationships you cultivated and the reputation you built. As a leader, it's crucial to focus on the quality of your relationships, for they are the foundation upon which your legacy will stand. Results are temporary; relationships are enduring.

Building and maintaining relationships is not a one-time effort. It's a continuous process that requires time, energy, and commitment. The rewards, however, are immeasurable. By investing in your relationships, you create a strong foundation for success in both your personal and professional life. The work may be challenging, but the payoff is worth every bit of effort.

Conversations: The Building Blocks of Relationships

Great relationships start with great conversations. The quality of the conversations you have is a direct reflection of the strength of your relationships. Leaders who understand the art of conversation are better equipped to build meaningful connections.

Conversations are not just about exchanging information; they're about sharing experiences, emotions, and ideas. They're the vehicle through which we express ourselves and connect with others. Learning how to keep a conversation alive—how to listen, respond, and engage —is a skill that takes a lifetime to master.

The Pursuit of Lifelong Connection

The pursuit of building and maintaining relationships is never-ending. It requires a commitment to understanding others, being open to new perspectives, and continuously improving your communication skills. As a leader, this journey is not just about personal growth—it's about creating a legacy of strong, meaningful relationships that will endure long after your career ends.

In the end, the number of people who truly matter to you is the truest measure of success. Your relationships are your legacy. They are the enduring connections that define who you are and what you leave behind. So, invest in them wisely, nurture them consistently, and watch as they become the foundation of a life well-lived.

BLUEPRINT FOR ADDING VALUE

Authentic relationships are the foundation of meaningful connections, and they go beyond mere transactions or surface-level interactions. These relationships demand effort, intentionality, and a genuine desire to add value to another person's life. It's not enough to simply exchange pleasantries or offer the occasional piece of advice. Real relationships thrive when we actively seek to better someone's life, whether it's through introducing them to new ideas, offering support, or simply being present when they need us most.

The truth is, good relationships don't just happen on their own. They require consistent work and thoughtfulness. Building and maintaining these connections is not just about offering solutions or comfort—it's about continuously finding ways to add value in diverse and sometimes unexpected ways.

Expanding the Concept of Value

One way to think about adding value in a relationship is to broaden our perspective on what support looks like. Too often, we fall into the trap of offering value in the same few ways, which can lead to stagnation. To truly enrich our relationships, we need to be creative and diverse in how we contribute to others' lives.

Consider these varied approaches to adding value:

- *Offering Guidance and Counsel:* Sometimes, the most valuable thing you can offer is your wisdom. This could be through direct advice or by sharing your experiences in a way that helps someone navigate their own challenges.
- *Introducing New Opportunities*: Whether it's connecting someone to an event, a resource, or a person who could impact their life positively, opening doors for others is a powerful way to add value.
- *Providing Encouragement*: Simple words of support, especially in moments of doubt or challenge, can have a profound effect. Encouragement isn't just about cheerleading; it's about

genuinely believing in someone's potential and letting them know it.

- *Sharing Knowledge*: From market trends to industry insights, sharing what you know can help others make informed decisions. This might also include offering a different perspective that broadens their understanding.
- *Offering Radical Honesty:* Sometimes, the most valuable thing you can offer is the truth, even when it's difficult. Radical honesty, delivered with care, can help someone see what they might be missing.
- *Being a Stand-In:* There are times when someone might need you to step in for them, whether in a meeting, a project, or even a difficult conversation. Offering to be that stand-in shows a deep level of support.
- *Sharing Humor and Perspective:* Laughter is a powerful tool in building connections. Sharing a sense of humor or a different perspective can lighten someone's load and offer a fresh way of seeing things.
- *Investing Time and Skills*: Volunteering your time or expertise to help someone through a tough situation is one of the most tangible ways to add value.
- *Celebrating Successes*: Don't underestimate the power of celebrating someone's achievements. Acknowledging their hard work and successes validates their efforts and strengthens your connection.
- *Providing Mentorship:* Taking the time to mentor someone, offering guidance and sharing your own experiences, can be a game-changer in their personal and professional development.
- *Completing Tasks Together*: Whether it's a project they're struggling with or a simple task, offering your help not only lightens their load but also reinforces the bond between you.
- *Sharing Passions and Hobbies:* Introduce someone to what you love, and you might open up a new avenue of joy for them. Sharing your passions can create a deeper, more personal connection.

- *Offering Personalized Recommendations:* A well-considered suggestion—be it a book, a restaurant, or a travel destination—can show someone that you really know and care about their tastes and interests.
- *Providing Thoughtful Feedback:* Feedback, when delivered thoughtfully, helps others grow. Whether it's through talent assessment or constructive criticism, your insights can guide them toward improvement.

The Value-Driven Leader

The best leaders excel at adding value to relationships in diverse ways. They understand that relationships are a two-way street, where both parties invest in each other's growth and success. These leaders don't just wait for opportunities to help; they actively seek them out, knowing that by investing in others, they are also investing in themselves.

A leader who consistently finds new ways to help and support those around them fosters deep, meaningful connections that transcend mere transactions. These authentic relationships become the bedrock of a strong, collaborative environment where everyone thrives.

In the end, authentic relationships are not about keeping score or seeking immediate rewards. They are about the long-term investment in others—helping, supporting, and adding value without expecting anything in return. This selfless approach is the key to building and maintaining relationships that are truly meaningful and rewarding.

So, remember, it's the small, thoughtful gestures that often have the biggest impact. When you invest in others with no immediate benefit in mind, you're not just building a relationship; you're creating a foundation for something much more significant. The effort you put in now will pay dividends in the form of stronger, more authentic connections that enrich both your life and the lives of those around you.

Key Actions

- **Actively Listening**: Engage fully in conversations by giving your full attention, acknowledging the other person's feelings, and responding thoughtfully.
- **Being Consistent and Reliable**: Show up consistently in the relationship, following through on promises and being dependable in both good and challenging times.
- **Expressing Genuine Appreciation**: Regularly acknowledge and express gratitude for the other person's contributions, efforts, and presence in your life.
- **Maintaining Open and Honest Communication**: Foster trust by being transparent, sharing your thoughts and feelings openly, and encouraging the same from others.
- **Prioritizing Mutual Growth:** Focus on helping both yourself and the other person grow, encouraging continuous learning, and supporting each other's personal and professional development.

Discussion Questions

1. What does it mean to you to add value in a relationship, and how do you personally strive to do this in your own connections?
2. Can you share an example of a time when someone added unexpected value to your life? How did that impact your relationship with them?
3. How do you maintain consistency and reliability in your relationships, especially during challenging times?
4. In what ways can we encourage more open and honest communication in our relationships, both personally and professionally?
5. How do you balance the need for mutual growth in a relationship with the demands of everyday life? What strategies do you use to ensure both parties benefit from the connection?

Practice Exercises

1. Active Listening Practice

- **Objective**: Improve your ability to fully engage in conversations and understand others' perspectives.
- **How to Do It**: Choose a conversation partner and commit to practicing active listening for a week. During your interactions, focus entirely on what they are saying without interrupting. After they finish speaking, summarize what you heard and ask follow-up questions to show your engagement. Reflect on how this changes the quality of your conversations.

2. Consistency and Reliability Challenge

- **Objective**: Build trust by becoming more dependable and consistent in your relationships.
- **How to Do It**: Identify one area in a key relationship where you could be more consistent—this could be in communication, support, or follow-through on commitments. For the next month, consciously work on being reliable in this area. Keep a journal to track your progress and any feedback or changes you notice in the relationship.

3. Value-Adding Brainstorm

- **Objective**: Cultivate creativity in finding new ways to add value to your relationships.
- **How to Do It**: Set aside 30 minutes each week to brainstorm ways you can add value to the lives of the people around you. Think about different actions, gestures, or resources you could offer. Choose one idea each week and put it into practice. Afterward, reflect on how this impacted your relationship and how the other person responded.

FREQUENCY OVER INTENSITY

We live in a world that's constantly pulling us in different directions. The demands of work, family, and everything in between can make it easy to overlook the relationships that matter most. We often convince ourselves that quality time is the key to keeping these relationships strong. While quality is important, research and experience suggest that the frequency of our interactions plays a much more significant role in deepening our connections.

The Power of Repeated Interactions

Think about the people you see every day—your colleagues, clients, family members. The bonds you form with them are often built on small, consistent interactions rather than occasional grand gestures. Whether it's a quick chat in the hallway, a brief phone call, or a simple text message, these interactions create a sense of familiarity and comfort. Over time, this regularity builds trust and strengthens relationships in ways that infrequent, high-quality time just can't match.

The best leaders understand this. They don't wait for the perfect moment to engage with their teams, clients, or loved ones. Instead, they make it a habit to connect frequently, even if those connections are brief. These small, repetitive moments of interaction lay the foundation for deeper, more meaningful relationships.

A Lesson from the Rolodex

There's a story about an assistant who worked for a highly successful business executive in the 1980s. Part of this assistant's job was to scan the environment and identify opportunities for the executive to reconnect and add value to the relationships in their Rolodex. This included high-profile individuals like Jacqueline Onassis. The assistant would flag these opportunities and help the executive write letters, sometimes sending out up to 300 per week. This relentless dedication to maintaining relationships was a key factor in the executive's success.

The lesson here is clear: successful relationships are cultivated through frequent, meaningful contact. It's not about waiting for the right moment or having long, deep conversations—it's about showing up consistently, even in small ways.

The Math of Relationships: 15 Times 2 > 1 Times 30

Let's break it down with a simple equation: 15 times two is greater than one times 30. While this may not make sense mathematically, it's a powerful way to illustrate a point. Fifteen two-minute interactions are far more effective in building a relationship than one 30-minute interaction. Why? Because each small interaction builds on the last, creating a cumulative effect that deepens the connection.

Imagine you have two leaders, each given two hours to build a meaningful relationship with a new client. The first leader decides to spend the entire two hours at a lunch or ballgame—one long, quality interaction. The second leader takes a different approach, breaking those two hours into smaller chunks spread over two months. They spend 20 minutes over coffee, then 10 minutes on a follow-up phone call two weeks later. Next, there's a 20-minute text exchange about a current event. Over time, these frequent, smaller interactions create a stronger bond. Leader two likely has a much more solid relationship with the client than leader one.

The Importance of Variety and Consistency

While frequency is key, it's also important to vary the way you interact. The best leaders don't rely on just one method of communication. They surround face-to-face conversations with other forms of contact —phone calls, text messages, emails, even handwritten notes. This variety keeps the relationship fresh and ensures that the lines of communication are always open.

But remember, it's not just about throwing more interactions into the mix. It's about being thoughtful and intentional with each one. The goal isn't to overwhelm the other person but to create a rhythm of regular, meaningful contact that builds trust and deepens the relationship.

Quality Still Matters, But Frequency Matters More

Let's not completely dismiss the importance of quality time. Of course, spending meaningful time with someone is essential for a strong, healthy relationship. But when it comes to deepening those relationships, frequency is what makes the biggest impact. It's the consistent, ongoing interactions that truly build the bond.

So, the next time you find yourself thinking you don't have enough time to invest in your relationships, consider breaking up your time into smaller, more frequent interactions. Send a quick text, make a brief phone call, or schedule a short coffee break. These small efforts, repeated over time, can make all the difference.

In the end, relationships are like any other investment. The more frequently you contribute, the more they grow. So, keep showing up, keep reaching out, and watch your connections deepen in ways you never thought possible.

Key Actions

- **Frequent Interaction**: Prioritize regular, ongoing interactions with colleagues, clients, and loved ones, even if they are brief, to build familiarity, comfort, and trust.
- **Varied Communication Methods**: Use a variety of communication methods, such as face-to-face conversations, phone calls, text messages, emails, and handwritten notes, to keep the relationship fresh and maintain consistent contact.
- **Intentional and Thoughtful Engagement**: Be deliberate and mindful in each interaction, ensuring that the contact is meaningful and not overwhelming.
- **Consistent Presence**: Make it a habit to connect with important individuals frequently, rather than waiting for the perfect moment or focusing only on long, quality interactions.
- **Breaking Up Time**: Instead of relying on single, lengthy interactions, break up your time into smaller, more frequent interactions to create a cumulative effect that deepens relationships.
- **Maintenance of Relationships**: Recognize the importance of regularly maintaining and cultivating relationships, understanding that small, consistent efforts contribute significantly to long-term success.
- **Intentional Relationship-Building:** Make an effort to identify opportunities to reconnect and add value to relationships, similar to the executive's practice of sending frequent, meaningful correspondence.

Discussion Questions

1. How do you currently balance quality and frequency in your relationships, both personal and professional? Which do you think has had a greater impact on the strength of those relationships?

2. Can you recall a time when frequent, small interactions led to a stronger relationship than a single, high-quality interaction? How did those repeated contacts build trust and connection?

3. In what ways can leaders incorporate more frequent interactions into their daily routines without overwhelming themselves or others?

4. How does the use of varied communication methods (e.g., texts, calls, face-to-face meetings) impact the depth of your relationships? Which methods do you find most effective for maintaining consistent contact?

5. What strategies can you implement to identify and create opportunities for frequent, meaningful interactions with key individuals in your life or organization?

Practice Exercises

1. Daily Micro-Check-Ins

- **Objective**: Increase the frequency of contact with key individuals in your life or organization.
- **How to Do It**: Choose three people—such as a colleague, client, or family member—whom you want to strengthen your relationship with. Set aside five minutes each day to check in with each person. This could be through a quick text, an email, or a brief face-to-face conversation. The key is to keep it casual and consistent. Track your interactions over a month and reflect on how these small check-ins have impacted the relationship.

2. Diverse Communication Methods Challenge

- **Objective**: Improve the variety of communication methods you use to maintain relationships.
- **How to Do It**: For the next two weeks, make a conscious effort to use different communication methods with the same person. For instance, start with an in-person chat, follow up with a text, send an email, and then a handwritten note. Pay

attention to how each method affects the interaction and the overall relationship. At the end of the two weeks, evaluate which methods were most effective and why.

3. Relationship Frequency Planner

- **Objective**: Develop a habit of intentional, frequent interactions.
- **How to Do It**: Create a simple weekly planner where you list the key people in your life or organization. Next to each name, schedule specific times for brief interactions throughout the week. These interactions could be as short as a five-minute phone call or as long as a 20-minute coffee meeting. Review your planner at the end of the week to see how well you adhered to your schedule and adjust for the following week. This exercise helps build a routine of consistent contact.

NURTURE CONVERSATIONS

The power of conversation in building and maintaining relationships can't be overstated. Engaging in meaningful dialogue lays the groundwork for connections that have the potential to be rich, rewarding, and long-lasting. In many ways, the quality of a relationship is a direct reflection of the quality of the conversations that sustain it. Similarly, the depth and strength of those conversations can mirror the strength of the relationship itself.

But here's the problem: we often let these conversations fade away. Life gets busy, priorities shift, and the once-vibrant exchange of ideas and experiences quietly dwindles. We may not always know where a relationship could lead, but one thing is certain—maintaining connections with interesting, intelligent, and experienced individuals can open doors to new opportunities, valuable learning experiences, and further connections. This is why it's crucial to be mindful of which conversations and relationships we choose to keep alive.

The Importance of Consistency

So, how do the most skilled leaders go about maintaining these important conversations? The answer lies in consistency and the value added to the relationship over time. It's not just about having a great chat once; it's about sustaining that dialogue and ensuring it continues to thrive. If both parties consistently contribute value to the relationship, it's possible to keep the conversation going for years, even without frequent face-to-face interaction or shared experiences.

Take a common scenario: Imagine you attend a conference and, by chance, end up sitting next to someone with whom you strike up a conversation. You discover shared interests—children the same age, similar job responsibilities, and a mutual love for certain activities. The conversation is engaging, and you decide to meet for coffee later. During that coffee meeting, you find even more common ground, from shared travels to mutual acquaintances. The connection feels natural, and the conversation flows effortlessly.

You agree to meet for breakfast the next morning to continue the conversation. Again, the dialogue is easy, and there's a genuine connection. By the end of the conference, you exchange contact information, fully intending to stay in touch.

But then, life happens. Time passes, and you don't hear from the person. They cross your mind occasionally, but you take no action. Months later, you find yourself in their city or are reminded of them by something random. You decide to reach out, maybe with a phone call or text. But there's no response. It's disappointing, and you might wonder what went wrong.

Adding Value to Sustain Relationships

The truth is, without consistent communication and effort to add value to the relationship, it's easy for it to fade away. The best leaders recognize this and make a concerted effort to maintain frequent contact with the people they value. This could be as simple as regular check-ins, sharing articles or resources that might interest the other person, or just reaching out to see how they're doing.

When you show a genuine, ongoing interest in someone else's life or work and actively contribute to the relationship, you're keeping the conversation alive. This holds true even when face-to-face interaction isn't possible. The key is in the consistency and the value you add—whether it's a thoughtful note, a relevant article, or a simple "How's everything going?"

Applying This in Professional Relationships

This process isn't limited to personal relationships. Professional connections require the same level of attention and care. You might have a colleague, client, or business partner you don't see often, but by consistently adding value to the relationship through communication, support, and shared insights, you can keep that connection strong.

The next time you find yourself in a conversation with someone you'd like to stay connected with, think about how you can consistently add value. It takes effort, but the reward of a rich, meaningful relationship is well worth it. After all, the relationships we choose to nurture today could shape the opportunities and experiences we encounter tomorrow.

Key Actions

- **Engage in Meaningful Conversations**: Focus on having deep and meaningful conversations that lay the foundation for strong relationships.
- **Be Consistent in Communication**: Regularly communicate with the people you want to maintain a relationship with, even if it's just through brief check-ins.
- **Add Value to the Relationship**: Consistently contribute something of value to the relationship, whether it's sharing useful resources, offering support, or simply showing genuine interest.
- **Be Mindful of Relationships to Nurture**: Identify and prioritize the conversations and relationships that are worth maintaining and nurturing over time.
- **Sustain Dialogue Over Time**: Keep the conversation going over the long term, even without frequent face-to-face interaction, by staying engaged and adding value.
- **Apply These Behaviors in Professional Contexts**: Use the same approach in professional relationships as in personal ones, maintaining regular communication and adding value to keep the connection strong.

Discussion Questions

1. How do you currently approach maintaining relationships with people you value? Are there any strategies from this section that you could implement to improve your consistency in communication?
2. What are some ways you can add value to a relationship that may not involve face-to-face interaction? How can these actions keep the conversation and connection alive?
3. Think about a relationship in your life that has faded over

time. What steps could you have taken to prevent this, and how might you revive the conversation now?

4. In your professional life, how do you differentiate between relationships worth nurturing and those that aren't? What criteria do you use to make these decisions?

5. Discuss the challenges of maintaining consistent communication in today's busy world. How can leaders overcome these challenges to ensure they are building and sustaining meaningful relationships?

Practice Exercises

1. Daily Connection Check-In

- **Objective**: Build the habit of consistent communication with key individuals in your network.
- **How to Do It**: Set aside 10 minutes each day to reach out to someone in your personal or professional network. This could be a simple text, email, or LinkedIn message to check in, share an interesting article, or offer support. Rotate through your contacts to ensure you're maintaining connections with a variety of people.

2. Value-Add Challenge

- **Objective**: Practice adding value to your relationships consistently.
- **How to Do It**: Choose three people you want to strengthen your relationship with. Over the next month, find one way each week to add value to each of these relationships. This could be through sharing relevant information, offering assistance, or simply providing encouragement. Track your efforts and note any changes in the strength of these connections.

3. Reflect and Reconnect

- **Objective**: Reignite and sustain fading relationships.
- **How to Do It**: Identify three relationships that have faded over time but are worth rekindling. Reflect on why these connections dwindled and what value you can now bring to the table. Reach out with a thoughtful message, acknowledging the lapse in communication, and express a genuine interest in reconnecting. Plan to follow up regularly to rebuild and maintain the relationship.

SHAPE TOMORROW, TODAY

Conversations are more than just exchanges of information—they are opportunities to lay the groundwork for future interactions. Every conversation, whether casual or formal, is a stepping stone that can lead to the next. But for many, the chance to build upon a dialogue is often missed. So, how can you ensure that today's conversation naturally sets the stage for tomorrow's?

The Power of Purposeful Dialogue

Every conversation should serve a purpose beyond the immediate exchange. When engaging in a discussion, it's crucial to think beyond the moment and consider how this conversation can be a bridge to the next. This mindset shifts your approach from simply communicating to strategically building ongoing dialogues.

For example, imagine you're in a meeting with a potential client. The immediate goal might be to understand their needs and offer solutions. But while you're doing this, you can also be thinking about what's next. Maybe you mention a follow-up call to dive deeper into a specific issue, or you suggest a future meeting to review progress. By doing so, you're not just ending the conversation; you're setting up the next one.

Planting Seeds for the Next Interaction

Effective communicators are always planting seeds for future interactions. They introduce topics, ask questions, or propose ideas that naturally lead to the next conversation. This isn't about manipulation; it's about creating continuity and keeping the relationship active.

Consider a scenario where you're catching up with a colleague over coffee. As the conversation winds down, you might say, "I'd love to hear more about your upcoming project—how about we schedule another chat next week to discuss it?" This simple suggestion not only gives the current conversation a purpose but also ensures there's a reason to reconnect soon.

Leaving Conversations Open-Ended

One of the most effective ways to ensure a conversation leads to another is by leaving it open-ended. This doesn't mean being vague; rather, it's about intentionally leaving room for follow-up. When you end a conversation with a question, a pending decision, or an unresolved issue, you create a natural reason to continue the dialogue.

Take, for example, a leader who is discussing a new initiative with their team. Instead of wrapping up the meeting with a summary, they might say, "I'd like to hear your thoughts on this over the next few days—let's regroup next week to finalize our approach." This approach keeps the conversation alive and sets the expectation that it will continue.

The Art of Strategic Follow-Up

Following up isn't just a courtesy; it's a strategic move that solidifies the connection and sets the stage for the next interaction. When you follow up on a conversation, you're showing that you value the relationship and are committed to keeping it going.

Let's say you've just had a productive conversation with a new contact at a networking event. Sending a quick message the next day, referencing something you discussed, and suggesting a time to meet again is a powerful way to keep the momentum going. This simple act of follow-up turns a single conversation into the beginning of an ongoing relationship.

Creating a Continuous Loop

The ultimate goal is to create a continuous loop of conversations, where each interaction naturally leads to the next. This approach requires foresight and intentionality but pays off in the form of stronger, more enduring relationships.

In every conversation, ask yourself: What can I do now to ensure this dialogue continues? Whether it's planting seeds, leaving things open-ended, or making a strategic follow-up, each step is an investment in the future of the relationship.

Key Actions

- **Engage in Purposeful Dialogue**: Approach every conversation with the mindset that it can lead to future interactions. Focus on how the current exchange can serve as a bridge to the next.
- **Plant Seeds for Future Interactions**: Introduce topics, ask questions, or propose ideas that naturally lead to a follow-up conversation.
- **Leave Conversations Open-Ended**: Intentionally leave room for future dialogue by ending the conversation with a question, a pending decision, or an unresolved issue.
- **Practice Strategic Follow-Up**: After a conversation, follow up in a timely manner to solidify the connection and set the stage for the next interaction.
- **Create a Continuous Loop:** Continuously think about how to keep conversations going by building on each interaction, ensuring a seamless flow from one dialogue to the next.

Discussion Questions

1. How can you ensure that your current conversations are purposeful and lead to future interactions? Can you think of a recent conversation where you could have applied this approach?
2. What are some practical ways to plant seeds during a conversation that encourage a follow-up discussion? Can you share an example of when this worked for you?
3. Why is it important to leave conversations open-ended, and how can doing so impact the long-term relationship?
4. How do you typically follow up after a conversation, and how might you improve your follow-up strategy to keep the dialogue going?
5. In what ways can creating a continuous loop of conversations enhance your personal and professional relationships? How can you apply this strategy in your current role?

Practice Exercises

1. Purposeful Conversation Mapping

- **Objective**: To develop the habit of identifying and planning future interactions during conversations.
- **How to Do It**: After each conversation you have, take a few minutes to reflect on the discussion. Write down at least one potential follow-up topic or question that could naturally lead to the next interaction. Practice this with both casual and professional conversations. Over time, you'll start recognizing opportunities to keep the dialogue going while you're still in the moment.

2. Planting Seeds Exercise

- **Objective**: To improve your ability to introduce topics or questions that encourage future conversations.
- **How to Do It**: During your next five conversations, consciously introduce a topic or question that could lead to a follow-up discussion. For example, you might mention an upcoming project or ask for someone's opinion on a future event. Afterward, track which of these seeds resulted in continued dialogue and analyze what made them effective.

3. Strategic Follow-Up Practice

- **Objective**: To enhance your follow-up strategy and ensure conversations continue.
- **How to Do It**: After each significant conversation, commit to sending a follow-up message within 24 hours. In your message, reference something specific from the conversation and propose a future interaction, such as a meeting, call, or even just a check-in. Review your follow-up messages over time to see how often they lead to continued conversations and adjust your approach as needed.

SURPRISE CONGRATULATIONS

Offering congratulations might seem like a small act, but it can have a significant impact, especially when it comes from someone unexpected. As leaders, our words carry weight, and recognizing the achievements of others, even those we don't know well, can create lasting bonds and inspire greatness.

Why Congratulations Matter

Congratulations are more than just a polite gesture; they are a way of showing that we see and value the accomplishments of others. Whether it's a major milestone like a promotion or a personal achievement like learning a new skill, taking the time to acknowledge these moments can make a difference. People are constantly achieving things worthy of recognition, and by congratulating them, we're not just acknowledging their success—we're also reinforcing a culture of appreciation and encouragement.

The Unexpected Impact

There's something special about receiving congratulations from an unexpected source. It's one thing to be acknowledged by someone you know well, but when a compliment or recognition comes from someone you barely know, it can leave a deep impression. This is particularly true in professional settings, where a leader's words can motivate and inspire others far beyond the immediate moment.

Consider the story of Tommy Hutton, a young player in the Dodgers organization. In his first major league game, Tommy had a rough start —he struck out, grounded out, and popped out. As he sat in the dugout, feeling a mix of disappointment and relief, the reporters began to swarm.

But in the midst of the chaos, a legendary figure, Sandy Koufax, made his way through the dugout to find Tommy. Despite never having met Tommy before, and with Tommy not even having his name on his jersey or locker, Koufax congratulated him on his debut. He told Tommy he believed he'd have a wonderful career with the Dodgers.

That simple act of congratulations made a huge impact on Tommy—it was a moment he never forgot, and it fueled his commitment to the Dodgers organization for years to come.

How Leaders Can Make a Difference

As leaders, we have a unique opportunity to make a lasting impact on those around us. Our congratulations carry more significance because people look up to us and value our opinions. A few thoughtful words, a handwritten note, or a brief conversation can make someone's day, and more importantly, it can strengthen our relationship with them.

But it's not just about congratulating those we know well. The real power lies in recognizing the achievements of people we don't know, or don't know well. It's a small act that can create a ripple effect, encouraging others to strive for excellence and fostering a culture of mutual respect and appreciation.

Making Congratulations a Habit

To make congratulations a consistent part of your leadership style, set a simple goal: congratulate someone you don't really know once a week. It doesn't have to be elaborate—a quick note, an email, or a few words in passing can suffice. The key is sincerity. When people feel that your congratulations are genuine, it deepens the connection and reinforces a positive culture within your team or network.

The Lasting Impact

Congratulating others, particularly those outside your immediate circle, is a powerful way to build and strengthen relationships. It shows that you're paying attention, that you value the contributions of everyone around you, and that you're committed to fostering a culture of recognition and encouragement.

So, don't be afraid to reach out and congratulate someone you don't know well. It's a small gesture, but it can have a lasting impact—not just on them, but on your own growth as a leader. By making a habit of recognizing others, you're not just building relationships; you're also building a reputation as someone who values people and their achievements. And that's the kind of leader people remember.

Key Actions

- **Recognizing Achievements Regularly**: Acknowledge both major and minor accomplishments of others, showing that you value their efforts and successes.
- **Offering Congratulations to Unexpected Sources**: Don't limit your recognition to just those you know well; congratulate people you don't know well or at all, as this can have a profound and lasting impact.
- **Leveraging the Influence of Leadership**: As a leader, understand that your congratulations carry significant weight and can inspire and motivate others, so use this influence thoughtfully.
- **Making Congratulations a Habit**: Set a goal to regularly congratulate someone you don't really know, ensuring that this practice becomes a consistent part of your leadership style.
- **Being Sincere in Your Praise**: Ensure that your congratulations are genuine and heartfelt, as sincerity deepens connections and reinforces a positive culture.

Discussion Questions

1. How can regularly congratulating people, even those you don't know well, impact the culture within a team or organization?
2. Why do you think receiving congratulations from an unexpected source, like a leader or someone you don't know well, leaves a lasting impression?
3. What are some practical ways to make congratulating others, especially those outside your immediate circle, a consistent habit in your daily routine?
4. How does the sincerity of congratulations influence the

effectiveness of the gesture? Can you share an example from your experience?

5. As a leader, how can you use your influence to create a culture of recognition and encouragement within your organization?

Practice Exercises

1. Weekly Recognition Journal

- **Objective**: Develop the habit of recognizing and congratulating others regularly, particularly those outside your immediate circle.
- **How to Do It**: At the end of each week, write down at least three accomplishments or positive actions you noticed from colleagues, acquaintances, or even strangers. For each entry, write a brief note or email congratulating the person on their achievement. This practice helps you become more mindful of the achievements of those around you and reinforces the habit of offering sincere congratulations.

2. Random Acts of Recognition

- **Objective**: Improve your ability to offer genuine congratulations to people you don't know well.
- **How to Do It**: Once a week, make it a point to congratulate someone you don't interact with regularly. This could be a colleague from a different department, a service provider, or even someone you follow on social media who has achieved something noteworthy. The goal is to step out of your comfort zone and practice recognizing achievements beyond your immediate circle.

3. Leadership Congratulation Log

- **Objective**: Enhance your awareness of the influence your words have as a leader and practice using that influence positively.

- **How to Do It**: Create a log where you track instances where you've congratulated someone, noting the context, your relationship with the person, and the impact (if any) that the congratulation had. Reflect on these instances weekly to understand how your words as a leader can inspire and motivate others, and to identify opportunities to make your congratulations more impactful.

GRATITUDE IN ENDINGS

Leadership isn't just about making tough decisions and steering the ship—it's also about the small, often overlooked moments that make a big difference. One of these moments is how you end a conversation. Successful leaders understand that how you close a dialogue can have a lasting impact. It's not just about saying goodbye; it's about leaving people feeling appreciated and valued. That's where gratitude comes into play.

Ending on a High Note

Imagine finishing every conversation with a note of appreciation. This might sound simple, but it's incredibly effective. By expressing thanks at the end of a discussion—whether it's for the person's time, their input, or simply their presence—you create a positive closing that lingers. It's like adding an uplifting crescendo to a piece of music. This final note resonates, reinforcing a sense of goodwill and building stronger connections.

Think about it: when someone thanks you at the end of a meeting, you leave with a good feeling. You're more likely to remember that interaction positively, and it makes you want to engage with that person again. It's a small gesture, but it can turn routine exchanges into relationship-building opportunities.

Transforming Apologies into Gratitude

Gratitude doesn't have to be reserved for the end of conversations. It can also be a powerful tool in situations where we typically default to apologies. For instance, instead of saying, "I'm sorry for being late," try saying, "Thank you for your patience." This subtle shift changes the focus from your mistake to the other person's kindness. It's a way of acknowledging their understanding rather than highlighting your own shortcoming.

This practice isn't just about avoiding the word "sorry." It's about creating a culture where people feel recognized and appreciated, even in less-than-ideal circumstances. When leaders replace apologies with gratitude, they set a tone of mutual respect and understanding. It's a simple change, but it can alter the dynamics of a conversation, making it more positive and constructive.

Embracing Disagreements with Thanks

Disagreements are inevitable in any workplace, but how leaders handle them can make all the difference. Instead of becoming defensive or dismissive, successful leaders see disagreements as opportunities for growth. When someone challenges their ideas, they don't shut down; they express gratitude.

Thanking someone for their perspective, especially when it differs from your own, shows that you value diverse viewpoints. It encourages open dialogue and makes people feel safe to speak up. This approach fosters a more collaborative environment where innovation can thrive. After all, when people know their opinions are valued—even if they're not always agreed with—they're more likely to contribute meaningfully to the team.

The Bigger Picture: Why Gratitude Matters

So, why is gratitude so essential for leaders? It's more than just good manners; it's a cornerstone of emotional intelligence. Emotional intelligence is the ability to recognize and manage your own emotions, as well as the emotions of others. By expressing gratitude, leaders show that they're attuned to the feelings and needs of their team. They demonstrate that they understand the impact of their words and actions.

Gratitude also plays a crucial role in building a positive organizational culture. When people feel appreciated, they're more engaged and motivated. They're more likely to go the extra mile, not because they have to, but because they want to. This sense of being valued leads to higher job satisfaction and lower turnover rates. In short, a little gratitude goes a long way in creating a thriving workplace.

Cultivating a Culture of Gratitude

Gratitude isn't just a leadership tactic; it's a mindset. Leaders who consistently express appreciation create an environment where everyone feels seen and valued. This doesn't happen overnight, but with conscious effort, it can become a natural part of your leadership style.

Start by making gratitude a habit. Whether you're ending a conversation, addressing a mistake, or navigating a disagreement, look for opportunities to express thanks. Over time, you'll find that these small acts of appreciation add up, transforming not just your relationships, but your entire organization.

Remember, gratitude is more than a polite gesture—it's a powerful tool that can enhance your leadership and strengthen your team. By ending conversations on a positive note, replacing apologies with thanks, and embracing disagreements with appreciation, you can build a more collaborative, respectful, and productive workplace. And in the process, you'll discover that gratitude doesn't just begin with endings—it begins with you.

Key Actions

- **Ending Conversations with Gratitude**: Successful leaders make it a habit to end every conversation on a positive note by expressing gratitude and appreciation.
- **Replacing Apologies with Gratitude**: Instead of defaulting to apologies, leaders shift the focus by expressing thanks, such as saying "Thank you for your patience" instead of "I'm sorry for being late."
- **Thanking Others During Disagreements**: When faced with disagreements, leaders express gratitude for differing perspectives, valuing diverse viewpoints and fostering open dialogue.
- **Cultivating a Habit of Gratitude**: Leaders consistently look for opportunities to express appreciation in various situations, making gratitude a natural part of their leadership style.

- **Fostering a Culture of Appreciation**: By regularly showing gratitude, leaders create a work environment where everyone feels valued, leading to higher engagement, motivation, and job satisfaction.

Discussion Questions

1. How can ending conversations with a note of gratitude impact the overall morale and relationships within a team?
2. In what ways can replacing apologies with expressions of gratitude change the dynamics of workplace interactions?
3. How does thanking others for their differing perspectives during disagreements contribute to a more collaborative work environment?
4. What are some practical strategies leaders can use to consistently cultivate a habit of gratitude in their daily interactions?
5. How can fostering a culture of appreciation through regular expressions of gratitude lead to higher engagement and motivation among team members?

Practice Exercises

1. Gratitude Journaling

- **Objective**: To develop the habit of expressing gratitude consistently.
- **How to Do It**: At the end of each day, take five minutes to reflect on your interactions with others. Write down three specific instances where you expressed gratitude or where you could have expressed gratitude. Focus on how you ended conversations, handled disagreements, or replaced apologies with thanks. Over time, this exercise will help you naturally incorporate gratitude into your daily interactions.

2. Transforming Apologies into Thanks

- **Objective**: To practice shifting from apologizing to expressing gratitude.
- **How to Do It**: Over the next week, consciously replace apologies with expressions of gratitude in your conversations. For example, if you're late to a meeting, instead of saying, "I'm sorry I'm late," say, "Thank you for waiting." Keep a log of these instances, noting how the shift in language affected the interaction and the other person's response. Review the log at the end of the week to reflect on the impact.

3. Thanking During Disagreements

- **Objective**: To become comfortable with expressing gratitude during disagreements.
- **How to Do It**: During meetings or discussions where disagreements arise, practice acknowledging and thanking others for their differing viewpoints. For instance, say, "Thank you for bringing that perspective; it helps me see things from a different angle." After each meeting, take a few minutes to reflect on how this approach influenced the tone of the discussion and whether it led to a more constructive outcome.

DON'T OVERSTEP

Respecting boundaries and authority is vital for fostering healthy, productive relationships with our peers. This concept, often referred to as the "Venturi rule," highlights the importance of acknowledging and honoring each other's space, whether it's professional or personal. It's about knowing when to defer to others, understanding the weight of their responsibilities, and never doing anything that might disrespect their dignity or undermine their position.

Boundaries and Respect

In both professional and personal settings, everyone has their own territory—clients, projects, family, or social circles. These are spaces where they hold authority, and where they need to be seen and respected by those around them. When you step into someone else's territory, your role is to support them, not overshadow them. This is where respect and deference become crucial.

Imagine a colleague who manages a critical project. If you step into their space, your actions should reinforce their authority, not challenge it. Even if you have a suggestion or criticism, how you communicate it matters. You should never make them look bad in front of their team or clients. Instead, find ways to uplift them, ensuring their leadership remains intact.

Honoring Authority and Space

The Venturi rule extends beyond just professional interactions. It's equally important in personal relationships. Disrespecting someone in their own space—be it their home, social circle, or family dynamic— can lead to conflict and strained relationships. This is particularly true in close-knit environments where roles and hierarchies are more nuanced.

Let's take a family scenario: Imagine visiting a sibling who is the primary caretaker for elderly parents. While there, your words and actions should support their role, not undermine it. Criticizing them in front of the parents or making decisions on their behalf without consultation could create tension and erode trust. Respect their territory as the caretaker and collaborate in a way that reinforces their authority.

Building Respect and Trust

To truly respect someone's territory, you need to go beyond just avoiding conflict. It's about actively listening, understanding their perspective, and supporting their goals. When in someone else's space, it's your responsibility to help them succeed. That might mean offering assistance, providing encouragement, or simply staying out of their way when appropriate.

One key behavior to adopt is treating someone as if they are the king or queen of their domain when you are in their territory. This doesn't mean you can't be candid or offer feedback, but it does mean timing and delivery are everything. Outside of their space, you can engage in honest discussions, but inside, your focus should be on making them shine.

The Venturi rule is more than just a guideline; it's a strategy for creating an environment of mutual respect and trust. By recognizing and honoring each other's boundaries, you build a foundation for strong, collaborative relationships. This respect fosters an atmosphere where everyone can thrive, leading to more effective teamwork and a more harmonious working environment.

By holding the Venturi rule sacrosanct and respecting the territories of others, you create a culture of mutual respect. This respect isn't just about being polite; it's about recognizing the value of boundaries and using them to build stronger, more trusting relationships with your peers. Whether in the boardroom or the living room, respecting territory is the key to effective collaboration and lasting success.

Key Actions

- **Recognize Territory**: Understand that everyone has areas where they hold authority, whether it's at work, in social settings, or at home. Respect these spaces by acknowledging their importance and deferring to those who manage them.

- **Support, Don't Overshadow**: When in someone else's space, your role is to support, not overshadow. Let them lead and focus on actions that reinforce their authority and credibility.
- **Make Them Shine**: Treat others as if they are the rulers of their domain. Your presence in their territory should make them look good, not small. Offer help, but ensure it elevates them in the eyes of their team, clients, or family.
- **Respect First, Feedback Later**: Save candid feedback for a time when it won't undermine their authority. Respect the space they operate in and provide your insights when it won't damage their standing.
- **Build Trust Through Respect:** Consistently respecting others' boundaries builds trust, which is the cornerstone of any strong relationship. Over time, this trust enables deeper collaboration and more successful outcomes.

Discussion Questions

1. What are some common challenges you've faced when trying to respect others' boundaries and authority in professional or personal settings? How did you address these challenges?
2. Can you share an example of a time when someone respected or disrespected your territory? How did it impact your relationship with that person?
3. In what ways can leaders foster a culture where the Venturi rule is respected and upheld by everyone on the team?
4. How can you balance being honest and candid with providing support and deference when you're in someone else's territory? Where is the line between offering helpful feedback and overstepping boundaries?
5. What strategies can you use to ensure that your actions consistently support and reinforce others' authority when you're in their domain? How can you apply these strategies in your current role or relationships?

Practice Exercises

1. Territory Mapping

- **Objective**: Identify and understand the territories of your peers, colleagues, or family members.
- **How to Do It**: Make a list of the key people you interact with regularly. For each person, identify the areas where they hold authority or responsibility (e.g., specific projects, family roles, social circles). Reflect on your past interactions with these individuals. Consider if there were moments when you might have unintentionally stepped into their territory without proper respect. Write down ways you can better support them in their domain going forward, ensuring you respect their boundaries and reinforce their authority.

2. Role Reversal Practice

- **Objective**: Develop empathy and better understand how it feels to have your territory respected or disrespected.
- **How to Do It**: Partner with a colleague, friend, or family member for this exercise. Choose a scenario where you typically hold authority or responsibility (e.g., leading a meeting, organizing a family event). Switch roles with your partner, allowing them to take the lead while you take on a supporting role. During the exercise, consciously practice deference, offering support without overshadowing their leadership. Afterward, discuss how each of you felt in your respective roles, focusing on moments when you felt respected or disrespected. Use this feedback to refine how you approach others' territories in the future.

3. Respectful Feedback Simulation

- **Objective**: Practice delivering feedback in a way that respects others' territory and authority.

- **How to Do It**: Choose a recent situation where you needed to give feedback to someone in their domain. Recreate the scenario in your mind or with a partner, focusing on how you might deliver the feedback while still honoring their authority. Practice using specific language that acknowledges their role and contributions, offering suggestions or critiques in a way that supports rather than undermines. If possible, role-play with a trusted colleague or mentor who can give you feedback on how well you respected the other person's territory during the exercise. Reflect on the exercise and adjust your approach as needed, ensuring that your feedback in real-life situations is both constructive and respectful.

QUICK TRANSITIONS MATTER

Leadership is a constant balancing act. From managing a team meeting one minute to dealing with a crisis the next, the ability to quickly and smoothly transition between different situations and conversations is a critical skill. The best leaders don't just move from task to task; they shift with purpose, leaving behind any baggage and fully immersing themselves in what's in front of them.

The Power of Being Present

One of the most important aspects of making these quick transitions is the ability to be fully present in each moment. Imagine a day filled with back-to-back meetings, some of which might be challenging or emotionally charged. If you carry the frustration or stress from one conversation into the next, it's likely to spill over, affecting your performance and the dynamic of the next interaction.

Great leaders recognize this and practice a kind of mental reset between engagements. By focusing on the present, they're able to leave behind what just happened and bring their full attention and energy to the task or person at hand. This not only improves their effectiveness but also signals respect and attentiveness to those they're interacting with, which strengthens relationships.

Mindfulness: Your Transition Tool

Mindfulness is the cornerstone of making these transitions smooth and effective. It's about being fully aware and engaged in the present moment, rather than being distracted by what's already happened or what's coming next. This doesn't require hours of meditation; simple, focused breathing exercises or even taking a moment to clear your thoughts before entering a new situation can make all the difference.

For instance, before walking into a meeting, take a deep breath, acknowledge any lingering emotions from the previous interaction, and then consciously let them go. This small act can clear your mental slate and help you approach the new conversation with a fresh perspective.

Adapting to Different Roles

Leaders wear many hats. One moment you're guiding your team; the next, you're a negotiator, a mentor, or even a spouse or parent. Each role requires a different mindset and approach. The ability to transition quickly and effectively between these roles is what sets successful leaders apart.

Think of each role as a different game, each with its own rules and strategies. Being mindful of these shifts and making a conscious effort to adapt your approach can help you excel in each role, rather than letting one bleed into another, causing confusion or mixed signals.

The Importance of Fast Transitions

Quick transitions aren't just about efficiency; they're about maintaining the quality of your interactions. When you linger too long in the emotions or mindset of a previous conversation, you risk bringing negativity or distraction into the next. This can affect not only your mood but also the tone of the new interaction, potentially undermining the relationship or the outcome you're aiming for.

To avoid this, it's crucial to draw sharp lines between engagements. A useful strategy is to incorporate transitional activities into your routine. These can be as simple as a walk around the office, a trip to grab a coffee, or even a few moments of quiet reflection. Use this time to mentally close the chapter on the previous conversation, reset your focus, and set an intention for the next one.

Learning from Experience: The Case of Steve Young

Steve Young, the legendary football player and coach, offers a powerful example of the impact of quick transitions. On the field, Young learned that dwelling on the last play—whether it was a success or a failure—was counterproductive. The key to his success was his ability to move on immediately and focus on the next play with a clear mind. This lesson translated seamlessly into his post-playing career, where the ability to transition quickly between different roles and responsibilities became one of his strengths.

Young's story underscores a vital point: quick transitions are not just about moving on; they're about being ready for what's next, fully engaged and unburdened by what just happened.

Making Quick Transitions Part of Your Leadership Toolkit

As a leader, your ability to transition smoothly and quickly between different situations and conversations can be the difference between thriving and just surviving. It's a skill that can be honed with practice, mindfulness, and intentionality.

Start by incorporating simple mindfulness techniques into your day. Use transitional activities to clear your mind and refocus your energy. Remember, each interaction is a fresh start, an opportunity to fully engage and connect with the people around you. By mastering the art of quick transitions, you'll not only become a more effective leader but also build stronger, more productive relationships with your peers, team, and everyone you interact with.

In leadership, quick transitions aren't just about moving from one task to another—they're about doing so with purpose, presence, and a clear mind. By letting go of past interactions and focusing on the present moment, you can bring your best self to each new situation, strengthening relationships and driving success.

Key Actions

- **Being Fully Present**: Focus on the present moment, leaving behind any baggage from previous interactions to engage fully in the current conversation or task.
- **Practicing Mindfulness**: Use mindfulness techniques, such as deep breathing or brief moments of reflection, to reset your mind before transitioning into a new situation.
- **Adapting to Different Roles**: Recognize the different roles you play throughout the day and consciously adjust your approach to fit each role effectively.
- **Drawing Sharp Lines Between Engagements**: Incorporate transitional activities, like a quick walk or a coffee break, to

mentally close one chapter and prepare for the next, ensuring you don't carry over negative emotions or distractions.

- **Setting Intentions for Each New Interaction:** Before entering a new conversation or meeting, take a moment to set a clear intention for what you want to achieve, helping you stay focused and effective.

Discussion Questions

1. How do you currently manage transitions between different tasks or conversations during your day, and what impact do you think it has on your effectiveness as a leader?
2. What role does mindfulness play in your daily routine, and how could incorporating simple mindfulness techniques improve your ability to stay present and focused during transitions?
3. Can you think of a time when carrying over emotions from one interaction negatively impacted another? How could you have handled the transition more effectively?
4. In what ways do you consciously adapt your behavior or mindset when shifting between different roles, such as leader, mentor, or family member? How does this adaptability influence your relationships?
5. What transitional activities could you introduce into your routine to help you mentally reset and set clear intentions for each new interaction or task?

Practice Exercises

1. Mindful Transition Practice

- **Objective**: Improve your ability to reset and refocus between tasks or conversations.
- **How to Do It**: Before moving from one meeting or task to the next, take 1-2 minutes to practice mindful breathing. Sit or stand still, close your eyes, and take deep breaths, focusing solely on the sensation of breathing. As you breathe in,

imagine drawing in calm and focus; as you breathe out, release any tension or lingering thoughts from the previous interaction. This will help you clear your mind and prepare for the next situation with a fresh perspective.

2. Role-Switching Reflection

- **Objective**: Enhance your ability to adapt to different roles throughout the day.
- **How to Do It**: At the end of each day, reflect on the different roles you played—such as leader, mentor, negotiator, or family member. For each role, write down one thing you did well and one area where you could improve. Consider how you adapted (or could have adapted) your approach to fit each role better. Over time, this exercise will help you become more aware of how to transition smoothly between different roles and improve your effectiveness in each.

3. Intentional Transition Planning

- **Objective**: Develop the habit of setting clear intentions for each new interaction.
- **How to Do It**: Before each meeting or conversation, take 30 seconds to identify the main objective you want to achieve. Ask yourself: What's the purpose of this interaction? What outcome am I aiming for? How can I best contribute to this discussion? Write down a brief note or mentally affirm your intention. This practice helps you stay focused and ensures that each interaction is purposeful, allowing for smoother transitions and more effective engagements.

DISAGREEING WITHOUT BEING DISAGREEABLE

Disagreeing isn't the problem; it's how we disagree that can make or break relationships, teams, and even entire organizations. As a leader, mastering the art of disagreeing agreeably is crucial. This skill allows you to voice your opinions, challenge ideas, and engage in constructive debate without alienating others or diminishing their perspectives. It's about balancing assertiveness with respect, and it's a key ingredient in building a culture of trust and collaboration.

The Power of Validation

The best leaders don't shy away from disagreement; they lean into it with a mindset of mutual respect. A critical first step in disagreeing agreeably is validating the other person's viewpoint. This doesn't mean you have to agree with them, but it does mean acknowledging their right to hold their opinion. A simple way to do this is by making them feel heard and understood. For instance, you might say, "I can see why you feel that way" or "Your perspective makes sense given your experience."

This kind of validation sets the stage for a more productive conversation. It shows that you respect the other person's right to their opinion, even if you're about to offer a different viewpoint. It's disarming because it takes the defensive edge off the conversation. Instead of gearing up for a confrontation, both parties can engage in a dialogue.

Disagree, But With Grace

Once you've validated the other person's perspective, you can introduce your differing view. The key here is to do it with grace and tact. Instead of saying, "You're wrong," try framing your disagreement in a way that shows you're open to a discussion rather than a debate. For example, "I used to see it that way too, but over time, I've come to a different conclusion."

This approach does two things: it acknowledges that you've considered the other person's viewpoint, and it shows that your opinion isn't fixed.

It opens the door for a conversation where both parties can explore their ideas without feeling threatened.

Show Appreciation

Another powerful tool in disagreeing agreeably is expressing appreciation. Acknowledge the other person's thoughtfulness, the effort they put into their argument, or the way they articulated their points. Even if you don't agree with the content, you can still appreciate the process. This might sound like, "I really appreciate the careful thought you put into this" or "You've made some strong points, and I value your input."

This not only softens the disagreement but also reinforces that the relationship is more important than any single point of contention. It's a subtle reminder that, while you may disagree on a specific issue, you're on the same team.

Be Sincere, Not Passive-Aggressive

It's essential to be genuine in your approach. Disagreeing agreeably isn't about being passive-aggressive or insincere. It's not about sugarcoating your opinions or pretending to agree when you don't. It's about being honest in a way that maintains the dignity and respect of both parties.

To do this effectively, you need to be in tune with the other person's feelings and needs. Pay attention to their reactions and adjust your approach if necessary. If you sense that they're becoming defensive, try to steer the conversation back to common ground. The goal is to disagree in a way that strengthens the relationship, not weakens it.

Fostering a Culture of Respect

When leaders model the behavior of disagreeing agreeably, they set the tone for the entire organization. It encourages open communication and collaboration, even when opinions differ. This is especially vital in today's complex and fast-paced business environment, where the ability to work effectively with others is more critical than ever.

For leaders with deep expertise in a particular area, this can be challenging. It's easy to fall into the trap of believing that your experience and knowledge mean your opinion is the only valid one. But effective leadership isn't about being the smartest person in the room; it's about creating an environment where all voices are heard, and all perspectives are considered.

The Bottom Line

Disagreeing agreeably is more than just a nicety; it's a leadership necessity. It's about creating a culture where people feel respected, even when they disagree. By mastering this skill, leaders can foster an environment of trust and collaboration, leading to better decisions and stronger relationships.

In the end, it's not about winning the argument; it's about finding the best path forward—together. And that's what true leadership is all about.

Key Actions

1. **Validate the Other Person's Viewpoint**: Acknowledge the other person's right to hold their opinion. Make them feel heard and understood before introducing your differing view.
2. **Disagree with Grace:** Frame your disagreement in a way that shows openness to discussion rather than confrontation. Use phrases that acknowledge the other person's perspective while introducing your own.
3. **Express Appreciation**: Acknowledge the other person's effort, thoughtfulness, or the way they articulated their points, even if you disagree with the content.
4. **Be Sincere, Not Passive-Aggressive**: Be genuine in your approach; avoid being passive-aggressive or insincere. Stay in tune with the other person's feelings and adjust your approach if necessary.
5. **Foster a Culture of Respect**: Model the behavior of disagreeing agreeably to set the tone for open communication and collaboration within the organization. Encourage a culture where all voices are heard, and all perspectives are considered.

Discussion Questions

1. How can leaders effectively validate someone's opinion without compromising their own viewpoint?
2. In what ways does disagreeing with grace impact the dynamics of a team or organization?
3. How can expressing appreciation during a disagreement change the tone of the conversation?
4. Why is sincerity important when disagreeing agreeably, and how can leaders ensure they are being genuine in their approach?
5. How can fostering a culture of respect and open communication improve decision-making and collaboration within an organization?

Practice Exercises

1. Perspective-Taking Dialogue

- **Objective**: To improve your ability to validate others' viewpoints and disagree gracefully.
- **How to Do It**: Find a partner and choose a topic where you have differing opinions. Spend a few minutes explaining your perspective while your partner listens. Then, switch roles. After both perspectives have been shared, practice responding with validation, such as acknowledging the other person's right to their opinion, before introducing your own differing view. Focus on using phrases that validate and respect the other person's perspective.

2. Appreciation Statements Practice

- **Objective**: To develop the habit of expressing appreciation during disagreements.
- **How to Do It**: Reflect on recent disagreements or discussions where differing opinions were shared. Write down statements that could express appreciation for the other person's effort or

thoughtfulness. For example, "I appreciate the careful thought you put into this." Practice incorporating these statements into your daily interactions, especially during disagreements, to create a habit of respectful acknowledgment.

3. Active Listening and Sincerity Drill

- **Objective**: To enhance your ability to listen actively and respond sincerely during disagreements.
- **How to Do It**: Engage in a conversation where a disagreement is likely to arise. Focus on actively listening to the other person without interrupting or planning your response. After they've finished speaking, summarize what you've heard to ensure understanding, then respond with a sincere and respectful disagreement if necessary. Pay attention to the other person's reactions and adjust your tone and approach to maintain a constructive and respectful dialogue.

VALUES OVER INCIDENTS

Confrontation is an inevitable part of any relationship, whether personal or professional. It's that moment when something feels off, when someone crosses a line, and you know it needs to be addressed. But here's the thing: confrontation isn't just about calling out a specific incident. It's about the deeper values and standards that the incident represents.

Let's break this down.

The True Purpose of Confrontation

Confrontation often gets a bad rap. People see it as negative, something to avoid unless absolutely necessary. But in reality, it's a critical tool for maintaining the integrity of any relationship. When someone believes that a rule, standard, or value has been violated, confrontation is the mechanism to address it.

Imagine a scenario where someone breaks a confidence by sharing something that was told to them in private. Sure, the act of sharing is the incident. But the real issue isn't just that they blabbed—it's that they violated a core value of trust. That's where the focus should be.

The Difference Between Disagreement and Confrontation

It's easy to confuse confrontation with disagreement, but they're not the same thing. Disagreements are a normal, healthy part of any relationship. They're about differences of opinion, which can often be resolved through discussion, negotiation, and compromise.

Confrontation, on the other hand, is more serious. It's not about differing views; it's about a specific behavior that goes against the agreed-upon values of the relationship. It's your way of saying, "This isn't just a difference of opinion—this is a breach of what we stand for."

The Emotional Response to Confrontation

Nobody likes being confronted. It triggers a defensive response, a gut reaction to protect oneself from criticism. This often leads to arguments, denials, or even counter-confrontations. It's human nature to want to deflect responsibility or avoid accountability when put on the spot.

But here's the kicker: those reactions don't solve the problem. They just bury it, letting it fester and potentially causing even more damage down the line. Effective leaders understand this and approach confrontation differently.

Confronting Values, Not Just Behavior

Strong leaders know that when you confront someone, it shouldn't just be about the incident at hand. It should be about the underlying values that the incident threatens. By focusing on values, you're not just addressing a one-time mistake—you're reinforcing the principles that guide the entire relationship.

Let's say an employee shows up to a client meeting unprepared. Sure, you could chew them out for not doing their homework. But what if, instead, you framed the conversation around the value of prepared-ness? You might ask questions like, "What do we owe our clients in terms of preparation? How does this align with our commitment to excellence?" This shifts the focus from the mistake to the bigger picture —what you stand for as a team.

Why Confrontation Matters

Confrontation isn't about blame or making someone feel bad. It's about addressing a problem head-on, finding a solution, and moving forward with a stronger, more resilient relationship. It's about holding people accountable not just for their actions, but for the values those actions represent.

The next time you find yourself needing to confront someone, remember this: it's not just about what they did—it's about what their actions say about your shared values. Use the moment as an opportu-nity for growth, for reinforcing what really matters in your relationship or organization.

By shifting the focus from incidents to values, you turn confrontation from a negative experience into a positive, constructive one. It's not just about fixing what's broken—it's about building something better together.

Key Actions

- **Addressing Confrontation as a Necessary Part of Relationships**: Recognizing that confrontation is essential in maintaining the integrity of personal and professional relationships.
- **Focusing on Values Over Incidents**: Confronting not just the specific behavior or action, but the underlying values and standards that the incident represents.
- **Differentiating Between Disagreement and Confrontation**: Understanding that disagreement is about differing opinions, while confrontation addresses a breach of agreed-upon values.
- **Managing Emotional Responses to Confrontation**: Acknowledging that defensiveness is a natural reaction to confrontation, but it doesn't solve the problem.
- **Using Confrontation to Reinforce Values**: Framing confrontations around the values that guide the relationship, rather than just the specific incident.
- **Viewing Confrontation as an Opportunity for Growth**: Using confrontation not to assign blame but to strengthen relationships by addressing and reinforcing shared values.

Discussion Questions

1. Why is it important to focus on underlying values rather than just specific incidents during a confrontation?
2. How can leaders effectively manage the natural defensive reactions that people have during confrontations?
3. In what ways can reframing a confrontation around shared values lead to better outcomes for both parties involved?
4. How can distinguishing between disagreement and confrontation help in maintaining healthier relationships?

5. What strategies can be used to ensure that confrontations become opportunities for growth rather than moments of blame or criticism?

Practice Exercises

1. Values-Based Reflection

- **Objective**: To develop the ability to identify and articulate the values underlying specific behaviors.
- **How to Do It**: Reflect on a recent conflict or confrontation you've experienced, either personal or professional. Write down the specific incident, and then list the values or standards that were challenged by this behavior. Consider how you could have addressed the situation by focusing on these values rather than just the incident itself.

2. Role-Playing Confrontations

- **Objective**: To practice managing emotional responses and focusing on values during confrontations.
- **How to Do It**: Partner with a colleague or friend and take turns role-playing a confrontation scenario. One person plays the role of the leader, and the other plays the role of the person being confronted. The leader should practice addressing not only the specific behavior but also discussing the values that were compromised. Afterward, switch roles and provide feedback to each other on how well the values were addressed and how the emotional responses were managed.

3. Crafting Value-Centric Conversations

- **Objective**: To improve your ability to frame conversations around shared values rather than focusing solely on incidents.
- **How to Do It**: Think of a current or upcoming situation where you anticipate the need for confrontation. Draft a

conversation outline where you lead with the values that are important to your relationship or organization. Plan how you will bring these values into the discussion to address the specific behavior or incident. Practice this conversation in your mind or with a peer before the actual confrontation takes place.

CHAPTER 7
LEAD CHANGE, DON'T JUST MANAGE IT

Change is inevitable, both in life and in business. It's a journey from the known to the unknown, and that can be unsettling. When organizations undergo change, it often stirs up feelings of fear, discomfort, and even resistance—especially among those who have experienced change before and found it challenging.

Change management has been a formal discipline for decades, yet it still faces pushback. Part of the problem lies in the language we use. Words like "transformation" can carry heavy connotations, often misunderstood or viewed with suspicion. The way we talk about change matters. Clear, direct communication about the reasons for change and its goals is crucial to making the transition smoother.

The Reality of Change

Change management isn't just about rolling out new systems or processes. It's about people. Successful change management requires careful planning and the involvement of everyone affected—leaders, front-line employees, customers, and other key stakeholders. A clear vision for the change must be established and communicated in a way that resonates with everyone involved.

Building support for change is essential, and that starts with effective communication. People need to understand not just the what, but the why behind the change. Addressing concerns and objections head-on is part of this process. Resistance is natural, but it can be mitigated by listening to and understanding the perspectives of those who are hesitant. Adjusting the change plan based on feedback isn't a sign of weakness; it's a strategic move that can increase buy-in and ultimately, the success of the initiative.

The Role of Leadership

Leadership is the linchpin of successful change management. Leaders must not only drive the change but embody it. They need to model the behaviors they want to see throughout the organization. This goes beyond just talking the talk—leaders must walk the walk. Transparency, openness to feedback, and a willingness to take risks are all part of this.

One common pitfall for leaders is the use of jargon like "change" or "transformation." These words can trigger resistance because they're often associated with disruption and uncertainty. Instead, focus on the specific outcomes and improvements the change will bring. Frame the conversation around progress and growth rather than just change for its own sake.

Building the Skills to Adapt

For change to take root, people need the right tools. This means investing in training and development programs that build the necessary skills and capabilities within the organization. But it's not just about formal training—creating a culture of continuous learning and adaptation is key. Employees need to feel supported as they navigate the changes, with opportunities to learn and grow along the way.

The book *Who Moved My Cheese?* became a popular metaphor for adapting to change, highlighting how flexibility and a positive mindset can help individuals and teams thrive during transitions. While it's a bit of a cliché, the core message still holds true: adaptability is critical to long-term success.

Making Change Sustainable

One of the biggest challenges in change management is ensuring that changes stick. It's one thing to implement a change, but quite another to make sure it endures. Sustainability requires ongoing effort—monitoring, evaluation, and a readiness to make adjustments as circumstances evolve. Change isn't a one-and-done event; it's a continuous process.

This means creating a culture that not only accepts change but also expects it. By fostering an environment of ongoing learning and adaptation, organizations can better weather the inevitable storms of change. The only constant in life and business is change itself, and those who learn to navigate it effectively will position themselves for success in a rapidly evolving world.

Embrace the Inevitable

Navigating change is never easy, but it is necessary. Organizations that proactively approach change—by involving all stakeholders, communicating effectively, demonstrating strong leadership, and building the right skills—will be better equipped to succeed. Remember, the only thing that doesn't change is the need to change. By embracing this reality, you can turn the challenge of change into an opportunity for growth.

REPETITION OVER WORDS

Change is inevitable in business. Whether it's adapting to new technology, adopting a fresh strategy, or rethinking processes, organizations constantly face the need to evolve. But even when change is clearly necessary, one of the biggest obstacles in its path is the power of existing norms within an organization. These norms—deeply ingrained patterns of behavior—are the backbone of a strong culture, but they can also be the chains that hold progress back.

Norms don't just exist; they persist. They carry on even when new people join the organization or when leadership changes hands. The way things have "always been done" can become a powerful deterrent to innovation and adaptation. But how do you break free from the hold of old norms? The answer lies not in words, but in actions—specifically, in the power of repetition.

Repetition Over Rhetoric

Talking about change is easy. Leaders can advocate, preach, and promote new ideas until they're blue in the face, but words alone rarely shift behavior. That's because people are naturally skeptical of change. If they feel like they're being sold something, their guard goes up. They start looking for flaws, questioning motives, and generally resisting the very thing they're being asked to embrace.

So, how do you overcome this resistance? You show them, over and over again, what the new way looks like. Repetition is the real change-maker. When people see the same behavior modeled consistently, it starts to sink in. It becomes familiar, and eventually, it becomes the new norm.

The Magic of Ten

There's something almost magical about the number ten when it comes to forming new habits. Research suggests that if you do something ten times in a row, you begin to establish a new pattern in your mind. It's as if your brain needs those ten repetitions to separate from the old way of doing things and accept the new behavior as the default.

This means that to effectively create new norms, you need to build routines that allow for repetition. Training sessions, regular reinforcement, and rewards for sticking to the new behavior all contribute to this process. The more opportunities people have to practice the new behavior, the more likely it is to stick.

The Role of a Champion

Every successful change initiative needs a champion—someone who believes in the new way and is committed to making it happen. This person doesn't just talk about change; they embody it. They're the ones who remind the organization of its commitment to the new norms, who encourage others to keep practicing until the new behavior becomes second nature.

The champion plays a crucial role in ensuring that the new norm is repeated enough times to take root. They're the ones who keep the momentum going, who don't let people slide back into old habits when the going gets tough.

Patience and Persistence

Change doesn't happen overnight. Even with a strong champion and plenty of repetition, people will need time to adjust. It's essential to be patient during this transition. The best leaders understand that the hold of old norms is strong, and they approach the process with persistence and support. They know that if they keep at it, the new behavior will eventually replace the old.

The Key to Lasting Change

In the end, repetition is the key to forming new norms. By consistently enforcing the new behavior, it becomes the new standard, and over time, people adjust without even realizing it. Establishing routines, providing reinforcement, and having a champion for the change all contribute to the repetition needed to create lasting norms.

Leaders who understand the power of norms and the role of repetition in changing them are the ones who successfully navigate their organizations through periods of change. They don't just talk about new ways of doing things—they show them, again and again, until those new ways become the norm. And in doing so, they ensure that their organizations are not just keeping up with change but leading it.

Key Actions

- **Modeling New Behaviors Consistently**: Demonstrating the desired behavior repeatedly to help it become the new norm.
- **Building Routines for Repetition**: Creating opportunities for people to practice new behaviors regularly, through training sessions, reinforcement, and rewards.
- **Championing the Change**: Having a dedicated individual who embodies the change and reminds others to commit to the new norms.
- **Patience and Persistence**: Understanding that change takes time and consistently supporting the transition to new behaviors without rushing the process.
- **Using Repetition as a Tool:** Recognizing that repeated actions, especially in sets of ten, help to establish new habits and norms within the organization.

Discussion Questions

1. How can leaders effectively model new behaviors in a way that encourages the rest of the organization to follow suit?
2. What specific routines or practices could be implemented in your organization to ensure that new behaviors are consistently repeated?
3. Why do you think repetition, particularly around the "magic number ten," is so critical in forming new norms? Have you seen this play out in your own experiences?
4. In what ways can a 'champion for change' influence the success of a new initiative within an organization? Can you

identify someone in your organization who could take on this role?

5. What strategies can leaders use to maintain patience and persistence when trying to establish new norms, especially when faced with resistance or slow progress?

Practice Exercises

1. Behavior Modeling Challenge

- **Objective**: Improve your ability to model new behaviors consistently.
- **How to Do It**: Choose one new behavior you want to establish within your team. For the next ten days, intentionally model this behavior in every interaction, meeting, and communication. Track how often you demonstrate this behavior and note any changes in how others respond. Reflect on how your consistent actions influence your team's adoption of the new behavior.

2. Repetition Routine Builder

- **Objective**: Develop routines that reinforce new behaviors.
- **How to Do It**: Identify a specific change or new norm you want to establish in your organization. Design a routine that incorporates this change into daily or weekly activities. For example, if the goal is to improve meeting efficiency, create a new agenda format and practice it in every meeting for the next ten sessions. Track adherence and gather feedback to refine the routine.

3. Champion Role Play

- **Objective**: Enhance your ability to champion change within your organization.
- **How to Do It**: Select a colleague or team member to role-play with you. Take turns being the "champion" for a

hypothetical change initiative. As the champion, practice motivating and reminding your partner of the new behavior, ensuring it is repeated consistently. Afterward, discuss the effectiveness of your approach and identify areas for improvement. Repeat this exercise with different scenarios to build versatility in championing various types of change.

ACTION OVER ATTITUDE

Conventional wisdom has long held that to inspire meaningful change, you must first change someone's beliefs. The idea is that if you want to change behavior, you must first win over the mind. But what if this traditional model has it backward? What if action, not belief, is the true catalyst for change?

Recent research and real-world examples suggest that behavior, not belief, should come first. When people experience the positive effects of a new behavior, their attitudes and beliefs naturally begin to shift. In other words, by acting first, you can shape attitudes and foster lasting change.

Experience Drives Belief

One of the key arguments for prioritizing behavior is the simple power of experience. When someone tries a new action and sees the benefits firsthand, it becomes easier to change their beliefs about that action.

Take, for example, a person who's been advised to reduce their salt intake for health reasons. If you start by asking them to track their salt intake and make small adjustments, they might not be fully convinced at first. But as they begin to experience lower blood pressure and better health, their attitude toward a low-salt diet starts to shift. The benefits they observe become the proof that fuels their belief in the change.

This experience-driven belief is often more potent than a belief that's been argued into existence. Seeing is believing, as the saying goes, and by taking action first, people see the results for themselves.

Making Change Manageable

Another advantage of the behavior-first approach is that it's far less intimidating than trying to change someone's beliefs from the get-go. Changing a belief system is no small feat, especially when those beliefs are deeply ingrained. It can feel overwhelming, even insurmountable.

But behavior? That's a different story. Small actions are far less daunting and easier to commit to. By asking someone to take small, manageable steps—like cutting back on salt or practicing daily mindfulness—you make the process of change more approachable. These small actions, repeated consistently, can lead to big shifts over time.

Small Actions, Big Impact

So, how do you put this behavior-first model into practice? It starts with small, consistent actions that align with the change you're aiming to achieve. The key is to make these actions simple enough to be incorporated into daily life and to reinforce them through positive feedback or rewards.

For example, imagine you're trying to cultivate a more compassionate team culture. Instead of preaching the virtues of compassion, you could start by encouraging team members to perform small acts of kindness. Maybe it's as simple as giving a shout-out to a colleague who helped with a project or leaving a note of thanks on someone's desk. Recognizing and rewarding these actions creates a ripple effect, gradually building a culture where compassion is the norm.

Crafting a Supportive Environment

Beyond individual actions, the environment plays a critical role in sustaining behavior-driven change. People are more likely to stick with new behaviors when they're supported by their surroundings—both physically and socially.

This might mean providing the tools and resources that make the desired behaviors easier, like offering reusable water bottles to encourage environmental responsibility or setting up a reward system for teams that hit their collaboration targets. It could also involve creating social norms that reinforce the behavior, such as a company-wide initiative where everyone is encouraged to use reusable bags or participate in community service.

When the environment supports the behavior, the behavior, in turn, reinforces the belief.

Rewriting the Script: Action Shapes Attitude

The traditional belief-first model has its place, but it's not the only way to inspire change. By flipping the script and focusing on behavior first, you can create a powerful momentum that leads to lasting change. Small, consistent actions—backed by a supportive environment—allow people to experience the benefits of change, which in turn shapes their beliefs and attitudes.

In the end, action is a powerful tool for transformation. So, if you want to inspire change, start by taking that first step. The beliefs will follow.

Key Actions

- **Behavior-First Approach**: Instead of trying to change beliefs first, focus on changing behaviors. Action can lead to belief changes as individuals experience the benefits of the new behavior.
- **Experience Drives Belief**: When people engage in a behavior and see positive outcomes, their beliefs and attitudes naturally shift. Direct experience is often more convincing than arguments or persuasion.
- **Small, Manageable Steps**: Changing behavior is less overwhelming than trying to change beliefs. Small, consistent actions are easier to adopt and can lead to significant changes over time.
- **Reinforcement Through Positive Feedback**: Reinforcing small behaviors with recognition or rewards helps to solidify the behavior and gradually build a culture that reflects the desired change.
- **Supportive Environment**: Creating an environment that encourages and supports the desired behaviors is crucial. This includes providing resources, establishing social norms, and making it easy for people to engage in the behaviors.
- **Action Shapes Attitude**: The idea that taking action first can lead to belief changes, rather than the other way around, is a powerful approach to inspiring lasting change.

Discussion Questions

1. How might the behavior-first approach be more effective than traditional belief-first models in creating lasting change within an organization?
2. Can you share an example from your experience where a small change in behavior led to a significant shift in beliefs or attitudes, either personally or professionally?
3. What are some practical ways leaders can create an environment that supports and reinforces the desired behaviors in their teams or organizations?
4. How do you think the concept of "experience drives belief" could be applied to overcoming resistance to change in a workplace setting?
5. In what ways can recognizing and rewarding small, consistent behaviors lead to a larger cultural shift within a team or organization?

Practice Exercises

1. Behavior Tracking and Reflection

- **Objective**: To understand the impact of small behavior changes on beliefs and attitudes.
- **How to Do It**: Choose a small behavior you want to change (e.g., reducing sugar intake, increasing daily steps). Track this behavior consistently for two weeks. At the end of each day, reflect on how this behavior made you feel and any changes in your attitude toward the behavior. After two weeks, assess how your beliefs about this behavior have shifted as a result of your actions.

2. Small Acts of Recognition

- **Objective**: To practice reinforcing positive behaviors within a team or group setting.

- **How to Do It**: Over the next week, actively look for small, positive behaviors in your team or among colleagues (e.g., someone going out of their way to help another, showing initiative, or being particularly collaborative). Each time you observe one, provide specific recognition—either publicly or privately. Reflect on how this recognition affects the individual and the team dynamic over time.

3. Environmental Design for Behavior Change

- **Objective**: To create an environment that supports and encourages desired behaviors.
- **How to Do It**: Identify a behavior you want to encourage in yourself or others (e.g., reducing waste, increasing focus during work). Design or modify your environment to make this behavior easier to perform (e.g., placing recycling bins within easy reach, creating a distraction-free workspace). Monitor how these environmental changes impact the consistency and ease of the behavior over a month and adjust as needed to further support the desired action.

EXPAND COMFORT ZONES

Leadership isn't just about steering the ship; it's about constantly preparing the crew for whatever lies ahead. One of the most critical tasks of an effective leader is making change less of a jolt and more of a journey. The best leaders don't just manage change—they create a culture where change feels natural, even welcome. They do this by expanding the boundaries of their team's thinking, ensuring that the organization remains open to new ideas, new practices, and new perspectives.

The Danger of Tight Boundaries

When leaders set narrow boundaries and foster a culture that dismisses outside information, they inadvertently cultivate resistance to change. It's easy to become insulated, taking pride in "our way" of doing things. But that's a recipe for stagnation. The most successful leaders understand that innovation doesn't happen in isolation. Inspiration and excellence often come from unexpected places, and it's the leader's job to ensure their team is receptive to these external influences.

Making Openness the Norm

Creating a culture that's comfortable with change starts with normalizing the idea that valuable insights can come from outside the organization. Don't wait for a crisis to force your team to look outward. Instead, make it a regular practice to seek out new ideas and perspectives. This proactive approach keeps your team ahead of the curve, ready to adapt as industries and markets evolve.

One practical way to encourage this is by establishing a normative expectation that your team regularly engages with peers outside the organization. For instance, ask your team members to identify and connect with three counterparts from competitor organizations. Hosting these peers for informal discussions can expose your team to different ways of thinking and operating, creating a continuous flow of fresh ideas into your organization.

The Power of Diversity and Inclusion

Expanding boundaries isn't just about looking outside the organization; it's also about broadening the range of voices and experiences within your team. Promoting diversity and inclusion is critical. A diverse team brings a wide array of perspectives, which leads to more creative problem-solving and innovation. But diversity alone isn't enough. Inclusion ensures that every team member feels valued and heard, which in turn makes them more comfortable with change. When people feel included, they're more likely to engage with new ideas and embrace new ways of working.

Leading by Example: A Practical Approach

Let's put theory into practice. Imagine your team is about to shift to a new matrix structure—a change that could be met with resistance. Instead of pushing the change through and hoping for the best, take a different approach. Ask your team to survey other organizations that have successfully implemented a similar structure. Have them bring this knowledge back and share it with the team in an open discussion. This not only broadens the team's understanding of the new structure but also emphasizes that the change has been successfully tried elsewhere. This approach makes the unfamiliar feel more familiar, easing the transition and making the change more comfortable.

Another example might be during the early stages of a project. Instead of relying solely on internal expertise, encourage your team to seek out best practices from other industries or even competitors. For instance, hosting a breakfast with peers from different companies to discuss shared challenges and solutions can spark new ideas and approaches that your team might not have considered.

Prioritizing Execution Over Ownership

When change is on the horizon, it's easy for teams to become territorial. People often feel a sense of ownership over their methods and ideas, which can create friction when new approaches are introduced. As a leader, it's your job to shift the focus from ownership to execution. The goal isn't to preserve the status quo but to find the best way forward, regardless of where the idea originates. By emphasizing execution—getting the job done well, regardless of whose idea it was—you create a culture where change is seen as a pathway to success, not a threat to personal pride.

Cultivating a Change-Ready Culture

Ultimately, expanding boundaries to make change more comfortable is about fostering a culture of continuous learning and openness. It's about creating an environment where new ideas are not just tolerated but actively sought out, where diversity and inclusion are celebrated, and where execution takes precedence over ownership.

Leaders who expand boundaries ensure their teams are not just reacting to change but anticipating and embracing it. They create a culture where change isn't something to be feared—it's something to be welcomed as an opportunity for growth and improvement. By expanding the boundaries of what's possible, these leaders make change not just comfortable, but exciting.

Key Actions

- **Expanding Boundaries:** Encourage the team to look beyond internal practices and seek inspiration and ideas from external sources.
- **Promoting Openness to Outside Information:** Make it a regular practice for the team to engage with peers outside the organization to gather new perspectives and ideas.
- **Fostering Diversity and Inclusion:** Build a diverse team and ensure everyone feels included and valued, leading to more creative problem-solving and greater comfort with change.
- **Encouraging Continuous Learning:** Normalize the pursuit of new knowledge and ideas, making it a regular part of the team's culture to seek out fresh insights.
- **Prioritizing Execution Over Ownership:** Shift the focus from defending personal methods and ideas to finding the best approach for successful execution, regardless of where the idea originates.

- **Leading by Example:** Implement practical steps, such as engaging with competitors or surveying other organizations, to help the team feel more comfortable with impending changes.
- **Creating a Change-Ready Culture:** Cultivate an environment where change is welcomed as an opportunity for growth, rather than something to be feared.

Discussion Questions

1. How can leaders balance the need for external inspiration with maintaining a strong internal culture?
2. In what ways can promoting diversity and inclusion within a team lead to better adaptation to change?
3. What strategies can leaders use to shift the team's focus from ownership of ideas to successful execution?
4. How can leaders effectively encourage continuous learning within their teams?
5. What role does a leader's example play in creating a culture that is comfortable with change?

Practice Exercises

1. Peer Exchange Breakfasts

- **Objective**: To broaden your team's perspectives by engaging with peers outside the organization.
- **How to Do It**: Identify three professionals in similar roles at competitor organizations. Arrange a casual breakfast meeting to discuss challenges, best practices, and innovative ideas. Encourage your team members to lead these discussions, gather insights, and share them with the team afterward.

2. Diversity Perspective Challenge

- **Objective**: To promote diversity and inclusion within your team by valuing different perspectives.

- **How to Do It**: Organize a monthly team meeting where each member presents a solution to a current problem from the viewpoint of a different demographic or cultural perspective. This exercise encourages team members to think outside their usual mindset and consider a broader range of solutions.

3. Execution Over Ownership Workshop

- **Objective**: To shift the focus from idea ownership to successful execution.
- **How to Do It**: Conduct a workshop where team members collaborate on a project, but with a twist—each person contributes to an idea that wasn't originally theirs. The goal is to emphasize the importance of refining and executing ideas regardless of who proposed them. Afterward, debrief the group to discuss how this experience changed their approach to collaboration and ownership.

KEEP THE GOOD, CHANGE THE REST

Change is one of the most challenging aspects of leadership. Whether you're leading a family, a team, or an entire organization, you know how unsettling change can be. Yet, as a leader, you also know that change is essential for growth. The trick is to balance it with something familiar—something that doesn't change—to help people navigate the transition more comfortably.

The Masters: A Case Study in Balancing Tradition and Innovation

One of the best examples of balancing tradition with change is the Masters golf tournament. The Masters is steeped in tradition. The Green Jacket, awarded to the champion, and the champions' dinner are iconic elements that have remained unchanged for decades. These traditions create a sense of continuity and stability, offering a familiar touchstone for both players and fans.

However, the Masters is also one of the most progressive events in the world of golf. From constantly updating the course to adopting new camera angles and engaging with modern advertisers, the Masters evolves while still honoring its traditions. This balance between tradition and innovation keeps the tournament relevant and exciting, without alienating its core audience. It's a powerful lesson for any leader: change doesn't have to mean abandoning what works.

Why Stability Matters in a Changing World

Imagine working in an environment where everything is in flux. New policies are rolled out every week, team structures are constantly shifting, and even the company's core mission seems to change with the seasons. It's exhausting, and more importantly, it's destabilizing. People begin to question their place in the organization and, ultimately, their identity.

This is why it's critical to preserve certain elements that don't change, even as you introduce new ideas and processes. When you anchor your team in tradition, you give them something to rely on. It's like having a lighthouse in a storm; no matter how rough the seas get, they have a point of reference to guide them.

The Power of Rituals and Traditions

Traditions and rituals are not just quaint leftovers from the past; they serve a crucial function in providing a sense of belonging and continuity. In the context of an organization, these rituals could be as simple as starting every meeting with a reflection on the company's core values. This practice reinforces what matters and helps team members find purpose and meaning in their work.

For example, think about a family that goes on vacation to the same place every year. This ritual provides a sense of security and continuity for the children, giving them the confidence to explore the world without fear. The same principle applies in the workplace. When employees know there are certain things they can count on—like a consistent set of values or a recurring company event—they're more open to embracing change in other areas.

Stability as a Foundation for Progress

The ultimate takeaway for leaders is simple: if you want people to embrace change, you need to provide them with some things that never change. These constants act as a foundation, giving your team the confidence to explore new ideas and adapt to new circumstances.

Stability isn't the enemy of progress; it's the bedrock that makes progress possible. By preserving certain traditions and providing a sense of stability, you create an environment where change is not only possible but welcomed. And as a leader, you should recognize the importance of these unchanging elements in your own life as well. After all, the best way to lead others through change is by showing them how to find stability in their own lives.

So, the next time you're faced with the challenge of implementing change, remember this: change doesn't have to be a complete overhaul. Sometimes, the most effective way to move forward is by keeping one foot firmly planted in the past.

Key Actions

- **Balancing Tradition with Change**: Leaders should maintain certain traditions while introducing new ideas, ensuring that change doesn't mean abandoning what works.
- **Preserving Stability**: Maintaining some unchanging elements within the organization provides employees with a sense of continuity, which helps them feel secure during times of change.
- **Implementing Rituals and Traditions**: Regular practices, such as starting meetings with a reflection on core values, help reinforce what matters and provide a sense of belonging and continuity.
- **Providing Familiar Touchstones**: Leaders should create familiar reference points, like consistent values or recurring events, to help team members feel grounded even as other things change.
- **Recognizing the Importance of Stability**: Stability should be seen as a foundation that enables progress, rather than an obstacle to change.
- **Emphasizing the Power of Rituals in Personal Life**: Leaders should also apply the principle of stability in their personal lives, such as maintaining family traditions, to provide a sense of security and confidence in exploring new challenges.

Discussion Questions

1. How can leaders identify which traditions or rituals are essential to preserve when introducing change within an organization?
2. In what ways can balancing stability and change help reduce resistance among team members during periods of organizational transformation?
3. Can you think of examples from your own experience where maintaining a tradition helped ease the transition through a significant change? How did it impact the team?

4. How might leaders ensure that the rituals and traditions they choose to maintain continue to serve the organization's evolving needs and values?

5. How can leaders apply the concept of balancing tradition and change in their personal lives to better handle uncertainties and challenges?

Practice Exercises

1. Identify and Preserve Key Traditions

- **Objective**: To practice balancing tradition and change by identifying key elements worth preserving in your organization or team.
- **How to Do It**: Start by making a list of all the traditions, rituals, and core values in your organization. Reflect on which of these elements are most crucial to the team's identity and should be preserved. Engage in a discussion with your team or peers about why these elements are important and how they can serve as anchors during periods of change.

2. Incorporate Rituals into Your Routine

- **Objective**: To reinforce stability and continuity by introducing or reinforcing rituals within your team or organization.
- **How to Do It**: Choose a simple, meaningful ritual to integrate into your daily or weekly routine, such as starting meetings with a reflection on core values or recognizing achievements. Apply this ritual consistently over several weeks and observe its influence on team morale and stability. Gather feedback from your team on the ritual's impact and make adjustments as needed to ensure it remains meaningful and relevant.

3. Evaluate Change Initiatives with Stability in Mind

- **Objective**: To practice balancing change with stability by evaluating change initiatives through the lens of tradition.
- **How to Do It**: When planning a change initiative, consider all the existing traditions, values, or rituals that might be affected. Think about how you can preserve these elements while still implementing the necessary changes. Develop a plan to communicate both the change and the preservation of key traditions to your team, emphasizing the importance of continuity alongside progress.

BUILD ON WHAT WORKS

We're all guilty of looking for the next big thing—the shiny new solution that promises to solve our problems. But often, the real secret to success lies not in reinventing the wheel, but in building on what's already working. In today's fast-paced, ever-changing business landscape, the ability to recognize and expand on existing strengths within an organization can be a powerful catalyst for meaningful and lasting change.

The Power of What's Already Working

When facing the challenge of change, most leaders instinctively focus on what needs fixing. They spend their energy identifying problems, gaps, and weaknesses. While this approach has its place, it's often more effective to focus on what's already going well. The idea is simple: by identifying and amplifying the successes that align with your desired outcomes, you create a strong foundation on which to build the change you want to see.

Consider this: within every organization, there are pockets of success —teams, processes, or individuals who are already embodying the changes you wish to see on a larger scale. These examples are your proof points. They show that the change is not just possible; it's already happening. By highlighting these successes, you can create a sense of optimism and possibility throughout the organization.

But here's the trick—these success stories aren't always obvious. Sometimes, they're buried deep within different departments, teams, or even across different geographies. As a leader, it's your job to actively seek them out. This might mean visiting different offices, talking to frontline employees, or digging into data that's often overlooked. The goal is to find those bright spots and bring them into the light.

Building Momentum Through Success

Once you've identified what's working, the next step is to build on it. When people see that their efforts are recognized and supported by leadership, they're more likely to engage with the change process. This recognition can create a ripple effect, encouraging others to follow suit. Success breeds success, and before you know it, you have momentum on your side.

This approach is not just about patting people on the back—it's strategic. By investing in what's already working, you create a virtuous cycle. The initial success inspires further engagement, which leads to even greater success. It's like a snowball effect: as it rolls down the hill, it gathers more snow, gaining size and speed.

Applying the Approach to Relationships

This strategy isn't limited to organizations; it works in personal relationships, too. If you want to encourage a change in behavior— whether with a partner, a friend, or a colleague—it's often more effective to highlight when they're already exhibiting the behavior you desire. For instance, if you want your partner to communicate more openly, recognize and appreciate the moments when they do. This acknowledgment acts as a positive reinforcement, making them more likely to repeat the behavior.

By focusing on what's already working, you're not only encouraging more of that behavior, but you're also fostering an environment where change feels achievable. It's a subtle yet powerful way to guide someone towards the outcome you want.

The Key to Lasting Change

At the end of the day, change is hard. But by focusing on what's already working, you're giving yourself—and your team—a head start. This approach provides tangible proof that the change is possible, creating a sense of hope and optimism that's crucial for long-term success.

Moreover, by building on existing strengths, you're not starting from scratch. You're reinforcing what's already good, which is far more sustainable than trying to fix everything that's broken. This way, you create a solid foundation for lasting change, whether in your organization or in your personal relationships.

So, the next time you're faced with the challenge of driving change, resist the urge to focus solely on what's wrong. Instead, look for what's right, expand on it, and let it serve as the cornerstone of your efforts. In doing so, you'll not only make change more attainable but also set the stage for a future where success is the norm, not the exception.

Key Actions

- **Identify and Amplify Successes**: Focus on what's already working well within the organization, team, or relationship, and build upon those successes.
- **Actively Seek Out Proof Points**: Look for examples of success that align with the desired change, even if they are not immediately obvious or easily found.
- **Recognize and Highlight Existing Strengths**: Acknowledge and bring attention to successful behaviors, processes, or practices that can serve as a foundation for further change.
- **Build Momentum Through Positive Reinforcement**: Use the recognition of existing successes to create a ripple effect, encouraging further engagement and participation in the change process.
- **Apply the Strategy to Relationships**: In personal interactions, recognize and appreciate instances when desired behaviors are already being exhibited to encourage more of that behavior.
- **Create a Sense of Hope and Optimism**: Leverage the successes to foster a positive environment where change feels achievable and sustainable.
- **Reinforce Existing Strengths Rather Than Fixing Weaknesses:** Focus on expanding and strengthening what is already good, rather than trying to fix everything that is broken.

Discussion Questions

1. How can leaders effectively identify and amplify the successes

already present within their organization, especially when these successes are not immediately obvious?

2. What are some specific examples of "proof points" in your organization or team that could be leveraged to inspire broader change?

3. In what ways can recognizing and highlighting existing strengths create momentum for further change, both in professional and personal settings?

4. How can the approach of expanding on what already works be applied to relationships outside of the workplace, and what potential challenges might arise?

5. Why is it often more sustainable to build on existing strengths rather than focusing solely on fixing weaknesses, and how can this mindset be cultivated among team members?

Practice Exercises

1. Success Scouting

- **Objective**: Improve your ability to identify and amplify existing successes within your team or organization.
- **How to Do It**: Spend one week actively observing your team or organization, focusing on finding at least three examples of behaviors, processes, or outcomes that align with your desired change. Document these examples, noting why they are successful and how they could be expanded upon. Share these examples with your team in a meeting or through a written communication, highlighting their significance and discussing ways to build on them.

2. Positive Reinforcement in Relationships

- **Objective**: Practice reinforcing desired behaviors in personal or professional relationships to encourage more of the same.
- **How to Do It**: Identify a behavior you would like to see more of in a particular relationship, such as timely communication

or collaboration. Over the course of two weeks, consciously recognize and verbally acknowledge when the other person exhibits this behavior. Reflect on how this positive reinforcement affects the relationship and whether it leads to an increase in the desired behavior.

3. Momentum Building Challenge

- **Objective**: Develop the skill of creating momentum by focusing on and expanding existing strengths within your team.
- **How to Do It**: Choose a current project or initiative within your team that has shown signs of success. Organize a workshop or brainstorming session with your team to discuss what has worked well so far. Collaboratively develop a plan to expand on these successes, setting specific goals for how to leverage the strengths identified. Implement the plan and track the progress over the next month, noting any increase in engagement or success as a result.

SMALL WINS, BIG PROGRESS

When it comes to driving change within an organization, the idea of focusing on small wins and incremental progress might seem like common sense, but it's a strategy that's often overlooked. Leaders, eager to make a big impact, sometimes chase after monumental victories, overlooking the power of steady, consistent progress. However, creating change one win and one step at a time can be far more effective for motivating employees and building momentum toward lasting transformation.

The Power of Progress

People thrive on progress. The feeling that they're moving forward, even in small ways, can be a powerful motivator. Recognizing and celebrating small victories along the way not only maintains momentum but also keeps the team engaged in the process. For instance, imagine a leader who wants to improve communication within their organization. Instead of trying to overhaul the entire system overnight, they might start by introducing one new communication tool or method. They implement it, monitor the results, and celebrate the improvements, however small, before moving on to the next step.

This approach not only makes the change process more manageable but also gives employees a sense of accomplishment at each stage. When people see that their efforts lead to tangible results, they're more likely to stay committed to the larger goal.

Building Momentum Through Small Wins

Momentum in change management is like a snowball rolling downhill —it starts small but can build into something powerful. Leaders can help create this momentum by being attuned to when people embrace change and by actively looking for small signs of progress. It's not just about waiting for a major milestone to celebrate; it's about recognizing the little things that indicate the team is moving in the right direction.

For example, a fast-food chain undergoing a business transformation might begin by focusing on the basics: improving cleanliness, efficiency, team morale, and customer service. These are foundational elements that, when improved, set the stage for bigger changes like introducing new products or services. As each area sees improvement, the team's confidence grows, making them more receptive to further changes.

Breaking Down the Change Process

Change rarely happens in one sweeping motion. More often, it's the result of many small, deliberate steps. Leaders who break down the change process into smaller milestones not only make the overall goal seem less daunting but also create opportunities to celebrate along the way.

Consider a company that aims to boost customer satisfaction. Instead of setting a lofty goal of a 20% increase in satisfaction ratings, they might set smaller, more achievable goals—like a 1% increase each month. These incremental goals are easier to achieve and maintain, and they provide a steady stream of positive reinforcement for the team.

By breaking down the change process, leaders can keep the focus on continuous progress rather than waiting for one big success. This approach makes the journey less overwhelming and more sustainable.

Charting the Path to Victory

A clear roadmap is essential for navigating any change. Before diving into the change process, it's crucial to map out the small steps and wins that will lead to the ultimate goal. This not only helps keep the team focused but also makes it easier to recognize and celebrate those small victories along the way.

For instance, if a company is working to improve its product development process, the leader might outline specific milestones such as reducing development time by 10%, improving cross-functional collaboration, or increasing the frequency of feedback loops. Each of these milestones represents a small victory on the way to the larger goal and provides an opportunity to reinforce the positive changes being made.

The Key Actions for Success

To make this approach effective, leaders must be vigilant in identifying small wins and celebrating them with the team. This doesn't mean throwing a party for every minor achievement, but rather acknowledging the progress in meaningful ways—whether it's through a simple shoutout in a meeting, a note of thanks, or a small reward.

Additionally, it's important for leaders to help their teams see how these small wins connect to the larger goal. When employees understand how their actions contribute to the bigger picture, they're more likely to feel invested in the outcome.

Framing success in terms of progress, rather than focusing on what hasn't been achieved yet, also plays a significant role in maintaining motivation. A positive, forward-looking mindset helps the team feel more empowered and less discouraged by the inevitable setbacks that come with any change process.

The Big Picture

Creating change one win and one step at a time isn't just about making progress—it's about building a culture of continuous improvement. By focusing on small, incremental steps, leaders can maintain momentum, keep their teams engaged, and drive lasting change. The small victories may seem insignificant on their own, but together, they create a powerful force that propels the organization toward its ultimate goals.

In the end, it's not just about reaching the finish line—it's about the journey. Celebrating progress, however small, keeps everyone motivated and moving forward. And in the world of change management, that's what truly makes the difference.

Key Actions

- **Recognize and Celebrate Small Wins**: Leaders should actively look for and acknowledge small victories throughout the change process to maintain momentum and keep the team engaged.

- **Break Down the Change Process into Smaller Milestones**: Instead of focusing solely on a large, final goal, leaders should break the process into manageable steps, making progress more achievable and less overwhelming.
- **Create a Roadmap of Small Wins**: Chart out specific milestones and steps that will lead to the ultimate goal, helping to maintain focus and recognize progress.
- **Connect Small Wins to the Larger Goal**: Leaders should help their teams understand how each small victory contributes to the overall objective, increasing their investment in the process.
- **Maintain a Positive, Forward-Looking Mindset**: Frame success in terms of progress rather than focusing on what hasn't been achieved yet, which helps to keep the team motivated and empowered.
- **Be Vigilant in Identifying Small Signs of Progress:** Leaders should be attuned to even minor signs of progress and use them to build momentum and create a sense of optimism within the team.

Discussion Questions

1. How can leaders effectively identify and celebrate small wins without losing sight of the larger goal?
2. What are some practical ways to break down a large organizational change into smaller, more manageable milestones?
3. How can leaders ensure that employees understand the connection between small victories and the overall success of a project or initiative?
4. What are the potential risks of focusing too much on small wins, and how can these be mitigated?
5. In your experience, how does maintaining a positive, forward-looking mindset impact the success of a change initiative?

Practice Exercises

1. Small Wins Journal

- **Objective**: Develop the habit of recognizing and celebrating small victories.
- **How to Do It**: At the end of each day, write down three small wins or progress points that occurred. These could be personal achievements, team accomplishments, or positive developments within your organization. Reflect on how these small wins contribute to larger goals and consider how you might acknowledge or celebrate them with your team.

2. Milestone Mapping

- **Objective**: Improve your ability to break down large goals into smaller, manageable steps.
- **How to Do It**: Take a current project or initiative you're working on and break it down into smaller milestones. Identify the key steps needed to reach each milestone and create a timeline for achieving them. Review this map regularly, adjusting as needed, and use it to guide your progress and communication with your team.

3. Connection Building Exercise

- **Objective**: Enhance your ability to connect small wins to the larger goal and communicate this effectively to your team.
- **How to Do It**: After identifying a small win or milestone, take time to articulate how this achievement ties into the broader objectives of your team or organization. Practice explaining this connection to a colleague or in a team meeting. Focus on making the link clear and compelling, showing how small successes contribute to the bigger picture.

FOLLOWERS DRIVE CHANGE

Leadership is often painted as the driving force behind innovation and progress within an organization. The common belief is that leaders, with their vision and authority, are the primary catalysts for change. But here's the truth: change doesn't happen just because a leader says so. Real change takes hold when the first followers—those early adopters who jump on board with a new idea—begin to influence their peers. These first followers often have more sway over the group than the leaders themselves.

The Power of the First Follower

The first follower is often the unsung hero of change. While leaders might set the direction, it's the first follower who validates the leader's vision and makes it relatable to others. They're the ones who make a leader's idea seem less risky and more achievable. The first follower's endorsement turns an idea into a movement.

Why is this? Because people are naturally skeptical of change, especially when it's driven by someone at the top. They want to see that someone they trust, someone in the trenches with them, believes in the new direction. This trust doesn't automatically lie with the top brass; it lies with the colleague who sits next to them, the person who understands the day-to-day realities of their work.

Identifying Key Opinion Leaders

So, how do leaders harness the power of first followers? The first step is identifying who these key opinion leaders are within your organization. These aren't always the people with the fancy titles or the most years of experience. They're the ones others naturally turn to for advice or guidance. Their opinion holds weight because they've earned the trust and respect of their peers.

Leaders who want to drive change need to build strong relationships with these influencers. This doesn't mean using them as mere tools to push through an agenda. It means genuinely engaging with them, listening to their concerns, and addressing their needs. If you can get these key individuals on board, they'll do the heavy lifting of convincing others.

Building Relationships That Matter

Building relationships with key opinion leaders isn't a one-time task. It requires ongoing effort and authenticity. Leaders must be willing to have open, honest conversations with these individuals. Ask them what they think about the proposed changes. What are their concerns? What potential roadblocks do they see? And, most importantly, what can you do to help them succeed in their roles?

Leaders who take the time to understand the perspectives of these influencers can tailor their approach to meet the needs of the broader organization. This might mean providing additional resources, offering training, or simply being available to address concerns as they arise.

Communicating the Why

Once you have key opinion leaders on board, the next step is to communicate the value of the change to the entire organization. This isn't just about selling an idea; it's about making sure everyone understands why the change is necessary and how it benefits them. People are more likely to support a change when they see how it aligns with their own goals and the overall mission of the organization.

Leaders need to articulate the rationale behind the change clearly and compellingly. But more than that, they need to be prepared to address any concerns or resistance that might come up. Change can be unsettling, and it's the leader's job to ease those fears by providing reassurance and support.

Effective leadership isn't about being the loudest voice in the room or the one with the most authority. It's about recognizing the power of the first followers and leveraging their influence to drive change. The best leaders know that people are more likely to follow their peers than their bosses when it comes to adopting new ideas.

By building strong relationships with key opinion leaders, engaging them in the change process, and clearly communicating the value of the change, leaders can create an environment where new ideas take root and flourish. In the end, it's not just about leading; it's about empowering others to lead alongside you.

Key Actions

- **Recognizing the Power of First Followers**: Understand that change often gains momentum through the influence of first followers, not just the leader's vision.
- **Identifying Key Opinion Leaders**: Focus on identifying who the key opinion leaders are within the organization, those who naturally influence their peers.
- **Building Relationships with Influencers**: Engage with key opinion leaders through open, honest conversations, addressing their concerns and providing support.
- **Genuinely Engaging and Listening**: Leaders should authentically engage with opinion leaders, listen to their concerns, and tailor their approach based on this feedback.
- **Communicating the Rationale for Change**: Clearly articulate the reasons behind the change, aligning it with the organization's goals and addressing potential concerns.
- **Empowering Others to Lead:** Shift the focus from solely leading to empowering others within the organization to become leaders in their own right.

Discussion Questions

1. How can identifying and engaging with key opinion leaders influence the success of change initiatives within an organization?
2. In what ways can a leader effectively build trust and rapport with first followers to drive change?
3. What are the potential risks of relying too heavily on first followers to implement change, and how can leaders mitigate these risks?
4. How does the role of a first follower differ from that of a

leader when it comes to promoting new ideas and strategies within an organization?

5. What strategies can leaders use to effectively communicate the rationale for change and address resistance from the broader organization?

Practice Exercises

1. Identify and Engage Opinion Leaders

- **Objective**: Improve your ability to recognize and build relationships with key influencers within your organization.
- **How to Do It**: Identify three individuals in your organization who are seen as informal leaders or trusted by their peers. Schedule one-on-one meetings with each of them to discuss their perspectives on a recent or upcoming change. Listen to their concerns, ask for their input on how the change can be successfully implemented, and explore ways to involve them in the process.

2. Practice Clear Communication of Change

- **Objective**: Develop your skill in articulating the rationale behind changes in a way that resonates with your team.
- **How to Do It**: Take a recent change initiative within your organization and craft a brief presentation or written communication that clearly explains the reasons behind the change, how it aligns with the organization's goals, and how it benefits the team. Share this with a colleague or mentor for feedback, then refine it based on their suggestions.

3. Role-Playing First Follower Engagement

- **Objective**: Enhance your ability to effectively engage and influence first followers during a change process.
- **How to Do It**: Pair up with a colleague or peer and role-play a scenario where you introduce a significant change to your

team. In this role-play, your partner acts as a key opinion leader or first follower. Practice engaging them in a conversation about the change, addressing their concerns, and persuading them to support and advocate for the change among their peers. Afterward, discuss what worked well and what could be improved.

TOLERANCE'S HIDDEN WEIGHT

Leadership is hard work. It's not about handing down orders from on high or basking in the glow of past successes. It's about navigating obstacles, most of which are people-related. One of the toughest hurdles? Dealing with resistance to change.

There's an old saying that goes, "You're only as strong as the worst behavior you're willing to tolerate." It's true. A leader's power to drive change doesn't hinge on their vision or charisma alone—it depends on their ability to confront those who resist that vision. If you're unwilling to address the naysayers and the rule-breakers, you're setting yourself— and your entire team—up for failure.

The Hidden Saboteurs

In any organization, resistant individuals are like anchors, dragging down progress. They may not be overt in their resistance; sometimes, it's the subtle refusal to adapt that does the most damage. These people become symbols of defiance, and their attitude can ripple through the team, undermining morale, culture, and performance.

When resistance festers unchecked, it sends a clear message: "This behavior is acceptable." And that's when things start to unravel. It's not just about the one person who won't get on board; it's about the credibility of the leader who allows it to happen.

One leader I spoke with had a rather dark-humored sign on their desk: "Some people are only alive because it's against the organizational law to kill them. And a leader's job is to kill them." The message was provocative but clear: resistance must be confronted head-on. Of course, this isn't about physical harm—it's about challenging the behavior that threatens to derail your team.

Addressing the Elephant in the Room

Ignoring resistance is like ignoring a ticking time bomb. You might hope it defuses itself, but it rarely does. The best leaders know this. They don't shy away from conflict or pretend that resistance doesn't exist. They confront it, sometimes in creative ways.

There are two basic approaches to dealing with resistant individuals: outlast them or remove them.

- **Outlasting Resistance:** This doesn't mean ignoring the problem. It means engaging with those around the resistant individual, building a coalition of the willing. Sometimes, by isolating the resistance, you can outmaneuver it. This works when the person in question is more of a passive resistor, someone whose influence is waning.
- **Removing Resistance:** This doesn't necessarily mean firing someone. It could mean reassigning them to a different role where their influence is minimized, stripping away the privileges or status that enable their resistance. In some cases, it might involve sidelining them so that their impact is neutralized.

The point is, you can't allow someone to opt out of change while expecting everyone else to buy in. If you do, you're sending mixed messages, and people will take notice. Your authority erodes every time you let resistance slide.

The Visionary Test

For change to happen, people need to believe in it. But more importantly, they need to believe in you. There's a saying, "We don't buy the vision before we buy the visionary." As a leader, your ability to inspire change depends on your credibility. If your team sees you tolerating bad behavior, that credibility takes a hit.

When you let a few team members play by their own rules—skipping meetings, shirking responsibilities, or just doing the bare minimum— it undermines everyone else's trust in you. They start asking themselves, "Why should I go the extra mile when so-and-so gets away with doing nothing?" That's a dangerous question to let hang in the air.

Political reasons often tie a leader's hands. Maybe the resistant person has a senior sponsor, critical technical skills, or is close to retirement. But letting these reasons dictate your actions can be fatal to your leadership. The moment your team sees you bending to these pressures, they start doubting your ability to lead.

The Silent Saboteurs

Most teams have at least one or two "protected" individuals—people who seem untouchable, regardless of their behavior. These individuals can destroy a leader's credibility faster than almost anything else. It's not just about them being resistant to change; it's about the message their immunity sends to everyone else.

Why should anyone else engage in the change when you allow these people to opt out? Why should they trust you to lead them when you're not even holding everyone to the same standard?

Taking Action: The True Test of Leadership

Resistance to change isn't just an obstacle; it's a test of your leadership. The best leaders don't just recognize the symbolism of resistant individuals—they act on it. They know that their ability to drive change is directly tied to their willingness to confront and, if necessary, remove those who stand in the way.

Remember, you're only as strong as the worst behavior you're willing to tolerate. So, ask yourself: What are you tolerating that's holding your team back? And what are you going to do about it?

Leadership isn't about making everyone happy; it's about making the hard choices that drive progress. If you're serious about leading change, you need to be serious about confronting resistance. Because if you don't, you're not just tolerating bad behavior—you're endorsing it.

Key Actions

- **Confronting Resistance:** Leaders must directly address individuals who resist change rather than ignoring or avoiding the issue.
- **Setting Clear Expectations:** Leaders should not allow any team members to opt out of the change process, as this undermines the entire effort.

- **Outlasting Resistance:** Engaging with the broader team to isolate and outmaneuver resistant individuals rather than confronting them directly.
- **Removing Resistance:** Finding ways to neutralize the influence of resistant individuals, such as reassigning them to different roles or removing their privileges.
- **Maintaining Credibility:** Leaders must consistently enforce standards and not tolerate bad behavior, as allowing it can erode their credibility.
- **Avoiding Favoritism:** Leaders should avoid protecting certain individuals, regardless of their status or skills, as this sends a negative message to the rest of the team.
- **Building Trust:** By addressing resistance and holding everyone to the same standard, leaders build trust and reinforce their authority.
- **Making Hard Choices:** Effective leadership involves making difficult decisions, especially when it comes to confronting resistance within the team.

Discussion Questions

1. Why is it essential for leaders to confront resistance directly rather than ignoring it?
2. How can leaders balance the need to address resistant behavior with the risk of disrupting team dynamics?
3. In what ways can protecting certain individuals within an organization harm a leader's credibility?
4. What strategies can leaders use to effectively neutralize the influence of resistant individuals without resorting to termination?
5. How does the behavior of a leader in dealing with resistance impact the overall trust and morale of the team?

Practice Exercises

1. Behavior Audit

- **Objective:** Identify and address the worst behaviors tolerated within your team.
- **How to Do It:** Start by listing the behaviors within your team that you find most detrimental to progress, even if they seem minor. Rank them based on their impact on team dynamics and overall performance. Choose one behavior to address each week. Create a plan to confront and correct this behavior, whether through a direct conversation, setting new expectations, or restructuring responsibilities. Reflect on the outcomes at the end of the week and adjust your approach as needed.

2. Role Reassignment Simulation

- **Objective:** Practice removing resistance by reallocating roles and responsibilities.
- **How to Do It:** Begin by identifying a hypothetical or real-life resistant individual within your organization. Design a plan to reassign their role or adjust their responsibilities in a way that minimizes their negative influence. Consider the potential reactions from the individual and the broader team and plan your communication strategy accordingly. If possible, simulate the conversation with a trusted colleague or mentor to refine your approach. Implement the reassignment if feasible, or note the lessons learned from the exercise for future use.

3. Credibility Check-In

- **Objective:** Strengthen your leadership credibility by consistently enforcing standards.
- **How to Do It:** Conduct a self-assessment of how consistently you enforce standards across your team. Identify any

instances where you might have shown favoritism or allowed certain behaviors to slide. Set a goal to address one area where your enforcement has been inconsistent. Communicate your expectations clearly to the team, emphasizing the importance of holding everyone to the same standard. Over the next month, monitor your actions to ensure you are consistent in addressing behaviors that conflict with the team's values or goals. At the end of the month, evaluate the impact of your efforts on team morale and trust in your leadership.

START SMALL, SCALE FAST

Change is a constant in any organization, but managing it well can be tricky. One strategy that can make the process smoother is to start small and scale fast. This approach involves introducing change in bite-sized, manageable chunks, testing them in controlled environments, and then expanding rapidly once the concept has been proven. It's a way to minimize risk, maximize learning, and build momentum.

The Power of Starting Small

Starting small allows leaders to test changes in a low-risk setting. It's like dipping your toes in the water before diving in. By breaking down change into smaller pieces, you can see what works and what doesn't without overwhelming the team or risking major disruptions. This approach helps identify potential issues early, giving you the chance to smooth out the rough edges before rolling the change out on a larger scale.

But starting small isn't just about minimizing risk—it's also about building support. When team members see a change working in a smaller setting, they're more likely to become advocates for it. They've had a chance to witness the benefits firsthand, and this can turn them into champions for broader adoption.

To keep the momentum going, give the initial small-scale change an expiration date. This creates a natural checkpoint for the team to reassess, refine, and commit to the change once they've seen its value. It turns a trial run into a stepping stone for broader buy-in, fostering a sense of ownership and engagement among team members.

Aligning with Values and Culture

No matter how well a change is executed on a small scale, it won't succeed if it clashes with the company's values and culture. Alignment is crucial. If the change doesn't resonate with what the organization stands for, it will face resistance. Leaders need to ensure that any change, no matter how small, fits seamlessly with the company's identity and the needs of its customers.

It's also important to think about the customer experience. Will this change improve the way customers interact with your business? Will it meet their needs? These questions should guide your strategy from the very beginning. Change that enhances the customer experience is much more likely to be embraced by everyone involved.

Scaling Fast: When the Time Is Right

Once a change has proven successful on a small scale, it's time to act quickly. The goal is to take what you've learned from the test case and apply it across the organization before the momentum fades. Use the small-scale success as a blueprint, a proof of concept that shows what's possible. This evidence can be powerful in convincing others of the change's value.

Gaining buy-in for a larger rollout is at least half the battle. When you can point to a tangible success, it becomes easier to bring others on board. They've seen it work; now it's just a matter of scaling that success.

A Practical Example

Consider a team introducing a new mobile application to streamline communication. Instead of launching it company-wide right away, they test it with a small group. Over three months, they work out the bugs and refine the user experience. By the time it's rolled out across the entire organization, it's a well-oiled machine. The initial users, who have seen it improve their workflow, become the app's biggest advocates, making the larger rollout smoother and more successful.

Driving Meaningful Change

Starting small and scaling fast isn't just a strategy—it's a mindset. It's about being methodical in your approach to change, focusing on alignment with core values, and always keeping the customer's experience in mind. When done right, it's a way to drive meaningful progress while minimizing the risk of disruption.

Remember, change management is as much about gaining buy-in as it is about implementing the change itself. Use the success of small-scale efforts to build support and make a compelling case for broader adoption. In the end, this approach can turn what might have been a daunting task into a series of manageable, successful steps forward.

Key Actions

- **Start Small**: Introduce changes in manageable, small-scale chunks to minimize risk and identify potential issues early on.
- **Test in Controlled Environments**: Implement changes in a controlled setting to learn what works and what doesn't before expanding the change organization-wide.
- **Build Support and Advocacy**: Use the success of small-scale changes to turn team members into advocates, fostering buy-in and a sense of ownership.
- **Set Expiration Dates for Small-Scale Changes**: Create natural checkpoints for reassessment and refinement, encouraging team commitment once the change has been proven effective.
- **Ensure Alignment with Company Values and Culture**: Verify that changes align with the organization's values and culture to avoid resistance and increase the likelihood of success.
- **Focus on Customer Experience**: Consider how changes will impact customers, ensuring that they meet customer needs and enhance their experience.
- **Scale Quickly After Success**: Once a change has been validated on a small scale, rapidly expand it across the organization to capitalize on momentum.
- **Use Success as Evidence for Broader Adoption**: Leverage the success of small-scale changes to build support for broader implementation, making the case for organization-wide adoption.

Discussion Questions

1. What are some potential risks of implementing large-scale changes without first starting small? C
2. How can setting an expiration date for small-scale changes help in building team commitment and refining the change?
3. In what ways can alignment with company values and culture influence the success or failure of a change initiative? How have you seen this play out in your organization?
4. How can leaders effectively use small-scale successes as a tool to gain broader support for larger change initiatives?
5. What strategies can be employed to ensure that changes positively impact the customer experience?

Practice Exercises

1. Pilot Project Planning

- **Objective**: To practice starting small by planning and executing a pilot project.
- **How to Do It**: Identify an area in your organization where a change is needed. Design a small-scale pilot project that can be tested with a limited group. Outline the objectives, key metrics for success, and a timeline with an expiration date for the pilot. After executing the pilot, gather feedback, make necessary adjustments, and prepare a plan for scaling up based on the results.

2. Values Alignment Check

- **Objective**: To ensure that proposed changes align with your organization's values and culture.
- **How to Do It**: When planning a change, create a checklist of your organization's core values. Evaluate the proposed change against this list, identifying any potential conflicts or alignments. For each value, write down how the change supports or challenges it. Use this analysis to refine the

change initiative, ensuring it aligns with the organization's cultural principles.

3. Customer Experience Mapping

- **Objective**: To enhance the impact of changes on customer experience.
- **How to Do It**: Choose a recent or upcoming change initiative and create a customer journey map that outlines how the change will affect different touchpoints in the customer experience. Identify potential pain points and areas of improvement. Adjust the change initiative as necessary to enhance customer satisfaction and address any negative impacts. Review the results with your team and discuss further enhancements.

PRE-SELL CHANGE

Change is a fact of life, both in and out of the workplace, but that doesn't make it any easier to manage. Resistance is almost guaranteed, especially if people feel blindsided or left out of the decision-making process. To navigate these challenges, savvy leaders know that the key to successful change lies in pre-selling the idea before it even becomes a pressing issue. By involving the people who will be affected early on, leaders can build trust, gain buy-in, and smooth the path for a smoother transition.

The Power of Early Engagement

One of the most effective ways to overcome resistance is to engage people well before the change is on the horizon. Early engagement isn't just about sharing the plan; it's about involving people in the process, making them feel like active participants rather than passive recipients. This approach fosters a sense of ownership and can turn potential detractors into advocates for the change.

To do this, leaders must facilitate open and mature conversations about the change. Transparency is crucial—be clear about why the change is necessary, what it will involve, and how it will impact everyone, both positively and negatively. But transparency alone isn't enough. Listening is just as important. Take the time to understand people's concerns and work collaboratively to address them. This two-way dialogue not only builds trust but also enhances the credibility of the change initiative.

Formalizing Commitment: The Power of a Promise

Once you've engaged people and addressed their concerns, the next step is to formalize their commitment. This isn't about coercion; it's about creating a sense of accountability. Formal commitments can take many forms—written agreements, contracts, or even a verbal pledge—but the key is to make the commitment explicit.

One effective tool for securing commitment is the concept of a "Ulysses Contract." Named after the Greek hero who tied himself to the mast of his ship to resist the Sirens' call, a Ulysses Contract is a preemptive agreement that locks in a decision with little room for renegotiation. By committing to the change upfront, individuals and teams reduce the likelihood of backtracking when the going gets tough. It's a way of ensuring that people stick to their commitments, even when faced with the inevitable challenges that come with change.

Creating Urgency with Hard Deadlines

In addition to formal commitments, setting hard deadlines is another way to keep the momentum going. Deadlines create a sense of urgency, making it clear that the change isn't just a distant idea but a real, impending event that requires immediate attention. This urgency can help to overcome inertia and push people to act.

However, it's important to be strategic about when these deadlines are set. People are generally more reasonable and open to change when it's still far off in the future. As the implementation date approaches, anxiety and self-interest can take over, making rational decision-making more difficult. That's why the best leaders negotiate and secure commitments well in advance, during a time when people are more likely to consider the broader impact and less likely to be driven by immediate concerns.

Strategic Timing: Negotiating Before Change Becomes Urgent

The timing of these discussions and commitments is crucial. As change looms closer, people tend to become more self-interested and resistant. But when the change is still in the distant future, they're more likely to think rationally and consider what's best for everyone involved.

This is why the most effective leaders plant the seeds of change long before it's scheduled to take place. By forging agreements in a neutral climate, free from the pressures of impending change, leaders can lay the groundwork for a smoother, more rational dialogue. This early groundwork creates a foundation of trust and mutual understanding that will pay dividends when the time for change finally arrives.

Laying the Foundation for Successful Change

Change doesn't have to be a battle. By pre-selling the idea, engaging people early, and securing formal commitments, leaders can turn potential resistance into enthusiastic support. Setting hard deadlines and using tools like Ulysses Contracts further ensure that people stay on track and follow through on their commitments.

But the real secret lies in timing. By negotiating agreements well before the change is imminent, leaders can foster a more rational, less self-interested approach to change. This proactive approach not only makes the change itself more successful but also strengthens the trust and credibility of leadership, paving the way for future initiatives.

In the end, successful change management is less about forcing change and more about guiding people through it. By engaging early, committing formally, and timing strategically, leaders can create a smoother, more effective transition that benefits everyone involved.

Key Actions

- **Engage People Early**: Involve those affected by the change well before it is implemented to build ownership and reduce resistance.
- **Facilitate Open and Transparent Conversations**: Be clear about the reasons for the change, its potential impact, and listen to people's concerns to build trust and credibility.
- **Formalize Commitment**: Secure explicit commitments through written agreements, contracts, or verbal pledges to create accountability.
- **Utilize a Ulysses Contract**: Implement preemptive agreements that lock in decisions with little room for renegotiation, ensuring compliance even when challenges arise.
- **Set Hard Deadlines**: Establish firm deadlines to create urgency and ensure timely action, while being mindful of when these deadlines are set.

- **Strategically Time Negotiations**: Negotiate and secure commitments well in advance of the change to take advantage of a more rational and less self-interested mindset.
- **Plant the Seeds of Change Early:** Begin discussions and agreements long before the change is imminent to foster a foundation of trust and rational dialogue.

Discussion Questions

1. Why is it important to engage people early in the change process, and how can early involvement help reduce resistance to change?
2. How can leaders ensure that their conversations about change are open, transparent, and effective in building trust? Can you share an example from your experience?
3. What are the benefits of formalizing commitments through agreements or contracts when implementing change? How might this approach influence accountability?
4. How can the concept of a Ulysses Contract be applied in a business setting to ensure adherence to change initiatives? What are the potential advantages and challenges of using this strategy?
5. Why is timing crucial when negotiating change, and how can early negotiations help leaders foster a more rational and collaborative approach to change management?

Practice Exercises

1. Stakeholder Engagement Simulation

- **Objective**: To improve your ability to engage and involve stakeholders early in the change process.
- **How to Do It**: Identify a hypothetical or upcoming change initiative in your organization. Create a plan to engage key stakeholders by mapping out who should be involved, what information needs to be communicated, and when to engage them. Role-play conversations with a colleague or mentor

where you practice explaining the change, addressing concerns, and seeking input. Reflect on the outcomes and adjust your approach for future engagements.

2. Drafting a Ulysses Contract

- **Objective**: To develop your skills in formalizing commitments and creating accountability.
- **How to Do It**: Choose a scenario where commitment to a decision or change is crucial. Draft a Ulysses Contract that outlines the commitment, the reasons behind it, and the consequences of not adhering to it. Present the contract to a team or group (real or hypothetical) and discuss its potential impact. Evaluate how this approach could be used in real-life situations to secure commitment to change initiatives.

3. Strategic Timing Workshop

- **Objective**: To practice strategic timing in negotiating change commitments.
- **How to Do It**: Create a timeline for a major change initiative, focusing on when to have key discussions and secure commitments. Consider the psychological impact of timing and how people's willingness to commit might change as the implementation date approaches. Role-play scenarios where you negotiate agreements at different points in the timeline, noting the differences in responses and outcomes. Analyze which timing strategies were most effective and why.

CHAPTER 8
CULTIVATE A PLAYER-LED TEAM

Leadership isn't just about having someone at the helm making decisions. Real leadership goes beyond titles and roles, permeating every level of a team. Whether it's a sports team, a corporate group, or just friends working toward a common goal, the true strength of any team lies in its ability to harness leadership from every member. This concept, often referred to as player-led leadership, can transform a group of individuals into a dynamic, adaptable force capable of achieving more than any single person could on their own.

The Essence of Player-Led Leadership

Player-led leadership isn't about delegating tasks or merely making decisions. It's about cultivating a culture where every team member feels empowered and expected to lead in their own way, regardless of their official position. When leadership is distributed across the team, it encourages a diversity of ideas and perspectives, leading to more creative and effective solutions. This approach also allows individuals to play to their strengths, contributing in ways that best utilize their unique talents.

Successful teams—whether in business, sports, or any other domain—often exhibit this kind of leadership. In these teams, leadership is fluid;

it's not tied to one person but can shift based on the situation and the strengths of the team members involved. This kind of flexibility is crucial in today's fast-paced, unpredictable environment.

Flexibility and Adaptability

One of the most significant advantages of player-led leadership is its inherent flexibility. Different challenges require different approaches, and a team that relies on a single leader may find itself at a disadvantage. In contrast, a team where leadership is shared can adapt more readily. For instance, if a particular challenge arises that falls within the expertise of a specific team member, that person can step up and take the lead, even if they aren't the designated leader. This allows the team to respond to challenges in the most effective way possible, leveraging the best available resources.

This flexibility also fosters resilience. In the face of setbacks, a player-led team can adjust and pivot more quickly because leadership is not centralized. This decentralized approach to leadership ensures that the team remains agile and responsive, capable of navigating the inevitable obstacles that arise.

Empowering the Individual

Player-led leadership also offers significant benefits to individual team members. By encouraging leadership at all levels, team members are given the opportunity to develop their own leadership skills. This not only boosts their confidence but also increases their investment in the team's success. When everyone feels a sense of ownership, they are more likely to go the extra mile and contribute in meaningful ways.

However, this approach isn't without its challenges. It requires a high level of trust and respect among team members, as well as open, honest communication. Leaders must be willing to step back and allow others to lead, which can be difficult for those who are used to being in control. It also requires a leader who is secure enough in their own abilities to take responsibility for the team's failures, even when those failures result from decisions made by others. This kind of vulnerability is essential for building trust and creating a culture where player-led leadership can thrive.

Cultivating a Culture of Trust

The foundation of successful player-led leadership is trust. Without it, team members will be hesitant to step up and lead, fearing that their decisions will be second-guessed or undermined. Leaders can cultivate this trust by being transparent, setting clear goals and expectations, and recognizing and rewarding contributions. It's also crucial for leaders to lead by example, demonstrating the behaviors they want to see in their team.

In addition to trust, leaders must invest in the development of their team members. This means not only focusing on individual strengths but also providing the support and coaching necessary to help team members grow. When team members feel supported, they are more likely to take on leadership roles, which ultimately leads to a more cohesive and successful team.

Avoiding the Pitfalls of "Dirty Empowerment"

It's important to note that not all empowerment is created equal. "Dirty empowerment" occurs when leaders give the appearance of empowering their team members but still retain control over decisions. This type of pseudo-empowerment can be damaging, as it undermines trust and stifles the initiative. True player-led leadership requires leaders to genuinely trust their team members and give them the freedom to make decisions without constantly seeking approval.

Breaking Through to Success

Player-led leadership is not the easiest approach to implement, but it's one of the most effective. By fostering a culture of trust, encouraging leadership at all levels, and avoiding the pitfalls of dirty empowerment, teams can achieve breakthroughs that wouldn't be possible under a more traditional, top-down leadership model. It's about creating an environment where everyone is both a leader and a follower, depending on what the situation demands.

When done right, player-led leadership transforms a team into a resilient, adaptable, and highly effective unit, ready to tackle any challenge that comes their way. The journey to this level of leadership might be challenging, but the rewards—both for the team and the individuals within it—are well worth the effort.

EXPRESS VALUES DAILY

Values are more than just words on a wall—they're the lifeblood of any team or organization. They shape the culture, guide decisions, and set the standard for behavior. But values only matter if they're lived out daily. It's not enough to identify them; they need to be expressed consistently to build a strong, unified culture.

Identifying Your Team's Core Values

The process of determining team values starts with a conversation. Gather the team and discuss what principles matter most. This isn't a box-ticking exercise—it's about defining what you stand for. Keep the list short. If you have too many values, they become hard to remember and even harder to live by. Once you've nailed down the key values, make sure everyone is on board. Alignment is crucial. If your team isn't united on these values, they'll be meaningless.

Bringing Values to Life

Once you've established your values, it's time to bring them to life. Values shouldn't be abstract concepts; they should be woven into the fabric of your team's daily activities. This can take many forms—from the way decisions are made to how team members are recognized and how challenges are tackled.

For example, a professional services firm might value client-centricity. To keep this top of mind, the team could start each day with a leader sharing a client testimonial. This daily ritual reinforces the importance of prioritizing client needs. On an athletic team, where "playing unselfishly" might be a core value, players could be encouraged to point out the teammate who helped them score. This not only celebrates teamwork but also builds a sense of unity.

Creative Expressions of Values

Creativity plays a big role in how values are expressed. The more personalized and meaningful the expressions, the stronger the impact. Some teams use rituals or ceremonies. Take the U.S. Supreme Court, for instance. They value collegiality, and before every session, they engage in a ritual of 36 handshakes. It's a simple act, but it reinforces respect and camaraderie among the justices.

Other teams might focus on daily actions. Showing respect, striving for excellence, and acknowledging contributions are all ways to express values in the everyday rhythm of work. The key is to find expressions that resonate with your team and consistently reinforce them.

Leading by Example

Effective teams are led by value-driven leaders who don't just talk about values—they live them. John Wooden, the legendary UCLA basketball coach, was a master at this. He didn't just preach about character and teamwork; he embodied these values, and his teams followed suit. Leaders set the tone. If they're committed to the values, the team will be too.

Reinforcing Values Regularly

It's not enough to set values and forget them. They need to be reinforced constantly. Regular team meetings, discussions, and everyday actions should all reflect the team's core values. This repetition helps embed the values into the team's culture, making them second nature.

Values should also inform every aspect of the team's work—decisions, evaluations, hiring, and strategy. There's no one-size-fits-all when it comes to values; they need to align with the team's goals and priorities. It's the leader's job to ensure these values are clear and that the team understands and embraces them.

Making Values a Way of Life

Expressing values daily through messages, rituals, competitions, activities, and drills helps keep them alive. These expressions should become a natural part of how the team operates. Whether it's how you start meetings, celebrate wins, or onboard new members, these rituals help your team internalize the values and live them out.

Over time, these practices become part of the team's identity, just like we have in our organization under "The B:Side Way." This isn't just about compliance; it's about creating a culture where everyone feels connected and committed to the same standards.

Fostering a Value-Driven Culture

You can't force a team to gel, but you can create an environment where they want to. When values are clear and consistently reinforced, team members start holding each other accountable. It's no longer just the leader's job—it becomes a collective responsibility.

A value-driven culture is a strong foundation for success. It unites the team, fosters accountability, and aligns everyone towards common goals. When a team lives its values, it's not just doing the work; it's living the mission every single day.

Key Actions

- **Identifying Core Values:** Engage in a team discussion to determine and agree on a few key principles that the team stands for.
- **Bringing Values to Life:** Consistently incorporate the identified values into daily activities, decisions, and team interactions.
- **Creative Expression of Values:** Use rituals, ceremonies, or daily actions to express and reinforce team values in a meaningful and personalized way.
- **Leading by Example:** Leaders should embody the team's values, setting the tone for the rest of the team to follow.
- **Reinforcing Values Regularly:** Frequently revisit and reinforce the team's values through meetings, discussions, and everyday actions to ensure they become ingrained in the team culture.
- **Making Values a Way of Life:** Integrate values into all aspects of team operations, including how meetings are conducted, successes are celebrated, and new members are onboarded.
- **Fostering Accountability:** Encourage team members to hold

each other accountable to the values, creating a collective responsibility for upholding the team's standards.

Discussion Questions

1. What are the core values that our team currently embodies, and are there any additional values we should consider integrating?
2. Can you share examples of how we've successfully brought our values to life in our daily work? Where do you see opportunities for improvement?
3. How can we get more creative in expressing our values through rituals, ceremonies, or daily actions to make them more meaningful and impactful?
4. In what ways can our leaders better model our team's values, and how does this influence the overall team culture?
5. How do we ensure that our values are regularly reinforced and that team members hold each other accountable to these standards? What steps can we take to strengthen this process?

Practice Exercises

1. Core Value Alignment Workshop

- **Objective:** To identify and align the team's core values.
- **How to Do It:** Schedule a dedicated workshop with your team. Start with an open discussion where each team member shares the values they believe are most important. Then, narrow down the list to 3-5 key values that resonate with everyone. Make sure there's consensus on the selected values and discuss how these can be reflected in daily work.

2. Daily Value Reflection

- **Objective:** To integrate and reinforce team values in daily actions.

- **How to Do It:** Begin each workday with a brief reflection or team huddle focused on a specific value. Ask each team member to share a recent example of how they've lived this value in their work. Rotate the focus to different values each day to ensure consistent reinforcement and application.

3. Value-Driven Leadership Challenge

- **Objective:** To practice leading by example and embedding values in leadership actions.
- **How to Do It:** For one week, consciously model the team's core values in all interactions, decisions, and communications. At the end of each day, take five minutes to reflect on how well you embodied the values. Identify areas for improvement and set specific goals for the next day. Encourage feedback from team members on how well the values are being demonstrated by leadership.

SHARED LEARNING BUILDS TRUST

Shared experiences are the backbone of strong teams. When people come together to learn and grow, something magical happens: they build trust. Trust isn't just about knowing someone will get the job done; it's about understanding their strengths, weaknesses, and how they'll react in different situations. This kind of deep trust comes from shared learning experiences.

The Power of Shared Experiences

Shared experiences aren't just for fun; they're essential for team development. When team members step out of their daily grind and engage in activities together, whether it's a social outing, a workshop, or a volunteer project, they create a bond that goes beyond the office walls. These experiences allow team members to see each other in new lights, breaking down barriers and fostering a deeper connection.

Learning Together: The Foundation of Team Cohesion

One of the most valuable aspects of shared experiences is the opportunity to learn together. When a team tackles a new challenge or dives into a new subject as a unit, it creates a sense of collective knowledge. This shared learning isn't just about acquiring new skills; it's about understanding each other's thought processes and problem-solving styles. It's about building a shared language and set of experiences that the team can draw on in the future.

For example, imagine a team that spends a day in a hands-on workshop learning a new software tool. As they struggle and succeed together, they're not just learning the tool; they're learning how each person approaches challenges, who steps up as a leader, and who excels at finding creative solutions. This knowledge becomes invaluable when the team faces a real-world problem and needs to work together efficiently.

Breaking the Routine: The Role of Novelty

Routine can be the enemy of creativity and engagement. When teams are stuck in the same patterns, it's easy for motivation to wane. Shared experiences inject a sense of novelty and excitement into the team dynamic. Whether it's a new challenge or simply a change of scenery, these experiences can reinvigorate a team and reignite their passion for the work they do.

Think about long-term projects that can become monotonous over time. Introducing a shared learning experience, like an offsite retreat or a new team-building activity, can break up the routine and provide a much-needed boost. It's not just about taking a break; it's about refocusing the team's energy and reminding them of their shared goals.

Building Trust Through Shared Learning

Trust isn't built overnight, and it certainly doesn't come from a single team-building exercise. It's developed over time through consistent, positive interactions. Shared experiences are a powerful way to accelerate this process. When team members learn together, they build a sense of predictability and understanding. They see how their colleagues handle pressure, how they collaborate, and how they communicate.

This predictability is crucial for trust. When you know how someone will react in a given situation, you can rely on them. This kind of trust is essential for high-performing teams. It allows team members to take risks, knowing that their colleagues will support them. It also creates a safe environment where team members can be honest and open without fear of judgment.

Creating Shared Experiences: A Leader's Role

As a leader, it's your responsibility to create these shared experiences. It takes planning and creativity, but the payoff is worth it. Start by thinking about your team's values and goals. What kind of experiences would resonate with them? What skills do they need to develop? From there, you can brainstorm activities that align with these objectives.

Some ideas might include:

- *Team-Building Activities*: These can be as simple as a group lunch or as complex as an escape room challenge. The key is to choose activities that encourage collaboration and communication.

- *Offsite Learning Events:* Workshops, seminars, or even conferences can provide valuable learning experiences outside the usual work environment.
- *Volunteer Projects:* Giving back to the community as a team can build a sense of purpose and unity.
- *Social Outings:* Sometimes, the best way to build trust is through informal, low-pressure activities like a team hike or a game night.

Whatever you choose, make sure everyone has the opportunity to participate. Inclusivity is key to creating a sense of team.

Why It Matters

In the end, shared learning experiences are about more than just having fun or acquiring new skills. They're about building a foundation of trust that allows a team to perform at its best. When team members trust each other, they communicate more openly, collaborate more effectively, and support each other through challenges.

As a leader, fostering these experiences is one of the most powerful tools at your disposal. By bringing your team together in new and meaningful ways, you're not just creating memories; you're building a stronger, more cohesive team capable of achieving great things together.

Key Actions

- **Engaging in Shared Experiences**: Encourage team members to participate in activities that go beyond their regular work, such as social outings, workshops, or volunteer projects, to build deeper connections.
- **Learning Together as a Team**: Facilitate opportunities for the team to learn new skills or tackle challenges together, fostering a sense of collective knowledge and understanding.

- **Breaking the Routine**: Introduce novelty into the team's routine through shared experiences, helping to maintain motivation and engagement.
- **Observing and Understanding Team Members**: Pay attention to how team members handle different situations during shared experiences to build trust through predictability and understanding.
- **Creating a Safe Environment**: Promote an atmosphere where team members feel comfortable taking risks and being honest, knowing they have the support of their colleagues.
- **Planning and Facilitating Shared Experiences**: As a leader, take an active role in organizing and facilitating shared experiences that align with the team's values and goals.
- **Ensuring Inclusivity**: Make sure that all team members have the opportunity to participate in shared experiences, fostering a sense of unity and belonging.

Discussion Questions

1. How have shared experiences, such as team outings or workshops, impacted the trust and cohesion within your team? Can you share specific examples?
2. In what ways can learning together as a team help you better understand each other's strengths and working styles? How can we apply this understanding to improve our collaboration?
3. How do you think breaking the routine with novel activities can help maintain your team's motivation and creativity, especially during long-term projects?
4. What are some ways we can ensure that your shared experiences are inclusive and meaningful for everyone on the team? How can we improve participation?
5. As a team, what kinds of shared experiences or learning opportunities would you like to see more of in the future? How can these activities help you achieve our goals?

Practice Exercises

1. Team Reflection Sessions

- **Objective**: To build trust and understanding among team members by reflecting on shared experiences.
- **How to Do It**: After a shared experience, gather the team for a reflection session. Encourage each team member to share what they learned, how the experience impacted their understanding of their colleagues, and how they can apply these insights in their daily work. Use open-ended questions to facilitate discussion, and ensure everyone has the opportunity to contribute.

2. Role-Switching Challenges

- **Objective**: To deepen understanding of each team member's strengths and challenges by experiencing their roles.
- **How to Do It**: Organize a role-switching day where team members take on each other's tasks or responsibilities for a short period. This could be done in pairs or within small groups. After the exercise, discuss as a team what each person learned about the other's role, and how this understanding can improve collaboration and trust.

3. Inclusive Activity Planning

- **Objective**: To improve your ability to create inclusive and meaningful shared experiences for the team.
- **How to Do It**: Plan a team activity that aligns with your team's values and goals. Before finalizing, gather input from all team members on what types of activities they would find engaging and meaningful. After the event, solicit feedback on how inclusive and beneficial the experience was, and use this feedback to refine future activities. Repeat this process regularly to continuously improve your planning skills.

CONVERSATIONS OF INQUIRY

Conversations are the lifeblood of any team. But not all conversations are created equal. To build a high-performing team, you need to cultivate conversations that go beyond surface-level exchanges. You need to dive into inquiry and dialogue.

The Power of Inquiry and Dialogue

Most of us are familiar with conversations where the primary goal is to advocate for our own ideas. We state our points, defend them, and often, without realizing it, dismiss or discredit opposing viewpoints. These advocacy-based conversations are common, but they rarely lead to the kind of deep understanding and trust that high-performing teams need.

Dialogue, on the other hand, is different. It's about inquiry—asking questions to genuinely understand other perspectives, rather than trying to win an argument or come to a quick conclusion. In a dialogue, the focus shifts from pushing an agenda to exploring an issue collaboratively. This shift is crucial because it creates space for team members to share their thoughts openly, feel heard, and contribute to a deeper understanding of the challenges at hand.

Why Dialogue Matters

Why should teams invest time in dialogue? Because avoiding tough conversations leads to unresolved issues and festering tensions. When we don't address sensitive topics, we miss out on the opportunity to grow as a team. Engaging in dialogue, however, allows team members to voice their concerns, explore different perspectives, and ultimately build trust.

Trust isn't just a feel-good concept; it's the foundation of any successful team. When team members trust each other, they're more likely to share ideas, take risks, and support one another. This trust leads to better decision-making and a stronger, more cohesive team. Without it, teams are prone to miscommunication, misunderstandings, and missed opportunities.

Practical Steps to Foster Inquiry and Dialogue

So how do you cultivate a culture of inquiry and dialogue in your team? Start by making time for it. Set aside moments in meetings where the goal isn't to solve a problem but to explore it. Encourage your team to ask questions that don't have straightforward answers. For example, instead of focusing on "How do we fix this?" ask, "Why is this happening?" or "What are we missing?"

Creating an environment where everyone feels comfortable sharing is also key. This means establishing a space where team members know their voices will be heard without judgment. It's not about creating a "safe space" in the clichéd sense, but rather fostering a culture where open, honest conversation is the norm. Make it clear that every opinion is valued, even if it challenges the status quo.

Incorporating inquiry-based questions into your team's daily conversations can transform the way you work together. These questions should be designed to dig deeper, uncover root causes, and open up new avenues for discussion. Questions like "What assumptions are we making?" or "How might others view this situation?" encourage a broader perspective and a more collaborative approach to problem-solving.

Building a Culture of Dialogue

The best teams are those that can talk about anything—no topic is too sensitive, no issue too complex. When you cultivate a culture of inquiry and dialogue, you equip your team to handle challenges head-on, build stronger relationships, and achieve better outcomes.

Remember, dialogue isn't just about understanding others—it's also about building a collective understanding. When team members feel that their perspectives are valued and their voices are heard, they're more engaged, more committed, and more willing to go the extra mile.

In the end, the ability to have open, honest, and inquiry-based conversations is what separates good teams from great ones. By focusing on dialogue, you're not just addressing the issues at hand; you're laying the groundwork for long-term success.

Key Actions

- **Shifting from Advocacy to Inquiry**: Focus on understanding other perspectives rather than pushing your own agenda.
- **Making Time for Dialogue**: Set aside specific times in meetings to explore issues rather than just making decisions.
- **Encouraging Open Sharing**: Create an environment where team members feel comfortable sharing their thoughts and opinions without fear of judgment.
- **Asking Inquiry-Based Questions**: Use questions designed to dig deeper, uncover root causes, and encourage broader perspectives.
- **Building Trust Through Conversation**: Engage in open and honest dialogue to build trust and strengthen team relationships.

Discussion Questions

1. How can we shift our team's focus from advocacy-based conversations to inquiry-driven dialogue in our daily interactions?
2. What are some specific examples where open dialogue led to better decision-making or stronger relationships within our team?
3. How can we create an environment where everyone feels comfortable sharing their thoughts, especially on sensitive or difficult topics?
4. What inquiry-based questions can we start incorporating into our meetings to encourage deeper thinking and exploration of issues?
5. In what ways can building trust through dialogue improve our team's overall performance and cohesiveness?

Practice Exercises

1. Shift to Inquiry

- **Objective**: Develop the habit of asking questions that promote deeper understanding rather than pushing your own viewpoint.
- **How to Do It**: In your next team meeting, focus on asking questions rather than offering solutions or opinions. For instance, instead of suggesting how to fix a problem, ask, "What factors are contributing to this issue?" or "How do you think we should approach this challenge?" Reflect on how the conversation changes when you prioritize inquiry over advocacy.

2. Create a Dialogue Session

- **Objective**: Practice fostering a space for open dialogue where all team members can share their perspectives.
- **How to Do It**: Dedicate a portion of your next meeting to a "Dialogue Session" where the goal is not to reach a decision but to explore a topic deeply. Choose a complex or sensitive issue, and encourage everyone to share their thoughts without judgment. Focus on listening and understanding rather than responding. After the session, debrief on how the experience felt and what insights were gained.

3. Practice Active Listening

- **Objective**: Improve your ability to listen actively and understand others' perspectives during conversations.
- **How to Do It**: In your daily interactions, consciously practice active listening. This means fully concentrating on the speaker, understanding their message, responding thoughtfully, and remembering what was said. Avoid interrupting or preparing your response while the other

person is speaking. After the conversation, summarize what you heard to ensure you understood correctly. Over time, this will enhance your ability to engage in meaningful dialogue.

INSTANT ACCOUNTABILITY

Building high-performing teams is crucial for success in any organization. One of the key ingredients in this recipe is creating a culture of instant accountability and mutual respect. These two elements are not just nice-to-haves—they're essential for any team aiming for excellence.

The Power of Instant Accountability

Instant accountability means taking ownership of your actions—good or bad—without delay. It's about acknowledging mistakes as soon as they happen, which sets the stage for learning and growth. This is not just about covering your own bases; it's about fostering an environment where everyone feels responsible for the team's success.

The Navy Blue Angels, an elite flight demonstration squadron of the United States Navy, provide a stellar example of this principle in action. They practice what's called "calling a safety," where each team member is expected to identify and call out their own mistakes during a critique session immediately after a performance. No one hides their errors; instead, they openly discuss them, making corrections on the spot. This approach not only drives continuous improvement but also builds trust within the team. When everyone is held accountable, it sets a standard that's hard to beat.

Why Instant Accountability Matters

Accountability and respect are two sides of the same coin. When team members own up to their mistakes, it demonstrates trust and respect within the team. Conversely, when there's a lack of accountability, you often find a lack of respect—and the results can be disastrous. Teams that fail to hold themselves accountable quickly fall into a cycle of underperformance. Members start to fear taking risks or making decisions, knowing they won't be backed up or, worse, that their mistakes will be swept under the rug.

Leaders play a pivotal role in establishing this culture. They must create an environment where team members feel safe to admit their mistakes and work together to fix them. This isn't about coddling; it's about setting clear expectations and encouraging openness. When team members know they won't be unfairly criticized but instead will be supported in making things right, they're more likely to take ownership and contribute positively to the team's goals.

The Link Between Respect and Performance

Respect is the foundation of any strong team, and it's closely linked to accountability. When people respect one another, they're more likely to engage in honest, productive conversations. They don't shy away from tough topics or sugarcoat feedback. Instead, they tackle issues head-on, knowing that it's all in the service of making the team better.

However, when disrespect enters the picture, everything changes. Conversations become superficial, trust erodes, and the team's cohesion falls apart. Leaders who allow disrespect to fester—whether it's due to a lack of character or competence—are sending a clear message: that some people are above accountability. This undermines the entire team and can even lead to resistance against the leader's direction.

Addressing disrespect is no easy task, but it's one that leaders must take on if they want to maintain a strong team. Sometimes, this means making the hard call to remove a team member who consistently undermines the group's cohesion. Other times, it's about helping that person rebuild trust with the rest of the team. Either way, it's about ensuring that respect remains a cornerstone of the team's culture.

The Role of Leaders in Fostering Accountability

Leaders aren't just responsible for holding others accountable—they need to hold themselves to the same standard. A great leader admits their own mistakes just as quickly as they expect others to. This sets a powerful example and reinforces the idea that everyone is in this together.

But leaders also need to be vigilant about respect. They must be quick to address any signs of disrespect within the team, whether it's a casual comment that crosses the line or a deeper issue that's been simmering under the surface. When leaders act swiftly and decisively, they show that respect isn't just a word on a poster—it's a core value that everyone must uphold.

Key Actions

- **Taking Ownership of Mistakes**: Team members are expected to acknowledge and take responsibility for their mistakes immediately, without delay.
- **Encouraging Open Critique**: Creating an environment where team members feel safe to critique themselves and others, fostering continuous improvement.
- **Practicing "Calling a Safety"**: A behavior modeled by the Navy Blue Angels where team members identify and call out their own mistakes during a critique session immediately after a performance.
- **Building Trust Through Accountability**: Establishing a culture where accountability is linked to mutual respect and trust among team members.
- **Promoting Honest Conversations**: Encouraging honest, productive conversations that address tough issues directly, with the goal of improving team performance.
- **Addressing Disrespect Swiftly**: Leaders must act quickly to address any signs of disrespect within the team, whether it's minor or significant.
- **Leading by Example**: Leaders should model the behavior they expect from their team, including admitting their own mistakes and holding themselves accountable.
- **Creating a Safe Environment for Feedback**: Leaders must create an environment where critique is expected, and team members feel comfortable admitting mistakes and working together to find solutions.
- **Making Tough Decisions When Necessary**: Leaders may need to remove team members who consistently undermine respect and accountability within the team.
- **Fostering Mutual Respect**: Cultivating respect as a core value that drives accountability, honest communication, and team cohesion.

Discussion Questions

1. What strategies can leaders use to establish a culture of instant accountability within a team?
2. How does taking immediate ownership of mistakes influence trust and respect among team members?
3. What challenges might arise when addressing disrespect within a team, and how can leaders effectively manage these situations?
4. How does the practice of "calling a safety" contribute to accountability and continuous improvement in a team setting?
5. Why is it crucial for leaders to model accountability, and what impact does this have on the team's overall culture?

Practice Exercises

1. Mistake Acknowledgment Drill

- **Objective**: Improve your ability to take immediate ownership of mistakes.
- **How to Do It**: At the end of each day, reflect on any mistakes or missteps you made during the day. Write them down and note how you addressed (or could have addressed) them immediately. Share these reflections with a trusted colleague or mentor to practice openly acknowledging mistakes in a safe environment.

2. Accountability Partner Sessions

- **Objective**: Foster mutual accountability and trust within your team.
- **How to Do It**: Pair up with a colleague and commit to a weekly 15-minute check-in. During this time, each person shares one area where they fell short and what they are doing to improve. This exercise builds the habit of accountability and reinforces the importance of owning mistakes.

3. Respect and Feedback Role-Play

- **Objective**: Strengthen your ability to address disrespect and give constructive feedback.
- **How to Do It**: Set up a role-play scenario where you practice addressing a team member who has shown signs of disrespect or needs constructive feedback. Focus on being direct, specific, and maintaining respect throughout the conversation. Afterward, discuss the experience with an observer or your role-play partner to get feedback on your approach.

MANAGING HIGH PERFORMERS

Managing a team comes with its own set of challenges, but one of the toughest is figuring out how to handle high-performing individuals. These are the folks who have the drive to excel, the skills to back it up, and the hunger for recognition. They can be the engines that drive your team forward, but they can also be the source of friction if not managed carefully.

On one side, you want to push and support your top performers—they're the ones who can elevate the entire team's performance. On the other, you have to make sure you don't alienate the rest of the team in the process. It's a balancing act, and the stakes are high. Get it right, and you've got a powerhouse team. Get it wrong, and you risk creating a divided group that's more focused on internal competition than on achieving shared goals.

Everyone on the Team Matters

One of the bedrock principles of great leadership is the belief that everyone on the team matters. It's not just about the stars; it's about every single member. The best leaders treat each person with respect, give them a voice, and create opportunities for them to contribute. It doesn't matter if they're the top performer or someone who's still finding their footing—everyone's input is valuable.

Why is this so important? Because when people feel heard and valued, they're more likely to buy into the team's mission. They're more likely to put in the extra effort, share ideas, and support their teammates. In short, they're more likely to become part of a cohesive, high-performing unit.

The Same Rules Apply to Everyone

Another key to managing a successful team is ensuring that everyone plays by the same rules. This doesn't mean treating everyone exactly the same—that would be unfair and unrealistic. What it does mean is holding everyone to the same standards and expectations.

Let's say responsiveness to clients is a core value for your team. That means everyone, from the top performer to the newest member, needs to meet the same expectations when it comes to responding to clients. No one gets a pass just because they're good at something else. When everyone is held to the same standards, it fosters a sense of fairness and unity within the team. No one feels like there are different rules for different people, and that's critical for maintaining trust and morale.

Recognizing and Rewarding High Performers—Fairly

Here's where things get tricky. High performers do deserve special recognition and sometimes special treatment. They're the ones who often go above and beyond, and they can drive the team to new heights. Maybe they get more responsibility, more access to important information, or more face time with leadership. That's okay—up to a point.

The key is to make sure that this recognition doesn't cross the line into favoritism. If other team members start to feel like they're being side-lined or that there are "first-class" and "economy" seats on the team, you've got a problem. The challenge for leaders is to find ways to reward high performers without disenfranchising others. This might mean being transparent about why certain individuals are getting certain opportunities and making sure that all team members have a path to similar rewards if they step up.

Creating a Culture of Accountability

One of the biggest barriers to team success is the fear of making mistakes. If team members are afraid to fail, they won't take risks, and they won't innovate. That's why creating a culture of accountability is so important. In a culture of accountability, mistakes aren't something to be hidden or feared—they're something to be acknowledged, learned from, and moved past.

Instant accountability is a powerful tool in this regard. When team members are encouraged to own up to their mistakes as soon as they happen, it creates an environment where everyone is learning and growing together. It also levels the playing field because it's not just the lower performers who are held accountable; everyone, including the leader, is expected to admit their missteps.

This kind of environment fosters mutual respect. When leaders hold themselves to the same standards as everyone else and are willing to admit when they've messed up, it sends a powerful message. It tells the team that accountability isn't just a buzzword—it's a core value. And when accountability is a core value, teams are more resilient, more innovative, and ultimately more successful.

The Big Picture: Building a Cohesive, High-Performing Team

In the end, the goal of any team leader is to build a group that's more than just the sum of its parts. That means managing the tension between recognizing and rewarding high performers and making sure that everyone feels valued and included. It means creating an environment where everyone plays by the same rules, where accountability is expected and respected, and where mistakes are seen as opportunities to learn and grow.

By focusing on these principles, leaders can create teams that are not only high-performing but also cohesive, resilient, and ready to take on whatever challenges come their way. The result? A team where everyone feels like they matter and where everyone is playing by the same rules—because that's what it takes to win.

Key Actions

- **Respecting and Valuing Every Team Member**: Treat every individual on the team with respect and give them opportunities to contribute, regardless of their performance level.
- **Applying the Same Standards and Expectations to Everyone**: Ensure that all team members are held to the same standards and expectations, creating a sense of fairness and unity.
- **Recognizing and Rewarding High Performers Fairly**: Acknowledge and reward high performers appropriately while

being mindful not to alienate or disenfranchise other team members.

- **Creating a Culture of Accountability**: Encourage instant accountability, where team members are expected to admit mistakes quickly and learn from them, fostering a learning environment.
- **Leading by Example**: As a leader, hold yourself to the same standards as your team members, admitting mistakes and being transparent about your actions.
- **Fostering Mutual Respect:** Build an environment of mutual respect by treating everyone equally and encouraging a culture where accountability and learning from mistakes are valued.

Discussion Questions

1. How can leaders ensure that every team member feels valued and respected, even if they are not top performers?
2. What are the potential risks of applying different rules or standards to high performers, and how can these risks be mitigated?
3. In what ways can leaders recognize and reward high performers without creating a divide within the team?
4. How does fostering a culture of accountability contribute to a team's overall success, and what strategies can leaders use to encourage this culture?
5. Why is it important for leaders to hold themselves to the same standards as their team members, and what impact does this have on team dynamics?

Practice Exercises

1. Conduct a "Roundtable Feedback" Session

- **Objective**: To ensure all team members feel valued and respected.

- **How to Do It**: Schedule a roundtable session where each team member is given the opportunity to share their thoughts, ideas, and concerns. As the leader, actively listen and encourage participation from everyone, especially those who are quieter or less assertive. After the session, reflect on how you can incorporate their feedback into your leadership approach.

2. Create a "Fairness Audit" Checklist

- **Objective**: To apply consistent standards and expectations across the team.
- **How to Do It**: Develop a checklist that outlines the key standards and expectations for your team, such as response times, quality of work, and collaboration. Regularly review this checklist to ensure that you are applying these standards uniformly across all team members. Identify any areas where you may be unconsciously favoring certain individuals and make adjustments as necessary.

3. Practice "Instant Accountability" with Your Team

- **Objective**: To foster a culture of accountability.
- **How to Do It**: Start by modeling instant accountability yourself. When you make a mistake, openly admit it to your team and discuss what you've learned from it. Encourage your team members to do the same by creating a safe environment where mistakes are seen as learning opportunities rather than failures. Regularly hold brief sessions where the team discusses recent mistakes and the lessons learned from them.

PEER-TO-PEER RECOGNITION

Peer recognition is a cornerstone of strong team culture. When praise comes from those who work alongside us, it carries a special weight. Our peers know the ins and outs of our daily challenges, and their recognition signifies a deep, mutual respect. It's not just about feeling good; it's about feeling valued by the very people who understand our work the best.

Why Peer Recognition Matters

Recognition from peers goes beyond simple acknowledgment. It validates our contributions and reinforces our sense of belonging within the team. When peers appreciate our efforts, it tells us that we're on the right track and that our work matters. This validation strengthens team bonds, creating a sense of equality and shared purpose. It's not about hierarchy or titles; it's about respect and appreciation for the work we do together.

The Missing Piece: Formal Mechanisms

Despite its importance, peer recognition often falls by the wayside in many organizations. Without a formal system, it can be tough for team members to regularly acknowledge each other's contributions. This isn't because they don't value each other, but rather because the opportunities to express that value aren't built into the team's daily routines.

The Leader's Role in Fostering Peer Recognition

Here's where leadership comes into play. Team leaders have the power to cultivate an environment where peer-to-peer recognition thrives. By promoting open communication and encouraging team members to recognize each other's efforts, leaders can weave appreciation into the fabric of the team culture.

Simple practices can make a big difference. For example, incorporating "shout-outs" in regular meetings where team members can highlight the contributions of their peers is a great start. Leaders can also introduce formal mechanisms like peer-nominated awards or recognition programs that celebrate individual and collective achievements. These initiatives don't just make recognition possible; they make it expected.

The Ripple Effect: Benefits of Peer Recognition

Incorporating peer recognition into the team's culture yields significant benefits. It shifts the focus from competition to collaboration, driving morale and motivation upward. When team members regularly acknowledge each other's efforts, it builds a foundation of trust and respect that's essential for effective teamwork.

This trust is particularly crucial when tackling complex projects or navigating challenges. Teams that recognize and appreciate each other's strengths are better equipped to work together seamlessly. They're more likely to offer support when it's needed and to rely on each other's expertise, leading to more successful outcomes.

Creating a Culture of Accountability

Recognition isn't just about celebrating successes; it's also about owning mistakes. To build a truly cohesive team, leaders must foster a culture where accountability is valued as much as praise. This means creating an environment where team members feel safe admitting their mistakes and learning from them.

One effective practice is promoting instant accountability. Encourage team members to call out their own mistakes as soon as they happen. This approach not only prevents small issues from becoming bigger problems but also reinforces a culture of transparency and continuous improvement.

When team members are open about their missteps, it fosters a deeper sense of trust and respect. They know they can count on their peers for support, not judgment. This, in turn, strengthens the team's ability to grow together and tackle challenges head-on.

Peer recognition is more than just a feel-good practice—it's a powerful tool for building stronger, more effective teams. By encouraging open appreciation and creating a culture of accountability, leaders can transform their teams into high-performing units where trust, respect, and collaboration are the norms. In this kind of environment, team members don't just work together—they thrive together.

Key Actions

- **Peer Recognition**: Valuing and acknowledging the efforts of colleagues, which reinforces mutual respect and strengthens team bonds.
- **Validation and Belonging**: Recognizing contributions from peers to confirm one's worth and sense of belonging within the team.
- **Leadership in Peer Recognition**: Leaders promoting open communication and encouraging team members to recognize each other's efforts.
- **Formal Mechanisms for Recognition**: Implementing systems like "shout-outs," peer-nominated awards, or recognition programs to make peer appreciation a regular part of team culture.
- **Collaboration Over Competition**: Fostering an environment where teamwork and mutual support are prioritized over individual competition.
- **Trust and Respect**: Building trust and respect among team members by regularly acknowledging strengths and contributions.
- **Instant Accountability**: Encouraging team members to immediately own and address their mistakes to promote transparency and continuous improvement.
- **Supportive Culture**: Creating a safe environment where team members feel comfortable admitting mistakes, leading to stronger team cohesion and growth.

Discussion Questions

1. How does peer recognition impact team morale and performance?
2. What are some effective ways leaders can encourage peer-to-peer recognition within a team?

3. Why is it important to have formal mechanisms for peer recognition in an organization?
4. How does a culture of instant accountability influence trust and transparency within a team?
5. In what ways can peer recognition help shift a team's focus from competition to collaboration?

Practice Exercises

1. Daily Peer Recognition

- **Objective**: To build the habit of recognizing and appreciating your peers regularly.
- **How to Do It**: Each day, take a moment to observe the contributions of your team members. Identify one specific action or effort by a colleague that you genuinely appreciate. Share your recognition with them directly, either in person, via email, or during a team meeting. Be specific about what you appreciated and why it mattered.

2. Peer Recognition Journaling

- **Objective**: To reflect on and internalize the impact of peer recognition.
- **How to Do It**: Keep a journal dedicated to recording instances of peer recognition—both giving and receiving. At the end of each week, review your entries and reflect on how these moments affected team morale and your own sense of connection to the team. Consider how you can continue to foster a culture of appreciation.

3. Accountability Partner Practice

- **Objective**: To cultivate a culture of instant accountability within your team.
- **How to Do It**: Pair up with a colleague to act as accountability partners. Commit to sharing any mistakes or

challenges you encounter with your partner as soon as they happen. Work together to find solutions and support each other in learning from these experiences. This practice will help reinforce a transparent and supportive team environment.

UNDERSTANDING BUILDS CLOSENESS

In leadership, everyone talks about empathy and charisma as if they're the magic keys to success. They're good to have, but they aren't the whole story. Some of the most effective leaders aren't the warmest or most charming people. Instead, they set high standards, pay attention to the smallest details, and push their teams to excel. These qualities don't always make them likable, but they do make them effective.

So, how do these leaders manage to inspire their teams? How do they build the kind of relationships that make people want to go the extra mile? The answer lies in a deep understanding of the people they lead.

Understanding Beyond Empathy

Empathy is about putting yourself in someone else's shoes. It's important, but it only scratches the surface. To build strong relationships, you need to go deeper. You need to understand the people on your team as individuals—their histories, motivations, and unique perspectives. This isn't about being their best friend; it's about recognizing what makes them tick.

Start by paying attention to the little things. Ask about their lives outside of work, but don't just ask for the sake of asking. Listen to the answers. Notice the details that others might overlook. Maybe someone's been quiet in meetings lately—find out why. Perhaps another team member consistently goes above and beyond—learn what drives them. This isn't just about being a caring leader; it's about gathering the insights that will help you lead more effectively.

Building Relational Closeness Through Understanding

To balance high standards with relational closeness, you need to show that you care about your team members as people, not just as cogs in the machine. Here's how:

1. *Ask Thoughtful Questions:* Move beyond the surface-level questions. Instead of just asking how someone's weekend was, ask about what they're passionate about outside of work. If

they mention a challenge, follow up later to see how they're doing. This shows you're genuinely interested in them as individuals.

2. *Be Transparent and Vulnerable*: Share your own experiences, especially the difficult ones. When you're open about your own challenges, it creates a space where others feel comfortable being open, too. This builds trust and shows that you're not just a leader, but a fellow human being.

3. *Understand Their Backstories:* Everyone has a story that shapes who they are today. Take the time to learn these stories. You don't need to know every detail, but understanding the key events that have influenced your team members can help you relate to them on a deeper level. It also allows you to tailor your leadership approach to better suit their needs and motivations.

4. *Acknowledge Individual Contributions:* People want to feel seen and valued for what they bring to the table. Recognize not just the outcomes but the effort and thought behind them. When you acknowledge what makes each person unique, you're reinforcing their sense of belonging and importance to the team.

Relational Closeness as a Leadership Strategy

You don't need to fully understand or relate to every person on your team—no one expects that. But making the effort to connect, to see them as individuals, goes a long way. This effort, combined with your high standards and attention to detail, builds a foundation of trust and respect.

When people feel understood, they're more likely to buy into your vision and push themselves to meet the high expectations you've set. They're also more likely to collaborate effectively with others, leading to a stronger, more cohesive team.

In the end, deep understanding isn't just about making people feel good—it's about creating the kind of relational closeness that drives real results. So, take the time to get to know your team, show that you care, and watch how it transforms your leadership and your team's success.

Key Actions

- **Ask Thoughtful Questions**: Go beyond surface-level inquiries and ask about what truly matters to your team members, showing genuine interest in their passions and challenges.
- **Listen and Notice Details**: Pay close attention to your team members' responses and behaviors, noticing the small things that might reveal more about their state of mind and motivations.
- **Be Transparent and Vulnerable**: Share your own experiences and challenges to create an environment of trust and openness.
- **Understand Team Members' Backstories**: Take the time to learn about the key events and experiences that have shaped your team members, helping you relate to them on a deeper level.
- **Acknowledge Individual Contributions**: Recognize and value the unique efforts and thought processes behind each team member's contributions, reinforcing their importance to the team.

Discussion Questions

1. How can leaders balance the need for high standards with the importance of building strong, personal relationships with their team members?
2. What are some practical ways to go beyond surface-level empathy and develop a deeper understanding of your team members?
3. How does sharing your own experiences and vulnerabilities as a leader impact your team's trust and openness?
4. In what ways can understanding the backstories of your team members improve your ability to lead them effectively?

5. How can acknowledging individual contributions reinforce a team member's sense of belonging and motivate them to perform at their best?

Practice Exercises

1. Deep Listening Practice

- **Objective**: Improve your ability to listen attentively and pick up on subtle cues from your team members.
- **How to Do It**: Set aside time during one-on-one meetings to focus entirely on listening. Ask open-ended questions and practice active listening by summarizing what the other person says and reflecting it back to them. Pay attention to their tone, body language, and any underlying emotions. After the conversation, take a few minutes to jot down what you learned about the person that you didn't know before.

2. Personal Connection Journaling

- **Objective**: Develop a habit of learning and remembering key details about your team members.
- **How to Do It**: Create a journal or digital document where you note down personal and professional details about each team member, such as their interests, challenges, and key life events. Review and update these notes regularly. Before meeting with team members, review your notes to help you ask meaningful questions and show genuine interest in their lives.

3. Storytelling and Vulnerability Exercise

- **Objective**: Enhance your ability to build trust and openness through sharing your own experiences.
- **How to Do It**: Reflect on your personal and professional experiences, particularly those that were challenging or taught you important lessons. Choose one story to share with your

team in a relevant context—such as a team meeting or a one-on-one session. Focus on being open about your emotions and what you learned from the experience. Afterward, observe how sharing this story impacts your relationship with your team.

SAFE RISKS DRIVE GROWTH

The fishbowl effect is what happens when team members feel like they're constantly being watched and judged. It's like working in a glass box where every move is scrutinized. This leads to a culture of fear where people are hesitant to speak up or share ideas. They worry about being judged, ridiculed, or even punished for making mistakes. When that fear takes hold, innovation stalls, and growth becomes impossible.

So, how do you break the cycle? The answer lies in creating a culture of safety—a place where team members feel secure enough to take risks, make mistakes, and learn from them. This doesn't happen by accident. It requires intentional leadership and practices that make safety a core value.

Embrace Mistakes Immediately

One of the most effective ways to build this kind of environment is through instant accountability. This means encouraging team members to own their mistakes the moment they happen. Rather than waiting for someone else to point it out or hoping it goes unnoticed, team members are expected to step up and say, "I missed the mark here, and here's what I learned."

Instant accountability shifts the focus from blame to learning. When mistakes are acknowledged quickly, they lose their power to create fear. Instead of dwelling on what went wrong, the team can immediately pivot to understanding why it happened and how to prevent it in the future. This kind of environment turns mistakes into valuable lessons rather than points of contention.

The Role of Leaders: Set the Tone

Leaders play a crucial role in creating a safe environment. If you're in a position of power, your actions and attitudes set the tone for the entire team. If you react to mistakes with anger or disappointment, you'll create a culture of fear. But if you treat mistakes as a natural part of the learning process, your team will follow suit.

It's not enough to say that mistakes are okay—you have to show it. Share your own experiences of failure and what you learned from them. When your team sees that even the leader isn't perfect, they'll feel more comfortable admitting their own missteps. This vulnerability fosters trust and encourages more open communication.

Storytelling: The Power of Shared Experiences

Storytelling is a powerful tool for creating safety. When leaders share personal stories of failure, they humanize themselves. They show that they're not infallible, and they create a space where vulnerability is acceptable.

Encourage your team to share their own stories. When people see that others have faced challenges and come out the other side, they're more likely to take risks themselves. This shared experience builds empathy and understanding within the team, making it easier for everyone to communicate openly.

Shift the Focus: From Punishment to Growth

In a culture of safety, the focus isn't on punishing mistakes but on learning from them. This requires a fundamental shift in how feedback is delivered. Instead of reprimanding someone for what they did wrong, focus on what they can do better next time.

Use a "more of, less of" approach. Highlight the behaviors or actions that were effective and should be repeated, and point out the ones that need to be adjusted. This approach is not only constructive but also actionable, giving team members clear guidance on how to improve without making them feel like they're under a microscope.

Why Safety Matters

Creating a culture of safety isn't just about making people feel good—it's about driving performance. When team members feel safe, they're more likely to take risks, and risk-taking is essential for innovation. A team that's willing to experiment, fail, and try again is a team that's capable of achieving great things.

But it all starts with safety. If your team feels like they're in a fishbowl, they'll never take the risks needed to push boundaries and achieve excellence. As a leader, it's your responsibility to break the glass and create an environment where everyone feels secure enough to give their best.

In the end, creating safety is about fostering a culture where mistakes are seen as opportunities for growth, not as failures. It's about making sure your team knows that they can take risks, speak up, and be themselves without fear of judgment or punishment. When you achieve that, you'll have a team that's not just safe—but unstoppable.

Key Actions

- **Leadership Vulnerability**: Leaders should openly share their own experiences of failure to create a culture of safety and trust.
- **Supportive Feedback**: Shift the focus from punishment to growth by using a "more of, less of" approach when giving feedback.
- **Storytelling and Shared Experiences**: Use storytelling to create empathy and understanding, making it easier for team members to communicate openly.
- **Encouraging Risk-Taking**: Foster an environment where team members feel safe to take risks, knowing that mistakes are seen as opportunities for learning, not judgment.

Discussion Questions

1. How can instant accountability be effectively implemented within a team, and what challenges might arise in encouraging team members to own their mistakes immediately?
2. In what ways can leaders demonstrate vulnerability without undermining their authority, and how does this impact the overall culture of safety within a team?

3. How does the "more of, less of" approach to feedback differ from traditional methods, and why might it be more effective in fostering growth and improvement?

4. What role does storytelling play in building trust within a team, and how can leaders use their personal experiences to encourage more open communication among team members?

5. How can a culture that encourages risk-taking and views mistakes as learning opportunities contribute to a team's overall success, and what steps can leaders take to create such an environment?

Practice Exercises

1. Leadership Storytelling Practice

- **Objective**: Build trust and openness within your team by sharing personal experiences of failure and learning.
- **How to Do It**: Identify a recent mistake or challenge you've faced. Prepare a brief story that highlights what went wrong, how you handled it, and what you learned. Share this story in a team meeting or one-on-one with a colleague. Observe the reactions and follow up by inviting others to share their own experiences. Repeat this exercise regularly to normalize vulnerability and foster a culture of shared learning.

2. Constructive Feedback Simulation

- **Objective**: Improve your ability to deliver growth-focused feedback using the "more of, less of" framework.
- **How to Do It**: Pair up with a colleague or team member and role-play a feedback session. Start by identifying a recent situation where feedback is needed. Practice delivering feedback using specific, actionable language that highlights what the person should do "more of" and what they should do "less of." Afterward, switch roles and provide feedback on how the session was handled. Reflect on the effectiveness of

the approach and refine your technique in subsequent simulations.

3. Risk-Taking Encouragement Exercise

- **Objective**: Foster a culture of innovation by encouraging team members to take calculated risks.
- **How to Do It**: Set aside time in a team meeting for a "risk-sharing" session. Encourage each team member to share one idea or project they've been hesitant to pursue due to fear of failure. Discuss as a group how these risks could be approached and mitigated, focusing on the potential learning outcomes rather than the possibility of failure. Reflect on the discussions and work to implement one or more of these ideas, reinforcing the value of risk-taking within the team.

TEAM SUCCESS OUTSIDE WORK

Success breeds success. When a team experiences success together, they develop a strong sense of identity as winners. This identity creates a winning attitude that spills over into their work. But in the hustle of daily business, opportunities for team success can be limited by deadlines, quotas, and the grind of the routine. That's where smart leadership comes in—creating opportunities for the team to succeed away from their regular work can foster camaraderie, build resilience, and ignite a winning attitude that fuels productivity.

Creating Success Beyond the Office Walls

The idea is simple: give your team a chance to win together in a setting that's outside of their day-to-day responsibilities. This doesn't mean you need to organize extravagant events or complicated outings; it can be anything that brings the team together for a shared goal. Think about a range of activities—from outdoor adventures that push physical limits to lighthearted challenges like escape rooms, cooking competitions, or even charity work. The key is to find something that allows the team to collaborate, have fun, and achieve success together.

When a team wins together in these settings, they start to see each other differently. They recognize strengths they might not have noticed before and develop a deeper respect for each other's abilities. This shift in perspective can reveal hidden talents and foster a culture of support and encouragement. It's no longer just about meeting deadlines; it's about succeeding as a unit.

Reversing the Spiral of Struggle

What if your team is struggling? It happens. Morale dips, productivity wanes, and before you know it, failure starts to feel like the norm. This is where a leader's ability to step in and shift the dynamic is crucial. By taking the team out of the office and into a different environment, you can reset their mindset. Success in a different setting can rekindle confidence and give the team a fresh perspective on their work.

For instance, imagine a team that's been underperforming for months. They're demoralized, and the downward spiral feels inevitable. Now, picture them tackling a challenge they're not used to—maybe it's building a structure in a timed challenge or working together to solve a complex puzzle. When they succeed, even in a small way, it can spark a renewed sense of purpose. They see that they *can* win, and that belief starts to rebuild their confidence. They return to the office with a different energy, one that says, "We've got this."

The Ripple Effect of a Winning Team

The benefits of these offsite successes don't just stay with the team—they ripple out across the entire organization. A team that believes in its ability to win is more productive, more innovative, and more engaged. They tackle challenges with a positive mindset and deliver results that contribute to the overall success of the company. And this winning attitude is contagious. Other teams see the energy and camaraderie, and they want in on it. Before long, you've created a culture where success isn't just hoped for—it's expected.

Leading the Charge

Great leaders understand that fostering a winning attitude isn't just about what happens inside the office. By intentionally creating opportunities for the team to succeed together in different settings, they build bonds that strengthen the team's identity. These experiences not only make the team more cohesive but also instill a sense of pride and confidence that translates directly into their work.

When your team sees themselves as winners, they carry that attitude into everything they do. They become more than just a group of individuals—they become a force that drives the organization forward. That's the power of team success away from the work.

Key Actions

- **Creating Opportunities for Team Success Outside of Work**: Leaders should intentionally create chances for their teams to succeed in settings outside of regular work activities.

- **Choosing Diverse Activities**: Select a variety of activities, ranging from physical challenges to fun, team-building exercises, that allow the team to collaborate and succeed together.
- **Building Camaraderie and Strengthening Relationships**: Foster stronger relationships within the team by engaging in activities that encourage collaboration and mutual respect.
- **Reversing Negative Momentum**: Use offsite successes to rebuild confidence and morale in a struggling team, helping them reset their mindset and renew their sense of purpose.
- **Fostering a Winning Attitude**: Encourage a team mindset that sees success as achievable and expected, which in turn enhances productivity and innovation.
- **Leveraging Success for Organizational Impact**: Understand that the positive effects of team success extend beyond the immediate team and can influence the broader organizational culture.
- **Leading with Intent**: Recognize the importance of leadership in creating and guiding opportunities for team success, which ultimately strengthens the team's identity and contributes to the organization's success.

Discussion Questions

1. How can leaders identify the right type of offsite activities that will resonate with their team and foster a winning attitude?
2. What are some examples of team-building activities that have had a lasting positive impact on team dynamics in your experience?
3. How can a leader effectively use offsite successes to rebuild morale and confidence in a struggling team?
4. In what ways can the winning attitude developed through offsite team successes be sustained and integrated into daily work practices?

5. What are the potential challenges or drawbacks of organizing offsite team-building activities, and how can they be mitigated?

Practice Exercises

1. Design a Team-Building Activity

- **Objective**: To develop the ability to create meaningful and impactful team-building activities.
- **How to Do It**: Identify a challenge or goal your team is currently facing. Brainstorm and design an offsite activity that aligns with this challenge and encourages collaboration and success. Consider the interests and strengths of your team members when planning the activity. Implement the activity with your team, then gather feedback to evaluate its effectiveness and adjust future activities accordingly.

2. Facilitate a Debriefing Session

- **Objective**: To improve skills in guiding team reflection and extracting lessons from offsite successes.
- **How to Do It**: After conducting a team-building activity, schedule a debriefing session. Prepare open-ended questions that encourage team members to reflect on their experiences, what they learned, and how they can apply those lessons to their work. Lead the discussion, ensuring that all voices are heard and that the conversation remains focused on growth and development. Summarize key takeaways and discuss how the team can carry their winning attitude into their daily tasks.

3. Develop a Follow-Up Plan

- **Objective**: To ensure that the positive effects of offsite activities are sustained and integrated into the team's work.

- **How to Do It**: After an offsite success, create a follow-up plan that includes specific actions or habits the team should continue to practice. Set short-term and long-term goals based on the strengths and insights gained from the activity. Regularly check in with the team to track progress, celebrate small wins, and make adjustments as needed. Encourage the team to share their successes and challenges in implementing the follow-up plan, fostering ongoing collaboration and improvement.

A GREAT TEAM LEADS ITSELF

There's a certain freedom in knowing that a great team can function just as well whether the leader is in the room or not. The goal is to build a team that operates smoothly and makes decisions effectively, regardless of whether the leader is present. Unfortunately, some teams struggle without their leader, becoming what's known as a "leader-centric" team—a sign that the leader hasn't done enough to empower their members to step up and take charge.

The Problem with Leader-Centric Teams

A leader-centric team is one that leans too heavily on its leader for guidance. Every decision, every conversation, and every move hinges on the leader's input. This creates a bottleneck, slowing down progress and stifling the team's potential. Worse yet, when the leader is unavailable, the team flounders, unsure of how to proceed. This dependency can be a crutch, holding back both the team and the leader from reaching their full potential.

The Power of Player-Led Teams

As I mentioned in the introduction to this chapter, the "player-led" team is where the magic happens. Here, every member is empowered to lead, take ownership, and contribute to the team's success. These teams don't just survive in the leader's absence—they thrive. Decisions are made swiftly, conversations flow naturally, and progress continues uninterrupted. Thomas Kail and Lin-Manuel Miranda, the creative minds behind *Hamilton*, understood this well. They fostered an environment where everyone's input was valued, leading to one of the most successful productions in history.

Shifting the Mindset: From "My" Team to "Our" Team

Creating a player-led team starts with a fundamental shift in the leader's mindset. It's no longer about *my* team; it's about *our* team. Every member has a role to play, and every voice matters. This requires the leader to let go of the reins a bit and trust their team to take the lead. It means recognizing that the team's success doesn't solely rest on the leader's shoulders—it's a collective effort.

Building Ownership and Empowerment

Fostering a player-led team isn't just about delegation; it's about building a culture of ownership and empowerment. Start by involving all team members in decision-making processes. Ask for their input during meetings, listen to their ideas, and encourage them to take charge of their work. Autonomy is key. When team members feel they have the freedom to make decisions, they're more likely to take initiative and push the team forward.

Testing the Waters: The Absence Test

A simple way to gauge whether your team is player-led or leader-centric is to step away and see how they function without you. If the team continues to perform at a high level, making decisions and driving progress without missing a beat, you've done your job. But if things start to falter in your absence, it's a clear sign that more work is needed to empower your team.

Leading by Letting Go

Creating a player-led team requires leaders to embrace a new way of thinking. It's about shifting from being the central figure in every decision to becoming a facilitator who empowers others to lead. By doing so, you create a team that's resilient, adaptable, and capable of sustaining success without your constant presence. In the end, a great team doesn't wait for the leader—they're already out in front, paving the way to success.

Key Actions

- **Empowerment of Team Members**: Encouraging and enabling all team members to take ownership of their roles and responsibilities, making decisions independently without relying solely on the leader.
- **Involving Team Members in Decision-Making**: Actively seeking input from all team members during meetings and

decision-making processes, ensuring everyone's voice is heard and valued.

- **Building a Culture of Autonomy**: Granting team members the autonomy to make decisions and manage their tasks, which fosters initiative and drives the team forward.
- **Shifting from "My" Team to "Our" Team**: Adopting a mindset that recognizes the team's success as a collective effort, not just dependent on the leader's contributions.
- **Testing Team Independence**: Stepping back to observe how the team functions in the leader's absence, using this as a measure of the team's autonomy and leadership capabilities.
- **Leading by Letting Go**: Transitioning from being the central figure in all decisions to a facilitator who supports and empowers others to lead.

Discussion Questions

1. What are the potential risks of having a leader-centric team, and how can these risks impact the overall performance and morale of the team?
2. How can leaders effectively shift their mindset from viewing the team as "my" team to "our" team?
3. In what ways can a leader foster a culture of autonomy and ownership within the team?
4. What are some practical strategies for involving team members in decision-making processes?
5. How can a leader evaluate whether their team is truly player-led?

Practice Exercises

1. Delegate Decision-Making

- **Objective**: To practice empowering team members by involving them in decision-making processes.
- **How to Do It**: Identify a decision that you would typically make yourself and delegate it to a team member or a group

within the team. Provide them with the necessary context, but allow them to take ownership of the decision-making process. Afterward, review the outcome together and discuss what went well and what could be improved.

2. Absence Simulation

- **Objective**: To assess how well your team operates without your direct involvement and to identify areas for improvement in fostering a player-led environment.
- **How to Do It**: Choose a project or a meeting where you typically play a central role and deliberately step back. Observe how the team handles the situation without your input. Take notes on their decision-making, communication, and problem-solving abilities. Later, discuss with the team what they experienced and how they felt during your absence.

3. Rotate Leadership Roles

- **Objective**: To encourage team members to take on leadership roles and responsibilities, thereby fostering a player-led team culture.
- **How to Do It**: Implement a rotating leadership model for a specific project or during regular team meetings. Assign different team members to lead the discussion, make decisions, or manage the project for a set period. Provide them with guidance as needed, but allow them to take the lead. After each rotation, have a debriefing session to discuss what they learned and how the experience can benefit the team as a whole.

CHAPTER 9
MASTER TIME, LEAD WITH FOCUS

Time is the one resource every leader wishes they had more of, but the clock never stops ticking. Effective leadership isn't about having more time—it's about making better use of the time you do have. The best leaders understand that while they can't control time, they can control how they spend it. And that's what separates those who lead from those who merely manage.

Prioritize Like Your Life Depends on It

The secret to effective time management lies in prioritization. It's easy to get lost in a sea of tasks, but not all tasks are created equal. The most successful leaders ruthlessly focus on what truly matters, cutting through the noise to identify the key activities that will drive the most value. This isn't about doing more in less time; it's about doing the right things with the time you have.

Start by identifying your top priorities—the tasks that align with your long-term goals and make the biggest impact. Then, guard your time fiercely. Distractions are the enemy of productivity, and even well-meaning interruptions can derail your focus. By eliminating the non-essential, you create space for deep, meaningful work that moves the needle.

Delegate to Elevate

Effective leaders know they can't do it all. Delegation isn't just about offloading tasks; it's about empowering your team and leveraging their strengths. By trusting others to handle what they're capable of, you free up your own time to focus on the high-level decisions that only you can make.

But delegation requires more than just passing the baton—it requires trust, communication, and clarity. When done right, delegation not only lightens your load but also helps your team grow, making everyone more efficient and effective.

Balancing the Now and the Next

Leadership is a balancing act between the urgent demands of today and the strategic goals of tomorrow. Effective time management requires you to navigate both short-term tasks and long-term objectives with equal finesse. This means being adaptable, ready to shift gears when necessary, and always keeping an eye on the bigger picture.

Regularly re-evaluate your goals and adjust your priorities as needed. The ability to pivot is crucial in a fast-paced environment where change is the only constant. By staying flexible and focused, you ensure that your time is spent in alignment with what truly matters, both now and in the future.

Stress Less, Lead More

Time management isn't just about squeezing more productivity out of your day—it's also about managing stress. Poor time management is a surefire way to increase stress, which can lead to burnout and diminish your effectiveness as a leader.

To stay on top of your game, you need to make self-care a priority. Regular breaks, exercise, and mindfulness practices can help you maintain your energy and focus. Remember, a leader who is burned out can't lead effectively. By managing your stress, you not only protect your well-being but also set an example for your team.

Your Time, Your Values

Ultimately, how you spend your time is a reflection of your values. Your calendar doesn't lie—it shows what you consider important. As a leader, it's crucial to align your time with your values and priorities. When you do, every minute becomes an opportunity to create value, make an impact, and lead with purpose.

In the end, time management isn't just a skill—it's a mindset. It's about being intentional with every moment, making decisions that reflect your highest priorities, and leading in a way that maximizes both your time and your impact.

DAILY PROGRESS, BIG IMPACT

Time management is a constant struggle for most leaders. There are always more tasks, more responsibilities, and more demands than there are hours in the day. It's easy to get caught up in the whirlwind of urgent but unimportant tasks and lose sight of what truly matters. That's where the "rocks in a jar" metaphor comes in—a simple yet powerful reminder to focus on your biggest priorities first.

What Really Matters

The essence of the "rocks in a jar" metaphor is straightforward: imagine your day as a jar, and your tasks as rocks, pebbles, and sand. The big rocks represent your most important tasks—those that align with your long-term goals and values. Pebbles are the less critical tasks, and the sand represents the minor, often trivial, things that tend to fill our time. If you fill the jar with sand first, there's no room for the big rocks. But if you start with the big rocks, the smaller things can fill in around them.

This metaphor highlights a crucial point: not all tasks are created equal. Effective leaders understand that success comes from consistently working on what truly matters, not just what's most urgent. By identifying your "big rocks"—the key priorities that will drive your success—you ensure that your efforts are aligned with your goals. These big rocks are the tasks that, when accomplished, will make the most significant impact on your work and life.

Daily Progress, No Matter What

It's not enough to identify your big rocks; you have to make progress on them every day. This is where many leaders stumble. They get caught up in the small stuff—emails, meetings, putting out fires—and push their big priorities to the back burner. But the key to effective time management is chipping away at your big rocks daily, no matter how busy you get.

One strategy is to break your big rocks into smaller, manageable chunks. It's easier to carve out time for a 30-minute task than to block out an entire afternoon. By doing a little bit each day, you build momentum and make steady progress. Over time, these small efforts compound, leading to significant achievements.

Routine, Flexibility, and Focus

Leaders who master the "rocks in a jar" approach don't just prioritize—they build routines that support their priorities. They create a daily or weekly rhythm that ensures their big rocks are addressed first, not last. This might mean dedicating the first hour of your workday to your most critical task or setting aside a specific block of time each week for strategic planning.

But routines alone aren't enough. Life happens, priorities shift, and unexpected demands arise. That's why flexibility is just as important as routine. Effective leaders know when to stick to their schedule and when to adapt. They don't rigidly cling to their plans when circumstances change; instead, they reassess and adjust, ensuring their big rocks stay in focus even as they respond to new challenges.

Minimizing distractions is another essential piece of the puzzle. In a world full of constant interruptions, staying focused on your big rocks requires discipline. This might mean turning off notifications, setting boundaries during deep work periods, or even stepping away from the office when you need uninterrupted time to think and plan.

Make Every Minute Count

The "rocks in a jar" metaphor isn't just a clever analogy; it's a practical approach to making the most of your time. By starting with your biggest priorities, breaking them down into manageable pieces, and creating routines that support consistent progress, you can ensure that your time is spent on what truly matters.

And remember, it's not about perfection. It's about making steady, incremental progress every day. Some days you'll move mountains; other days, it might feel like you barely made a dent. But as long as you keep chipping away at your big rocks, you'll find that over time, those small efforts add up to something truly significant.

The bottom line? Focus on what matters, make progress every day, and be flexible enough to adapt when necessary. By doing this, you'll not only manage your time more effectively, but you'll also create more value in your role, achieve your goals more efficiently, and ultimately lead a more fulfilling, purpose-driven life.

Key Actions

- **Identify Your Big Rocks**: Focus on the most important tasks that align with your long-term goals and values.
- **Make Daily Progress**: Chip away at your big rocks every day, even if only in small, manageable chunks.
- **Build Supportive Routines**: Establish daily or weekly routines that prioritize your big rocks first, ensuring consistent progress.
- **Stay Flexible**: Adapt to changing circumstances and reassess your priorities when necessary, while keeping your big rocks in focus.
- **Minimize Distractions**: Implement strategies to minimize interruptions and maintain focus on your big rocks during deep work periods.
- **Embrace Incremental Progress:** Recognize that steady, incremental progress on your big rocks will add up over time, leading to significant achievements.

Discussion Questions

1. What are your "big rocks" in both your professional and personal life, and how do you ensure they take priority in your daily routine?
2. How do you break down large, critical tasks into smaller, manageable chunks to make daily progress? Can you share a specific example?
3. In what ways have you built routines that help you focus on your most important tasks?
4. How do you balance the need for routine with the flexibility to adapt when priorities shift or new challenges arise?

5. What strategies do you use to minimize distractions and stay focused on your big priorities, especially during periods of deep work?

Practice Exercises

1. Identify and Prioritize Your Big Rocks

- **Objective**: To develop the habit of consistently identifying and prioritizing your most important tasks.
- **How to Do It**: At the start of each week, list all the tasks you need to accomplish. Identify the top three tasks that will have the most significant impact on your long-term goals—these are your "big rocks." Schedule dedicated time each day to work on these tasks before anything else. At the end of the week, reflect on your progress and adjust as needed.

2. Daily Chunking and Progress Tracking

- **Objective**: To improve your ability to break down large tasks into manageable chunks and track your daily progress.
- **How to Do It**: Take one of your big rocks and break it down into smaller tasks that can be completed in 30 minutes or less. Each day, spend at least 30 minutes working on one of these smaller tasks. Track your progress in a journal or digital tool, noting what you accomplished and any obstacles you encountered. Review your progress weekly to see how these small steps add up.

3. Focus and Distraction Management

- **Objective**: To strengthen your ability to stay focused on your priorities and minimize distractions.
- **How to Do It**: Choose one day this week to practice deep work. Identify a two-hour block of time where you'll focus exclusively on one of your big rocks. Before starting, eliminate potential distractions—turn off notifications, close

unnecessary tabs, and let others know you're unavailable. After the session, reflect on your ability to stay focused and note any distractions that occurred. Use this insight to improve your focus in future sessions.

BEYOND THE TO-DO LIST

We all know the feeling—our brains are juggling a million things at once, and inevitably, some of them slip through the cracks. To-do lists are often the first line of defense against forgetfulness, helping us keep track of what needs doing. But if you want to elevate your game as a leader, a simple to-do list won't cut it. You need something more powerful: a tracking list.

Why Your Brain Isn't Your Best Organizer

Here's the truth: your brain is fantastic at generating ideas but terrible at holding onto them. The human mind isn't built for storing and recalling every little task or responsibility, especially when you're juggling multiple roles. To-do lists help with this, but they're inherently limited. They often become a dumping ground for random tasks without any context or prioritization.

To truly stay on top of your game—and the game of those you lead—you need to move beyond the to-do list. That's where the tracking list comes in.

What Is a Tracking List?

A tracking list isn't just a collection of tasks; it's a comprehensive overview of everything that demands your attention, either now or in the future. This includes:

- *Ongoing Responsibilities*: Tasks that need to be revisited periodically, like weekly reports or regular meetings.
- *Delegated Tasks:* Items that you've handed off to others but still need to monitor.
- *Future Deadlines:* Things that don't require immediate action but need to be on your radar.
- *Personal Goals:* Long-term objectives that require consistent attention and progress.

Unlike a to-do list, which often just contains isolated tasks, a tracking list provides context. It shows you not only what needs to be done but also why it's important, who's responsible, and when it needs to happen.

Leading with a Tracking List

Great leaders don't just manage their own tasks—they also keep tabs on the work of their team. Your tracking list should include not only your own responsibilities but also the major tasks and goals of those you lead. This doesn't mean micromanaging; it means having a clear understanding of what everyone is working on and how it aligns with the broader goals of the organization.

When you track your team's progress, you're in a better position to offer support and guidance. You can anticipate potential roadblocks, recognize when someone needs encouragement, and ensure that everyone is moving in the same direction.

Different Forms, Same Purpose

Your tracking list can take whatever form works best for you. It could be a digital document, a series of notes in a notebook, or even a specialized app designed for project management. The key is to choose a format that you can easily update and access. Consistency is crucial; if you don't regularly review and update your tracking list, it loses its effectiveness.

The Art of Prioritization

One of the biggest advantages of a tracking list is its ability to help you prioritize. When you see everything laid out—your tasks, your team's responsibilities, upcoming deadlines—you can make informed decisions about what needs your attention first. This allows you to allocate your time more effectively, focusing on what truly matters rather than getting bogged down in the minutiae.

Making It Work for You

The beauty of a tracking list is that it's adaptable. You can customize it to fit your specific needs and the unique demands of your role. The important thing is to start using it. Don't get hung up on creating the "perfect" system right out of the gate. The system that works is the one you actually use and refine over time.

The Bigger Picture

At the end of the day, a tracking list is more than just a tool—it's a mindset. It's about staying organized, being proactive, and leading with intention. When you track not just what you need to do, but also what your team is doing and where everything stands, you're setting yourself up for success.

In a world where it's easy to get overwhelmed by the sheer volume of responsibilities, a tracking list is your secret weapon. It gives you clarity, helps you manage your time, and ensures that nothing important falls through the cracks. Whether you're managing a project, leading a team, or just trying to keep your own life in order, a tracking list is an invaluable tool that can help you stay on top of it all.

So, go ahead—ditch the simple to-do list and upgrade to a tracking list. Your future self will thank you.

Key Actions

- **Moving Beyond To-Do Lists**: Recognizing that a simple to-do list is insufficient for effective leadership and opting for a more comprehensive tracking list.
- **Creating a Tracking List**: Developing a list that includes not just tasks, but ongoing responsibilities, delegated tasks, future deadlines, and personal goals.
- **Tracking Team Progress**: Including the responsibilities and progress of team members in the tracking list to offer better support and guidance.
- **Regular Review and Updates**: Consistently reviewing and updating the tracking list to ensure it remains effective and relevant.
- **Prioritizing Tasks**: Using the tracking list to make informed decisions about what tasks or responsibilities need attention first.

- **Choosing a Format That Works**: Adapting the tracking list to a format that is easy to update and access, whether digital or physical.
- **Adopting a Proactive Mindset:** Viewing the tracking list as a tool for staying organized, being proactive, and leading with intention

Discussion Questions

1. How does a tracking list differ from a traditional to-do list, and why is it considered more effective for leaders?
2. What challenges might arise when trying to track not only your own responsibilities but also those of your team members? How can these challenges be addressed?
3. How do you prioritize tasks on your tracking list when faced with multiple high-priority items? What criteria do you use to determine what comes first?
4. In what ways can regularly reviewing and updating your tracking list contribute to better time management and overall productivity?
5. What formats or tools have you found most effective for maintaining a tracking list, and how do they help you stay organized?

Practice Exercises

1. Daily Tracking Review

- **Objective**: To build the habit of regularly updating and reviewing your tracking list.
- **How to Do It**: Set aside 10 minutes at the start and end of each day to review your tracking list. In the morning, identify the top three priorities for the day. In the evening, update the list with any progress made, new tasks, or delegated responsibilities. Reflect on what worked well and where adjustments are needed for the next day.

2. Delegation Check-In

- **Objective**: To improve your ability to track and support the progress of tasks you've delegated to others.
- **How to Do It**: Choose a project or task that you've delegated to a team member. Schedule a weekly check-in where you discuss their progress, any challenges they're facing, and how you can support them. After each check-in, update your tracking list with new information and adjust your support strategy as needed.

3. Prioritization Drill

- **Objective**: To enhance your ability to prioritize tasks effectively using your tracking list.
- **How to Do It**: Take your current tracking list and identify five tasks with varying levels of importance and urgency. Rank these tasks in order of priority, explaining your reasoning for each choice. After completing this exercise, reflect on how you made your decisions and consider any adjustments to your prioritization criteria for future tasks.

UNSTRUCTURED TIME IS POWER

We often think of unstructured time as a luxury, a reward for when all our work is done. But what if unstructured time is actually one of the most valuable tools for boosting productivity? It's a counterintuitive idea, but one worth exploring. Let's dive into why unstructured time might be your most productive time and how to harness it to achieve more.

The Space to Think Deeply

In today's world, distractions are everywhere. From constant notifications to the demands of our day-to-day responsibilities, finding a moment to think deeply is rare. This is where unstructured time shines. Without a rigid schedule dictating our every move, we can step back and allow our minds to settle on the big picture. It's in these quiet moments, free from interruptions, that some of our most valuable insights emerge.

Consider how difficult it is to solve complex problems when you're constantly being pulled in different directions. When you carve out unstructured time, you create a space where you can focus on the challenges at hand, often leading to breakthroughs that structured, task-oriented time can't offer.

The Creative Wanderings of the Mind

Unstructured time isn't just about deep thinking; it's also about letting your mind wander. Our brains are naturally inclined to make connections when they're not under pressure. Think about the times you've had your best ideas—maybe it was in the shower, during a walk, or while you were engaged in a mindless task. These moments of unintentional creativity happen because your brain is given the freedom to explore without the constraints of a specific goal.

This wandering is essential for innovation. When you allow your mind to drift, you open the door to new ideas and perspectives. It's like giving your brain permission to play, which can lead to creative solutions that structured thinking might miss.

The Myth of Constant Busyness

In our culture, there's a pervasive belief that being busy equates to being productive. We fill our calendars with meetings, tasks, and obligations, often leaving little room for anything else. But busyness doesn't necessarily mean effectiveness. In fact, constantly being "on" can lead to burnout and hinder your ability to think strategically.

True productivity isn't just about doing more; it's about doing what matters most. Unstructured time allows you to step back, assess what's really important, and ensure you're working on the right things. It's a shift from working hard to working smart, where the emphasis is on quality over quantity.

Integrating Unstructured Time into Your Routine

Making unstructured time a regular part of your life requires intentionality. It's not something that will happen on its own—you have to create space for it. One effective strategy is to schedule it just like you would any other important activity. For example, block out an hour three times a week for "free thinking time." During this hour, disconnect from your phone and computer, and allow yourself to reflect on the bigger issues or challenges you're facing.

This isn't wasted time; it's a strategic investment in your long-term productivity. By deliberately setting aside time for unstructured thinking, you give yourself permission to slow down and think deeply, which can lead to more thoughtful and creative outcomes.

Recognizing the Value of Different Types of Time

Not all time is created equal. Some tasks require intense focus and concentration, while others are more routine and don't demand as much mental energy. By recognizing the difference, you can prioritize your most critical work during your peak productive hours and reserve less structured tasks for when your energy naturally dips.

Unstructured time fits into this model perfectly. It's not about abandoning structure altogether but about knowing when to let go of the reins. Understanding that unstructured time can be just as valuable—if not more so—than structured, task-oriented time is key to maximizing your productivity.

Embracing Unstructured Time

Unstructured time might just be the secret weapon you've been overlooking in your quest for productivity. As cognitive psychologist Amos Tversky wisely noted, "You waste years by not being able to waste hours." By intentionally creating space for unstructured time, you allow your brain to function at its highest capacity, free from the constant noise and demands of everyday life.

Incorporating unstructured time into your routine isn't about being lazy or unproductive; it's about being strategic. It's about knowing when to swim against the current and when to let the current carry you. By dedicating time for reflection, creative thinking, and strategic planning, you can unlock new levels of productivity and innovation.

So, next time you feel the pressure to fill every moment with activity, remember the power of unstructured time. It might just be the most productive time you have.

Key Actions

- **Carve Out Unstructured Time for Deep Thinking**: Schedule dedicated time free from distractions to focus on big-picture challenges and strategic thinking.
- **Allow Your Mind to Wander**: Embrace moments of unintentional creativity by engaging in activities that don't require intense focus, allowing your brain to explore new ideas.
- **Prioritize Quality Over Quantity**: Shift from constantly staying busy to focusing on what matters most, recognizing that effectiveness isn't about doing more but about doing the right things.
- **Schedule "Free Thinking Time" Regularly**: Intentionally block out time in your calendar for unstructured thinking, ensuring it doesn't get overshadowed by other tasks.

- **Differentiate Between High-Focus and Low-Focus Tasks**: Recognize that different tasks require different levels of mental energy and prioritize high-focus work during peak productive hours.
- **Recognize the Strategic Value of Unstructured Time**: Understand that unstructured time is not wasted but is a valuable tool for enhancing creativity, problem-solving, and overall productivity.

Discussion Questions

1. How do you currently incorporate unstructured time into your routine, and what impact has it had on your productivity and creativity?
2. Can you recall a time when allowing your mind to wander led to a significant breakthrough or creative idea? How did that experience shape your view on the value of unstructured time?
3. Why do you think our culture often equates busyness with productivity, and how can we shift our mindset to value quality over quantity in our work?
4. How do you differentiate between high-focus and low-focus tasks in your daily schedule? What strategies do you use to ensure you're prioritizing the most important work during your peak productive hours?
5. What challenges do you face in scheduling and protecting unstructured time in your calendar, and how can you overcome these obstacles to make it a regular part of your routine?

Practice Exercises

1. Scheduled Reflection Time

- **Objective**: Improve your ability to think deeply and strategically by dedicating time to unstructured thinking.

- **How to Do It**: Schedule a one-hour block three times a week where you disconnect from all devices and focus solely on reflecting on key challenges, goals, or projects. Use this time to brainstorm, mind-map, or simply think without any specific agenda. Document any insights or ideas that emerge during this time.

2. Mindful Wandering

- **Objective**: Cultivate creativity by allowing your mind to wander freely.
- **How to Do It**: Engage in an activity that requires minimal focus, such as walking, showering, or doing a simple chore. During this time, avoid intentionally thinking about work or problems. Instead, let your mind drift naturally. After the activity, jot down any ideas or thoughts that came to you during this period.

3. Task Prioritization Drill

- **Objective**: Develop the ability to distinguish between high-focus and low-focus tasks and allocate time accordingly.
- **How to Do It**: At the start of each day, list out all tasks you need to accomplish. Label each task as either "High-Focus" or "Low-Focus" based on the mental energy required. Prioritize your high-focus tasks during your peak productivity hours (e.g., morning for most people) and schedule low-focus tasks for later in the day. Reflect at the end of the week on how this practice influenced your overall productivity and stress levels.

UNINTERRUPTED FOCUS IS KEY

In our constantly connected world, finding the time to work without distractions feels like a luxury. Notifications, emails, and the ever-present buzz of technology pull us in a thousand different directions. It's no wonder that staying focused on important tasks can feel nearly impossible. But there's a method to cut through the noise: working in uninterrupted chunks of time.

The Concept: Chunking Your Time

At its core, chunking time means setting aside a specific block of time to focus on a single task without any interruptions. This could be 30 minutes, 45 minutes, or even a full hour. The key is to choose a duration that allows you to fully immerse yourself in the work without checking the clock or giving in to distractions.

The idea behind chunking isn't just about getting work done—it's about getting into a state of flow. Flow is that magical zone where you're completely absorbed in what you're doing. Time seems to slip away, and your productivity soars. To achieve this, you might need to find a quiet spot, block out noise with headphones, turn off your phone, or let others know you're not to be disturbed.

Finding Your Focus Rhythm

Everyone's ability to focus is different. Some people can dive into a task for an hour or more without coming up for air, while others need a break every 30 minutes to stay sharp. It's all about finding your focus rhythm. Experiment with different time blocks and see what works best for you. Maybe you'll discover that you're most productive in the early morning or late at night, or that 50-minute sessions with 10-minute breaks are your sweet spot.

Prioritize and Protect Your Time

Working in uninterrupted chunks of time only works if you're focusing on the right tasks. That's where prioritization comes in. Before you start your day, identify the most critical tasks that need your attention. Whether it's writing a report, strategizing for a big project, or simply clearing out your inbox, make sure your most important work gets your best time.

A good example of this is a leader who arrives at the office early every morning. By starting the day at 7 a.m. and working undisturbed for the first hour, they tackle high-priority tasks before the chaos of the day begins. This approach allows them to set the tone for the day, achieve more in less time, and feel a sense of accomplishment before most people have had their first cup of coffee.

Creating a Distraction-Free Environment

To work in uninterrupted chunks of time, you need the right environment. That might mean closing your office door, working from a quiet room, or even going to a place where you know you won't be interrupted. It's also important to enlist the help of those around you. Let your team know when you need focus time, so they can avoid interrupting you. If you work from home, communicate with family members about your need for quiet during certain hours.

Sometimes, creating this environment is as simple as putting your phone on airplane mode or using apps that block distracting websites. The goal is to eliminate anything that might pull you out of your flow.

The Exponential Impact of Focused Time

The benefits of working in uninterrupted chunks of time are clear. Not only do you get more done in less time, but you also open the door to deeper creative insights and higher-quality work. When you're fully focused on a task, you're more likely to catch mistakes, think critically, and come up with innovative solutions.

And there's a cumulative effect, too. The more you practice working in these focused blocks of time, the better you become at it. You train your brain to switch into focus mode more quickly, making it easier to enter that productive flow state.

Working in uninterrupted chunks of time is about more than just productivity. It's about giving yourself the space to think deeply, solve problems creatively, and do your best work. In a world full of distractions, this approach is a powerful tool to help you stay on track and achieve your goals.

To get started, experiment with different time blocks, prioritize your tasks, and create a distraction-free environment that supports your focus. With practice, you'll find that working in chunks of uninterrupted time becomes a natural part of your routine, leading to greater productivity and a sense of accomplishment that can transform your workday.

Key Actions

- **Chunking Time**: Setting aside specific blocks of uninterrupted time to focus on a single task.
- **Finding Your Focus Rhythm**: Experimenting with different time durations to discover the most effective focus period for yourself.
- **Prioritizing Tasks**: Identifying and focusing on the most critical tasks first, ensuring that your best time is spent on high-priority work.
- **Creating a Distraction-Free Environment**: Eliminating potential distractions by finding a quiet workspace, using noise-blocking tools, turning off devices, or communicating your need for focus time to others.
- **Enlisting Support**: Asking others around you (colleagues, family members, etc.) to respect your focus time and avoid interruptions.
- **Maintaining Consistency:** Regularly practicing working in uninterrupted time chunks to improve focus and productivity over time.

Discussion Questions

1. How do you currently manage distractions in your work environment, and what strategies have you found most effective for maintaining focus?

2. What time of day do you find yourself most productive, and how can you structure your day to maximize uninterrupted work periods during this time?

3. How do you prioritize your tasks, and how might working in uninterrupted chunks of time enhance your ability to tackle high-priority tasks?

4. What challenges do you face in creating a distraction-free environment, and how can you overcome these obstacles to improve your focus?

5. Have you experimented with different time blocks for focused work? What duration works best for you, and how does it impact your overall productivity?

Practice Exercises

1. Focus Block Challenge

- **Objective**: To identify and optimize your ideal focus period for uninterrupted work.
- **How to Do It**: Start by setting a timer for 30 minutes and work on a single task without any distractions. Gradually increase the time in subsequent sessions (e.g., 45 minutes, 60 minutes) until you find the duration that allows you to maintain the highest level of focus. Record your observations after each session, noting your level of concentration, productivity, and any challenges faced. Adjust the time as needed to find your optimal focus block.

2. Priority Mapping

- **Objective**: To improve your ability to prioritize tasks effectively.
- **How to Do It**: At the beginning of each day, list all the tasks you need to accomplish. Next, categorize them into high, medium, and low priority based on their importance and deadlines. Choose the top three high-priority tasks and dedicate uninterrupted chunks of time to each, starting with

the most critical. At the end of the day, review your progress and reflect on how prioritizing impacted your productivity.

3. Environment Optimization Drill

- **Objective**: To create a workspace that minimizes distractions and maximizes focus.
- **How to Do It**: Identify all potential distractions in your current work environment (e.g., noise, interruptions, phone notifications). Develop a plan to eliminate or reduce these distractions. This could include setting up a dedicated workspace, using noise-canceling headphones, or setting boundaries with others during focus times. Practice working in this optimized environment for a week and track your ability to maintain focus and productivity. Make adjustments as necessary to improve your setup.

DISCIPLINE YOUR TECH

We live in an era where technology is omnipresent, weaving itself into every corner of our lives. From the constant buzz of social media to the ceaseless stream of emails and notifications, it's become nearly impossible to go a single day without being interrupted by some form of electronically mediated communication. While technology offers incredible benefits, it can also overwhelm us, diminish our empathy, and leave us feeling perpetually distracted. The challenge is to not let technology dictate the terms of our lives but instead to impose our own rules on its use.

Why You Need to Set Your Own Rules

The crux of the issue lies in the relentless nature of today's tech. Unlike earlier technological advancements, which diffused slowly enough for society to establish norms and rules, modern innovations spread at lightning speed. Think back to the introduction of the telephone—it took decades for this technology to become widespread, allowing time for society to develop guidelines around its use. We had rules about when and where to use the phone, how long calls should last, and when it was appropriate to call someone. These social conventions helped people manage the impact of the telephone on their lives.

Contrast that with today's environment. Innovations like email, text messaging, and social media have diffused so quickly that society hasn't had time to establish universal rules. The result? We're at the mercy of these technologies, responding to others as quickly as the medium allows, often at the expense of our own productivity and well-being. Without personal rules, the flood of information can erode our ability to focus and get things done.

Create Focused Time Blocks

One of the most effective ways to regain control is to create chunks of uninterrupted, focused time. This strategy, known as time-blocking, involves setting aside dedicated periods—perhaps as short as 45 minutes—where you eliminate distractions and fully engage in a specific task. During these blocks, notifications are turned off, phones are silenced, and the digital noise is pushed aside. The goal is to enter a state of flow where you can be entirely present and productive.

Time-blocking is a powerful tool for enhancing productivity and reducing stress. By setting boundaries around your work time, you can accomplish more in less time and feel a greater sense of accomplishment at the end of the day. This simple practice can transform how you interact with technology, turning it from a source of constant interruption into a tool that supports your goals.

Impose Sanctions on Your Technology Use

Another key strategy is to impose sanctions on your own technology use. This means setting limits on when and how you engage with your devices. For example, you might decide to enable "Do Not Disturb" mode during certain hours of the day or disable notifications entirely during focused work periods. You could also create specific rules for yourself, such as no screens during meals or no emails on weekends unless absolutely necessary.

These self-imposed sanctions are not about rejecting technology but about using it on your own terms. By deliberately choosing when and how to engage with your devices, you can create a healthier relationship with technology that allows you to protect your time and mental space.

Build a Culture of Respect with Others

Managing your relationship with technology isn't just a solo endeavor—it's also about setting expectations with those around you. By establishing clear rules and communicating them with colleagues, friends, and family, you can create a culture of mutual respect for each other's time and focus. For instance, you might let others know that you don't respond to emails after 8:00 PM or that you prefer not to engage in deep conversations over text. These boundaries help others understand and respect your need for uninterrupted time.

When everyone is on the same page, it becomes easier to maintain a balanced and fulfilling life. Encouraging those around you to set their own rules can also foster a more mindful and intentional use of technology within your community.

Practical Examples of Technology Rules

Here are some practical examples of rules you might consider:

- *No screens during meals:* Focus on the people around you, not your devices.
- *No emails on weekends*: Unless requested or absolutely necessary, avoid work-related communication during your personal time.
- *Keep your phone out of the bedroom*: Promote better sleep and relaxation by leaving your phone in another room.
- *Disable notifications during focus blocks*: Silence your devices to stay in the zone during important tasks.
- *No deep conversations over text:* Save meaningful discussions for in-person or at least phone conversations.
- *Set specific times to check messages:* Avoid the trap of constantly checking your phone by designating times to catch up on messages.

Take Back Control of Your Life

It's crucial to remember that technology is a tool meant to serve you, not the other way around. By setting your own rules and creating focused time blocks, you can shackle technology and reclaim control of your time and productivity. These rules are personal and should be tailored to what works best for you. Take the time to reflect on your relationship with technology and decide what boundaries will help you live a more balanced and fulfilling life.

By making deliberate choices about your technology use and setting clear boundaries, you can create a healthier, more intentional relationship with the digital world. Remember, the power to control your technology lies in your hands—use it wisely.

Key Actions

- **Create Focused Time Blocks**: Set aside dedicated periods of uninterrupted time for specific tasks, eliminating distractions by turning off notifications and silencing devices to enhance productivity.
- **Impose Sanctions on Technology Use**: Set limits on when and how you engage with your devices, such as using "Do Not Disturb" mode or disabling notifications during certain hours.
- **Build a Culture of Respect with Others**: Establish clear rules and communicate them with colleagues, friends, and family, setting expectations for when you are available and encouraging them to set their own boundaries.
- **Implement Practical Technology Rules:** Avoid screens during meals, keep your phone out of the bedroom, designate specific times to check messages, and save deep conversations for in-person or phone interactions.

Discussion Questions

1. What personal technology rules have you implemented to manage your time and focus?
2. How do you set and maintain boundaries around technology use with colleagues, friends, and family?
3. What strategies can you use to create more effective time blocks in your daily routine?
4. How can creating a culture of respect around technology use benefit personal and professional relationships?
5. What role do leaders play in shaping social norms around responsible technology use?

Practice Exercises

1. Time-Blocking Exercise

- **Objective**: Improve focus and productivity by dedicating uninterrupted time to specific tasks.
- **How to Do It**: Start by identifying your most important tasks for the day. Allocate specific time blocks (e.g., 45 minutes to an hour) for each task, ensuring that you eliminate all potential distractions during these periods. Turn off notifications, close unnecessary tabs, and set your phone to "Do Not Disturb." After each block, take a short break before starting the next one. Reflect on how this focused time improves your ability to complete tasks efficiently.

2. Technology Sanction Challenge

- **Objective**: Establish and maintain personal rules for technology use to improve your focus and well-being.
- **How to Do It**: Choose one or two specific sanctions to impose on your technology use for a week. For example, decide not to check your phone during meals or to disable email notifications during certain hours. Track your adherence to these rules and note any changes in your productivity, stress levels, and overall well-being. At the end of the week, assess the impact and adjust your rules as needed.

3. Boundary Setting with Others

- **Objective**: Enhance your ability to set and communicate boundaries regarding technology use with others.
- **How to Do It**: Identify a situation where you need to establish clearer boundaries with colleagues, friends, or family members about your technology use (e.g., not responding to emails after 8:00 PM). Write down the boundary you want to

set and practice how you will communicate it. Then, have a conversation with the relevant person(s) to set this boundary. Observe their response and your ability to maintain the boundary over time. Reflect on the experience and consider any adjustments needed for future interactions.

ALTERNATE TASKS FOR FRESH THINKING

We've all heard about the supposed wonders of multitasking. The idea that you can juggle several things at once and somehow get more done has been sold as a golden ticket to productivity. But here's the catch—multitasking doesn't work the way we've been led to believe. In fact, it can backfire, leading to mistakes, distractions, and a noticeable dip in the quality of your work.

When you try to tackle multiple tasks simultaneously, your brain isn't actually handling them all at once. Instead, it's rapidly switching between them, and this constant toggling takes a toll. You end up spreading your focus too thin, which can lead to errors and leave you mentally drained. Over time, this mental exhaustion, known as cognitive fatigue, sets in, making it harder to maintain your productivity or even think clearly.

The Case for Alternate Tasking

Taking breaks is one way to combat this cognitive fatigue, but let's face it—finding time for a full-blown break can be tough, especially when your schedule is jam-packed. This is where alternate tasking, or what I like to call "ultra-tasking," comes into play. Unlike multitasking, which spreads your attention too thin, ultra-tasking is about chunking your activities into specific time blocks and varying the type of work you do throughout the day.

Imagine you spend an hour hammering away at a mentally taxing task like drafting a report. Your brain is likely feeling the strain, but your body might be itching for some movement. Rather than diving straight into another mental task, switch gears—go for a run, take a walk, or do something physical. This shift not only gives your mind a break but also helps reset your energy levels, making it easier to return to mental tasks with renewed focus.

The Science Behind It

Different types of work demand different kinds of energy. Mental tasks require cognitive effort, while physical tasks use up physical energy. By alternating between these kinds of activities, you're effectively giving one part of your brain a rest while engaging another. It's like giving your brain a mini-vacation without taking a full break from productivity.

Think about it this way: after reading a dense book for an hour, your brain might be ready to check out, but your body is still raring to go. That's the perfect time to switch from mental to physical activity. By doing so, you're not just preventing burnout—you're also keeping your mind sharp and avoiding that all-too-common crash that comes from too much focus on one type of work.

Why Ultra-Tasking Beats Multitasking

Ultra-tasking does more than just stave off cognitive fatigue—it also helps improve the quality of your work across the board. If you spend all day processing information without giving your brain a break, you might find that your creativity dwindles, your ability to lead conversations weakens, and even the task you've been focusing on starts to suffer. On the flip side, by varying your activities and keeping your brain engaged in different ways, you can maintain a higher level of mental clarity and productivity.

Consider this: When you switch from a mental task to a physical one, you're not just resting your mind—you're actively recharging it. This allows you to come back to your original task with a fresh perspective and renewed energy, often leading to better results.

How to Incorporate Ultra-Tasking Into Your Routine

Incorporating ultra-tasking into your daily routine is simpler than it sounds. Start by dividing your day into blocks of time dedicated to specific tasks. Within these blocks, vary the type of effort you're putting in. For instance, after spending an hour on a mentally demanding task, switch to something physical for a bit before returning to another mental task. This rhythm helps maintain a balance between cognitive and physical exertion, keeping both your mind and body in peak condition.

Remember, the key is not just to take breaks but to take the right kind of breaks. A break doesn't always have to mean stopping work entirely; sometimes, it's just about switching gears to give your brain a breather while keeping your productivity rolling. And as you alternate between different types of tasks, you'll find that your mind stays fresher, your focus sharper, and your overall productivity higher.

Ultra-tasking, or alternating the tasks you engage in throughout the day, is a powerful strategy for keeping your mind fresh and your productivity high. By varying your activities and taking strategic breaks, you can avoid the pitfalls of multitasking, prevent cognitive fatigue, and improve the quality of your work. It's not just about doing more— it's about doing better. Incorporate this method into your routine, and you'll find that your workday feels less draining and more fulfilling.

Key Actions

- **Avoid Multitasking**: Understand that multitasking spreads your focus too thin, leading to mistakes, distractions, and decreased quality of work.
- **Practice Ultra-Tasking**: Chunk different activities into specific time blocks and alternate between different kinds of effort, such as switching between mental and physical tasks.
- **Take Strategic Breaks**: Instead of full breaks, switch to a different type of task to give your brain a rest while maintaining productivity.
- **Balance Cognitive and Physical Effort**: Alternate between mental and physical activities to prevent cognitive fatigue and maintain energy levels.
- **Maintain Mental Clarity**: By varying activities throughout the day, keep your mind sharp and avoid the decline in creativity and effectiveness that can come from focusing on one type of work for too long.
- **Incorporate Ultra-Tasking Into Daily Routine**: Plan your day with time blocks for different types of tasks, ensuring a balance between cognitive and physical exertion.

- **Use Breaks Effectively**: Use breaks to switch gears rather than stopping work entirely, helping to recharge your mind and improve focus when returning to tasks.

Discussion Questions

1. How has your experience with multitasking affected your productivity, and what changes could you make to incorporate ultra-tasking into your daily routine?
2. In what ways do you think alternating between mental and physical tasks throughout the day could benefit your overall performance and well-being?
3. Can you identify a time when cognitive fatigue impacted the quality of your work? How might ultra-tasking have helped in that situation?
4. What challenges do you anticipate in adopting an ultra-tasking approach, and how might you overcome them to better balance your mental and physical energy?
5. How do you currently manage breaks in your workday, and how could you adjust your approach to make those breaks more strategic and beneficial?

Practice Exercises

1. Time-Blocking for Ultra-Tasking

- **Objective**: To develop the habit of alternating between different types of tasks to maintain mental clarity and productivity.
- **How to Do It**: At the beginning of your day, create a schedule that alternates between mental and physical tasks. For example, block out one hour for a mentally demanding task (like writing or analyzing data), followed by 30 minutes of physical activity (like a walk or light exercise). Continue this pattern throughout the day, adjusting the time blocks as needed based on the intensity of the tasks.

2. Mental and Physical Task Pairing

- **Objective**: To learn how to effectively pair mental and physical tasks for better overall performance.
- **How to Do It**: Identify a list of mental tasks (e.g., reading, writing, problem-solving) and physical tasks (e.g., stretching, cleaning, walking). Practice pairing them throughout your day. For instance, after a 45-minute session of focused reading, immediately switch to a 15-minute physical task like stretching. Track how these pairings affect your focus and energy levels.

3. Cognitive Fatigue Awareness and Response

- **Objective**: To build awareness of cognitive fatigue and practice responding with appropriate task shifts.
- **How to Do It**: Throughout your day, regularly check in with yourself to assess your mental energy. When you notice signs of cognitive fatigue (e.g., difficulty focusing, feeling mentally drained), switch to a different type of task. For example, if you're struggling to concentrate on a mental task, shift to something physical, like a brisk walk or a quick chore. Keep a journal to reflect on how these shifts impact your productivity and well-being.

LET GO TO MOVE FORWARD

We've all been conditioned to see procrastination as a sign of laziness or a lack of motivation. The word itself has a negative connotation, bringing to mind images of missed deadlines, last-minute scrambles, and half-baked work. But what if I told you that procrastination isn't always the enemy? In fact, there's a type of procrastination that can be your best friend—if you know how to use it.

The Flip Side of Procrastination: Prioritization

At its core, procrastination is about delaying or postponing tasks. But what if the reason you're putting something off isn't because you're avoiding it, but because you're prioritizing something more important? That's where proactive procrastination, or what I like to call strategic delay, comes into play.

Strategic delay is about consciously choosing to push certain tasks to the back burner so you can focus your energy and attention on the ones that really matter. It's a deliberate act, not a passive one. You're not just letting things slide; you're making a calculated decision about where to direct your efforts.

The Challenge of Letting Go

For those of us who thrive on getting things done, the idea of leaving tasks unfinished can feel like nails on a chalkboard. We're wired to check things off our to-do lists, to clear out our inboxes, to respond to every request that comes our way. But leadership demands a different approach.

As a leader, your job isn't just to do things; it's to do the right things. That means you need to be comfortable with the idea that some tasks —maybe even a lot of them—won't get done. You have to be willing to let go, to leave things undone, and to focus on what really moves the needle.

The Power of the "Must-Ignore List"

Here's where the "must-ignore list" comes in. Think of it as a reverse to-do list. Instead of listing what you need to accomplish, you're listing what you're choosing to ignore, at least for now. These are the tasks that, while they might be nice to complete, don't align with your top priorities.

The beauty of the must-ignore list is that it frees you from the pressure of trying to do everything. By consciously deciding what you won't do, you create space to focus on what truly matters. It's a simple but powerful tool that can transform how you approach your day.

Procrastination with Purpose

So how do you make this work in practice? Start by identifying the tasks that are most critical to your success. These are the ones that should get your full attention. Next, look at everything else on your plate and ask yourself, "Does this really need to be done right now? Or can it wait?"

If it can wait, put it on your must-ignore list. Don't worry about it. Don't stress over it. Just let it go. By doing this, you're not just procras-tinating—you're prioritizing. You're making a conscious choice to focus on what matters most.

The Art of Selective Ignoring

This isn't about shirking responsibility or being careless. It's about being strategic with your time and energy. Not every task is urgent, and not every task is important. By learning to selectively ignore the noise, you can zero in on the signals that truly matter.

And here's the thing: the more you practice this, the better you'll get at it. You'll start to see that the world doesn't end when you let a few things slide. In fact, you might find that by letting go of the less important stuff, you're able to achieve more in the areas that count.

Embracing the Unfinished

At the end of the day, effective prioritization isn't about getting everything done—it's about getting the right things done. It's about recognizing that some tasks will remain unfinished, and that's okay. What matters is that you've focused your efforts where they're needed most.

So, embrace the art of letting go. Use procrastination as a tool, not a crutch. Create your must-ignore list, and let it guide you toward greater productivity and efficiency. Remember, being a leader isn't about doing more—it's about doing what matters. And sometimes, that means leaving a few things undone.

Key Actions

- **Strategic Delay**: Consciously choosing to delay or postpone certain tasks in order to focus on more important and impactful ones.
- **Letting Go of Unfinished Tasks**: Being comfortable with leaving some tasks unfinished to prioritize what truly matters.
- **Creating a "Must-Ignore List"**: Developing a list of tasks that can be intentionally ignored to free up time and energy for higher-priority activities.
- **Selective Ignoring**: Deliberately ignoring less important tasks to focus on the signals that truly matter, rather than getting caught up in the noise.
- **Procrastination with Purpose**: Using procrastination as a tool for prioritization, ensuring that only the most critical tasks receive attention.
- **Embracing Unfinished Work:** Accepting that not all tasks need to be completed and recognizing that focusing on the right things is more important than doing everything.

Discussion Questions

1. How can strategic delay help you focus on what truly matters in your work? Can you share an example where this approach led to better outcomes?

2. What challenges do you face when trying to let go of unfinished tasks, and how can embracing the idea of a 'must-ignore list' help you overcome these challenges?

3. In what ways can selective ignoring improve your productivity and efficiency? How do you determine which tasks to ignore and which to prioritize?

4. How does the concept of procrastination with purpose differ from traditional procrastination, and how can it be applied to leadership roles?

5. How do you balance the need to complete tasks with the understanding that not everything needs to be done? What strategies do you use to ensure that your focus remains on the most important tasks?

Practice Exercises

1. Prioritization Audit

- **Objective**: To identify and focus on high-impact tasks.
- **How to Do It**: At the start of each week, list all your tasks and responsibilities. Categorize them into three groups: High Impact, Medium Impact, and Low Impact. Focus your efforts on the High Impact tasks first, moving on to Medium Impact only after the High Impact tasks are complete. At the end of the week, review your progress and adjust your priorities for the following week.

2. Create and Use a "Must-Ignore List"

- **Objective**: To practice intentional ignoring and improve focus.
- **How to Do It**: Identify tasks that are not critical to your immediate goals and put them on a "Must-Ignore List." Commit to ignoring these tasks for a set period (e.g., one week) and instead focus on your top priorities. Reflect on how this shift in focus affects your productivity and mental clarity.

3. Selective Ignoring Practice

- **Objective**: To strengthen your ability to focus on what truly matters.
- **How to Do It**: Throughout your day, when new tasks or requests arise, pause and ask yourself if they align with your top priorities. If they don't, consciously choose to ignore or delay them. Keep a journal of the decisions you make to ignore tasks and review it weekly to see how this practice has influenced your productivity and stress levels.

WHITE SPACE FOR ENERGY

Letting go is one of the toughest lessons to learn as a leader. The world often tells us that leaving things unfinished is a sign of failure, of procrastination. But that's a narrow view. The reality is that true productivity isn't about getting everything done. It's about getting the *right* things done. And sometimes, that means strategically ignoring certain tasks altogether.

Redefining Procrastination: The Shift to Prioritization

Procrastination has a bad rap. It's seen as the enemy of progress, a byproduct of laziness or lack of motivation. But let's flip that script. Procrastination, in its healthiest form, is really about prioritization. When you prioritize, you choose to focus on what matters most and push the rest aside. It's not about avoiding work; it's about making sure the work you do is impactful.

This is where the concept of *proactive procrastination* comes into play. It's a deliberate strategy where you consciously decide to delay or even ignore certain tasks to give your full attention to the ones that truly move the needle. Unlike the traditional procrastination that stems from avoidance, proactive procrastination is a tool for time management, a way to ensure your energy is spent wisely.

The Challenge of Letting Go

As leaders, we're wired to be doers. We thrive on checking things off our to-do lists, on being responsive and reliable. But leadership demands a different mindset. It requires the ability to distinguish between what's urgent and what's important—and sometimes, to let go of the urgent in favor of the important.

This shift isn't easy. The urge to tackle every task that comes your way can be overwhelming. But effective leadership means knowing when to step back, when to say, "This isn't worth my time right now." It's about recognizing that trying to do it all can lead to burnout and inefficiency, both for you and your team.

Creating Your Must-Ignore List

One of the most powerful tools in your leadership toolkit should be a **must-ignore list**. This isn't about neglecting your responsibilities; it's about consciously deciding which tasks can wait or be delegated so you can focus on higher priorities.

Here's how you can create your own:

1. *Identify Low-Impact Tasks:* These are the tasks that don't directly contribute to your main goals. They might be time-consuming, but they don't move the needle in a significant way.
2. *Delegate Where Possible:* If something is low on your priority list but still needs to be done, find someone else who can handle it. Delegation isn't just about offloading work; it's about empowering others to take ownership.
3. *Delay with Purpose:* Some tasks don't need immediate attention. If there's no pressing deadline, consider putting them on hold. The key is to do this intentionally, not out of avoidance.
4. *Reassess Regularly:* Your must-ignore list isn't set in stone. Regularly review and adjust it based on shifting priorities and new information.

The Positive Side of Procrastination

When used strategically, procrastination can be a powerful productivity tool. By selectively ignoring certain tasks, you free up mental space and energy to focus on what truly matters. It's about making deliberate choices that align with your goals, rather than getting bogged down by the minutiae.

Consider this: not all tasks are created equal. Some demand your immediate attention; others don't. The art of leadership lies in knowing the difference and acting accordingly.

The Takeaway

Learning to let go of tasks and leave things undone isn't about shirking responsibility. It's about mastering the art of prioritization. By embracing proactive procrastination and developing a must-ignore list, you can focus on the tasks that truly matter, increasing both your productivity and effectiveness as a leader.

Remember, true productivity isn't measured by how much you do but by how much you achieve. And sometimes, achieving more means doing less.

Key Actions

- **Prioritization Over Completion**: Focus on completing the most important tasks rather than trying to do everything.
- **Proactive Procrastination**: Intentionally delay or ignore less critical tasks to concentrate on high-impact work.
- **Letting Go**: Develop the ability to let go of tasks that aren't essential to your primary goals, even if they seem urgent.
- **Creating a Must-Ignore List**: Identify tasks that can be delayed or delegated to free up time for more critical responsibilities.
- **Delegation**: Empower others by delegating tasks that are less important to your core objectives.
- **Delaying with Purpose**: Delay tasks that don't require immediate attention, doing so intentionally and strategically.
- **Regular Reassessment**: Regularly review and adjust your must-ignore list based on shifting priorities and new information.
- **Selective Focus:** Concentrate your efforts on tasks that directly contribute to your main goals, ignoring distractions.

Discussion Questions

1. How do you currently differentiate between urgent tasks and important tasks in your daily work? What strategies do you use to prioritize effectively?

2. Can you share an example of a time when proactive procrastination helped you achieve a better outcome? How did ignoring certain tasks contribute to your success?

3. What challenges do you face when trying to let go of tasks that seem urgent but aren't truly important? How do you overcome these challenges?

4. How might creating a "must-ignore list" change the way you approach your workload? What tasks would you consider adding to such a list?

5. In what ways can delegation empower your team, and how do you decide which tasks to delegate versus handle yourself?

Practice Exercises

1. The Prioritization Matrix

- **Objective**: To practice distinguishing between urgent and important tasks.
- **How to Do It**: Each morning, create a simple matrix with four quadrants: Urgent & Important, Not Urgent & Important, Urgent & Not Important, Not Urgent & Not Important. List your tasks for the day in the appropriate quadrants. Focus your time on the tasks in the Urgent & Important quadrant, while consciously deciding which tasks can be ignored, delayed, or delegated.

2. Must-Ignore List Creation

- **Objective**: To develop the habit of identifying and setting aside low-priority tasks.
- **How to Do It**: At the start of each week, review your to-do list and identify at least three tasks that can be ignored or delayed. Write these tasks on a separate "must-ignore list" and set them aside. Revisit this list at the end of the week to see if any tasks still require your attention or if they resolved themselves.

3. Delegation Drill

- **Objective**: To improve your ability to delegate tasks effectively.
- **How to Do It**: Identify one task each day that you would typically handle yourself but that could be delegated. Choose a team member who could benefit from the experience and delegate the task to them, providing clear instructions and support. Reflect at the end of the day on how the delegation went and what you learned from the process.

SPEED UP TO SAVE TIME

Building relationships is at the core of any successful endeavor. But sometimes, the desire to connect can make it tough to know when to wrap things up. You might worry that ending a conversation too soon will come across as rude or uncaring. Here's the thing, though: People value clarity and respect for their time as much as you do. It's not just about being polite; it's about finding the right balance between engaging in meaningful conversation and managing your time effectively.

The Power of Symbols: Creating Consistent Endings

A powerful technique for managing conversations is the use of symbols —physical or verbal cues that consistently signal the end of a meeting or discussion. Symbols work because they create a pattern that others can easily recognize and understand. For example, you could place a small hourglass on your desk and flip it over when it's time to wind down. Or, you could use a consistent phrase like, "Let's recap what we've discussed," to indicate that the conversation is wrapping up.

Over time, these symbols become a natural part of your interactions. People will learn to associate these signals with the end of a conversation, making the transition smoother and less awkward for everyone involved. The key here is consistency—use the same symbol or phrase regularly, and it will become an expected and appreciated part of your communication style.

Making the Most of Every Interaction: Quality Over Quantity

Knowing when and how to end a conversation is just as crucial as knowing how to start one. It's not about the length of the conversation but the quality of it. By setting time constraints and employing symbols, you can manage your time more effectively without sacrificing the quality of your interactions.

This approach is not about rushing people; it's about being intentional with your time and theirs. Every conversation has a natural arc, and your role is to guide it gracefully to its conclusion. When you do this well, you'll find that your days are more productive, your relationships are stronger, and your impact is greater.

The Silent Impact of Respecting Time

Effective communication isn't just about what you say—it's also about how you manage the flow of conversation. People remember how you made them feel during an interaction, and part of that feeling comes from how you respected their time. By being mindful of how you end conversations, you show that you value both the person and the task at hand.

In the end, mastering the balance between relationships and time management isn't just a skill—it's essential. When you navigate this discomfort with grace and clarity, you'll find that both your relationships and your schedule will thank you.

Key Actions

- **Using Speed Up Cues**: Implementing subtle but clear signals, like "I have one last question before we wrap up," to guide the conversation toward its conclusion without being abrupt.
- **Setting Time Constraints**: Establishing a clear time limit at the beginning of a conversation to create a framework that keeps the discussion focused and efficient.
- **Balancing Approachability with Efficiency**: Striking a balance between being accessible and protecting your time by transparently communicating time constraints while remaining engaged and respectful.
- **Practicing Intentional Time Management:** Being deliberate in managing your time during conversations to ensure they are purposeful, productive, and respectful of everyone's time.

Discussion Questions

1. How can using "speed up cues" improve the productivity of

your conversations without making the other person feel rushed or dismissed?

2. What are some challenges you might face when setting time constraints at the beginning of a conversation, and how can you overcome them?

3. How do you strike the right balance between being approachable and protecting your time during important discussions?

4. In what ways can intentional time management during conversations lead to more effective leadership and stronger relationships with your team?

5. Can you share an experience where setting time constraints or using speed up cues positively impacted the outcome of a conversation? What did you learn from that experience?

Practice Exercises

1. Speed Up Cue Practice

- **Objective**: To become comfortable using speed up cues in conversations.
- **How to Do It**: In your next few meetings or conversations, consciously incorporate phrases like "I have one last question before we wrap up" or "Let's focus on the most important point." Start with low-stakes situations, such as casual conversations with colleagues, and gradually apply these cues in more formal or high-stakes settings. Reflect on how the other person responds and adjust your approach as needed to maintain a polite and productive tone.

2. Time Constraint Conversations

- **Objective**: To improve the efficiency and focus of your conversations by setting clear time constraints.
- **How to Do It**: Begin each of your next three meetings by clearly stating the amount of time you have available (e.g., "I've got 15 minutes, let's make the most of it"). Notice how

this affects the flow of the conversation and the focus of the participants. After each meeting, evaluate how well the time constraint worked and whether it helped keep the discussion on track. Adjust your approach based on your observations.

3. Balancing Approachability with Efficiency

- **Objective**: To refine your ability to balance being approachable with managing your time effectively.
- **How to Do It**: Select a few upcoming conversations where you expect the need to balance being open with managing time. Before the conversation, plan how you will communicate your availability and time constraints in a way that shows both respect and engagement. For instance, you could say, "I'm really interested in hearing your thoughts, and I want to ensure we focus on the key points given our time." After the conversation, reflect on how well you managed this balance and where you can improve in future interactions.

BALANCING TIME AND RELATIONSHIPS

For many leaders, especially those who thrive on building relationships, ending a conversation can feel awkward. You might worry that cutting things short will come across as rude or uncaring. But here's the truth: people appreciate clarity and respect for their time as much as you do.

The key is to balance your natural conversational skills with the need to manage your schedule. By mastering the art of the speed up cue and setting clear time boundaries, you can maintain strong relationships while also keeping your day on track. It's not about being abrupt; it's about being clear and purposeful.

The Power of Symbols: Creating Consistent Endings

Another strategy to consider is using a physical or verbal symbol to signal the end of a meeting or conversation. This could be something as simple as a small hourglass on your desk, which you turn over when it's time to wind down. Or it could be a consistent phrase like, "Let's recap what we've discussed," signaling that the conversation is wrapping up.

Symbols work because they create a consistent pattern that others can recognize. Over time, people will learn to associate these signals with the end of a conversation, making the transition smoother and less awkward for everyone involved.

Making the Most of Every Interaction

In leadership, knowing when and how to end a conversation is just as important as knowing how to start one. By using speed up cues, setting time constraints, and employing symbols, you can manage your time more effectively without sacrificing the quality of your interactions. Remember, it's not about rushing people—it's about being intentional with your time and theirs.

In the end, effective communication isn't just about what you say, but how you manage the flow of conversation. When you master this skill, you'll find that your days are more productive, your relationships are stronger, and your leadership is more impactful.

Key Actions

- **Respect for Time:** Recognize the importance of balancing meaningful conversations with effective time management. Understand that people value clarity and respect for their time as much as you do.
- **Use of Symbols:** Implement consistent physical or verbal cues (e.g., an hourglass or a phrase like "Let's recap what we've discussed") to signal the end of a conversation, making transitions smoother and less awkward.
- **Consistency in Communication:** Regularly use the same symbols or phrases to create a recognizable pattern, helping others understand when a conversation is concluding.
- **Intentional Time Management:** Be deliberate in managing your time and the time of others by setting clear time constraints without sacrificing the quality of interactions.
- **Guiding Conversations:** Recognize the natural arc of conversations and guide them gracefully to their conclusion, ensuring that both the person and the task are respected.
- **Quality Over Quantity:** Focus on the quality of interactions rather than their length, ensuring that conversations are meaningful and effective.
- **Mindfulness in Communication:** Be aware of how you manage the flow of conversation, ensuring that people feel valued, and their time is respected.

Discussion Questions

1. How do you balance building relationships with managing your time effectively during conversations?
2. How can the use of symbols, like a consistent phrase or physical cue, improve the way you end conversations?
3. What strategies do you use to ensure that your conversations are high in quality, even when time is limited?

4. What challenges do you face when trying to wrap up a conversation without appearing rude or abrupt?
5. How does being intentional with your time during conversations impact your productivity and relationships?

Practice Exercises

1. The Hourglass Exercise

- **Objective**: Improve your ability to manage time during conversations.
- **How to Do It**: Place an hourglass or timer on your desk during meetings or calls. Set it for a specific time limit (e.g., 15 minutes). As the time runs out, practice using a consistent phrase like, "Let's recap what we've discussed," to signal the end of the conversation. Reflect on how this impacts the flow of the conversation and the other person's response.

2. Consistent Closing Phrase Practice

- **Objective**: Develop a habit of using a consistent phrase to conclude conversations.
- **How to Do It**: Identify a phrase you feel comfortable using to wrap up conversations (e.g., "Before we finish…" or "To summarize…"). Practice using this phrase in every conversation for a week, whether in person, on the phone, or via email. Notice how this affects the transition from discussion to conclusion and any changes in how others respond.

3. Time-Bound Conversation Drill

- **Objective**: Enhance your ability to balance conversation quality with time management.
- **How to Do It**: Set up a mock conversation with a colleague or friend where you have a set time (e.g., 10 minutes) to discuss a topic. Use this time to practice being intentional

with your words and guiding the conversation towards a meaningful conclusion within the time limit. After the exercise, evaluate how well you managed both the quality of the conversation and the time constraint. Repeat with different time limits to build flexibility.

CHAPTER 10
GROW DAILY, LEAD BOLDLY

Leadership isn't a destination; it's a journey. The best leaders know that their growth and development must be ongoing. But let's be honest—change isn't easy. Breaking old habits and forming new ones can feel like an uphill battle. That's why the key to becoming a better leader lies in making strategic, incremental changes that stick.

Small Changes, Big Impact

Change doesn't have to be dramatic to be effective. In fact, the most lasting changes often start small. Our brains are creatures of habit, hardwired to resist the unfamiliar. So instead of trying to overhaul your leadership style overnight, focus on making one small adjustment at a time. Think of it as planting seeds—over time, those small changes will grow into significant improvements.

To make a change that lasts, replace an old habit with a new, positive one. Simply trying to stop doing something rarely works because it leaves a void. But when you swap out a negative behavior with a positive action, you're filling that space with something beneficial. This approach makes it easier to build new, healthier habits.

The Ripple Effect of Change

As a leader, your actions have a ripple effect on those around you. Sudden, drastic changes can unsettle your team, especially if they're used to a certain way of doing things. Consistency and predictability are comforting, so when you make changes, do so gradually. Introduce new behaviors slowly, and let them become part of the fabric of your daily interactions. This way, your team can adapt without feeling like the ground is shifting beneath their feet.

The Power of Focused Effort

When it comes to self-improvement, less is more. Trying to change multiple aspects of your leadership at once is a recipe for resistance—both from yourself and those you lead. Instead, pick one behavior to focus on for six to eight weeks. Practice it consistently, day in and day out. Just like taking a daily dose of medicine, this focused effort will embed the new behavior into your routine until it becomes second nature.

Authenticity Is Key

Your team knows you. They've seen you in action, and they have a sense of who you are as a leader. If you suddenly start behaving in ways that are out of character, it's going to raise eyebrows. That's why authenticity is crucial. The changes you make should feel like natural extensions of who you are, not forced or fake. By practicing new behaviors consistently over time, you can integrate them into your leadership style in a way that feels genuine and true to yourself.

Building a Foundation for Growth

Leadership is about constant evolution. The best leaders don't rest on their laurels—they're always looking for ways to improve. By making small, strategic changes, you can steadily enhance your leadership skills. Focus on one behavior at a time, replace old habits with new, positive ones, and be mindful of the impact your changes have on your team. Most importantly, stay authentic. Over time, these incremental improvements will compound, making you a stronger, more effective leader.

The Journey Continues

Self-improvement isn't a one-time project; it's a lifelong commitment. By taking small steps every day, you can make significant strides in your leadership journey. Remember, the goal isn't to become a different leader overnight—it's to become a better version of the leader you already are. Keep refining, keep growing, and keep leading with authenticity and purpose.

EMBRACE THE IDENTITY

Labels matter. They shape how we see ourselves and how others see us. In the workplace, the label "leader" carries particular weight. It's more than just a title; it's a mindset, a way of being. When we start calling ourselves leaders, we begin to act like leaders, and that shift in behavior can lead to significant change and progress.

Embrace the Label

One of the most effective ways to grow into the role of a leader is to embrace the label wholeheartedly. This isn't just about what you do at work. It's about how you lead in every aspect of your life—at home, in your community, and even in your personal relationships. By consistently stepping into leadership roles in all these areas, you begin to embody the characteristics of a leader. The more you see yourself as a leader, the more you act like one, and the more others will begin to see you that way too.

But this isn't just about self-empowerment. It's about the impact you have on others. When you start calling yourself a leader, you're setting an example. You're showing others what leadership looks like, and you're giving them permission to see themselves as leaders too. It's a ripple effect that can transform not just individuals, but entire teams and organizations.

Cultivate a Culture of Leadership

Labels are contagious. When you consistently refer to yourself and others as leaders, you create a culture that values and promotes leadership. This is especially important in organizations where leadership might traditionally be confined to those with specific titles or ranks. By democratizing the label of "leader," you encourage a culture where leadership is about action and influence, not just position.

To cultivate this culture, be intentional about how you use the label. Refer to yourself as a leader in conversations, introductions, and even on social media profiles. Make it a habit to acknowledge and celebrate leadership qualities in others. When someone steps up, even in small ways, recognize them as a leader. This reinforces the idea that leadership is not a rare trait, but something that can be developed and demonstrated by anyone.

Leadership is in the Doing

One of the most critical aspects of leadership is understanding that it doesn't come from a title—it comes from actions. Leadership is about the choices you make every day, the way you communicate, the way you support and inspire others. If you wait for someone else to give you the title of "leader," you're missing the point. Leadership isn't about waiting; it's about stepping up.

Consider this: every time you raise your hand for a task, volunteer to take the lead, or speak up in a meeting, you're practicing leadership. By consistently choosing to lead, you reinforce your identity as a leader to yourself and others. Don't wait for permission—start living the label now.

The Impact of Living the Label

Calling yourself a leader is just the beginning. The real change happens when you start living up to that label. It's not enough to say it; you have to show it in your actions. This means taking responsibility, making decisions, guiding others, and continually looking for ways to grow and improve. It means being the person others can rely on, whether in moments of crisis or in the day-to-day grind.

As you live the label, you'll find that others start to view you differently. They'll begin to look to you for guidance and inspiration. This, in turn, strengthens your leadership identity and further solidifies your role. It's a positive feedback loop: the more you lead, the more you're seen as a leader, and the more opportunities you'll have to lead.

Creating a Lasting Legacy

Finally, by consistently referring to yourself and others as leaders, you're doing more than just shaping your own identity—you're contributing to a larger culture of leadership. This culture doesn't just benefit you; it benefits everyone around you. When leadership becomes a shared value, organizations become more resilient, innovative, and successful. People feel empowered to take initiative, solve problems, and drive progress.

In the end, the label of "leader" is more than just a word. It's a call to action. It's a challenge to step up, to take responsibility, and to make a difference. By embracing this label, by living it out every day, you're not just making a permanent change in yourself—you're creating a ripple effect that can lead to progress and positive outcomes for everyone around you.

So, don't wait for someone else to call you a leader. Start calling yourself one today. And watch how it changes not just your life, but the lives of those around you.

Key Actions

- **Embrace the Label**: Actively identify and refer to yourself as a leader in all areas of your life—work, home, community—to reinforce your leadership identity.
- **Lead in All Areas of Life**: Step into leadership roles consistently, whether at work, at home, or in the community, to embody the characteristics of a leader.
- **Set an Example for Others**: By calling yourself a leader, you model leadership behavior and encourage others to see themselves as leaders too.
- **Cultivate a Culture of Leadership**: Use the label "leader" to create an environment where leadership is valued and encouraged, regardless of titles or positions.
- **Acknowledge Leadership in Others**: Recognize and celebrate leadership qualities in others to promote a broader understanding of leadership.
- **Take Action**: Understand that leadership comes from daily actions, choices, decisions, and communication, not from titles.
- **Raise Your Hand for Leadership Tasks**: Volunteer for tasks, take the lead in projects, and speak up in meetings to practice leadership.

- **Live Up to the Label**: Consistently demonstrate leadership through responsibility, decision-making, and guiding others.
- **Create a Lasting Legacy**: By embracing the label of leader and encouraging others to do the same, contribute to a culture of leadership that drives progress and positive outcomes.

Discussion Questions

1. How do you think embracing the label of "leader" in all areas of your life can impact your personal and professional growth?
2. In what ways can acknowledging leadership qualities in others help to create a culture of leadership within an organization?
3. What are some practical steps you can take to begin living up to the label of leader in your daily actions and decisions?
4. How can we encourage a broader definition of leadership that goes beyond titles and formal positions within our teams or communities?
5. What challenges might arise when you start calling yourself a leader, and how can you overcome them to effectively embody the role?

Practice Exercises

1. Leadership Self-Reflection Journal

- **Objective**: To consciously embrace the label of leader and reflect on how your daily actions align with this identity.
- **How to Do It**: Each evening, take 10-15 minutes to journal about your day. Focus on moments where you exhibited leadership—whether it was making a decision, guiding a team, or stepping up in a challenging situation. Reflect on how these actions reinforce your identity as a leader and identify areas where you can improve. This practice will help you internalize the label and recognize leadership opportunities in everyday life.

2. Leadership Labeling Exercise

- **Objective**: To actively recognize and reinforce leadership qualities in yourself and others.
- **How to Do It**: Throughout the week, make it a point to label specific actions as "leadership" when you see them in yourself or others. For instance, if a colleague volunteers for a challenging task, acknowledge it by saying, "That's great leadership." Similarly, when you make a decisive choice, mentally affirm, "This is me leading." This exercise helps solidify the concept that leadership is not just about titles but about actions.

3. Leadership Role-Playing

- **Objective**: To practice stepping into leadership roles and making leadership decisions in a controlled environment.
- **How to Do It**: With a group or on your own, create scenarios where leadership is required—such as resolving a team conflict, guiding a project, or making a strategic decision. Role-play these scenarios, consciously taking on the role of the leader. If possible, get feedback from others on your performance, focusing on how effectively you embodied leadership qualities. This exercise builds confidence and helps you become more comfortable in leadership roles.

REWIRE THROUGH CONSISTENCY

Repetition isn't just a tool—it's the foundation of mastery. Whether you're an athlete, a musician, or a leader, the key to excellence lies in doing the same thing over and over until it becomes second nature. This process rewires your brain, creating new neural pathways that make behaviors and skills automatic. It's how you move from fumbling through a task to performing it with fluidity and confidence.

Take a moment to think about the professionals at the top of their fields. What sets them apart? It's not just raw talent; it's the hours, days, and years they've spent honing their craft through repetition. Athletes run drills until their bodies move on instinct. Musicians practice scales until their fingers fly across the keys without conscious thought. And leaders? They develop their skills in the same way—through deliberate, consistent practice.

The Science Behind Repetition

When you engage in a behavior repeatedly, you're not just building muscle memory; you're also strengthening the connections in your brain. Each time you perform a task, you create and reinforce neural pathways. Myelin, a fatty substance in the brain, plays a crucial role in this process. It wraps around nerve fibers, insulating them and making the transmission of nerve impulses faster and more efficient. The more you practice, the thicker the myelin becomes, and the quicker and more precise your actions become.

This is why repetition is so effective. It doesn't just help you remember how to do something; it literally changes the structure of your brain to make that task easier and more automatic. Over time, what was once a conscious effort becomes an unconscious habit.

Focus on Small, Granular Changes

But here's the catch: trying to change too much at once is a recipe for failure. The brain thrives on focus. When you concentrate on one small change at a time, you give your brain the chance to build those new neural pathways without getting overwhelmed. It's like carving a path through the woods. If you try to carve out multiple trails at once, you'll end up with a mess of half-finished paths. But if you focus on one trail, walking it over and over, it becomes clear and easy to follow.

This is why drills are so powerful. They break down complex skills into manageable chunks that you can practice repeatedly until they're second nature. Think of a martial artist practicing a single move against a wooden dummy, or a surgeon perfecting sutures on an orange before ever picking up a scalpel in the operating room. These drills may seem simple, but they are the building blocks of mastery.

Consistency Is Key

To reap the benefits of repetition, you need consistency. Set aside specific times for practice, and make it a non-negotiable part of your routine. Whether it's 10 minutes a day or an hour a week, the key is to show up, no matter what. This consistency not only reinforces the habit but also signals to your brain that this is important, something worth prioritizing.

Motivation is crucial here. Without a clear goal, it's easy to lose steam. Know why you're practicing and what you want to achieve. Keep that goal in mind, and remind yourself of it whenever you feel your motivation slipping.

A Practical Example: Mastering Note-Taking

Let's bring this idea home with a practical example. Imagine you're a leader who wants to improve your note-taking abilities during meetings. At first, it might feel overwhelming—trying to listen, think, and write all at once can be chaotic. But through repetition, you can train yourself to become a master note-taker.

Start by keeping notes during every meeting. It'll be rough at first. You might miss key points, or struggle to keep up with the pace of the conversation. But over time, you'll develop your own system—perhaps you create shorthand symbols, or maybe you find a way to structure your notes that works for you. As you repeat this process, meeting after meeting, you'll find that you're not just getting better at note-taking; you're actually changing the way you listen and process information.

Eventually, it becomes second nature. You walk into a room, and your brain automatically starts organizing and capturing the flow of conversation without conscious effort.

The Path to Mastery

Repetition is more than just doing the same thing over and over. It's about deliberate practice—focusing on small, specific actions that lead to big improvements over time. It's about being consistent, staying motivated, and having a clear goal in mind. And most importantly, it's about rewiring your brain to make these new behaviors and skills automatic.

Whether you're looking to improve a leadership skill, learn a new hobby, or make a personal change, remember this: mastery isn't about instant results. It's about showing up, putting in the work, and letting repetition do its magic. The path to success is paved with small, consistent steps. So pick your focus, drill down, and practice, practice, practice. The more you repeat, the more you rewire your brain—and the closer you get to mastering whatever it is you set out to achieve.

Key Actions

- **Engage in Repetition**: Consistently practice a behavior or skill to develop muscle memory and reinforce neural pathways in the brain.
- **Break Down Skills into Manageable Chunks**: Focus on small, specific tasks or drills to build mastery over time.
- **Focus on One Change at a Time**: Concentrate on making small, granular changes rather than trying to tackle too many things at once.
- **Maintain Consistency**: Set aside specific times for practice and make it a regular, non-negotiable part of your routine.
- **Stay Motivated with Clear Goals**: Keep a clear objective in mind to stay focused and committed to the practice.
- **Create Personal Systems**: Develop personalized methods or systems (e.g., shorthand symbols for note-taking) through repetition to improve efficiency and effectiveness.

- **Practice Deliberately**: Approach practice with intention, focusing on specific actions that lead to improvement and mastery.
- **Let Repetition Rewire Your Brain**: Understand that consistent repetition will eventually make behaviors and skills automatic, leading to long-term mastery.

Discussion Questions

1. How has repetition influenced your personal or professional development?
2. What is the significance of focusing on small, specific changes when developing new skills?
3. Why is maintaining consistency in practice important for achieving mastery?
4. How can the concept of rewiring your brain through repetition be applied to leadership skills?
5. What personal systems or habits have you developed through repetition to enhance your effectiveness?

Practice Exercises

1. Daily Micro-Practice

- **Objective**: To reinforce small, specific behaviors through consistent repetition.
- **How to Do It**: Identify one small skill or habit you want to improve. For example, if you're working on better note-taking, commit to practicing this skill every day in a low-stakes environment, such as during a personal meeting or when reading a book. Focus on capturing key points concisely. Set aside 10-15 minutes each day for this practice, and track your progress over time.

2. Focused Drill Sessions

- **Objective**: To build muscle memory and reinforce neural pathways for a specific skill.
- **How to Do It**: Choose a skill you want to master, like giving clear and concise feedback. Break it down into its components (e.g., structuring feedback, using specific examples, maintaining a neutral tone). Dedicate time each week to practice this skill in isolation through role-playing scenarios or written exercises. Repeat each component multiple times until it feels natural.

3. Weekly Reflection and Adjustment

- **Objective**: To refine and improve your practice routine by evaluating progress and making necessary adjustments.
- **How to Do It**: At the end of each week, take 15-20 minutes to reflect on your practice sessions. Consider what worked well and where you encountered challenges. Adjust your approach as needed, whether it's focusing more on a particular aspect of the skill or tweaking your practice routine for better results. Use this reflection time to set specific goals for the following week's practice.

NAMING DRIVES GROWTH

There's a hidden power in names—one that goes beyond mere identification. Nomenclature, the act of naming, is more than a way to classify things; it's a tool that allows us to understand, influence, and ultimately control our world. This principle is not only true in science but also in our personal lives and professional development.

Naming as a Catalyst for Change

Think about it: before you can change something, you have to recognize it. And to recognize it, you often need a name for it. Whether it's a bad habit, an underperforming process, or an area of personal growth, naming it is the first step toward acting on it. Once you put a label on something, it becomes tangible—a concept you can grasp, analyze, and, most importantly, modify.

This isn't just theory. It's a practical approach to change, one that's seen in everything from personal development to corporate culture. By assigning specific names to actions, behaviors, and processes, we gain the ability to dissect and improve them. It's the difference between vaguely knowing you need to "do better" and pinpointing that you need to "enhance your time management skills."

Building a Shared Vocabulary

In group settings, the power of naming things is amplified. A shared vocabulary within a team or organization fosters clarity and alignment. It transforms abstract ideas into actionable strategies and ensures that everyone is on the same page.

Take, for example, Amazon's principle of "disagree and commit." This phrase isn't just a catchy slogan; it's a powerful concept that shapes how decisions are made and executed within the company. By giving a name to the process of voicing concerns during a discussion and then fully committing to the final decision, Amazon has created a culture of honesty, collaboration, and forward momentum. This shared understanding of what it means to "disagree and commit" allows teams to move past disagreements and focus on execution without lingering resentment.

Language Shapes Motivation

The words we choose to describe our goals and actions don't just clarify —they motivate. Consider the difference between saying "I'm going to work out" versus "I'm going to enhance my fitness." The latter feels more purposeful, more aligned with a broader vision of health and well-being. It's a subtle shift, but it can make all the difference in how motivated you feel to stick with your routine.

This principle extends beyond fitness. In any area of life, deliberately choosing language that resonates with your goals can create a more compelling narrative. Words shape your perception of the task at hand, turning a chore into a meaningful pursuit.

The Precision of Naming in Behavior Change

Naming is not just about labeling; it's about precision. The more specific the name, the clearer the action. For example, in the realm of nutrition, it's not enough to just "eat better." Understanding terms like calories, carbohydrates, proteins, and fats gives you the tools to make informed choices. You can't control what you don't understand, and you can't understand what you haven't named.

Naming provides a framework for behavior change. When you know exactly what needs to change—be it a particular habit, thought pattern, or skill—you can develop a targeted plan to address it. It's the difference between a vague resolution to "get healthy" and a specific commitment to "reduce sugar intake and increase daily physical activity."

The Impact of Thoughtful Vocabulary

It's not just about naming things for the sake of it; the words we choose matter. Thoughtful vocabulary creates the conversation we need to have with ourselves and others. It paves the way for a clearer understanding of where we are, where we want to go, and how we plan to get there.

The principle of "disagree and commit" at Amazon is a perfect example of how a well-chosen phrase can encapsulate a complex process, making it easier for everyone to engage with it. Similarly, in your personal life, adopting a vocabulary that aligns with your goals can steer your thoughts and actions in the right direction.

Naming as a Pathway to Success

In the end, naming things is about more than just words; it's about taking control of your narrative. Whether in a corporate setting, a personal development journey, or a team environment, the names we assign to our actions and ideas have the power to shape outcomes.

So, next time you're faced with a challenge, start by naming it. Give it a label that captures its essence, and you'll find it much easier to tackle. Naming is the first step toward understanding, and understanding is the first step toward change. By deliberately choosing the words we use, we create the path we want to follow—one that leads to clarity, control, and ultimately, success.

Key Actions

- **Recognizing and Naming Issues**: Identify and label specific behaviors, habits, or processes as the first step toward addressing them.
- **Using a Shared Vocabulary**: Develop and use a common language within teams or organizations to ensure clarity and alignment.
- **Adopting Purposeful Language**: Choose words deliberately to create a motivating narrative that aligns with goals.
- **Being Specific in Naming**: Use precise terminology to clearly define actions and behaviors, allowing for targeted improvements.
- **Leveraging Thoughtful Vocabulary**: Use vocabulary that fosters understanding and drives the conversation toward desired outcomes.
- **Applying Named Concepts to Action**: Once a concept is

named, act on it with a clear plan for improvement or change.

Discussion Questions

1. How does naming behaviors or processes make them more tangible and easier to address?
2. How can a shared vocabulary within a team or organization enhance collaboration and alignment?
3. In what ways does the language we use to describe our goals and actions influence motivation and commitment?
4. Why is it important to be specific when naming behaviors or actions you want to change?
5. How can thoughtful vocabulary shape conversations and decisions in personal and professional contexts?

Practice Exercises

1. Behavior Identification and Naming

- **Objective**: Improve your ability to recognize and label behaviors or processes that need attention.
- **How to Do It**: At the end of each day, reflect on your actions and identify one behavior, habit, or process that you want to change or improve. Write it down and assign a specific name to it, such as "Procrastination Spiral" or "Meeting Efficiency." Over time, this will help you become more aware of areas for improvement.

2. Creating a Shared Vocabulary

- **Objective**: Develop a common language within your team or organization to enhance communication and alignment.
- **How to Do It**: In your next team meeting, introduce a new term or phrase that encapsulates a process or behavior you want the team to focus on, like "Quick Pivot" for adapting to changes or "Focused Follow-Up" for closing loops on tasks.

Encourage the team to use this language regularly in discussions to reinforce its meaning and importance.

3. Language Reframing for Motivation

- **Objective**: Practice reframing your goals and actions using more motivating and purposeful language.
- **How to Do It**: Take one of your current goals and rephrase it using language that feels more inspiring and aligned with your broader objectives. For example, instead of saying "I need to work out," reframe it as "I'm building my strength and resilience." Repeat this exercise with different goals to see how the change in language affects your motivation and commitment.

JUST KEEP GOING

Keeping a streak alive can be a game-changer when it comes to making lasting personal changes. It's about creating a consistent pattern of behavior that builds momentum and, over time, becomes a habit. The key is to start small, stay focused, and find ways to keep the streak going, even when things get tough.

Setting the Stage for Success

Before diving into any streak, it's crucial to set yourself up for success. Start by choosing a specific, achievable goal that aligns with what you want to change or improve. Whether it's working out regularly, learning a new language, or drinking more water, the goal should be clear and realistic. The trick here is to make the goal manageable so you're not overwhelmed from the get-go.

Once the goal is set, track your progress. One simple but effective technique is to use a visual aid, like a wall calendar, and mark each day you successfully hit your target. A red marker works wonders here—seeing those marks add up day by day can be incredibly motivating. It's a visual reminder that you're making progress, and the longer the streak, the more invested you become in not breaking it.

The Psychological Edge of Streaks

There's something about maintaining a streak that taps into our psychology. It's not just about the task itself but the pride and satisfaction that come with not breaking the chain. This feeling can be harnessed to push you through even when motivation wanes. You're not just doing it for the day—you're doing it to keep the streak alive, to protect the progress you've made.

One way to keep the pressure on, in a positive way, is to create a competition with yourself. Challenge yourself to beat your last streak or set a personal record. This could apply to anything—exercising more days in a row than last month, reading more pages each day, or even something as simple as not missing a single day of journaling.

Adapting and Overcoming Challenges

Of course, life happens. There will be days when sticking to your streak feels impossible. The key here is to be flexible and adaptable. If your original plan hits a snag, find a way to adjust without giving up entirely. Maybe you can't hit the gym because you're traveling—do a quick bodyweight workout in your hotel room instead. The point is to keep the streak going, even if it's in a modified form.

When setbacks occur, don't see them as failures but as opportunities to learn and improve. Maybe you didn't hit your water intake goal today. Instead of throwing in the towel, figure out what went wrong. Were you too busy? Did you forget to keep water handy? Make the necessary adjustments—carry a water bottle with you or set reminders on your phone. The next day, you'll be better prepared to keep the streak alive.

The Role of Environment

Your environment plays a huge role in whether you succeed in maintaining your streak. If your surroundings aren't conducive to your goals, you're setting yourself up for unnecessary struggle. Take a close look at your environment and make changes that support your efforts.

For example, if you're trying to read more, make sure your reading material is easily accessible. Place books where you can grab them quickly, like next to your bed or in your bag. If you're trying to eat healthier, stock your kitchen with healthy options and remove temptations. Small tweaks in your environment can make a big difference in keeping your streak alive.

The Commitment Factor

Maintaining a streak also requires a commitment—a promise to yourself that you'll stick with it, no matter what. This is where the idea of "disagree and commit" comes into play. It's a concept from Amazon, where team members can voice their concerns or objections about a decision, but once the decision is made, everyone commits fully to making it work.

You can apply this mindset to your streaks. There might be days when you don't feel like sticking to your routine, and that's okay. Acknowledge the resistance, but then commit to the process. Remind yourself of why you started the streak in the first place and how keeping it alive aligns with your bigger goals. It's about pushing through the resistance, not because it's easy, but because it's worth it.

Building a Streak That Lasts

In the end, the power of a streak lies in its ability to create lasting change. By setting specific goals, tracking your progress, adapting to challenges, and committing to the process, you can build momentum that carries you forward. It's not just about the streak itself but the habits and mindset you develop along the way.

So, start small, stay consistent, and keep that streak alive. Before you know it, what began as a simple goal will have transformed into a powerful new habit, one that drives you closer to your larger aspirations. And that's the real magic of keeping streaks alive.

Key Actions

- **Set Specific, Achievable Goals**: Begin with clear and realistic goals that align with what you want to change or improve.
- **Track Your Progress Visually**: Use a visual aid, like a wall calendar and a red marker, to track your daily progress and maintain motivation.
- **Create a Competition with Yourself**: Challenge yourself to maintain or surpass your streak, turning it into a personal competition.
- **Be Flexible and Adaptable**: When faced with challenges, modify your approach to keep the streak alive, even if it's in a different form.
- **Learn from Setbacks**: Instead of giving up, analyze setbacks to identify and make necessary adjustments for future success.
- **Optimize Your Environment**: Adjust your surroundings to support your streak by removing distractions and making resources easily accessible.

- **Commit to the Process**: Embrace the mindset of "disagree and commit," pushing through resistance to stick with your streak, even when it's difficult.
- **Focus on Consistency**: Prioritize maintaining the streak daily, as consistency is key to turning the behavior into a lasting habit.

Discussion Questions

1. How does tracking progress visually, like using a wall calendar, impact motivation to maintain a streak?
2. What role does adaptability play in maintaining a streak, especially when faced with challenges or setbacks?
3. How can optimizing your environment help in keeping a streak alive?
4. How do you balance the pressure of maintaining a streak with the need to avoid burnout?
5. What are the long-term benefits of maintaining a streak, and how do they contribute to building lasting habits?

Practice Exercises

1. Daily Goal Setting and Tracking

- **Objective**: To develop consistency in achieving small, daily goals.
- **How to Do It**: Choose a simple, daily goal that aligns with your larger objectives, such as drinking a certain amount of water or reading for 15 minutes. Use a calendar or journal to track each day you successfully complete the task. Mark each success with a visible symbol, like a checkmark or a star. Focus on maintaining the streak for a set period, like 30 days, and observe how the momentum builds.

2. Environment Optimization Challenge

- **Objective**: To learn how to create an environment that supports your goals.
- **How to Do It**: Identify one specific goal you're working on, such as exercising regularly or eating healthier. Spend 15 minutes each day for a week adjusting your environment to support this goal—remove distractions, place tools or resources in easy-to-access spots, or create reminders. At the end of the week, reflect on how these changes impacted your ability to maintain your streak.

3. Adaptability Practice

- **Objective**: To improve your ability to adapt and keep your streak alive in the face of challenges.
- **How to Do It**: For one week, anticipate potential obstacles that might interfere with your daily goal, such as a busy schedule or unexpected events. Each day, prepare a backup plan—identify a modified version of the task that you can still complete if the original plan falls through. Practice implementing this backup plan when needed and note how it helps you maintain your streak despite challenges.

CREATE AN ENVIRONMENT FOR CHANGE

Change is hard. No matter how strong your willpower or how noble your intentions, the environment around you can make or break your efforts to change. Whether it's in your personal life or at work, creating an environment that supports change is essential to making it stick. Let's dive into how you can shape your surroundings to set yourself up for success.

Your Environment Matters More Than You Think

When we talk about making changes, most people focus on mindset, discipline, or strategy. But the truth is, your environment plays a bigger role than you might realize. The space you occupy, the people you interact with, and even the tools at your disposal all influence your ability to change.

Your environment can either be an ally in your quest for change or an obstacle that constantly drags you back to old habits. The key is to become aware of the triggers that surround you—those little nudges that push you toward or away from your goals. Once you understand these triggers, you can take control and shape an environment that makes change not just possible, but inevitable.

Minimize Negative Triggers

The first step in creating a change-friendly environment is identifying and minimizing negative triggers. These are the things that, whether you realize it or not, sabotage your efforts. They could be physical distractions, emotional stressors, or even certain people in your life.

Let's say you're trying to have a productive conversation at work, but you're passionate about your idea, and your emotions start to take over. Suddenly, the conversation isn't about progress—it's about defending your viewpoint. The trigger here is your emotional investment in the idea, which makes it hard to listen and adapt.

On the flip side, if you're discussing someone else's proposal, you might find it easier to listen and contribute constructively because you're not as emotionally charged. By recognizing these emotional triggers, you can start to create an environment that keeps them in check. This might mean practicing mindfulness to stay calm during discussions or simply taking a step back when you feel your emotions flaring up.

But it's not just emotional triggers you need to watch out for. Physical triggers can be just as disruptive. If your workspace is cluttered or full of distractions, it's going to be tough to focus. The solution? Minimize these triggers by organizing your space and eliminating unnecessary distractions. The less you have pulling your attention away, the more energy you can devote to making meaningful changes.

Create Positive Triggers and Reinforce Them

Once you've minimized the negative, it's time to actively create and reinforce positive triggers—those elements in your environment that push you toward success.

Think about where and when you're most productive. Maybe it's in a quiet room, first thing in the morning before the world wakes up. Or perhaps you do your best thinking on a plane, where the lack of distractions allows you to focus deeply. Whatever your sweet spot is, seek it out and use it to your advantage.

One trick is to build routines that reinforce these positive triggers. If you know that a certain environment helps you focus, make it a habit to work there whenever you can. By consistently placing yourself in a setting that supports your goals, you're stacking the deck in your favor.

But it's not just about physical space. The people around you can be powerful positive triggers too. Surround yourself with those who uplift and motivate you, and distance yourself from those who drain your energy. If you're trying to make a big change, you don't need naysayers questioning your every move. Instead, seek out a support system that encourages your progress.

The Power of Tools and Resources

Finally, let's not forget the importance of having the right tools and resources at your disposal. You wouldn't try to build a house without the right materials, so why would you attempt to make a change without the tools you need?

If you're learning a new skill, make sure you have access to the best resources available—whether it's online courses, books, or mentors who can guide you. If you're trying to improve your health, invest in the right equipment, whether that's a gym membership, quality running shoes, or a set of resistance bands.

Creating an environment conducive to change isn't just about eliminating the bad and increasing the good. It's also about equipping yourself with the tools that make the journey smoother and more achievable.

Putting It All Together

Creating an environment that makes change possible isn't about one big overhaul. It's about making small, intentional adjustments that add up over time. Start by identifying and minimizing negative triggers, then actively create positive ones that reinforce your goals. Surround yourself with supportive people, and make sure you have the tools and resources you need.

Change doesn't happen in a vacuum. It happens in the real world, in the context of your environment. By shaping that environment to support your goals, you make change not just possible, but inevitable.

Key Actions

- **Identify and Minimize Negative Triggers**: Recognize the factors in your environment that hinder progress and actively work to reduce their impact.
- **Practice Mindfulness**: Use mindfulness techniques to stay calm and avoid letting emotions derail productive conversations or actions.
- **Organize Your Physical Space**: Keep your workspace tidy and free from distractions to improve focus and productivity.
- **Create and Reinforce Positive Triggers**: Identify

environments and situations that boost your productivity and make it a habit to engage in them regularly.

- **Build Supportive Relationships**: Surround yourself with people who uplift and motivate you, and limit interactions with those who drain your energy.
- **Equip Yourself with the Right Tools and Resources**: Ensure you have access to the necessary tools, resources, and knowledge to support your goals and make changes more achievable.

Discussion Questions

1. What are some negative triggers in your environment that hinder your ability to make positive changes?
2. How has your emotional investment in an idea affected your ability to have productive conversations?
3. In what ways does your physical workspace impact your productivity and ability to make changes?
4. Who in your life acts as a positive influence and supports your goals?
5. What tools or resources have been most effective in helping you achieve your goals?

Practice Exercises

1. Trigger Identification Journal

- **Objective**: Improve awareness of both positive and negative triggers in your environment.
- **How to Do It**: For one week, keep a daily journal where you note down moments when you felt particularly productive or unproductive. Reflect on the environmental factors, emotional states, or interactions that contributed to these feelings. At the end of the week, review your entries to identify common triggers, both positive and negative.

2. Mindful Workspace Organization

- **Objective**: Create a physical environment that supports focus and productivity.
- **How to Do It**: Set aside an hour to declutter and organize your workspace. Remove any unnecessary items that could serve as distractions. Arrange your space in a way that feels calming and conducive to work. Once your space is organized, spend 5 minutes each day maintaining it to reinforce the habit.

3. Supportive Network Mapping

- **Objective**: Strengthen relationships with positive influences and minimize exposure to negative ones.
- **How to Do It**: Draw a map of your current support network, listing people who positively influence your goals in one column and those who tend to drain your energy in another. Plan one actionable step to strengthen connections with those in the positive column, such as scheduling regular check-ins or collaborative projects. For those in the negative column, consider ways to limit interactions or reframe the relationship to reduce its impact on your goals.

JOURNAL FOR MOMENTUM

Journaling is more than just putting pen to paper; it's a powerful tool that can help you gain momentum and make meaningful changes in your life. Think of it as your personal playbook—a place where you can reinforce learning, track your progress, and capture the valuable insights that come your way. But like any tool, it's most effective when used correctly.

Reinforce Learning Through Reflection

One of the key benefits of journaling is that it forces you to re-articulate what you've learned. When you write down new information, you're not just recording it; you're processing it in your own words. This act of summarizing forces you to think critically about the material, helping you to better understand and retain it. It's a bit like teaching something to someone else—the very act of explaining it solidifies your grasp on the subject. Contrast this with simply reading or hearing information, which is often a passive process. Journaling makes it active, engaging your brain in a way that enhances memory and comprehension.

Tracking Progress: Turning Goals Into Reality

Journaling isn't just about reflecting on the past; it's also about planning for the future. By writing down your goals and the steps you're taking to achieve them, you make them tangible. A goal that's only in your head is easy to ignore or forget. But once it's on paper, it becomes a commitment. You can see it, touch it, and revisit it whenever you need a reminder. This process helps to internalize your objectives, making them feel more real and achievable.

Beyond goal-setting, journaling allows you to track your progress. You can look back and see how far you've come, which is incredibly motivating. It also gives you a chance to reflect on what's working and what isn't. Maybe you've hit a roadblock—journaling can help you analyze why and figure out your next steps. The simple act of writing things down also aids memory; we're much more likely to remember something we've written down than something we've only thought about.

Accountability in Action

Take the weight loss industry as an example. Countless experts recommend keeping a food journal as one of the most effective tools for losing weight. Why? Because it creates accountability. When you write down every single thing you eat, you're forced to confront your choices. You can't conveniently forget that late-night snack or pretend you didn't indulge in dessert. This same principle applies to any area of your life where you want to make changes. By documenting your thoughts, feelings, observations, and actions, you create a record that holds you accountable.

Capturing Insights and Observations

Journaling isn't just about you; it's also about the world around you. It's a way to capture other people's expressions, the ways they communicate, and how they interact with you. By writing down these observations, you become a more active participant in your own life. You begin to notice patterns, behaviors, and dynamics that you might otherwise miss. Over time, this practice can lead to deeper insights into not just how others operate, but how you relate to them.

Choosing the Right Journaling Method

Not all journaling is created equal, and finding the right approach is crucial. Some people thrive with structured formats, like bullet journals that combine to-do lists with reflections. Others prefer free-form writing, where they can let their thoughts flow without restriction. The key is to experiment and find what resonates with you. Whatever method you choose, the important thing is to make journaling a regular habit. Consistency is what turns journaling from a sporadic activity into a powerful tool for change.

The Momentum Multiplier

In the end, journaling is about driving momentum. It's about taking those small steps every day that add up to big changes over time. By reinforcing learning, tracking your progress, holding yourself accountable, and capturing valuable insights, you create a feedback loop that keeps you moving forward. And that's how real, lasting change happens—one journal entry at a time.

So grab a notebook, or open a new document on your computer, and start journaling today. The momentum you create might just surprise you.

Key Actions

1. **Reinforcing Learning Through Reflection**: Summarizing and re-articulating what you've learned in your own words to enhance understanding and retention.
2. **Tracking Progress**: Writing down goals and steps to achieve them, making them tangible and real, and revisiting them to measure progress and stay motivated.
3. **Creating Accountability**: Documenting actions, thoughts, and behaviors to hold yourself accountable for your choices and progress.
4. **Capturing Insights and Observations**: Noting down observations about others' behaviors and communication styles to gain deeper insights into your interactions and relationships.
5. **Choosing the Right Journaling Method**: Experimenting with different journaling formats to find one that works best for you, ensuring it becomes a consistent habit.
6. **Driving Momentum**: Using journaling as a tool to create a feedback loop that reinforces learning, tracks progress, and maintains accountability, leading to sustained momentum and lasting change.

Discussion Questions

1. How has journaling helped you reinforce learning or retain information in your life?
2. In what ways does writing down goals impact your motivation and ability to achieve them?

3. How do you think journaling can increase accountability in different areas of life?
4. How might journaling insights about others improve your communication skills or relationships?
5. Which method of journaling do you find most effective, and why?

Practice Exercises

1. Daily Reflection Writing

- **Objective**: Reinforce learning and improve information retention.
- **How to Do It**: At the end of each day, spend 10-15 minutes writing about what you learned that day. Summarize key takeaways in your own words, focusing on the most important lessons or insights. This could be from work, personal experiences, or something you read or heard.

2. Goal Tracking Journal

- **Objective**: Increase accountability and track progress toward your goals.
- **How to Do It**: Dedicate a section of your journal to your current goals. Each week, write down specific steps you've taken toward these goals and reflect on any progress or setbacks. Review your entries regularly to assess how far you've come and adjust your approach as needed.

3. Observation Notebook

- **Objective**: Capture insights about others to improve communication and relationships.
- **How to Do It**: Carry a small notebook with you, and whenever you notice something significant about how someone communicates or interacts with others, jot it down.

Reflect on these observations later, considering how they might influence your own communication or how you relate to others.

WATCH YOURSELF GROW

I can't stress enough how eye-opening it is to watch yourself in action. There's nothing quite like seeing yourself through the lens of a camera to bridge the gap between how you think you come across and how you actually do. From 2012 to 2018, I was on national TV every few weeks. It was a crash course in self-awareness. What I thought I was projecting often didn't match what the camera revealed. That disconnect was sometimes painful but always invaluable.

The Camera Doesn't Lie

The camera is an unflinching observer. It captures not just what you did but how you did it—your tone, your body language, your timing. It reveals the nuances that slip past your internal radar. And that's precisely why capturing yourself on video can be one of the most powerful tools for self-improvement.

We all have an image of ourselves in our minds. But that internalized view often falls short of reality. When you watch yourself on video, you're forced to confront the discrepancies. Maybe you thought you were coming across as confident, but the video shows you fidgeting or mumbling. Maybe you imagined you were making eye contact, but the video reveals your gaze was all over the place. The camera doesn't lie, and that honesty is what makes it such a powerful tool.

Self-Modeling: A Path to Replication

One of the biggest benefits of watching yourself on video is something called self-modeling. This is where you study your own successful actions to replicate them. It's like having a personalized playbook for success.

Take my son, for example. He's a golfer and uses an app to film his swing. Then, he watches the videos repeatedly, analyzing his tempo, his stance, the angle of his club—everything. This process not only boosts his confidence but also helps him refine and replicate those successful actions on the course. The same principle applies whether you're preparing for a big presentation, refining your sales pitch, or improving your tennis swing.

Preparation: Capture the Right Moments

To get the most out of self-modeling, you need to capture the right moments—what I call "game time." These are the instances when you're performing at your best. This could be anything from a conference call, a keynote speech, or even just a simple voicemail. The key is to have a clear idea of what you want to achieve and what you're looking for in the video.

Once you've captured your game time, the next step is to review it with a critical eye. What worked? What didn't? Where did you excel, and where did you fall short? The goal is to analyze your performance, identify the actions that led to success, and figure out how to replicate them consistently.

Fine-Tuning the Details

Watching yourself on video isn't just about the big picture—it's also about the finer details. Your body language, facial expressions, and tone of voice all play a huge role in how you're perceived. These nonverbal cues can make or break your performance, whether you're trying to land a big deal or simply connect with your audience.

For new behaviors, practicing in front of a mirror can be a helpful first step. But to truly nail those physical motions, expressions, or vocal tones, nothing beats watching yourself on video. It allows you to see exactly how you're coming across and make adjustments as needed. Over time, this practice will help you make these elements consistent, so they become second nature.

The Continuous Loop of Improvement

The process of watching yourself in action is a continuous loop: capture, analyze, practice, and repeat. The more you do it, the more refined your performance will become. The goal is to make the important details and smaller actions consistent with success. By reviewing these videos frequently, you'll be able to replicate your best behaviors more easily and achieve the results you're after.

So, set up that camera, hit record, and get ready to see yourself in a whole new light. It might be uncomfortable at first, but I promise it's worth it. There's no better way to close the gap between your aspirations and reality than by watching yourself in action.

Key Actions

- **Self-Awareness Through Video Review**: Watching yourself on video to gain an accurate understanding of how you come across versus how you think you come across.
- **Self-Modeling**: Analyzing and replicating successful actions by studying your own performance on video.
- **Capturing "Game Time" Moments**: Recording instances when you are performing at your best to analyze and learn from them.
- **Critical Self-Analysis**: Reviewing video footage with a critical eye to identify what worked, what didn't, and how to improve.
- **Attention to Non-Verbal Cues**: Focusing on body language, facial expressions, and tone of voice to enhance how you are perceived.
- **Consistent Practice and Refinement**: Continuously capturing, analyzing, and practicing behaviors to make successful actions consistent and second nature.
- **Repetition for Improvement**: Engaging in a loop of capturing, analyzing, practicing, and repeating to refine and improve performance over time.

Discussion Questions

1. How does the reality of seeing yourself on video differ from your internalized self-perception, and what surprised you the most when watching yourself in action?

2. In what areas of your life or work could self-modeling through video review have the most impact, and how would you go about implementing this practice?

3. What specific non-verbal cues (body language, facial expressions, tone of voice) have you noticed about yourself when watching a video, and how can you improve them?

4. How can you create opportunities to capture your "game time" moments, and what criteria would you use to determine which moments are worth reviewing?

5. Discuss a time when you used repetition and practice to refine a skill. How did capturing and analyzing your performance on video enhance or change that process?

Practice Exercises

1. Video Self-Review

- **Objective**: To improve self-awareness and refine personal performance by observing your actions in real-time situations.
- **How to Do It**: Choose a specific activity, such as giving a presentation, conducting a meeting, or practicing a skill like playing a sport. Record yourself during this activity using your phone or a camera. Watch the video afterward, focusing on your body language, tone of voice, and overall delivery. Take notes on what you did well and where you can improve. Repeat this exercise regularly, each time focusing on a different aspect of your performance.

2. Targeted Self-Modeling

- **Objective**: To replicate successful behaviors by analyzing and emulating your best performances.
- **How to Do It**: Identify a past performance where you felt you excelled—this could be anything from a successful sales pitch to a well-executed public speaking engagement. Watch a recording

of this event if available, or mentally replay it in your mind. Break down the specific actions and behaviors that contributed to your success. Practice these behaviors in a controlled environment, like in front of a mirror or with a small audience, aiming to replicate the success in future performances.

3. Non-Verbal Cue Enhancement

- **Objective**: To improve the consistency and effectiveness of your non-verbal communication.
- **How to Do It**: Record a short video of yourself speaking or performing a task, focusing specifically on your body language, facial expressions, and tone of voice. After watching the video, identify one non-verbal cue you want to improve, such as maintaining eye contact, reducing nervous gestures, or using more expressive facial expressions. Practice this specific cue in front of a mirror, gradually integrating it into your everyday interactions. Record a follow-up video to assess your progress and make further adjustments as needed.

ASK FOR A SECOND OPINION

One of the toughest things for leaders is letting others watch them in action. Whether it's a friend, spouse, or colleague, the idea of someone observing your performance can be intimidating. We all have a natural tendency to protect our vulnerabilities, but if you want to grow and improve, it's essential to let someone in.

The Importance of an Accountability Partner

Having someone to hold you accountable can be a game-changer. This doesn't mean just anyone—it needs to be someone who genuinely cares about your progress and knows you well enough to offer meaningful feedback. They should act as a source of insight, knowledge, and data, helping you stay on track and measure your growth.

One effective strategy is to establish regular check-ins with this person. These meetings aren't just about receiving feedback; they're about creating a consistent rhythm of reflection and improvement. It's a space where you can openly discuss your progress, share your challenges, and receive guidance on how to move forward.

Finding the Right Partner

It's crucial to find someone who can provide feedback in a non-evaluative environment. This could be a spouse, a close friend, or a coworker. The key is that this person understands you well enough to offer helpful insights without passing judgment. They should be able to offer gentle nudges in the right direction and reinforce your new behaviors or actions, even through subtle cues.

This person can act as a kind of secret partner in crime, discreetly supporting you as you work to improve. Their role isn't to criticize but to observe and provide constructive feedback that can help you grow. It's about having someone who's in your corner, rooting for your success while keeping you grounded.

Making Feedback Work for You

Inviting a friend or colleague to be your eyes and ears is a critical step in making lasting change. But it's not just about having someone watch you; it's about creating a feedback loop that fosters continuous improvement. Regular check-ins with a supportive partner and practicing self-modeling are both effective ways to hold yourself accountable and track your progress.

Remember, the goal isn't to seek validation but to seek growth. By finding the right partner and using their feedback constructively, you can enhance your leadership skills and make significant strides in your personal and professional development.

Take Action

So, how do you put this into practice? Start by identifying someone you trust—someone who can offer constructive feedback without making you feel judged. Set up a regular schedule for check-ins and commit to being open and honest during these sessions. Don't shy away from recording your performances either; these can serve as valuable learning tools.

Improvement is a journey, not a destination. By inviting a trusted partner into your process, you're taking an important step toward becoming the leader you aspire to be.

Key Actions

- **Allowing Others to Observe Your Performance**: Overcoming the discomfort of being observed by others to gain valuable insights and feedback.
- **Establishing Regular Check-Ins**: Setting up a consistent schedule with an accountability partner to discuss progress, challenges, and receive guidance.
- **Finding a Non-Evaluative Feedback Partner**: Choosing someone you trust, who knows you well and can offer helpful insights without passing judgment.

- **Receiving Constructive Feedback**: Being open to feedback that is supportive and aimed at fostering growth, rather than criticism.
- **Using Feedback to Improve**: Actively applying the feedback received to enhance your leadership skills and track your progress.

Discussion Questions

1. What challenges do you face when allowing others to observe your leadership performance, and how do you think overcoming these challenges could benefit your growth?
2. How do you currently seek feedback on your leadership style, and what could you do to make this process more structured and effective?
3. What qualities do you think are essential in a feedback partner, and how would you go about selecting the right person to provide you with constructive insights?
4. In what ways can regular check-ins with an accountability partner help you stay on track with your goals, and how might you integrate this practice into your routine?
5. How do you differentiate between constructive feedback that fosters growth and criticism that might be counterproductive, and how can you ensure that the feedback you receive is truly beneficial?

Practice Exercises

1. Role-Playing Feedback Sessions

- **Objective**: To practice receiving and applying feedback in a constructive manner.
- **How to Do It**: Partner with a trusted colleague or friend and simulate a feedback session. Present a recent challenge or project you've worked on, and ask them to provide feedback on your performance. Focus on staying open-minded and receptive during the session, then discuss how you can apply

the feedback. Repeat this exercise regularly to build your comfort level with receiving constructive criticism.

2. Scheduled Reflection and Check-In

- **Objective**: To create a consistent routine for self-assessment and feedback integration.
- **How to Do It**: Set a weekly or bi-weekly meeting with your accountability partner. During each check-in, review your recent activities, challenges, and successes. Ask for their observations and suggestions for improvement. After the session, write down key takeaways and actionable steps you can implement before the next check-in. Reflect on your progress at each meeting.

3. Observation and Feedback Journal

- **Objective**: To track feedback and your response to it over time.
- **How to Do It**: Start a journal where you record instances where you've received feedback. Include who provided the feedback, the context, what was said, and how you felt about it. Reflect on how you applied the feedback and what the outcome was. This exercise will help you become more aware of patterns in the feedback you receive and how effectively you're using it to improve. Review your journal periodically to identify areas for further development.

COUPLE BEHAVIORS FOR HABITS

Building new habits isn't easy. It takes more than just willpower to break old routines and establish new ones. The struggle often lies in the sheer effort required to change something that's been ingrained in us for years. But what if the key to success isn't about breaking old habits but replacing them with better ones?

Instead of fighting against an old habit, it's often more effective to introduce a new one in its place. This way, you're not just resisting a temptation; you're actively doing something different. One of the most effective methods for making this transition smoother is a technique called pairing.

The Power of Pairing

Pairing involves attaching a new behavior to an existing habit—one you already enjoy or find positive. This creates a natural bridge between the old and the new, making it easier to incorporate the desired behavior into your routine.

For example, let's say you want to start reading more. Instead of trying to carve out extra time in your day, pair this new habit with something you already do, like drinking your morning coffee. Every time you sit down with that cup of coffee, you pick up a book and read for a few minutes. Over time, the two actions become linked in your mind, and reading becomes a natural part of your morning ritual.

Pairing works because it leverages an existing routine, reducing the mental friction that comes with trying to establish something new. The key is to choose an activity you genuinely enjoy, as this positive association makes it easier to stick with the new habit.

Making the Most of Triggers

Another effective technique for reinforcing new habits is using triggers. A trigger is a specific event or situation that prompts the desired behavior. Think of it as a cue that reminds you to act in a certain way.

Let's say you're working on improving how you handle disagreements. You might set a trigger that whenever someone disagrees with you, it's your cue to respond calmly and constructively. The disagreement itself becomes a reminder to practice your new approach.

Triggers work because they create a direct link between a situation and a behavior, making it easier to remember and apply your new habit in real-life scenarios. The more consistent you are with responding to triggers, the more automatic the behavior becomes.

Combining Pairing and Triggers

Pairing and triggers don't have to work in isolation. In fact, using them together can supercharge your efforts to form new habits.

For example, if you're trying to establish a daily exercise routine, you could pair your workouts with something you enjoy, like listening to your favorite podcast or watching a TV show. At the same time, you could set a trigger, such as putting on your workout clothes right after you finish work. The pairing makes the exercise itself more enjoyable, and the trigger ensures you remember to do it.

This combination of enjoyment and consistency is powerful. By aligning your new habit with something you already love and setting clear reminders, you're stacking the odds in your favor. The new habit doesn't just feel like an obligation; it becomes something you look forward to, making it far more likely to stick.

Practical Examples of Pairing and Triggers

Here are some additional examples to help you see how pairing and triggers can work in your daily life:

1. *Reading More:* Pair reading with your morning coffee or tea. The drink becomes a cue to pick up your book.
2. *Exercising Regularly:* Listen to a favorite playlist or podcast only when you're working out. The audio content becomes the reward, making exercise more enjoyable.
3. *Healthy Eating:* Pair your meals with a favorite activity, like

watching a show or enjoying a walk afterward. The activity serves as a positive reinforcement for the healthy choice.

4. *Improving Communication:* Set a trigger for responding to emails or messages. For instance, whenever you receive an email, take a deep breath and approach your response with calm and clarity.

Creating new habits isn't just about willpower; it's about strategy. By coupling behaviors—pairing a new habit with an existing one and setting clear triggers—you create a system that supports and reinforces positive change. You're not just adding something new; you're weaving it into the fabric of your daily life.

Pairing and triggers work because they tap into the routines you already have, making it easier to adopt new behaviors without overwhelming yourself. And when you make the new habit enjoyable or at least less daunting, you're far more likely to succeed.

So next time you're struggling to form a new habit, don't just rely on sheer determination. Look for ways to couple behaviors and set triggers that make the process smoother, more enjoyable, and ultimately, more successful. The more you practice, the more these new habits will become second nature, leading to lasting change in your life.

Key Actions

- **Replacing Old Habits with New Ones**: Instead of trying to stop an old habit, introduce a new, more positive behavior to replace it.
- **Pairing New Behaviors with Existing Habits**: Attach a new behavior to an already established and enjoyable habit to make the new behavior easier to adopt.
- **Using Triggers to Reinforce New Habits**: Set specific events or situations as cues to prompt the desired behavior.
- **Combining Pairing and Triggers**: Utilize both pairing and triggers together to create a stronger and more consistent habit-forming process.

- **Making New Habits Enjoyable**: Align new behaviors with enjoyable activities to increase the likelihood of sticking to the new habit.
- **Setting Clear Reminders for New Behaviors**: Use consistent triggers to remind yourself to perform the new behavior, making it more likely to become automatic over time.

Discussion Questions

1. What existing habits in your routine could be paired with a new behavior to help reinforce the new habit?
2. How have triggers played a role in successfully forming new habits in your life?
3. What challenges arise when trying to replace old habits with new ones, and how might pairing and triggers address these challenges?
4. How does making a new habit enjoyable influence its adoption and long-term success?
5. How can the combination of pairing and triggers enhance the effectiveness of habit formation?

Practice Exercises

1. Habit Pairing Exercise

- **Objective**: To identify and pair a new habit with an existing positive routine.
- **How to Do It**: Choose a new habit you want to adopt (e.g., reading, exercising, meditation). Identify an existing habit that you already enjoy or do regularly (e.g., morning coffee, evening walk). Start practicing the new habit immediately after or during the existing one. Track your progress daily for a week and note how pairing the two habits affects your consistency.

2. Trigger Identification and Implementation

- **Objective**: To create specific triggers that prompt the desired behavior.
- **How to Do It**: Identify a behavior you want to reinforce (e.g., responding calmly in stressful situations, taking breaks during work). Choose a specific event or situation that can serve as a trigger (e.g., every time you receive an email, before starting a new task). Practice responding to the trigger with the desired behavior for one week, and reflect on how effectively the trigger helps you remember to practice the new habit.

3. Enjoyment Enhancement Exercise

- **Objective**: To make a new habit more enjoyable and therefore easier to maintain.
- **How to Do It**: Select a habit you find challenging to maintain (e.g., exercising, healthy eating). Pair it with an activity you enjoy (e.g., listening to music, watching a favorite show). For two weeks, consistently perform the new habit while engaging in the enjoyable activity. Pay attention to how your motivation and enjoyment levels change, and assess the impact on your habit formation.

DEVELOP A STUDY PRACTICE

Wisdom is often hailed as one of the most essential traits a leader can possess. It's what allows a leader to make sound decisions, inspire confidence, and guide their team effectively. But wisdom isn't something you're born with; it's something you cultivate. It comes from experience, learning, and, perhaps most importantly, reflection.

Leaders who aspire to be truly wise don't just passively consume information. They actively engage with it, documenting their insights, reflecting on what they've learned, and applying that wisdom in their daily lives. This process of documentation and review transforms ordinary knowledge into practical wisdom—a tool that can be used to navigate the complex challenges of leadership.

The Importance of Documenting and Reviewing Wisdom

Many people think wisdom is simply a byproduct of experience. While experience is crucial, wisdom requires more than just living through events—it demands a commitment to capturing and reflecting on the lessons those experiences teach.

The first step in cultivating wisdom is documentation. This isn't just about jotting down thoughts haphazardly; it's about creating a dedicated space for your insights, whether that's a physical journal, an electronic file, or a more structured commonplace book. The goal is to create a repository of the most valuable lessons and ideas you encounter.

But not all information is created equal. The key is to be selective. Only the most meaningful, well-articulated insights should make it into your collection. This ensures that your wisdom bank remains a place of high value, filled with practical and profound knowledge rather than cluttered with trivialities.

Once you've documented your insights, the next critical step is review. It's not enough to simply store this wisdom; you need to revisit it regularly. Set aside time, perhaps once a month, to go through your collection. This practice keeps your wisdom fresh, allowing you to reflect on how these insights apply to your current challenges and decisions. Over time, this review process deepens your understanding and embeds these lessons more firmly in your mind.

A Practical Approach to Cultivating Wisdom

To truly internalize and apply wisdom, successful leaders follow a three-step process:

Step One: Document Everything of Value, But Be Selective.

Whenever you encounter a meaningful insight—whether from a book, a conversation, or an experience—document it. But don't just capture everything; be discerning. Only include insights that are impeccably articulated and highly relevant.

Step Two: Distill the Best Insights Into Actionable Ideas.

As you accumulate these insights, take the time to distill them into bite-sized, actionable routines or principles. This could be as simple as a few key takeaways that you can apply immediately. The idea is to transform raw knowledge into something you can use in your day-to-day life.

Step Three: Collect, Store, and Regularly Review.

Once you've documented and distilled your wisdom, store it in an easily accessible format—whether it's a notebook, journal, or digital file. Make it a habit to review this collection regularly. This periodic review helps reinforce the lessons you've learned and allows you to see new connections or insights you might have missed before.

Example: Consider the approach of an athletic coach who records their practice plans after each session. By selecting the best drills and reviewing them monthly, they refine their training approach and continually improve. Similarly, a leader aiming to become an expert on pension plans might document insights from books, articles, and interviews. As their expertise grows, they regularly revisit their notes, uncovering nuances and deeper understanding that were initially hidden.

The Power of Reflection in Leadership

Wisdom isn't about having all the answers—it's about knowing how to find them and apply them effectively. By committing to a process of documentation, distillation, and regular review, leaders can transform their experiences and learnings into practical wisdom. This approach not only helps in making better decisions but also fosters continuous growth, ensuring that wisdom isn't just accumulated, but also applied.

In the end, wisdom is more than just knowledge. It's the thoughtful reflection on and application of that knowledge in the real world. And for leaders, that's what makes all the difference.

Key Actions

- **Actively Document Insights**: Leaders should create a dedicated space to document valuable insights, whether in a physical journal, electronic file, or commonplace book. The emphasis is on being selective and only capturing the most meaningful and well-articulated insights.
- **Be Selective in What You Document**: Not all information is worth keeping. Leaders should be discerning in what they include in their wisdom repository, ensuring it contains only high-value insights that can guide decision-making.
- **Regularly Review Documented Wisdom**: Set aside time, such as once a month, to review the insights and wisdom that have been documented. This regular review keeps the wisdom fresh and reinforces its application in daily life.
- **Distill Insights Into Actionable Ideas**: Transform raw knowledge into practical, bite-sized routines or principles that can be applied immediately. This distillation process makes the wisdom more accessible and actionable.
- **Apply Wisdom in Daily Life**: The ultimate goal of documenting and reviewing wisdom is to apply it in real-world situations, guiding decisions and actions in leadership and beyond.
- **Reflect on and Refine Insights**: Use the regular review

process to reflect on insights, uncover new connections, and refine understanding, leading to deeper wisdom over time.

Discussion Questions

1. How does the practice of documenting insights differ from simply taking notes, and why is it important for cultivating wisdom?
2. What criteria would you use to decide which insights are worth documenting and which should be excluded?
3. How can the regular review of documented wisdom impact decision-making and leadership effectiveness? Can you share a personal experience where this was evident?
4. In what ways can distilling insights into actionable ideas enhance your ability to apply wisdom in daily life? Can you provide an example of how you've done this?
5. What challenges might you face in maintaining a regular review practice, and how can you overcome these challenges to ensure wisdom is continuously cultivated and applied?

Practice Exercises

1. The Daily Insight Journal

- **Objective**: To develop the habit of documenting meaningful insights consistently.
- **How to Do It**: Set aside 10 minutes at the end of each day to reflect on what you've learned. Document one or two key insights or lessons from your day in a dedicated journal or digital file. Focus on articulating these insights clearly and concisely. Review your entries weekly to identify recurring themes or ideas that stand out.

2. Monthly Wisdom Review

- **Objective**: To reinforce learning by regularly revisiting documented insights.

- **How to Do It**: At the end of each month, schedule an hour to review the insights you've documented. As you review, highlight those that still resonate or have had a significant impact on your thinking. Consider how you've applied these insights over the past month and identify any new ways to incorporate them into your decision-making process.

3. Distillation and Application Workshop

- **Objective**: To practice distilling insights into actionable ideas and applying them in real-world scenarios.
- **How to Do It**: Choose three insights from your documented wisdom that you find particularly valuable. For each insight, distill it into a single actionable idea or principle that you can apply in your daily life or leadership role. Over the next week, focus on implementing these principles in specific situations. At the end of the week, reflect on the outcomes and refine the principles as needed for future use.

AFTERWORD

As you reach the end of The B:Side Way, I hope you're walking away with more than just a collection of ideas. This book isn't about abstract theories or distant ideals; it's about practical, actionable strategies that you can start using right now to lead with purpose and precision in every aspect of your life.

The B:Side Way is more than just a leadership philosophy—it's a way of thinking, acting, and being that transcends industries, roles, and titles. Whether you're at the helm of a large organization, running a small business, or simply striving to lead more effectively within your team or community, the principles we've explored together are designed to be both universal and adaptable. They are meant to serve as a foundation for growth, innovation, and success, regardless of where you find yourself on your professional or personal journey.

Throughout these pages, we've delved into the importance of owner-ship, accountability, and adaptability. We've discussed the value of embracing change not just as a necessity but as an opportunity for growth and innovation. We've also examined how continuous learning —both from our successes and our setbacks—can propel us forward, helping us to become more effective leaders and more fulfilled indi-viduals.

But these principles are not meant to remain confined to the pages of this book. They are tools to be wielded, practices to be embodied, and habits to be cultivated in your daily life. The real power of The B:Side Way lies not in the knowledge itself but in how you choose to apply it. Leadership is not about holding a certain title or having authority over others; it's about the choices you make, the example you set, and the impact you have on those around you.

Every decision, every conversation, every challenge is an opportunity to live out these principles. Whether you're leading a team through a complex project, mentoring a colleague, or simply navigating the day-to-day demands of your role, you have the ability to influence outcomes and inspire those around you. By practicing The B:Side Way, you can foster a culture of trust, drive meaningful growth, and make a lasting difference in your organization and beyond.

It's important to remember that leadership is a journey, not a destination. There will be moments of triumph and moments of challenge, but it's in the midst of these experiences that true growth occurs. The principles we've explored together are not a one-size-fits-all solution; they are a guide to help you navigate the complexities of leadership with clarity and confidence. As you continue to grow and evolve, so too will your understanding and application of these principles.

I encourage you to reflect on the ideas we've discussed, to revisit the exercises and practices outlined in this book, and to think critically about how you can integrate The B:Side Way into your own life. Start by making small, deliberate changes. Focus on one principle at a time, and gradually expand your practice. Over time, these small shifts will compound, leading to significant, positive transformations in your leadership and in your life.

As you embark on this journey, I want to remind you that you are not alone. The challenges you face, the questions you grapple with, and the successes you achieve are shared experiences among leaders everywhere. By committing to The B:Side Way, you are joining a community of individuals who are dedicated to leading with integrity, innovation, and impact. Together, we can create a ripple effect of positive change that extends far beyond our immediate circles.

In closing, I want to express my deepest gratitude to you, the reader. Thank you for investing your time and energy into exploring these concepts with me. Writing this book has been a deeply rewarding experience, one that has allowed me to distill years of learning, leading, and teaching into a framework that I hope will serve you well. It has also been a journey of growth and reflection for me, and I am profoundly grateful for the opportunity to share this journey with you.

As you move forward, I wish you courage in the face of challenges, curiosity in your pursuit of knowledge, and conviction in your commitment to lead with purpose and precision. Remember, the principles of The B:Side Way are yours to apply and adapt, and I have every confidence that you will use them to create meaningful and lasting impact.

Thank you, and here's to your continued success as you lead the B:Side Way.

Christopher Myers

ABOUT THE AUTHOR

Christopher Myers is a seasoned entrepreneur, CEO, and author with a deep passion for leadership and small business growth. As the Chief Executive Officer of B:Side Capital and B:Side Fund, he oversees one of the most active SBA lenders in the U.S., driving success for countless small businesses. In addition to his executive roles, Chris imparts his expertise as a Professor of Management and Entrepreneurship at Arizona State University's W.P. Carey School of Business and serves as an  Entrepreneur In Residence at Skysong Innovations.

Before his tenure at B:Side Capital, Chris guided the transformation of Yellow Express, an Australian logistics company, as its Interim Global CEO. He also co-founded BodeTree, a financial technology company that provided innovative solutions to small businesses until its successful exit in 2018.

Chris's insights into business and leadership have been featured across major platforms, including Entrepreneur Magazine, MSNBC, Fox Business, The Wall Street Journal, and Forbes. His thought leadership extends to The New York Times, TEDx, TechCrunch, and beyond, establishing him as a trusted voice in the industry.

A proud Arizona native, Chris graduated from Arizona State University with a degree in finance and furthered his studies in accounting and economics at Babeş-Bolyai University in Romania. His achievements were recognized in 2017 when he was inducted into the W.P. Carey School of Business Hall of Fame as its inaugural Young Alumni inductee.

ABOUT B:SIDE

B:Side is reshaping small business lending across the Western U.S. As a non-profit small business lender, we prioritize creating access to responsible capital for small businesses while serving as a trusted resource for lending institutions. Since 1990, we've helped over 5,000 small businesses, injecting more than $9 billion into the economy.

B:Side is about more than just small business loans. We're committed to empowering entrepreneurs, fostering innovation through technology, and driving economic growth in the communities we serve.

Discover more about our journey and the impact we're making at www.bside.org.

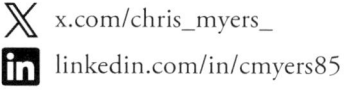

X x.com/chris_myers_

in linkedin.com/in/cmyers85

Made in United States
Troutdale, OR
11/20/2024

25092900R00310